Why Do You Need This New Edition?

6 good reasons why you should buy this new edition of *The Rich Get Rich and the Poor Get Prison.*

1. In the aftermath of the global financial meltdown Street protests, the authors pose the question, "Why aren't the tools of the criminal justice system being mobilized to protect Americans from predatory business practices and to punish those who cause widespread harm?"

2. The tenth edition includes extensive updating of statistics on criminal and noncriminal harms; it incorporates events and the results of the relevant research since the last edition.

3. The tenth edition starts each chapter with a helpful overview, so that students get an idea of what the main points of the chapter will be.

4. The tenth edition has an expanded section covering the reasons for the decline in crime rates.

5. The tenth edition has expanded definitions and explanations of key terms and ideas.

6. The tenth edition offers students access to MySearchKit, an online resource that offers book-specific learning objectives, chapter summaries, flashcards, and practice tests as well as activities to aid student learning and comprehension.

THE RICH GET RICHER AND THE POOR GET PRISON

IDEOLOGY, CLASS, AND CRIMINAL JUSTICE

Tenth Edition

THE RICH GET RICHER AND THE POOR GET PRISON

IDEOLOGY, CLASS, AND CRIMINAL JUSTICE

Jeffrey Reiman

American University

Paul Leighton

Eastern Michigan University

PEARSON

Boston Columbus Indianapolis New York San Francisco Upper Saddle River
Amsterdam Cape Town Dubai London Madrid Milan Munich Paris Montreal Toronto
Delhi Mexico City São Paolo Sydney Hong Kong Seoul Singapore Taipei Tokyo

Editorial Director: Craig Campanella
Editor in Chief: Dickson Musslewhite
Associate Editor: Mayda Bosco
Editorial Assistant: Joseph Jantas
Director of Marketing: Brandy Dawson
Marketing Manager: Jessica Lasda
Marketing Assistant: Zakiyyah Wiley
Production Project Manager: Debbie Ryan
Full Service Project Manager: Rashmi Tickyani/Aptara®, Inc.
Composition: Aptara®, Inc.
Central Design Manager: Jayne Conte
Printer/Binder/Cover: STP/Courier/Westford
Text Font: Palatino LT Std

Credits and acknowledgments borrowed from other sources and reproduced, with permission, in this textbook appear on the appropriate page within text.

Many of the designations by manufacturers and sellers to distinguish their products are claimed as trademarks. Where those designations appear in this book, and the publisher was aware of a trademark claim, the designations have been printed in initial caps or all caps.

Library of Congress Cataloging-in-Publication Data

Reiman, Jeffrey H.
  The rich get richer and the poor get prison : ideology, class, and criminal justice / Jeffrey Reiman, Paul Leighton. — 10th ed.
    p. cm.
  Includes index.
  ISBN-13: 978-0-205-13772-5
  ISBN-10: 0-205-13772-5
  1. Criminal justice, Administration of—United States.   2. Social classes—United States.
3. United States—Social policy.   I. Leighton, Paul, 1964–   II. Title.
  HV9950.R46 2013
  364.973—dc23

                                                                              2012029887

10 9 8 7 6 5 4 3

PEARSON

ISBN 10:   0-205-13772-5
ISBN 13: 978-0-205-13772-5

For Sue
and
For Satoko, Sala, and Aiko

For Sue
and
For Saeko, Sara, and Miki

BRIEF CONTENTS

CONTENTS

FIGURE AND TABLES

PREFACE TO THE TENTH EDITION

"Everything's f**ked up, and nobody goes to jail," notes *Rolling Stone* columnist Matt Taibbi in a March 3, 2011 piece aptly titled: "Why Isn't Wall Street in Jail? Financial crooks brought down the world's economy—but the feds are doing more to protect them than to prosecute them." That sentiment is apparently widely shared, and what started as a New York protest to occupy Wall Street turned into a global Occupy Wall Street protest movement. But while peaceful protesters are being arrested for disorderly conduct, those who created serious disorder in the world economy keep getting bonuses and go about business as usual.

For almost 35 years now, *The Rich Get Richer and the Poor Get Prison* has been raising the issue of economic inequality and asking, why aren't the tools of the criminal justice system being used to protect Americans from predatory business practices and to punish those well-off people who cause widespread harm?

The answer offered by *The Rich Get Richer and the Poor Get Prison* is that this is precisely how our criminal justice system is designed to function. It aims its weapons against the poor, while ignoring or treating gently the rich who prey upon their fellows. *The Rich Get Richer* invites readers to look at the American criminal justice system as if it were aimed, not at protecting us against crime, but at keeping before our eyes—in our courts and in our prisons, in our newspapers and on our TVs—a large criminal population consisting primarily of poor people. This serves the interests of the rich and powerful by broadcasting the message that the real danger to most Americans comes from people below them on the economic ladder, rather than from above. Looking at the criminal justice system this way makes more sense out of criminal justice policy than accepting the idea that the system is really aiming at protecting our lives and limbs and possessions. All of this is summed up by saying that *the rich get richer and the poor get prison.*

Supporting the thesis that the criminal justice system is aimed at maintaining a large visible population of poor criminals requires defending two main claims: First, that the system could reduce our high crime rates, but fails to do so; and second, that the system is biased against the poor at every stage. This second claim means that *for the same crimes*, the poor are more likely than the well-off to get arrested and, if arrested, more likely to be charged and, if charged, more likely to be convicted and, if convicted, more likely to be sentenced to prison and, if sentenced to prison, more likely to receive a long sentence. But it means even more: The bias against the poor starts earlier, at the point at which legislators decide what is to be a crime in the first place. Many of the ways in which the well-off harm their fellows (deadly pollution, unsafe working conditions, and some of the harmful practices that have led to the current financial crisis) are not even defined as crimes, *though they do more damage to life and limb, or take more money from people's pockets, than the acts that are treated as crimes.*

But what of the first claim, namely, that the system could reduce our high crime rates, but fails to do so? In recent years we have seen an enormous increase in the number of Americans behind bars and significant drops in our crime rates. We shall show that only a small fraction of this reduction is due to criminal justice policies, although some of it undoubtedly is. The thesis of *The Rich Get Richer* requires only that the criminal justice system fails to prevent enough crime so that there remains before our eyes a large population of poor criminals. And that is no less the case today than it was when the book was first written. Though crime is down these days, there is still plenty of it—much more than in countries similar to the United States in population density and wealth—and our citizens are still afraid of it. And our prisons are jammed full of people who are far poorer, and far more likely to have been unemployed or underemployed before entering prison, than their counterparts in the larger population.

Moreover, the criminal justice system—by which we always mean the whole system from lawmakers to law enforcers—continues not to implement programs that could alleviate the disabilities of poverty and dramatically reduce our high crime rates. And, as this book documents in detail, little has been done to make the harmful noncriminal acts of the well-off into crimes, or to reduce the bias against poor people caught up in the system. In short, though the system has had some success in reducing crime, it is still failing in the way that the thesis of *The Rich Get Richer* asserts: We still face the specter of a large and scary population of poor criminals. The criminal justice system still fails to protect us from the well-off by *not* treating their harmful acts as crimes. For all the changes of recent years, *the rich are still getting richer and the poor are still getting prison.*

In revising the book for the Tenth Edition, we have mainly tried to show the truth of this statement by bringing statistics comparing criminal and noncriminal harms (such as those caused by preventable occupational and environmental hazards) up-to-date, and by incorporating the results of the relevant research that has appeared since the last edition. As always, we have tried to introduce these updates with as little violation of the original edition's style and argument as possible.

This edition reports findings of studies published as recently as 2011. However, where we compare the relative danger of criminal versus noncriminal harms, we generally use figures for 2010, the latest year for which there are adequate statistics on both types of harm. When new statistics were not available, we have, where it seemed plausible, assumed that earlier statistics reflect continuing trends and enable projections from the past into the present. In all cases, we have kept our assumptions and estimates extremely conservative in order to keep the argument on the firmest ground. In addition to new studies and data, we also continue to report some of the most striking of the older studies. This shows how deep-seated the bias in our system is, and that the recent studies are not aberrations or about merely passing phenomena.

The preface to the last four editions noted the declining number of articles in scholarly sociology and criminology journals reporting on the relationship between economic status and arrest, conviction, and sentencing. The point bears repeating for this edition. When the First Edition of *The Rich Get Richer and the Poor Get Prison* appeared in 1979, there were many such studies, largely stimulated by President Johnson's establishment in 1965 of the President's Commission on Law Enforcement and the Administration of Justice. These studies consistently showed the presence of significant bias against lower-class suspects at every stage of criminal justice processing from arrest on. With each subsequent edition of *The Rich Get Richer*, the number of new studies on this topic has decreased, so that now, having once again reviewed every major journal (and many not-so-major ones) in the field, we find that the number of new studies has dwindled to a trickle. Nonetheless, the studies that do exist show the bias to be alive and well. Furthermore, this is also the tenth effort to arrive at an estimate of the total amount and cost of white-collar crime in the United States. There are organizations that study one or another type of white-collar crime, such as insurance fraud; but, while we are literally inundated with statistics on "common" crimes, there is no public or private agency that regularly measures the full extent of white-collar crime in all its varieties and issues a regular (not to mention annual) report. Social scientists who study the ways in which social problems are framed and addressed would do well to consider why we have so little research on economic bias in criminal justice and no measurement of the full extent of white-collar crime.

From reviewers' comments, we are happy to learn that the book continues to be used both by teachers who agree with its thesis and by those who do not. This is as it should be. *The Rich Get Richer* is meant to stimulate thought, pro and con, not to gather disciples. Over the years, reviewers have made numerous recommendations, many of which have been adopted, and which, we believe, have improved the book. Some of the recommendations—to discuss epistemology and scientific method, to present evidence conflicting with our theory alongside evidence that supports it, to provide detailed proposals for solving some of the problems that the book identifies in the criminal justice system, to call for overthrow of the capitalist system, and so on—have been resisted because following them would detract from the aim of the book. *The Rich Get Richer* is not meant to be a complete survey of the criminal justice system, and certainly not a complete survey of American social problems, and it is not meant to be a complete recipe for fixing either. Nor is it meant to be a balanced presentation of conservative and progressive views. The goal of *The Rich Get Richer* is more limited and more focused: *It is meant to show students that much that goes on in the criminal justice system violates their own sense of basic fairness, to present evidence that the system does not function in the way it says it does or in the way that students believe it should, and then to sketch a whole theoretical perspective from which they might understand these failures and evaluate them morally*—and to do it all in a short and relatively inexpensive book, written in plain language.

Although we have resisted changing the basic structure of this text, we have added discussion of many important events and authors, as well as many features to make the text more usable. Starting with the Third Edition, summaries and study questions were added; and with this Tenth Edition we have added chapter overviews at the start of the chapter to help prepare readers by highlighting the key points they will encounter. A summary at the end of the chapter helps reinforce the main points. The study questions at the end of the chapter require the student to recall what he or she has read and to think critically about it. The questions can be used by instructors for the purpose of testing and review, and by students as a way of making sure they have covered and thought about the most important issues in each chapter.

We also appreciate the need for supplementary materials, and they can be found in

- Appendixes I and II of this book
- An anthology of readings, *The Rich Get Richer: A Reader*, edited by Jeffrey Reiman and Paul Leighton (Boston: Pearson Education, Inc., 2010)
- At the author-maintained website, *http://www.paulsjusticepage.com/reiman. htm* and Paul Leighton's Twitter feed @poorgetprison (or https://twitter. com/#!/poorgetprison)

Appendix I to this book is a short essay by Jeffrey Reiman entitled, "The Marxian Critique of Criminal Justice." It is for those who want a larger theoretical context in which to place the thesis of *The Rich Get Richer*. The essay covers the ground from a general statement of Marxian theories of capitalism, ideology, and law, to a Marxian theory of criminal justice—and the ethical judgments about crime and criminals to which that theory leads. Many instructors have found this a handy and economical way of introducing their students to Marxian theory and its relation to criminal law and criminology. The essay addresses some of the same issues discussed in the main text of *The Rich Get Richer* and thus offers an alternative theoretical framework for understanding those issues. Although this alternative framework is compatible with that developed in the main text, the argument of *The Rich Get Richer* stands alone without it.

Appendix II, also authored by Jeffrey Reiman, is titled "Between Philosophy and Criminology." Like the first appendix, the second appendix is separate from the argument of the main text, but extends it in important ways. Unlike the first appendix, however, "Between Philosophy and Criminology" is a very personal statement. It aims, you might say, to stitch together the disparate parts of Reiman's intellectual life as a professional philosopher interested in criminal justice. He argues in it that criminology has a special need for philosophical reflection that other social sciences may not have, and he goes on to spell out the philosophical framework within which *The Rich Get Richer* stands. As with everything in this book, we will be as happy if this essay is used by those who criticize it as by those who agree with it.

In addition, an author-maintained website, managed by Paul Leighton, can be accessed at *http://www.paulsjusticepage.com/reiman.htm*. It contains chapter outlines and summaries with links to additional related resources, as well as Internet-based exercises for students. Several articles that we have written about corporate crime are available there. Readers can also access Paul's Twitter feed at the link above to explore current news items related to the ideas in this book.

Because we have revised rather than rewritten *The Rich Get Richer*, we are indebted to those who helped with the original edition. They are thanked in the following section, "Acknowledgments for the First Edition." Starting with the Ninth Edition, Paul Leighton joined Jeffrey Reiman as co-author of *The Rich Get Richer and the Poor Get Prison*. Paul, full professor of sociology, anthropology, and criminology at Eastern Michigan University, has assisted with the revisions of *The Rich Get Richer* since its Fourth Edition appeared almost two decades ago. Since then, Paul has taken on increasing responsibility for revising the book and, by now, his wide knowledge of the criminal justice system and of the literature of critical criminology are deeply interwoven into the text.

We are also indebted to Shigeru (Simon) Miyao, who translated the Ninth Edition of *The Rich Get Richer* into Japanese. When Mr. Miyao was pursuing his graduate degree in criminology in America, he came across *The Rich Get Richer*. He decided it was important enough to translate as a warning to his fellow citizens about policies and trends that Japan should avoid. Not only are we honored that he thought so highly of the book and grateful that he has made it available to a wider audience, we are also indebted to him for politely pointing out a range of technical errors, providing alternate URLs for ones no longer working, and offering better characterizations of information in some of the source material. Finally, Mr. Miyao suggested a series of translator's notes to help the Japanese readership better understand criminal justice terms and references to U.S. history and people. We are incorporating many of these into this edition to help both international and U.S. students who might lack background in certain subject areas. Mr. Miyao's work on the translation has been a gift to us, and this Tenth Edition is substantially improved because of it.

We appreciate the dedicated work of Dana Radatz, a doctoral student at the University of Omaha-Nebraska, on the index for this edition as well as her careful work implementing many of Mr. Miyao's suggestions. Seyed Mirmajlessi, a graduate student at Eastern Michigan University, was enthusiastic and thorough in gathering data, and helpful in getting the manuscript into final form for submission, and we are grateful to him for his efforts. The work of several past research assistants still lives on in this edition, so we thank Rachel (Songer) Stark, Carrie Buist, and Donna (Killingbeck) Selman. We also thank Karen Hanson, our editor at Allyn & Bacon, for her good counsel and hard work over many editions; and Debbie Ryan for ably handling the myriad tasks that must be addressed between submission of the manuscript and publication of the book. We are grateful to Sudeshna Nandy for her careful and expert editing. And we thank Rashmi Tickyani for coordinating the copyediting and review process.

Both Jeffrey and Paul thank their respective universities, American University and Eastern Michigan University, for providing them with the supportive and lively intellectual environments that have made this work possible and enjoyable over the years.

Jeffrey dedicates the book to his wife, friend, partner, and colleague, Sue Headlee, who continues to delight, encourage, inspire, and astonish him as she has for more than 35 years. Paul dedicates this book to his wife and best friend, Satoko, and their twins, Sala and Aiko, who further inspire him to work for a less violent society.

Jeffrey Reiman
and Paul Leighton

ACKNOWLEDGMENTS FOR
THE FIRST EDITION

This book is the product of seven years of teaching in the School of Justice (formerly, the Center for the Administration of Justice), a multidisciplinary criminal justice education program at American University in Washington, D.C. I have had the benefit of the school's lively and diverse faculty and student body. And, although they will surely not agree with all that I have to say, I have drawn heavily on what I have learned from my colleagues over the years and stand in their debt. In addition, more than is ordinarily recognized, a teacher receives guidance from students as they test, confirm, reject, and expand what they learn in class in the light of their own experience. Here, too, I am deeply indebted. My thanks go to the hundreds of students who have shared some part of their world with me as they passed through American University, and in particular to three students whose encouragement, loyalty, and wisdom are very much a part of the development of the ideas in this book: Elizabeth Crimi, Bernard Demczuk, and Lloyd Raines.

I express my gratitude to American University for providing me with a summer research grant that enabled me to devote full time to the book in the summer of 1976, when most of the actual writing was done. I am also grateful to Bernard Demczuk, who was my research assistant during the academic year 1975 to 1976 and who gathered much of the research data. I owe thanks as well to Cathy Sacks for ably and carefully typing the final manuscript.

Drafts of the manuscript for this book were read in whole or in part by (or to) Bernard Demczuk, Sue Hollis, Richard Myren, Lloyd Raines, Phillip Scribner, I. F. Stone, and John Wildeman. I am grateful for their many comments and I incorporate many of their recommendations in the final version. I have made my mistakes in spite of them.

Finally, for teaching me about artichokes, the meaning of history, and countless other mysteries, this book is dedicated to Sue Headlee Hollis.

J. R.
1979

MySearchLab®

SAVE TIME. IMPROVE RESULTS.

MySearchLab is a dynamic website that delivers proven results in helping individual students succeed. Its wealth of resources provides engaging experiences that personalize, stimulate, and measure learning for each student. Many accessible tools will encourage students to read their text, improve writing skills, and help them improve their grade in their course.

Features of MySearchLab

Writing

- Step by step tutorials present complete overviews of the research and writing process.

Research and Citing Sources

- Instructors and students receive access to the EBSCO ContentSelect database, census data from Social Explorer, Associated Press news feeds, and the Pearson bookshelf. Pearson SourceCheck helps students and instructors to monitor originality and avoid plagiarism.

eText and More

- *Pearson eText*—An e-book version of The Rich Get Richer and the Poor Get Prison: Ideology, Class, and Criminal Justice is included in MySearchLab. Just like the printed text, students can highlight and add their own notes as they read their interactive text online.
- *Primary Source [and/or Secondary] Documents*—A collection of documents, organized by chapter, are available on MySearchLab. The documents include head notes and critical thinking questions.
- *Gradebook*—Automated grading of quizzes helps both instructors and students monitor their results throughout the course.

ABOUT THE AUTHORS

Jeffrey Reiman is the William Fraser McDowell Professor of Philosophy at the American University in Washington, D.C. He was born in Brooklyn, New York, in 1942. He received his B.A. in philosophy from Queens College in 1963, and his Ph.D. in philosophy from Pennsylvania State University in 1968. He was a Fulbright Scholar in India during 1966–1967. He joined the American University faculty in 1970, in the Center for the Administration of Justice (now called the department of Justice, Law and Society of the School of Public Affairs). After several years of holding a joint appointment in the justice program and the Department of Philosophy and Religion, Dr. Reiman joined the Department of Philosophy and Religion full-time in 1988, becoming director of the Master's Program in Philosophy and Social Policy. He was named William Fraser McDowell Professor of Philosophy in 1990. He is a member of the Phi Beta Kappa and Phi Kappa Phi honor societies, and former president of the American University Phi Beta Kappa chapter. In addition to *The Rich Get Richer and the Poor Get Prison: Ideology, Class, and Criminal Justice*, Dr. Reiman is the author of *In Defense Of Political Philosophy* (1972), *Justice and Modern Moral Philosophy* (1990), *Critical Moral Liberalism: Theory And Practice* (1997), *The Death Penalty: For And Against* (with Louis P. Pojman, 1998), *Abortion and the Ways We Value Human Life* (1999), *As Free and as Just as Possible: The Theory of Marxian Liberalism* (2012), and more than 120 articles in philosophy and criminal justice journals and anthologies. He is also coeditor, with Paul Leighton, of the anthology *Criminal Justice Ethics* (2001).

Paul Leighton is a Professor in the Department of Sociology, Anthropology and Criminology at Eastern Michigan University. He received his B.A. in Criminal Justice from the State University of New York at Albany in 1986, and is indebted to Graeme Newman for helping to direct him away from law school to the Justice, Law, and Society program at American University. While at American University, he met Jeffrey Reiman and assisted with revisions of the fourth edition of *The Rich Get Richer and the Poor Get Prison*. He has worked on every edition since then. Dr. Leighton received his Ph.D. in Sociology and Justice from American University in 1995. He has been the North American Editor of *Critical Criminology: An International Journal,* and was named Critical Criminologist of the Year by the American Society of Criminology's Division on Critical Criminology. Dr. Leighton is the co-author of *Punishment for Sale* (with Donna Selman, 2010) and *Class, Race, Gender and Crime* (with Gregg Barak and Jeanne Flavin, Third Edition, 2010). He is also coeditor, with Jeffrey Reiman, of the anthology *Criminal Justice Ethics* (2001). In addition to his publications, Dr. Leighton is webmaster for StopViolence.com, PaulsJusticePage. com, and PaulsJusticeBlog.com. He is President of the Board of SafeHouse, the local shelter and advocacy center for victims of domestic violence and sexual assault.

Introduction
Criminal Justice through the Looking Glass, or Winning by Losing

The inescapable conclusion is that society secretly wants crime, needs crime, and gains definite satisfactions from the present mishandling of it.

—Karl Menninger, *The Crime of Punishment*[1]

A criminal justice system is a mirror in which a whole society can see the darker outlines of its face. Our ideas of justice and evil take on visible form in it, and thus we see ourselves in deep relief. Step through this looking glass to view the American criminal justice system—and ultimately the whole society it reflects—from a radically different angle of vision.

In particular, entertain the idea that the goal of our criminal justice system is not to eliminate crime or to achieve justice, *but to project to the American public a credible image of the threat of crime as a threat from the poor*. To accomplish this, the justice system must present us with a sizable population of poor criminals. To do that, it must fail in the struggle to eliminate the crimes that poor people commit, or even to reduce their number dramatically. Crime may, of course, occasionally decline, as it has recently—*but largely because of factors other than criminal justice policies*.

These last two statements must be explained. The news of declines in the crime rate has been quickly snatched up by leaders at all levels from the White House to the local police station as an occasion to declare the success of their crime-reduction policies. Later, we will point to a number of causes of the recent decline, such as the stabilization of the illegal drug trade and thus the reduction in drug-related violence, which have nothing to do with the success of criminal justice policies. If anything, the stabilization of the illegal drug trade is a sign of the failure of a long-standing justice policy, namely, the so-called war on drugs: Rather than the drug trade ending, that trade has become "business as usual." Nonetheless, we do not go so far as to say that criminal justice policy has made *no* contribution to the drop in crime rates.

In recent years, America has quadrupled its prison population and, in cities such as New York, allowed the police new freedom to stop and search

1

people they suspect. No one can deny that if you lock up enough people, and allow the police greater and greater power to interfere with the liberty and privacy of citizens, you will eventually prevent some crime that might otherwise have taken place. Later, we shall point out just how costly and inefficient this means of reducing crime is—in money for new prisons, in its destructive effect on inner-city life, and in increased complaints of police brutality. To be sure, these costly means do contribute *in some small measure* to reducing crime. Thus, when we say in this book that the criminal justice system is failing, our point is that it is failing to eliminate our high crime rates. We continue to see a large population of poor criminals in our prisons and courts, while our crime-reduction strategies do not touch on the social causes of crime. Moreover, our citizens remain fearful about criminal victimization even after the recent declines, and America's crime rate is still far above those of other industrial democracies around the world. We document this failure in Chapter 1, "Crime Control in America: Nothing Succeeds like Failure."

The reader should keep in mind that when we speak of the *criminal justice system*, we mean more than the familiar institutions of police, courts, and prisons. We mean the entire system that runs from the decisions of lawmakers about what acts are criminal, through the decisions of police about whom to arrest, all the way to the decisions of judges, juries, and parole boards about who will be in prison to pay for these acts.

You will rightly demand to know how and why a society such as ours would tolerate a criminal justice system that fails in the fight against crime. A considerable portion of this book is devoted to answering this question. Right now, however, a short explanation of how this upside-down idea of criminal justice was born will best introduce it.

Nearly 40 years ago, Jeffrey Reiman taught a seminar for graduate students titled "The Philosophy of Punishment and Rehabilitation." (The relationship between criminology and philosophy is discussed in Appendix II.) Many of the students were law-enforcement officers or working in the field of corrections as probation officers, prison guards, or halfway-house counselors. Together the class examined the various philosophical justifications for legal punishment, and then directed its attention to the actual functioning of our correctional system. For much of the semester, the class discussed the myriad inconsistencies and cruelties and the overall irrationality of the system. It discussed the arbitrariness with which offenders are sentenced to prison and the arbitrariness with which they are treated once there. It discussed the lack of privacy and the deprivation of sources of personal identity and dignity, the ever-present physical violence, as well as the lack of meaningful counseling or job training within prison walls. It discussed the harassment of parolees, the inescapability of the "ex-con" stigma, the refusal of society to let a person finish paying his or her "debt to society," and the absence of meaningful noncriminal opportunities for the ex-prisoner. Time and again the class confronted the bald irrationality of a society that builds prisons to prevent crime, knowing full well that they do not, and that does not seriously try to rid its prisons and post-release practices of those features that guarantee a high rate of *recidivism*, the return to crime by prison alumni. How could we fail so miserably? We are neither an evil nor a stupid nor an impoverished people. How could we continue to bend our energies and spend our hard-earned tax dollars on cures we know are not working?

Toward the end of the semester, the students were asked to imagine that, instead of designing a criminal justice system to reduce and prevent crime, they were to design one that would maintain a stable and visible "class" of criminals. What would it look like? The response was electrifying. Here is a sample of the proposals that emerged in the discussion.

1. It would be helpful to have laws on the books against drug use, prostitution, and gambling—laws that prohibit acts that have no unwilling victim. This would make many people "criminals" for what they regard as normal behavior and would increase their need to engage in *secondary crime* (the drug addict's need to steal to pay for drugs, the prostitute's need for a pimp because police protection is unavailable, and so on).

2. It would be good to give police, prosecutors, and/or judges broad discretion to decide who got arrested, who got charged, and who got sentenced to prison. This would mean that almost anyone who got as far as prison would know of others who committed the same crime but were not arrested, were not charged, or were not sentenced to prison. That would assure us that a good portion of the prison population would experience their confinement as arbitrary and unjust and thus respond with rage, which would make them more antisocial, rather than respond with remorse, which would make them feel more bound by social norms.

3. The prison experience should be not only painful, but also demeaning. The pain of loss of liberty might deter future crime. But demeaning and emasculating prisoners by placing them in an enforced childhood characterized by no privacy and no control over their time and actions, as well as by the constant threat of rape or assault, is sure to overcome any deterrent effect by weakening whatever capacities a prisoner had for self-control. Indeed, by humiliating and brutalizing prisoners, we can be sure to increase their potential for aggressive violence.[2]

4. Prisoners should neither be trained in a marketable skill nor provided with a job after release. Their prison records should stand as a perpetual stigma to discourage employers from hiring them. Otherwise, they might be tempted *not* to return to crime after release.

5. Ex-offenders' sense that they will always be different from "decent citizens," that they can never finally settle their debt to society, should be reinforced by the following means. They should be deprived for the rest of their lives of rights, such as the right to vote.[3] They should be harassed by police as "likely suspects" and be subject to the whims of parole officers who can at any time threaten to send them back to prison for things no ordinary citizens could be arrested for, such as going out of town, or drinking, or fraternizing with the "wrong people."

And so on.

In short, *when asked to design a system that would maintain and encourage the existence of a stable and visible "class of criminals," the students "constructed" the American criminal justice system!*

What is to be made of this? First, it is, of course, only part of the truth. Some steps have been taken to reduce arbitrary exercises of discretion in arrests and sentencing. And some prison officials do try to treat their inmates with dignity and to respect their privacy and self-determination to the greatest extent possible within an institution dedicated to involuntary confinement. Some prisons do provide meaningful job training, and some parole officers not only are fair but also go out of their way to help their "clients" find jobs and make it legally. And plenty of people are arrested for doing things that no society ought to tolerate, such as rape, murder, assault, or armed robbery, and many are in prison who might be preying on their fellow citizens if they were not. *All of this is true.* Complex social practices are just that: *complex.* They are rarely either all good or all bad. Nonetheless, the "successes" of the system, the "good" prisons, and the halfway houses that really help offenders make it are still the exceptions. They are not even prevalent enough to be called the beginning of the trend of the future. *On the whole, most of the system's practices make more sense if we look at them as ingredients in an attempt to maintain rather than reduce crime!*

This statement calls for an explanation. The one we offer is that the practices of the criminal justice system keep before the public the *real* threat of crime and the *distorted* image that crime is primarily the work of the poor. The value of this *to those in positions of power* is that it deflects the discontent and potential hostility of Middle America away from the classes above them and toward the classes below them. If this explanation is hard to swallow, it should be noted in its favor that it not only explains the dismal failure of criminal justice policy to protect us against crime, but also explains why the criminal justice system functions in a way that is biased against the poor at every stage from arrest to conviction. Indeed, even at an earlier stage, when crimes are defined in law, the system concentrates primarily on the predatory acts of the poor and tends to exclude or deemphasize the equally or more dangerous predatory acts of those who are well off.

In sum, we will argue that *the criminal justice system fails in the fight against crime while making it look as if crime is the work of the poor.* This conveys the image that the real danger to decent, law-abiding Americans comes from people below them, rather than from above them, on the economic ladder. This image sanctifies the status quo with its disparities of wealth, privilege and opportunity, and thus serves the interests of the rich and powerful in America—the very ones who could change criminal justice policy if they were really unhappy with it.

Therefore, it is appropriate to ask you to look at criminal justice "through the looking glass." On the one hand, this suggests a reversal of common expectations. Reverse your expectations about criminal justice and entertain the notion that the system's real goal is the very reverse of its announced goal.

On the other hand, the figure of the looking glass suggests the prevalence of image over reality. Our argument is that the system functions the way it does *because it maintains a particular image of crime: the image that it is a threat from the poor.* Of course, for this image to be believable there must be a reality to back it up. The system must actually fight crime—or at least some crime—but only enough to keep it from getting out of hand and to keep the struggle against crime vividly and dramatically in the public's view, never enough to substantially reduce or eliminate crime.

We call this outrageous way of looking at criminal justice policy the *Pyrrhic defeat* theory. A "Pyrrhic victory" is a military victory purchased at such a cost in troops and treasure that it amounts to a defeat. The Pyrrhic defeat theory argues that the failure of the criminal justice system yields such benefits to those in positions of power that it amounts to a victory. In what follows, we will try to explain the failure of the criminal justice system to reduce crime by showing the benefits that accrue to the powerful in America from this failure. From the standpoint of those with the power to make criminal justice policy in America, *nothing succeeds like failure.* We challenge you to keep an open mind and determine for yourself whether the Pyrrhic defeat theory does not make more sense out of criminal justice policy and practice than the old-fashioned idea that the goal of the system is to reduce crime substantially.

The Pyrrhic defeat theory has several components. Above all, it must provide an explanation of *how* the failure to reduce crime substantially could benefit anyone—anyone other than criminals, that is. This is the task of Chapter 4, "To the Vanquished Belong the Spoils: Who Is Winning the Losing War against Crime?" which argues that the failure to reduce crime substantially broadcasts a potent *ideological* message to the American people, a message that benefits and protects the powerful and privileged in our society by legitimating the present social order with its disparities of wealth and privilege, and by diverting public discontent and opposition away from the rich and powerful and onto the poor and powerless.

To provide this benefit, however, not just any failure will do. It is necessary that the failure of the criminal justice system take a particular shape. *It must fail in the fight against crime while making it look as if serious crime and thus the real danger to society are the work of the poor.* The system accomplishes this both by what it does and by what it refuses to do. Chapter 2, "A Crime by Any Other Name . . .," argues that the criminal justice system refuses to label and treat as crime a large number of acts of the rich that produce as much or more damage to life and limb than the crimes of the poor. Chapter 3, ". . . and the Poor Get Prison," shows how, even among the acts treated as crimes, the criminal justice system is biased from start to finish in a way that guarantees that, *for the same crimes,* members of the lower classes are much more likely than members of the middle and upper classes to be arrested, convicted, and imprisoned—thus providing living "proof" that crime is a threat from the poor. (A statement of the main propositions that form the core of the Pyrrhic defeat theory is found in Chapter 2 in the section titled "Criminal Justice as Creative Art.")

ONE CAUTION IS IN ORDER   The argument in Chapters 1 through 4 is not a "conspiracy theory." It is the task of social analysis to find patterns in social behavior and then explain them. Naturally, when we find patterns, particularly patterns that serve some people's interests, we are inclined to think of these patterns as *intended* by those whose interests are served, as somehow brought into being *because* they serve those interests. This way of thinking is generally called a *conspiracy theory.* Later we will say more about the shortcomings of this way of thinking and explain in detail how the Pyrrhic defeat theory differs from it. For the present, however, note that although we speak of the criminal justice system as "not wanting" to reduce crime and of the failure to reduce crime significantly as resulting in benefits to the rich and powerful in our society, *we are not maintaining that the rich and powerful intentionally make the system fail to gather up the resulting benefits.* Our view is rather that the system has grown up piecemeal over time and usually with the best of intentions. The unplanned and unintended overall result is a system that not only fails to substantially reduce crime, but also does so in a way that serves the interests of the rich and powerful. One consequence of this fact is that those who could change the system feel no need to do so. And thus it keeps on rolling along.

Our criminal justice system is characterized by beliefs about what is criminal, and beliefs about how to deal with crime, which predate industrial society. Rather than being anyone's conscious plan, the system reflects attitudes so deeply embedded in tradition as to appear natural. To understand why it persists even though it fails to protect us, all that is necessary is to recognize that, on the one hand, those who are the most victimized by crime are not those in positions to make and implement policy. Crime falls more frequently and more harshly on the poor than on the better-off. On the other hand, there are enough benefits to the wealthy from the identification of crime with the poor and the system's failure to reduce crime that those with the power to make profound changes in the system feel no compulsion nor see any incentive to make them. In short, the criminal justice system came into existence in an earlier epoch and persists in the present because, even though it is failing—indeed, because of the way it fails—it generates no effective demand for change. When we speak of the criminal justice system as "designed to fail," we mean no more than this. We call this explanation of the existence and persistence of our failing criminal justice system the *historical inertia* explanation, which Chapter 4 spells out in greater detail.

The concluding chapter presents an argument that the conditions described in Chapters 1, 2, and 3 (whether or not one accepts our explanation for them in Chapter 4) undermine the essential moral difference between criminal justice and crime itself. This chapter, called "Criminal *Justice* or *Criminal* Justice," makes some recommendations for reform of the system. These are not offered as ways to "improve" the system, but as the minimal conditions necessary to establish the moral superiority of that system to crime itself.

The Pyrrhic defeat theory is a child of the marriage of several ideas from Western social theory. Although this is discussed at greater length in what follows, it will serve clarity to indicate from the start the parents and the grandparents of this child. The idea that crime serves important functions for a society comes from Émile Durkheim. The notion that public policy can be best understood as serving the interests of the rich and powerful in a society stems from Karl Marx. From Kai Erikson is derived the notion that the institutions designed to fight crime instead contribute to its existence. From Richard Quinney comes the concept of the "reality" of crime as *created* in the process that runs from the definition of some acts as "criminal" in the law to the treatment of some persons as "criminals" by the agents of the law. The Pyrrhic defeat theory combines these ideas into the view that the failure of criminal justice policy becomes intelligible when we see that it creates the "reality" of crime as the work of the poor and thus projects an image that serves the interests of the rich and powerful in American society.

Though the Pyrrhic defeat theory draws on the ideas just mentioned, it changes them in the process. For example, the theory veers away from the traditional Marxist accounts of legal institutions insofar as those accounts generally emphasize the *repressive* function of the criminal justice system, whereas our view emphasizes its *ideological* function. Marxists tend to see the criminal justice system as serving the powerful by *successfully* repressing the poor. Our view is that the system serves the powerful by its *failure* to reduce crime, not by its success. Needless to add, insofar as the system fails in some respects and succeeds in others, these approaches are not incompatible. Nevertheless, in looking at the ideological rather than the repressive function of criminal justice, we will focus primarily on the image its *failure* conveys rather than on what it actually *succeeds* in repressing.[4] (A discussion of Marxian theory and its implications for ideology and criminal justice is found in Appendix I.)

Having located the Pyrrhic defeat theory in its family tree, we wish to say a word about the relationship between crime and economics. Our view is that the social order (shaped decisively by the economic system) bears responsibility for most of the crime that troubles us. This is true for all classes in the society, because a competitive economy that refuses to guarantee its members a decent living places pressures on all members to enhance their economic position by whatever means available. It degrades and humiliates the poor while encouraging the greed of the well-off.[5] Nevertheless, these economic pressures work with particular harshness on the poor because their condition of extreme need and relative lack of access to opportunities for lawful economic advancement vastly intensify for them the pressures toward crime that exist at all levels of our society.

These views lead to others that, if not taken in their proper context, may strike you as paradoxical. Evidence will be presented showing that there is a considerable amount of crime in our society at all socioeconomic levels. At the same time, it will be argued that poverty is a *source* of crime—we say "source" rather than "cause," because the link between poverty and crime is not a simple relationship between cause and effect. Poverty doesn't force poor people to commit crimes. Rather it confronts them with needs that they are less able than well-off people to satisfy legally, and it offers them fewer rewards for staying straight. Thus, they face pressures and incentives that make crime more tempting, and noncriminal avenues less appealing, than they are for better-off people. Consequently, while most poor people do not commit serious crimes, evidence suggests that the particular pressures of poverty lead poor people to commit a higher proportion (in relation to their number in the population) of the crimes that people fear, such as homicide, burglary, and assault. There is no contradiction between this and the recognition that those who are well-off commit many more crimes than is generally acknowledged, both the crimes widely feared and those not widely feared (such as white-collar crimes). There is no contradiction here, because, as will be shown, the poor are arrested far more frequently than those who are well-off when they have committed the same crimes, and the well-to-do are only rarely arrested for white-collar crimes. Thus, if arrest records were brought in line with the real incidence of crime, it is likely that those who are well-off would appear in the records far more than they do at present, even though the poor would still probably appear in numbers greater than their proportion of the population in arrests for the crimes people fear. In addition to this, we will argue that those who are well-off commit dangerous acts that are not defined as crimes and yet are as or more harmful than the crimes people fear. Thus, if we had an accurate picture of who is really dangerous to society, there is reason to believe that those who are well-off would receive still greater representation. On this basis, the following propositions will be put forth, which may appear contradictory if these various levels of analysis are not kept distinct.

1. Society fails to protect people from the crimes they fear by, among other things, refusing to alleviate the poverty that breeds them (documented in Chapter 1).

2. The criminal justice system fails to protect people from the most serious dangers by failing to treat the dangerous acts of those who are well-off as crimes (documented in Chapter 2), and by failing to enforce the law vigorously against the well-to-do when they commit acts that are defined as crimes (documented in Chapter 3).

3. By virtue of these and other failures, the criminal justice system succeeds in creating the image that crime is almost exclusively the work of the poor, an image that serves the interests of the powerful (argued in Chapter 4).

The view that the social order is responsible for crime does not mean that individuals are wholly blameless for their criminal acts or that we ought not have a criminal justice system able to protect us against them. To borrow an analogy from Ernest van den Haag, it would be foolhardy to refuse to fight a fire because its causes were suspect. The fact that society produces criminals is no reason to avoid facing the realization that many of these criminals are dangerous and must be dealt with. Also, although blaming society for crime may require that we tone down our blame of individual criminals, it does not require that we eliminate blame entirely or deny that they are responsible for their crimes. This is particularly important to remember because so many of the victims of the crimes of the poor are poor themselves. To point to the unique social pressures that lead the poor to prey on one another is to point to a mitigating, not an excusing, factor. Even the victims of exploitation and oppression have moral obligations not to harm those who do not exploit them or who share their oppression.

ABBREVIATIONS USED IN THE NOTES

Challenge The Challenge of Crime in a Free Society: A Report by the President's Commission on Law Enforcement and Administration of Justice (Washington, D.C.: U.S. Government Printing Office, February 1967).

Sourcebook Ann L. Pastore and Kathleen Maguire, eds. *Sourcebook of Criminal Justice Statistics*. References to earlier editions of this annual publication will be indicated by *Sourcebook*, followed by the year in the title. Earlier editions may have different editors. The *Sourcebook* is now only available in electronic form and can be accessed at *http://www. albany.edu/sourcebook/*.

StatAbst U.S. Census Bureau, *Statistical Abstract of the United States*. References to editions of this annual publication will be indicated by *StatAbst*, followed by the year in the title. It is available online at *http:// www.census.gov/prod/www/abs/statab.html*.

UCR U.S. Department of Justice, Federal Bureau of Investigation, *Crime in the United States* (commonly known as the Uniform Crime Reports). References to this annual report will be indicated by *UCR*, followed by the year for which the statistics are reported. As with the *Sourcebook*, there is no longer a print version of the *UCR*, but data back to 1995 can be accessed through *http://www.fbi.gov/about-us/cjis/ucr/ucr*.

BJS Bureau of Justice Statistics, a source of many reports cited in this book. The Bureau of Justice Statistics is an agency of the U.S. Department of Justice. It is part of the Justice Department's Office of Justice Programs, which also includes the Bureau of Justice Assistance, the National Institute of Justice, the Office of Juvenile Justice and Delinquency Prevention, and the Office for Victims of Crime. Reports of the Bureau of Justice Statistics are published by the U.S. Government Printing Office in Washington, D.C. The Bureau of Justice Statistics can be accessed online at *http://bjs.ojp.usdoj.gov/*.

Notes

1. Karl Menninger, *The Crime of Punishment* (New York: Viking, 1968).
2. Consider the following:

   Dr. Meredith Bombar, a social psychologist and associate professor of psychology at Elmira College, notes that it would be difficult intentionally to shape a more effective breeding ground for aggression than that which already exists in the average prison. In personal correspondence, Dr. Bombar writes, "When I teach Social Psychology class, I spend a week or so going over the social/learned causes of aggression (e.g., provocation, modeling, punishment, extreme frustration, roles and social norms calling for aggression, physical discomfort, crowding, presence of guns and other objects associated with aggression, etc.). After the students have digested that, I ask them to imagine a horrible fantasy world which would put together all of these known social/environmental causes of aggression. What would it be? A typical prison." (From Lee Griffith, *The Fall of the Prison: Biblical Perspectives on Prison Abolition* [Grand Rapids, MI: Eerdmans, 1993], p. 65 n.)

3. Almost 5 million American citizens are currently deprived of the right to vote because they have been convicted of a felony. See Jeffrey Reiman, "Liberal and Republican Arguments against the Disenfranchisement of Felons," *Criminal Justice Ethics* 24, no. 1 (Winter-Spring 2005): 3–18.

4. Since the 1960s, a new generation of Marxist theorists, primarily French, has begun to look specifically at the ideological functions performed by the institutions of the state. See, especially, Louis Althusser, "Ideology and Ideological State Apparatuses," in his *Lenin and Philosophy and Other Essays* (London: New Left Books, 1971), pp. 121–73; and Nicos Poulantzas, *Fascism and Dictatorship* (London: New Left Books, 1974), pp. 299–309. These writers refer to the pioneering insights of Antonio Gramsci into the ideological functions of state institutions. See Quintin Hoare and Geoffrey Nowell-Smith, eds., *Selections from the Prison Notebooks of Antonio Gramsci* (London: Lawrence and Wishart, 1971); and Carl Boggs, *Gramsci's Marxism* (London: Pluto Press, 1976). For other broadly Marxian analyses of the relationship between the state and ideology, see Ralph Miliband, *The State in Capitalist Society* (New York: Basic Books, 1969), pp. 179–264; and Jürgen Habermas, *Legitimation Crisis* (Boston: Beacon Press, 1975). A contemporary writer who takes seriously the ideological message of criminal justice practices is David Garland in *Punishment and Modern Society* (Chicago: University of Chicago Press, 1990), esp. Ch. 11, "Punishment as a Cultural Agent," pp. 249–76.

5. See, for example, John Braithwaite, "Poverty, Power, and White-Collar Crime: Sutherland and the Paradoxes of Criminological Theory," in Kip Schlegel and David Weisburd (ed.) *White-Collar Crime Revisited* (Boston: Northeastern University Press, 1992), pp. 78–107.

Crime Control in America
Nothing Succeeds Like Failure

Is it crime and punishment that go hand in hand?
Or does punishment feed the crime that plagues our land?

—Robert Johnson, *A Zoo Near You**

Failure is in the eye of the beholder.

—Anonymous

OVERVIEW

Chapter 1 has three main objectives: 1) to examine the exclusive focus on police and prison as the response to America's high crime rate, and the limited role they played in causing a decline in crime rates, 2) to review the "excuses" that are made for our high crime rates, and how we choose to have the crime rates we do, and 3) to outline the Pyrrhic defeat theory to explain the continued existence over decades of policies that fail to reduce crime. The subtitle of Chapter 1, "Nothing Succeeds Like Failure," highlights an important aspect of the larger argument: the criminal justice system is failing even if crime rates are down from all-time highs. "Tough on crime" policies had little to do with the reductions in crime rates, and mass incarceration had some "backfire" effects that promoted crime. Crime rates in the U.S. are still high compared to other developed countries. They are now down to the rates experienced during the 1970s, when crime was seen as an alarming problem. Policies targeting sources of crime (inequality, guns, prison, drug policy), and evidence-based policies about what works to reduce crime, have not been seriously considered. Ultimately, American criminal justice policy makes more sense if we look at the system as wanting to have high crime rates—there are groups for whom "crime pays" and for whom the system's failure is a success.

*By permission of BleakHouse Publishing.

DESIGNED TO FAIL

In the last 50 years, crime rates have gone up and down, although mostly up until the 1990s, and then down substantially. Current crime rates are still above what they were in the early 1960s, in spite of various "tough on crime" proposals that propelled the U.S. into "the largest prison expansion the world has ever known."[1] From 1980 to 2000, the U.S. built more prisons than it had in all of its history,[2] creating what has been called an incarceration binge, mass incarceration, hyperincarceration, and a *Plague of Prisons*.[3] The policies that led to the U.S. having the highest incarceration rate in the world obviously contributed something to lowering crime rates. But the contribution was modest at best, and it came at an enormous financial cost, heightened racial inequality and tensions, and added to a variety of social problems like the breakdown of inner-city communities. And while "getting tough on crime" is no longer the dominant theme in political discussions about criminal justice, the persistence of a failed policy for decades requires examination.

In response to rising crime rates during the 1960s, President Johnson proposed a number of initiatives addressing the *causes* of crime. These included antipoverty and economic opportunity programs that sought to spread the benefits of America's successful economy to more citizens. Programs that addressed social inequality were considered to be anticrime programs because they attacked crime's "root causes." Johnson declared: "There is something mighty wrong when a candidate for the highest office bemoans violence in the streets but votes against the war on poverty, votes against the Civil Rights Act, and votes against major educational bills that come before him."[4] President Nixon's "law and order" campaign explicitly rejected Johnson's strategy and in his 1970 State of the Union message, Nixon stated: "We must declare and win the war against the criminal elements which increasingly threaten our cities, our homes, and our lives."[5] The four years of Carter's Presidency were an exception to the "tough on crime" agenda (for example, he proposed eliminating penalties for possession of less than one ounce of marijuana).[6] But the "get tough" pattern resumed with Reagan's election as President in 1980 and continued through the 1990s—when crime rates started to decline—until the financial crisis of 2008.

During the 30 years in which crime rates were increasing, politicians never took responsibility for it. They played to voters' fears by advocating "law and order" or the many varieties of "getting tough on crime": more police, harsher sentences, mandatory minimums, three-strikes-and-you're-out laws (including expanding the number of offenses that count as strikes), and the increased use of capital punishment. When crime rates started to come down, however, politicians jumped to claim credit for the reductions. Franklin Zimring calls this "a version of 'heads I win, tails you lose,' in which decreases in crime are evidence that hard-line punishments work, whereas increases are evidence that they are needed."[7] For example, in his 1994 State of the Union Address, President Bill Clinton told us that

> while Americans are more secure from threats from abroad, I think
> we all know that in many ways we are less secure from threats here

at home. ... Violent crime and the fear it provokes are crippling our society, limiting personal freedom and fraying the ties that bind us.[8]

But then the good news began to arrive: A *New York Times* headline in 1996 announced, "A Large Drop in Violent Crime Is Reported."[9] The article said that President Clinton "asserted that his policies, including putting more police officers on the streets and regulating the sale of handguns and assault rifles, had helped contribute to the decline."

Less than two weeks later, *U.S. News & World Report* ran a cover article titled "Popgun Politics," asserting that neither President Clinton nor his opponent in the race for the presidency, Senator Bob Dole, was telling the truth about the crime issue. For example, while Clinton claimed that his policy of putting 100,000 new police on the street "played a big role in [the] recent crime drop," the magazine reported that "Clinton has won funding for 44,000 officers; [of whom] 20,000 are on the beat so far. Experts say that number could not have reduced crime much."[10] With officers working in shifts, taking vacations, and so on, it requires at least five officers to provide one officer on the street, around the clock, for a whole year.[11] So those 20,000 probably amount to no more than 4,000 new police on the streets around the clock.

Untroubled by such facts, President Clinton reported, in a 1997 radio address,

> We had a comprehensive plan to fight crime—to put 100,000 new community police officers on the street and tough new penalties on the books. ... This approach is working.
>
> This week the FBI reported that serious crime dropped another three percent last year, dropping for the fifth year in a row, the longest decline in more than 25 years. This is great news.

And how shall we respond to this news? Continues President Clinton: "Now that we've finally turned crime on the run, we have to redouble our efforts."[12] Then, two years later, in his 1999 State of the Union Address, the president was singing the same tune:

> I propose a 21st Century Crime Bill to deploy the latest technologies and tactics to make our communities even safer. Our balanced budget will help to put up to 50,000 more police on the street in the areas hardest hit by crime, and then to equip them with new tools from crime mapping computers to digital mug shots.[13]

Early in his first term, President George W. Bush noted the decline in crime and added, "[B]ut, unfortunately, American society is still far too violent. The violent crime rate in the United States remains among the highest in the industrialized world."[14] This speech was in the context of the president's *Blueprint for New Beginnings,* which included $821 million for prison construction and private prison space,[15] plus $140 million to support additional detention beds.[16] The declining crime rates coupled with the terrorist attacks of September 11, 2001, brought about the opposite of the situation described by President Clinton above. Americans became more concerned with threats from abroad, so crime became a low-priority issue. But a 2005 statement shows the administration's call for more of the same in its support for the Gang Deterrence and Community Protection Act: "Aggressive law enforcement and tougher sentencing laws bear a good deal of the responsibility for the precipitous reduction in crime rates, especially for violent crime, over the past decade."[17] The Department of Justice's 2006 budget noted the need for $1.2 billion to incarcerate larger numbers of prisoners because of "the aggressive enforcement of the Administration's law enforcement initiatives, and the resulting detainee population increase."[18]

As a candidate, Barack Obama did not repudiate the "get tough" policy of the last decades, but called for "a crime policy that's both tough and smart."[19] An article in *Politico* entitled "President Obama backing off strict crime policy" suggests a break with past federal crime policies, and it is significant that the harsh disparity in sentencing between crack and powder cocaine has recently been reduced from 100:1 to 18:1.[20] This change is the first reduction in drug sentences in decades, but the U.S. Sentencing Commission had been advocating for it since 1995. The other initiatives discussed in the article are merely *requests for reviews* of sentencing practices in general and of child pornography sentences in particular.[21] The results of these reviews may be reduced sentences, but the path from a request for review to recommendations to changes in law is long and uncertain.

Lest anyone believe that thinking about crime has changed since Clinton, Obama's Attorney General held a press conference to announce that crime was down in the first six months of 2011. His message: "We will continue to support our state, local and tribal partners and to implement the tough, smart policing policies that we know make a difference in the fight against violent crime."[22] Obama has supported greater levels of funding for the Community Oriented Policing Service (COPS) program started by Clinton to hire police officers, even though a 2005 report by the General Accounting Office found that "between 1993 and 2000, the overall crime rate declined by 26 percent, and the 1.3 percent decline due to COPS amounted to about 5 percent of the overall decline."[23] As a candidate, Obama said that the United States should "reduce the blind and counterproductive warehousing of non-violent offenders."[24] But according to a brief by the Justice Policy Institute, the 2010 Department of Justice budget "reduces spending on juvenile justice programs" and "increases spending on prisons, including 1,000 new contract beds (private prison providers) and two new federal prisons" that would add 4,800 new beds.[25]

More generally, the libertarian magazine, *Reason*, ran a cover story titled "Bummer: Barack Obama turns out to be just another drug warrior," which claims that (with the exception of crack sentences) Obama's drug policies "by and large have been remarkably similar to his predecessor's."[26] What makes the situation surprising is while holding other political offices before becoming President, Obama said "we can't incarcerate ourselves out of the drug crisis," that the war on drugs was "an utter failure," and he advocated decriminalization of marijuana.[27] According to a 2010 poll, 65 percent of Americans agree that the War on Drugs has been a failure and 52 percent favor legalization of marijuana.[28] But any shift in priorities that might signal a de-escalation of the drug war, like less enforcement and more treatment, "has not been perceptible in Obama's drug control budgets" says *Reason*. Even his policy on medical marijuana "is in some ways even more aggressively intolerant than George W. Bush's, featuring more frequent raids by the Drug Enforcement Administration (DEA), ruinous IRS audits, and threats of prosecution against, not only dispensaries, but anyone who deals with them."[29]

So, whether crime is a high-profile issue or a less visible one, the failed policies continue—even under those who seem to understand the problems with these policies. Sadly, state and local politicians have generally followed the direction set by our national leaders in promoting "tough on crime" solutions, at least until the financial crisis of 2008. Substantial declines in state and local budgets precipitated what is likely to be the first sustained reduction in incarceration in decades.[30] States are now scrambling to release nonviolent offenders and overhaul tough laws to reduce the flow of inmates into prison, which testifies to how little these laws contributed to public safety. Indeed, the paradigm shift from "tough on crime" to "smart on crime" is itself an admission that "tough on crime" was not smart.

Further, the sudden rush to embrace evidence-based policies should not obscure the level of irrationality that has been accepted as normal. The plain fact is that virtually no serious student of the crime problem believes we can arrest and imprison our way out of the crime problem, but that has been the predominant policy. Between 1980 and 2009, the number of persons incarcerated in state and federal prisons more than quadrupled, growing from 329,000 to more than 1.5 million. If we add those who are locked up in jails, there are now almost 2.3 million people behind bars in the United States, a number close to the entire population of states such as Utah or Nevada![31] In 2003, the Bureau of Justice Statistics reported that if 2001 incarceration rates remain unchanged, 11.3 percent of men and 32 percent of black men can expect to serve time in prison during their lifetime![32]

One troubling aspect of these policies is that the money used to fund the imprisonment boom has been taken from crime prevention, welfare, education, and medical treatment for the poor, thereby weakening programs that reduce crime in the long run. Criminologist William Chambliss writes that

> California, whose higher education system was once the envy of every other state, now is 'envied' by correctional officers and criminal justice employees, who saw an increase of more than 25,000 employees in the Department of Corrections workforce between 1984 and 1994; at the same time, there was a decline of more than 8,000 employees in higher education.[33]

By 2010, California spent 11 percent of its state budget on prisons and 7.5 percent on higher education, leading the then-Governor Schwarzenegger to propose an amendment to the state Constitution requiring it to spend more on higher education than prisons. The *Chronicle of Higher Education* notes "the proposal has a difficult road ahead."[34] The reforms it would mandate are even more far-reaching than the 2011 Supreme Court order to California to release 37,000 inmates to bring the system *down* to 137.5 percent of capacity, and remedy conditions that the Court found are causing "needless suffering and death."[35]

California was—and is—not alone: during the late 1980s and 1990s, spending for New York's public universities dropped by 29 percent while funding for prisons increased by 76 percent.[36] A 2008 study by the Pew Charitable Trusts notes that between 1987 and 2007, the amount that states spent on corrections increased by 127 percent (after correcting for inflation) while higher education expenditures increased by 21 percent. At the time of the report, five states spent as much or more on corrections than they did on higher education. The report, titled *One in 100* (referring to the number of Americans incarcerated compared to the adult population), finds that "prison costs are blowing holes in state budgets but barely making a dent in recidivism rates."[37] And what are the results? Violent crimes have declined since 1992, but crime rates are still very high. For example, in 1992, the FBI reported a violent crime rate of 758 per 100,000 persons in the population. In 2010 the FBI reported a decline in the violent crime rate to 404 per 100,000, just above what it was in 1972 (401 per 100,000).[38] Says criminologist Elliott Currie, "[T]he recent declines ... mainly represent a falling-off from an extraordinary peak."[39] And they have come down to rates that existed when far fewer Americans were locked up. In short, the crime reductions for which our leaders are now claiming credit are actually reductions from *very, very high* crime rates to rates that are merely *very high*.

For example, in 1999, the *Washington Post* ran a headline: "Crime Rates Down for the 7th Straight Year," but the news was not all good. The homicide rate was down to 6 per 100,000 inhabitants, a rate comparable to that in 1967, when it was thought to be a high rate. And while "[y]outh homicide rates are half of what they were five years ago," they are "twice as high as they were 15 years ago."[40] An even less comforting view appeared in another 1999 *Washington Post* article under the headline "Despite Rhetoric, Violent Crime Climbs":

> Rosy assessments of the nation's declining crime rate wrongly focus on the short-term drops from crime peaks early in the decade and ignore the overall rise of violence since the 1960s, according to a new report.
>
> The 30-year update of a landmark study by the National Commission on the Causes and Prevention of Violence found that violent crime in major cities reported to the FBI has risen by 40 percent since 1969.
>
> The new study is intended as a counterpoint to the drumbeat of optimistic reports describing the current drop in crime, and it offers a sober reminder that the United States still suffers from a historically high level of violence.[41]

This 1999 study was conducted by the Milton S. Eisenhower Foundation, an organization devoted to continuing the work of the original 1969 National Commission on the Causes and Prevention of Violence and the 1968 National Advisory Commission on Civil Disorders (Kerner Commission). The foundation study noted the strikingly higher rates of violent crime in the United States compared to other industrialized nations: "In 1995, handguns were used to kill 2 people in New Zealand, 15 in Japan, 30 in Great Britain, 106 in Canada, 213 in Germany, and 9,390 in the United States."[42] "The most optimistic view after looking at this," said foundation president Lynn A. Curtis, who also worked on the 1969 violence report, "is that we are in roughly the same ballpark now in the late 1990s as we were in the late 1960s, when everyone said crime is so bad we need a national commission to study it."[43] The difference is that in 1969, there were 197,136 individuals in state and federal prisons, but by 1999 that number had grown *over 700 percent* to 1,496,629—growth that has cost us billions of dollars, given prison records to huge numbers of nonviolent criminals, and torn up inner-city communities, but that has not made much of a difference in the amount of crime we have.[44]

Figure 1.1 illustrates these concepts by comparing the violent crime rate and incarceration rate (only of people in prisons—jail inmates are not included). If you look at the graph from 1990 onward, you get the misleading impression that higher incarceration rates led to lower levels of crime. The longer-term view reveals a more complex reality. During most of the

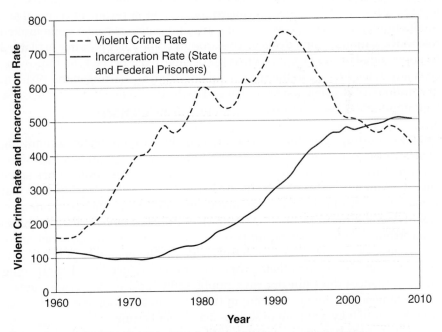

FIGURE 1.1   Violent crime rate and incarceration rate, 1960–2009.
Source: Sourcebook, Tables 3.106.2009 and 6.28.2009.

time, crime had an upward trend, while incarceration increased continually. Further, the graph shows that the current crime rate is far off its peak, but down to levels of the early 1970s. At that time, it had been increasing for more than a decade and was the subject of great concern, while that same level of violent crime is now a cause for celebration and complacency. As John DiIulio, President Bush's first director of the White House Office of Faith-Based and Community Initiatives, recently stated:

> America in 2010 is a half-century into massive public and private anticrime investments, tougher criminal sentencing policies, and security-seeking personal life style changes; yet, for all that, nationally, crime is not demonstrably lower today than it was 50 years ago, and in many places it is worse than it was when the national alarm about crime was first sounded. Since crime climbed on to the federal policy agenda in the early 1960s, successive government wars on crime and drugs have sacrificed once-sacred civil liberties. Today, nearly 2.5 million Americans live behind prison gates while tens of millions more live in gated communities.[45]

Understanding the Decline in Crime Rates

Although many Americans are confused about whether crime rates are increasing or decreasing, the overall pattern since 1992 has been declining crime rates. This reduction in crime only constitutes a "success" for the criminal justice system to the extent that the system caused the decline. A review of criminal justice literature, however, shows that prisons and police played a quite limited role in the national crime decline. The drop in crime rates is better explained by noncriminal justice factors, such as the decline in use of crack, an improving economy in the 1990s, and the removal of lead from air starting in the 1970s. In this section, we examine the factors linked to the declining crime rate to assess their importance. We'll start with the criminal justice response.

PRISONS   Putting someone in prison means they are no longer committing crimes in the community, so the growth in prison populations had some effect in reducing crime through incapacitation. But this strategy has some important limitations and side effects. For example, criminologists find that a small minority of offenders commit a disproportionate number of offenses. Identifying and incarcerating them improves public safety. Further increases in incarceration mean locking up people whose offenses and criminal histories are less serious, so there is a sharply diminishing benefit to public safety. Further, as offenders age, their propensity for crime declines. Lengthening prison sentences does not improve public safety and reduce crime rates if prison sentences were (as they are in the U.S.) already long enough to hold offenders until they aged out of serious and violent crime.

Prison also has some negative side effects that counteract some of its public safety benefits (these are also reviewed below in the discussion of prison as a source of crime). For example, prisons function as "schools for crime," by deepening an inmate's ties with other criminals, subjecting them to an environment that undermines personal responsibility and offers little rehabilitation. Ex-cons have reduced job possibilities because of the criminal record, and cynicism about the law and justice may reduce their commitment to obey the law. Prisons not only have criminogenic (crime-producing) effects on individuals, but also have effects on family formation and on community well-being. For example, the children of inmates do less well in school and are more likely to become delinquent; under conditions of mass incarceration, the moving back and forth of offenders between prison and home leads to community disorganization.[46]

In an article titled "The Limited Importance of Prison Expansion," William Spelman concludes, "The crime drop would have been 27 percent smaller than it actually was, had the prison build-up never taken place."[47] Richard Rosenfeld used different methods and concluded that the prison build-up was responsible for about 25 percent of the drop in crime rates.[48] In his detailed analysis, Harvard sociologist Bruce Western concludes that the "increase in the state imprisonment rate between 1993 and 2001 reduced the rate of serious crimes by 2 to 5 percent, about one-tenth of the 1990s crime drop."[49] Well-known criminologist Franklin Zimring emphasizes the cyclical nature of crime rates and suggests that a "best guess of the impact" of incarceration on crime rates "would range from 10% of the decline at the low end to 27% of the decline at the high end."[50] The few criminologists who think that the growth in imprisonment is responsible for more of the reduction in crime nevertheless concede that "the expansion of the inmate population certainly incurred exorbitant costs, both in terms of its disastrous impact on the lives of offenders and their families and in terms of the huge expenditure of tax revenue."[51]

Prison had only a modest effect on crime rates because American jurisdictions have always been highly likely to imprison violent offenders, so the incarceration binge swept up more people with less significant criminal histories. Incarcerating people who are less dangerous means there is less of an impact on public safety. Consider that

> the percentage of state prisoners incarcerated for violent offenses has actually declined from 57 percent to 48 percent. From 1980 to 1997, the number of violent offenders doubled, the number of nonviolent offenders tripled, and the number of drug offenders increased eleven-fold. At the end of 2001, there were an estimated 1.2 million nonviolent offenders locked up in America at a cost of more than $24 billion annually.[52]

Further, a large number of those admitted to prison were people who had their parole revoked for *technical* reasons, not because they were charged with or convicted of a new crime.

Another reason to be skeptical that the imprisonment binge had a significant impact on the crime rate is that the states with the fastest-growing prison populations did not have the greatest crime reductions. The point is made by Newt Gingrich, the former Speaker of the House and architect of the

1994 Republican "Contract with America," who once proposed legislation calling for life imprisonment for importing more than two ounces of marijuana.[53] He now notes that

> Over the past seven years, Florida's incarceration rate has increased 16 percent, while New York's decreased 16 percent. Yet the crime rate in New York has fallen twice as much as Florida's. Put another way, although New York spent less on its prisons, it delivered better public safety.[54]

More comprehensive reviews support the conclusion that there's no correlation between states that had the greatest growth in incarceration and those that had the greatest declines in crime rates.[55] Noted criminologist Joan Petersilia suggests that 10 to 15 percent of inmates could be safely released.[56] In reviewing the results of the research by a Working Group on the Economics of Crime, Philip J. Cook and Jens Ludwig ask, "What would we give up by reducing average sentence lengths back to 1984 levels? In terms of crime control, the answer may be: not all that much."[57]

POLICE   Another popular theory is that police contributed substantially to the decline in crime rates. In appraising this idea, keep in mind that the GAO found that the policy of hiring 100,000 police officers accounted for 5 percent of the reduction in crime. Remember, too, that the effect of police arresting and taking offenders off the street is accounted for in the discussion of prisons. Thus, the claim to be evaluated is that changes in police strategy—such as policing crime "hot spots," and aggressive enforcement of gun control laws—lowered crime rates. Research suggests such tactics can make a difference, yet there is not evidence that these tactics were implemented widely enough across the nation to have contributed to a substantial decline in the crime rate.[58]

One place where some experts are willing to credit police tactics with helping to reduce crime is New York City, where murder and felony rates decreased dramatically. Some of the credit for this is said to go to the aggressive policing encouraged by former New York City Police Commissioner William Bratton. This aggressiveness may have helped reduce crime, but it brought with it a 62 percent increase in the number of citizen complaints between 1994 and 1997 to the Civilian Complaint Review Board about police abuse, excessive force, and discourtesy.[59] To "black and Latino leaders who say some of Bratton's cops carry his aggressive style too far—'that's too damn bad,' says Bratton."[60]

On the other hand, Elliott Currie points out that many cities in California saw crime reductions when their police engaged in "more positive and community-oriented" activities, and that there are other "cities in which the police have done practically *nothing* that is new, and still the levels of violent crime have dropped strikingly."[61] John Conklin, in his book *Why Crime Rates Fell*, concurs that there is little to support a general link between policing and crime rates.[62]

NONCRIMINAL JUSTICE FACTORS   A variety of research attributes the decline in crime rates to factors other than criminal justice policies. Alfred Blumstein argues that the extreme growth in violence during the late 1980s and early 1990s was driven by a "homicide epidemic" made up primarily of murders committed by young men using guns. This was the period in which crack cocaine was introduced into inner cities. Juveniles were recruited into the drug business, in part because older drug dealers were being increasingly incarcerated, and the juveniles were "less vulnerable to the punishments imposed by the increasingly punitive adult criminal justice system."[63] At the same time there was a large influx of handguns into inner cities, often with higher power and faster action than traditional handguns. The mixture was highly volatile, because young men are not known for their peaceful dispute-resolution skills. Conflicts that previously would have been resolved by fists or knives were now increasingly solved with guns, indeed, often with extremely lethal semiautomatic pistols. During this period, homicide arrests for young men rose dramatically, while those for men 24 years old or older stayed relatively stable.

By 1993, murders started to decline, and so too did homicide arrests of young men. Though Blumstein acknowledges that the imprisonment binge played some role in this decline, he doubts that incarceration played more than a small role. First of all, crime was still rising in the 1980s when the prison population had already been growing for a decade. Second, the juveniles recruited into the drug trade were, on the whole, less likely to face incarceration due to their youth (32 is the median age of state prisoners). And, because these juveniles were frequently replacing less violent, older drug dealers who were incarcerated, the growth in imprisonment actually contributed to the increase in violence.[64] Blumstein observes,

> It is somewhat ironic that the growth in violence with handguns was at least partly a consequence of the drug war's incarceration of many of the older drug sellers. ... As older sellers were taken off the street, the drug market turned to younger individuals, particularly inner-city African-Americans. ... The reduction in age of the workers in the crack trade entailed a predictable increase in violence, as the inclination to deliberate before acting is simply less developed in the young.[65]

The peak in violent crime was also driven by turf wars between inner-city drug gangs. After enough fighting, more or less stable turf boundaries arise and the rate of violence subsides, not because the police have succeeded, but because the (surviving) drug dealers succeeded in creating a more stable inner-city business. The late James Fyfe, distinguished Professor of Criminology at the John Jay College of Criminal Justice and former New York City Police Captain, commented, "When a new illegal and profitable substance comes along, there is fighting and scratching for control. ... Then dealers kill each other off, and the market stabilizes and the amount of violence decreases."[66] So, while turf wars among drug gangs were a "staple of the late 1980s and early 1990s … such battles have now largely succumbed to what criminologist James Lynch terms the 'routinization of the drug trade'."[67]

Further crime reductions occurred as the popularity of crack cocaine declined, which reduced the profitability of drug markets and the associated violence. Blumstein notes: "As recognition of its deleterious effects became widespread, word spread through the streets that crack was an undesirable drug … diminishing the number of new users"; the reduction in the use of handguns by juveniles, credited to a combination of police pressure and action by community groups trying to clean up their neighborhoods; and the robust economy that "has provided legitimate job opportunities for [many young people], which has created incentives to avoid illegal activities."[68] The continued reduction in the use of crack and of methamphetamine may explain some of the recent declines in crime rates. The National Survey on Drug Use and Health reported that from 2006 to 2010, the number of methamphetamine users declined by more than half and cocaine users declined by about 40 percent.[69]

The final noncriminal justice factor to consider is the reduction in lead in the environment starting in the 1970s. Children growing up with lower levels of lead in their bodies are less aggressive and have fewer impulse control problems as teenagers and young adults. The accumulated data linking lead to permanent neurobehavioral disorders (especially through exposure of preschool children) was so strong that in 1974 the Environmental Protection Agency established a timetable for shifting to unleaded gasoline and preventing tons of lead in car exhaust from entering the air.

Environmental and health economist Jessica Reyes argues that "between 1992 and 2002, the phase-out of lead from gasoline was responsible for approximately a 56% decline in violent crime"—and "may cause further declines in the future."[70] The research of industrial economist David Nevin supports the conclusion that lead reduction was the biggest cause of reductions in crime. He found consistent and strong correlations between lead and violent crime, both in the U.S. and European nations, which switched to unleaded gas at different times.[71] Many people may be surprised that a decades-old regulatory act may have caused more of the decrease in crime rates than a recent criminal justice policy, but "within the field of neurotoxicology, Nevin's findings are unsurprising, said Ellen Silbergeld, professor of environmental health sciences at Johns Hopkins University," according to a *Washington Post* article.[72]

So, while politicians claim credit for the recent declines in crime, the real story appears to be that the enormous growth in our prison population over the last decades, coupled with questionable police tactics, may have contributed in some measure to the decline. But most of the decline can be attributed to factors beyond the criminal justice system, including a shift away from crack, periods of strong economic growth, extension of unemployment benefits during weak economic growth, and the public health initiative to remove lead from the environment. These factors together have contributed to reducing extremely high crime rates to rates that are lower, *but high nonetheless.* In short, crime is still rampant and, for all their crowing and claiming credit, neither politicians nor criminal justice policy makers have come close to changing this fact. The criminal justice system may win the occasional skirmish, but it is still losing the war against crime.

In sum, when we look behind the politicians' claims to have turned the tide against violence, the fact remains that criminal justice policy is failing to make our lives substantially safer. How are we to comprehend this failure? It appears that our government is failing to fulfill the most fundamental task of governance: keeping our streets and homes safe, assuring us of what the Founding Fathers called "domestic tranquility," and providing us with the minimum requirement of civilized society. It appears that our new centurions, with all their modern equipment and know-how, are no more able than the old Roman centurions to hold the line against the forces of barbarism and chaos. There are a number of ways in which to respond to this failure. One is to define it out of existence. For example, David Garland, responding to the claim that prisons have failed to reduce crime, contends that, if the prison is "evaluated in terms of its ability to deprive offenders of their liberty in accordance with a court order, to exclude them from society for a period of time, or to inflict mental suffering in ways which satisfy a punitive public ... , its only failures would be occasional escapes and unwanted leniencies."[73] To be sure, if all we ask of prisons is that they be prisons, that is, that they lock some people up for a while under unpleasant conditions, they succeed quite well. It should be clear, however, from the statements we have already cited from politicians defending increased imprisonment that our leaders assert that prisons will make our society safer by reducing crime. We should, then, hold prisons and the rest of the criminal justice system to this test. And when we do, they largely fail.

Another way to come to terms with this failure is to look at the *excuses* that are offered for it. This we will do—but mainly to show that they do not hold up!

One commonly heard excuse is that we can't reduce crime because our laws and our courts are too lenient. *Translation:* We are failing to reduce crime because we are not tough enough. Other excuses point to some feature of modern life, such as urbanization or population growth (particularly the increase in the number of individuals in the crime-prone ages of 15 to 24), and say that this feature is responsible for the growth in crime. *Translation:* We are failing to reduce crime because it is impossible to reduce crime.

Soon, we shall look at these excuses in greater detail and show that they do not explain our failure to reduce crime, and we will present evidence to support the claim that we could reduce crime and the harm it causes if we wanted to. So the question "How are we to comprehend our failure to reduce crime?" still stares us in the face. Examination of the excuses and of the rapidly growing body of knowledge about policies that are effective in reducing crime suggests that our failure is avoidable. What has to be explained is not why *we cannot* reduce crime, but why *we will not!* Oddly enough, this paradoxical result points us in the direction of an answer to our question.

Failure is, after all, in the eye of the beholder. The last runner across the finish line has failed in the race only if he or she wanted to win. If the runner wanted to lose, the "failure" is, in fact, a success. Here lies the key to understanding our criminal justice system. The failure of policies and institutions can serve vested interests and thus amount to success for them!

If we look at the system as "wanting" to reduce crime, it is an abysmal failure that we cannot understand. If we look at it as *not* wanting to reduce crime, it's a howling success, and all we need to understand is why the goal of the criminal justice system is to fail to reduce crime. If we can understand this, then the system's "failure," as well as its obstinate refusal to implement the policies that could remedy that "failure," becomes perfectly understandable. In other words, we can make more sense out of criminal justice policy by assuming that its goal is to maintain crime than by assuming that its goal is to reduce crime!

The remainder of this chapter explores the excuses for the failure to reduce crime and offers evidence to back up our assertion that there are policies that could reduce crime that we refuse to implement. We then briefly outline the relationship between the Pyrrhic defeat theory and the criminological theory of Kai Erikson and Émile Durkheim, to which it is akin. The chapter closes with a word on the work of Michel Foucault, whose views run parallel for a while to those defended in this book, before heading off in a different direction.

THREE EXCUSES THAT WILL NOT WASH, OR HOW WE COULD REDUCE CRIME IF WE WANTED TO

On July 23, 1965, President Lyndon Johnson signed an executive order establishing the President's Commission on Law Enforcement and Administration of Justice to investigate the causes and nature of crime, to collect existing knowledge about our criminal justice system, and to make recommendations about how that system might better meet "the challenge of crime in a free society." The commission presented its report to the president early in 1967, thick with data and recommendations. In the more than 40 years since the report was issued, more and more money has been poured into crime control, with the bleak results already outlined. When the commission wrote, it estimated that more than $4 billion was being spent annually at the national, state, and local levels to pay for police, courts, and correctional facilities in the fight against crime.[74] Since that time, the violent crime rate climbed from 200 per 100,000 in the population in 1965 to 404 in 2010, and the property crime rate went from 2,249 to 2,942 per 100,000.[75] The annual cost to the public of this brand of domestic tranquility was more than $227 billion by 2007, with 2.45 million persons employed by the criminal justice system.[76] BJS states that "if increases in total justice expenditure were limited to the rate of inflation (184%) since 1982, expenditures in 2003 would have been approximately $65.7 billion."[77] Thus, after adjusting for inflation, public expenditure on criminal justice has roughly tripled since 1965. And this doesn't even count the more than $100 billion spent each year on private security or the extra money people spend to live in gated communities.[78] Dollar for dollar, crime control is hardly an impressive investment—that is, if you think you are investing in crime reduction. (In Chapter 4, we comment on private prisons and the criminal justice-industrial complex that has financial interests in the continued expansion of the criminal justice system.)

Multiplying almost as fast as anticrime dollars are excuses for our failure to reduce crime significantly in the face of increased expenditure, personnel, research, and knowledge. Three excuses have sufficient currency to make them worthy of consideration as well as to set in relief the Pyrrhic defeat thesis, which we propose in their place.

First Excuse: We're Too Soft!

One excuse is that we are too soft on crime.[79] This view is widespread among laypersons (in 2003, 65 percent of the people polled thought courts were not harsh enough) and conservative critics of criminal justice policy (the late Ernest van den Haag, for example, claimed that "non-punishment is the major 'social' cause of crime").[80] This view is hard to disprove because, no matter how harsh we are, one can always say we should have been harsher. Nonetheless, the evidence is that U.S. policy has continued to get harsher from the 1970s "law and order" campaigns to the "war on crime," the "war on drugs," and other variations on "get tough on crime." The evidence presented above demonstrated that getting tougher had modest effects in reducing crime—and may have some criminogenic effect.

Further, comparisons across countries do not suggest that the U.S. is soft or lenient in any major respect: not in the range of acts covered by law (especially drug use and prostitution); not in the likelihood of arrest, of being charged, convicted, sentenced to prison; the actual time served in prison; and not in the likelihood of having parole or probation revoked (especially for technical reasons rather than because of a new crime).[81] At year-end 2009, the U.S. rate of incarceration (in jails and prisons) was 743 per 100,000 in the national population. For the United Kingdom, it was 155, for Germany 87, for Belgium 93, and for Canada (a society much like our own), it was 117 prisoners for every 100,000 persons in the national population.[82] Before and after the recent declines in crime, we had far greater percentages of our population under lock and key than comparably advanced European nations as well as our neighbor to the north.

Research suggests that our incarceration rates are not so different from those of other countries when compared with our higher crime rates and to the "level of lethal violence in the United States [that] is probably the highest in the Western world."[83] While all nations punish violent crime seriously, Oxford's *Crime and Public Policy* notes there is not moral consensus about whether recreational drug use should be a crime, so "the creation and enforcement of drug laws are seen more as policy decisions rather than as imperatives."[84] The U.S. is not unique in criminalizing drug possession and sales, but is more likely to use incarceration—in some "67 percent of drug cases, followed distantly by the Netherlands at 46 percent and Switzerland (38 percent)." Prison sentences were also longer (an average of 23 months), twice that in the countries with the next longest sentences (England and Wales).[85]

Such policy decisions stand in contrast to Portugal, which in 2001 decriminalized "the possession of *all* drugs, when deemed for personal use."[86] In 2003, Canada decriminalized possession of small amounts of marijuana, and started embracing "safe injection centers" for users of harder drugs.[87] In response to a government challenge, Canada's Supreme Court ruled unanimously that one project, Insite, should remain open: "Insite has saved lives and improved health without increasing the incidence of drug use and crime in the surrounding area. It is supported by the Vancouver police."[88]

But even if our incarceration rates stand in the same proportion to our overall crime rates as those of other countries, that still indicates that we are no more lenient than other modern nations. Nor, of course, should it be forgotten that we are the only Western industrialized nation that still has the death penalty, let alone (until 2005) the only such nation that executed people who had committed crimes while under the age of 18. At the close of 2010, the state and federal prison systems held 3,158 prisoners under sentence of death and executed 46 individuals that year.[89] On December 2, 2005, North Carolina carried out the 1,000th execution in the United States since the reinstatement of the death penalty by the U.S. Supreme Court in 1976. The United States also makes much more extensive use of the sentence of *life without the possibility of parole* than other Western nations.[90]

Finally, our incarceration rate doesn't include those who are currently on probation and parole. When these are added to those in jail or prison, the number of *adults* under some form of correctional supervision in 2010 was more than 7 million; that is, one of every 31 American adults—3.2 percent of the U.S. adult population—was incarcerated or on probation or parole. This represents almost a quadrupling of the number since 1980, when 1.84 million persons were under correctional supervision.[91] Our high rate of crime and lethal violence has persisted in the face of decades of getting tougher, leading one criminologist to characterize the get-tough approach to crime as a conservative social experiment that has been tested and shown to fail.[92]

Second Excuse: A Cost of Modern Life

Another excuse is that crime is an inescapable companion of any complex, populous, industrialized society. As we become more complex, more populous, more industrialized, and particularly more *urbanized*, we will have more crime as inevitably as we will have more ulcers and more traffic. These are costs of modern life, the benefits of which abound and clearly outweigh the costs. Crime, then, takes its place alongside death and taxes. We can fight, but we cannot win, and we should not tear our hair out about it.

This is less an explanation than a recipe for resignation. Furthermore, it does not account for the fact that other complex, populous, highly industrialized and technologically advanced nations such as Japan have crime rates that are considerably lower than ours. Japan has slightly less than half the U.S. population crowded onto a landmass less than 1/25 the size of the United States. In 2008, Japan had 1,297 homicides and about 28 violent offenses for every 100,000 inhabitants. That same year, the United States had 16,272 homicides and a violent crime rate of 456 for every 100,000 inhabitants.[93] In 2008, Tokyo, Japan, had a population of 12.9 million people and recorded 179 homicides; that same year, the entire state of Texas had 24.3 million people (almost twice the population of Tokyo) and 1,374 homicides—more than all of Japan.[94] In 2004, when the homicide rate in the United States was 5.6 per 100,000 inhabitants, Japan's rate was 0.5 per 100,000; Kenya had a rate of 6.7; Switzerland, 2.9; Denmark, 0.8; France, 1.6; and Canada, 2.0.[95] Currie summarizes the international data, stating that "even within the advanced industrial societies, the differences in levels of serious violent crime are extreme." Using homicide data, which he believes provides the most reliable comparisons, Currie says:

> The risks of dying by violence in the United States are more than double those of the next closest advanced industrial country—Canada—and roughly six times the average for the European Union. In the mid-2000s, they were 10 times higher than those in Germany or Austria, and 12 times those in the United Kingdom. ...
> The chances of dying by intentional violence among youth aged 15–29 years in the United States are 10 times those of the Netherlands and Denmark, 16 times those in Norway, and more than 25 times those in Germany. Indeed, the violent death rate for young Americans more closely resembles that of youth in Russia or some Latin American nations than it does the rest of the affluent industrial world.[96]

The "costs of modern life," or urbanization, excuse also fails to account for the striking differences in the crime rates *within* our own modern, complex, populous, and urbanized nation. Within the United States in 2010, the homicide rate ranged from 1 per 100,000 inhabitants in New Hampshire to 11.2 in Louisiana.[97] In 1968, *Time* magazine reported that

> Texas, home of the shoot-out and divorce-by-pistol, leads the U.S. with about 1000 homicides a year, more than 14 other states combined. Houston is the U.S. murder capital: 244 last year, more than in England, which has 45 million more people.[98]

By 2010, Texas (with 1,249 homicides) was in second place, ahead of Florida and New York (with 866 and 987, respectively), and behind California (with 1,809); and Houston's glory as murder capital had clearly faded. Houston reported 269 homicides for 2010, outdone by New York City (with 536), Los Angeles (293), and even Detroit (310).[99]

Such variations are not limited to murder. A comparison of violent and property crime rates for Standard Metropolitan Statistical Areas (SMSAs,

TABLE 1.1   Metropolitan Areas by Population and FBI Crime Rates, 2010

City	Population	Violent Crime Rate (Per 100,000 People)	Property Crime Rate (Per 100,000 People)
New York City	11,678,308	496	1,659
Houston, TX	5,978,213	620	3,944
Phoenix, AZ	4,229,275	371	3,535
Denver, CO	2,555,601	337	2,771
Boston, MA	1,908,436	565	2,409
Memphis, TN	1,313,722	1,007	4,625
Fresno, CA	926,736	537	4,251
Wichita, KS	621,313	582	3,799
Anchorage, AK	313,181	813	3,506
Farmington, NM	126,955	646	2,193

Source: UCR–2010, Table 6.

areas "made up of a core city with a population of 50,000 or more inhabitants and the surrounding county or counties which share certain metropolitan characteristics") reveals a striking *lack* of correlation between crime rate and population size (which we can take as a reasonable, though rough, index of urbanization and the other marks of modernity, such as complexity and industrialization, that are offered as explanations for the intractability of crime). See Table 1.1, in which metropolitan areas of different sizes and similar crime rates are ranked by population.

In other words, classifying crime with death and taxes and saying that it is an inevitable companion of modernity or urbanization will just not explain our failure to reduce it. Even if death and taxes are inevitable (unfortunately, not in that order), some die prematurely and some die suspiciously and some pay too much in taxes and some pay none at all. None of these variations is inevitable or unimportant. So too with crime. Even if crime is inevitable in modern societies, its rates and types vary extensively, and this is neither inevitable nor unimportant. Indeed, the variations in crime rates between modern cities and nations are proof that the *extent* of crime is not a simple consequence of urbanization. Other factors must explain the differences. These differences suggest that although some crimes may be an unavoidable consequence of urbanization, this in no way excuses our failure to reduce crime at least to the lowest rates reported in modern cities and nations.

Third Excuse: Blame It on the Kids!

A third excuse takes the form of attributing crime to young people, particularly young men between the ages of 14 and 25. This explanation goes as follows: Young people in our society, especially males, find themselves emerging from the security of childhood into the frightening chaos of adult responsibility. Little is or can be done by the adult society to ease the transition by providing meaningful outlets for the newly bursting youthful energy aroused in still immature and irresponsible youngsters. Hence, these youngsters both mimic the power of manhood and attack the society that frightens and ignores them by resorting to violent crime. Add to this several rapid increases in the population of this age group (such as the "baby boom"), and we have another explanation that amounts to a recipe for resignation: We can no more expect to reduce crime than we can hope to eradicate adolescence. We can fight crime, but it will be with us until we figure out a way for people to get from childhood to adulthood without passing through their teens.

Youngsters do show up disproportionately in crime statistics. In 1975, *Time* reported that "forty-four percent of the nation's murderers are 25 or younger, and 10 percent are under 18. Of those arrested for street crimes, excluding murder, fully 75 percent are under 25 and 45 percent are under 18."[100] In 2010, persons between the ages of 15 and 24 constituted 14 percent of the nation's population. They represented 39 percent of those arrested for all crimes.[101] However, there are problems with attributing crime to youth. The most important is that crime rates have grown faster than either the absolute number of young people or their percentage of the population. See Table 1.2, which compares national crime rates over the past 40 years with the percentage of the population represented by people aged 14 to 24.

TABLE 1.2   Crime Rates Compared with Youth Population, 1960–2005

Year	Violent Crime Rate (Per 100,000 Persons)	Property Crime Rate (Per 100,000 Persons)	14–24 Year Olds (% of Population)
1960	161	1,726	15.1
1970	364	3,621	19.9
1975	488	4,811	20.8
1980	597	5,353	20.4
1985	558	4,666	18.2
1990	730	5,073	16.2
1995	685	4,591	15.2
2000	507	3,618	15.4
2005	469	3,430	15.6
2010	404	2,942	14

Source: Sourcebook 2003, Table 3.106, pp. 278–79; *UCR–2005*, Table 1; *UCR–2010*, Table 1; *StatAbst—2011*, Table 8, p. 12; *StatAbst—2008*, Table 7, p. 10; *StatAbst—2001*, Table 11, p. 13; *StatAbst—1995*, p. 17; *StatAbst—1992*, pp. 14–15; and *StatAbst—1987*, p. 14.

Notice that, while there is some correlation between the rise and fall of crime rates and percentage of young people in the population, there are also important divergences: The percentage of young people in the population in 2000 was about what it was in 1960, yet the crime rate in 2000 was almost *four times higher* than that of 1960. Obviously, this growth in crime cannot be attributed to youth. The same can be said of the years 1970 and 1975, when young people's percentage in the population grew slightly, and crime rates soared. Or compare 1980 and 1990, when the youth percentage dropped more than 4 points and the violent crime rate grew significantly. In that same period, the number of 15 to 24 year olds decreased absolutely by 5,660,000, while the absolute number of Index crimes rose by over 1 million.[102] Similar discrepancies show up when the National Crime Victimization Survey (NCVS) is used.

What's more, the period of decline in the youth population coincided with an increase in serious crime in New York City; and even when crime rates went down recently, they never returned to the levels of the 1940s, when the percentage of young people aged 16 to 24 was about 14, roughly comparable to what it is now.[103]

We do not deny that a large number of crimes are committed by young people. The facts suggest, however, that although the number of youngsters in the populace has an important effect on crime rates, it cannot fully explain them or explain them away. That young people have higher rates of crime than older folks does not mean that young people always have the same rate of crime. When this group declined, crime went down, but not in proportion to the decline in the youth population. When this group was growing, the crime rates were growing faster. If crime increases faster (or decreases more slowly) than the youth population, that increase (or decrease) cannot be explained by the increase (or decrease) in youths. If the crime rate of 15–24 year olds changes, then this certainly is not explained by their youth. Something other than their youth or their numbers must explain why they are committing more crimes than people their age did in other periods.[104]

In any case, the greater likelihood of young people committing crime provides no excuse for failing to reduce the growth of crime at least to the rate at which the number of young people is growing (or shrinking). So another excuse for our failure fails to excuse. To get an idea of what criminal justice policy truly aimed at reducing crime might look like, let's look at the known sources of crime and the promising crime-prevention programs.

KNOWN SOURCES OF CRIME

Currie notes that the amount of crime and violence in a country is "strongly influenced by social policy and can be substantially mitigated, or exacerbated, by it." The level of crime in a society "represents a social and political choice—not simply an individual one, or even a reflection of abstract, impersonal forces operating pristinely above deliberate human intervention. In short, to a significant extent, we make the world of violence that surrounds us."[105]

We agree and argue that if the United States were serious about crime reduction, much more support would be given to policies that address the known sources of crime. Note that we say *sources* rather than *causes* because pathways to crime are less direct and more complicated than simple cause and effect. We know that poverty, slums, and unemployment are *sources* of street crime. We know that they breed alienation from social institutions, and that they reduce the likely rewards of going straight. But, we know as well that many, if not most, poor, unemployed slum dwellers do not engage in street crime. Yet, to say that this means we do not know that poverty and the other conditions discussed below are sources of violent crime is like saying that we do not know that a bullet in the head is deadly because some people survive or because we do not fully understand the physiological process that links the wound with the termination of life.

Poverty and Inequality

Those youngsters who figure so prominently in arrest statistics are not drawn equally from all economic strata. Although there is much reported and even more unreported crime among middle-class youngsters, the disturbing level of violent crime attributed to this age group is largely the work of poor inner-city youth. This is the group at the lowest end of the economic spectrum: unemployment hovers around 25 percent, with *under*employment (the percentage of persons either jobless or with part-time, low-wage jobs) still higher. This is a group with no realistic chance (for any but a rare individual) to enter college or amass sufficient capital (legally) to start a business or to get into the high-wage, skilled job markets. We know that poverty is a *source* of crime, and yet we do virtually nothing to improve the life chances of the vast majority of the inner-city poor. They are as poor as ever and are facing cuts in welfare and other services.

That poverty is a source of crime is not refuted by the large and growing amount of white-collar crime that we shall document later. In fact, poverty contributes to crime by creating need, while, at the other end of the spectrum, wealth can contribute to crime by unleashing greed. Criminologist John Braithwaite argues that economic inequality itself worsens crimes of the poor *and* of the well-off. It increases the opportunities for crimes by the well-off and reduces the likelihood they will be held accountable to the criminal law. At the same time, inequality increases the humiliation of the poor who are surrounded by visions of "the good life" and feel responsible for their failure to attain it.[106] And inequality has worsened in recent years.

The gap between rich and poor worsened during the 1980s and 1990s. In 1970, the poorest fifth of the nation's families received 5.5 percent of the aggregate income, and the richest fifth received 41.6 percent. By 2010, the share of the poorest fifth had declined to 3.3 percent, while that of the richest fifth had risen to 50.2 percent. In the period from 1980 to 2010, the share of the top 5 percent rose from 14.6 to 21.3 percent. By 2010, the number of Americans officially defined as being in poverty was 46.2 million (about 1 in

8 Americans), up from 30.1 million in 1990, and from 25.2 million in 1980.[107] (According to the Census Bureau, the 2010 number is "the largest number in the 52 years for which poverty estimates have been published.")[108] By 2010, 22 percent of American children were living in poverty, and in 2009 about 36 percent of black children and 33 percent of Latino children lived in families below the poverty level, compared with 12 percent of white children.[109]

These long-standing trends have worsened because of the 2008 financial crisis, which was the result of an aggressive policy of financial deregulation. The developments are also the predictable outcome of policies that cut services to the poor while reducing the taxes of the wealthy. In 1982, a group of 34 prominent economists sharply criticized then-President Reagan's economic policy as "extremely regressive in its impact on our society, redistributing wealth and power from the middle class and the poor to the rich, and shifting more of the tax burden away from business and onto low- and middle-income consumers."[110] At the same time, a study released by the Urban Institute concluded that "the Reagan administration's policies are not only aiding upper-income families at the expense of the working poor, but also are widening the gulf between affluent and poorer regions of the country."[111] The study maintained that the combined effect of the administration's tax and social service spending cuts was "to penalize working families near the poverty line who receive some federal benefits … creating 'major work disincentives'."

The tax cuts enacted by President George W. Bush had much the same effect because 25 percent of the benefits went to those with incomes in the top 1 percent, and nearly 50 percent of the benefits went to those with incomes in the top 10 percent. Using data from the Congressional Budget Office, the nonpartisan Center on Budget and Policy Priorities noted that between 1979 and 2001,

> the average after-tax income of the top one percent of households rose by a stunning $409,000, or 139 percent, after adjusting for inflation. This dwarfed the $6,300, or 17 percent, average increase among the middle fifth of the population, over this 22-year period, and the $1,100, or 8 percent, increase among the bottom fifth of the population.[112]

Furthermore, as unemployment has gone up and down over the past decades, unemployment at the bottom of society remains strikingly worse than the national average. For example, over the past 45 years, black unemployment has remained slightly more than twice the rate of white unemployment. In 1967, when 3.4 percent of white workers were unemployed, 7.4 percent of black workers were jobless. By 2011, 8 percent of white workers were unemployed compared to16.7 percent of blacks. Among those in the crime-prone ages of 16 to 19, 12 percent of white youngsters and 46.5 percent (almost one in every two) of black youngsters were jobless.[113]

Another place in which poverty and inequality are in evidence in America is in the distribution of wealth, that is, the value of people's total assets minus the debt that they have accumulated over their lifetimes. Edward Wolff writes that

> the equalizing trends of the 1930s–1970s reversed sharply in the 1980s. The gap between the haves and have-nots is greater now than at any time since 1929. The sharp increase in inequality since the late 1970s has made wealth distribution in the United States more unequal than in what used to be perceived as the class-ridden societies of northwestern Europe.[114]

In 2007, the most recent year for which data are available, the wealthiest 1 percent of American families owned 33.8 percent of total American wealth, and those immediately below them in the top 10 percent of the population owned another 37.7 percent of the wealth. The poorest 50 percent owned 2.5 percent of the wealth. These figures are on the conservative side because the survey on which they are based does not (for reasons related to sampling) include the *Forbes 400*, the wealthiest 400 Americans. In 2007, making that list required wealth of at least $1.3 billion. Together, these 400 people had almost 2.3 percent of all wealth.[115]

This conclusion is supported by research on income mobility, which is an important factor in determining class mobility and wealth. An economist with the Federal Reserve Bank of Chicago notes that "income mobility has declined in the last 20 years." The article, "The American Dream gains a harder edge," notes that most Americans do not believe mobility has declined, "but academic studies suggest that income mobility in the U.S. is no better than in France or Britain."[116] The *New York Times* series on class noted the same phenomenon and aptly summarized the research as: "Mobility happens, just not as rapidly as was once thought."[117]

In his important book, *Justice as Fairness*, John Rawls—the late Harvard moral and political philosopher called by some "the John Stuart Mill of the twentieth century"—discusses a form of society that he calls "welfare-state capitalism." In welfare-state capitalism, there is considerable inequality in wealth and income and only a minimum "safety net" for the poor—enough to make sure that their basic needs are satisfied, but no more than that. Rawls writes that in a capitalist welfare state, "there may develop a discouraged and depressed underclass many of whose members are chronically dependent on welfare. This underclass feels left out and does not participate in the public political culture."[118]

Can there be any doubt that Rawls is describing the United States here? Is there any wonder why a society that does no more than provide for the most basic needs of its poorest members (when it even does that much!)[119] also finds that those individuals commit crimes? Rawls's analysis shows us that economic inequality may result in crime, not simply from need, but by producing an impoverished class that feels "left out" of society and thus does not develop allegiance to its major institutions.

Writes Todd Clear, professor of criminal justice at Rutgers University, "Let's start investing in things that really reduce crime: good schools, jobs and a future for young parents and their children."[120] Why don't we?

Prison

We know that prison produces more criminals than it cures. As far back as 1973, the National Advisory Commission on Criminal Justice Standards and Goals recommended building no new adult prisons because "the prison, the reformatory and jail have achieved only a shocking record of failure. There is overwhelming evidence that these institutions create crime rather than prevent it."[121] Instead, the U.S. built a record number of prisons, and currently more than 70 percent of the inmates in the nation's prisons or jails are not there for the first time. The last time the Bureau of Justice Statistics did a major study, it found that 67.5 percent of inmates released in 1994, were rearrested within three years, "almost exclusively for a felony or serious misdemeanor" and almost 52 percent were back in prison.[122] A study by the Pew Charitable Trusts followed inmates released in 1999 and 2004 for three years. It used slightly different methodology than the BJS study, but concluded "that recidivism rates have been largely stable."[123] The finding is to be expected given the continued emphasis on warehousing[124] inmates rather than offering meaningful rehabilitation and helping them reintegrate into society. Indeed, prisons seem to do everything but give inmates the skills they will need to make it on the outside. Prison inmates are denied autonomy and privacy and are subjected to indignities and acts of violence as regular features of their confinement, all of which is heightened by overcrowding. As of the last day of 2010, 20 state prison systems were operating above the most generous measure of their reported capacity; the federal prison system was operating at 36 percent above capacity.[125] A study of prisons in four Midwestern states found that about one-fifth of male inmates reported "a pressured or forced sex incident while incarcerated. About nine percent of male inmates reported that they had been raped."[126]

The predictable result, as delineated by Robert Johnson and Hans Toch in *The Pains of Imprisonment*, "is that the prison's survivors become tougher, more pugnacious, and less able to feel for themselves and others, while its nonsurvivors become weaker, more susceptible, and less able to control their lives."[127] Prisoners are thus bereft of both training and capacity to handle daily problems in competent and socially constructive ways, inside or outside of prison. The organization Just Detention International (formerly Stop Prison Rape) reports, "Upon release, male prisoner rape survivors may bring with them emotional scars and learned violent behavior that continue the cycle of harm. Feelings of rage can be suppressed until release, when survivors may engage in violent, antisocial behavior."[128] According to a Human Rights Watch report titled "No Escape: Male Rape in U.S. Prisons," "the only way to avoid the repetition of sexual abuse, many prisoners assert, is to strike back violently." The report quotes a victim of prison rape saying, "People start to treat you right, once you become deadly."[129] In this way, prison makes inmates a greater harm to society than they were when they entered.

Once on the outside, burdened with the stigma of a prison record and rarely trained in a marketable skill, they find few opportunities for noncriminal employment open to them. Nor does this affect all groups in America alike. According to Michael Tonry, author of *Malign Neglect: Race, Crime and Punishment in America,* "By affecting so many young black men, American criminal laws have further undermined the black family and made it harder for black men to get an education and find good jobs." In his 2007 Presidential address to the American Society of Criminology, Professor Tonry went further: "If its aims were to reduce black men's chances of earning a decent living, or being successfully married and a good father, or being socialized into prosocial values, it is hard to know how the criminal justice system could do those things better."[130] In addition, a study by the Sentencing Project indicates that the enormous number of African–American men who have been convicted of felonies and, therefore, deprived of their right to vote, is "having a profound [negative!] impact on the black community's ability to participate in the political process."[131]

Because so much of the recent increase in imprisonment has been of inner-city black men who were involved in families and who had at least part-time legitimate employment at the time of their arrest and incarceration, social scientists are beginning to study the ways in which massive imprisonment is undermining the family and other community institutions, depriving children of male role models and women of potential husbands and support. Criminologists have found evidence suggesting that massive imprisonment may weaken inner-city institutions of informal social control *and thus lead to more crime in the long run.* Others argue that high levels of incarceration can weaken its stigma and thus the deterrent value of imprisonment; and incarceration can strengthen ties between prison gangs and offenders on the street.[132]

Can we honestly act as if we do not know that our prison system (including our failure to ensure a meaningful post-release noncriminal alternative for the ex-con) is a *source* of crime? Should we really pretend, then, that we do not *know* why ex-cons turn to crime? Recidivism does not happen because ex-cons miss their alma mater. In fact, if prisons are supposed to deter people from crime, one would expect that ex-prisoners would be the most deterred, because the deprivations of prison[133] are more real to them than to the rest of us. Recidivism is thus a doubly poignant testimony to the job that prison does in preparing its graduates for crime, yet we do little to change the nature of prisons or to provide real services to ex-convicts.

In his 2004 State of the Union Address, President Bush seemed to indicate that he understood at least a small part of the recidivism problem when he discussed the 600,000 inmates released back into society each year. He said, "We know from long experience that if they can't find work, or a home, or help, they are much more likely to commit more crimes and return to prison." The Second Chance Act finally became law in April of 2008, with authorized expenditures of $400 million over four years. When divided into the 2,400,000 inmates who would be released over that period, that amounts to about $167 per inmate. The 2012 budget for the Department of Justice reduced funding for this act from $100 million a year to $63 million,[134] at a time when more inmates are being released from prison because of cost-saving measures. That is hardly enough to ensure that America is "the land of the second chance—and when the gates of the prison open, the path ahead should lead to a better life."[135]

Guns

Most people know the expression "Guns don't kill people, people kill people." But guns make it much easier to kill people, so the huge stock of civilian guns (especially handguns) is a source of a firearm homicide rate in the United States that Oxford's *Crime and Public Policy* says is "extraordinarily high by the standards of other industrialized countries."[136] And, because the fatality rate for robberies using a gun is three times higher than for robberies with knives, and ten times higher than for robberies with other weapons, countries like Italy and Australia that have robbery rates comparable to the United States' have far fewer robberies that end up as homicides.[137]

Speaking about the extraordinary spate of deadly violence that we had in the late 1980s and early 1990s, Garen Wintemute puts it bluntly: "the entire increase in homicide in the United States through 1993 was attributable to firearm homicide."[138] Increasingly, this was due to highly lethal semiautomatic pistols (during the same period, the percentage of homicides with regular revolvers declined significantly). Hospitals reported an increase in gunshot wounds per victim and in the size of bullets removed. This phenomenon is closely linked to trends in handgun production. Starting in the late 1980s, American gun manufacturers started producing "high capacity, medium-caliber semiautomatic pistols that were also very inexpensive." Almost all were produced "by a small group of manufacturers in Southern California."[139]

A study by the nonpartisan National Research Council suggests that by 1999, the civilian gun stock was 258 million, with about 43 percent of households owning at least one.[140] Researchers from Harvard's School of Public Health estimated the number of privately owned firearms to be between 218 and 281 million. They note that "researchers have estimated about 25 guns per 100 people in countries such as Canada, New Zealand, Germany, France and Sweden. On the basis of current estimates from our survey, the U.S. has 93 guns per 100 people."[141]

The President's Crime Commission reported that, in 1965, "5,600 murders, 34,700 aggravated assaults and the vast majority of the 68,400 armed robberies were committed by means of firearms. All but 10 of 278 law enforcement officers murdered during the period 1960–65 were killed with firearms." The commission concluded that

> more than one-half of all willful homicides and armed robberies, and almost one-fifth of all aggravated assaults, involve use of firearms. As long as there is no effective gun-control legislation, violent crimes and the injuries they inflict will be harder to reduce than they might otherwise be.[142]

The situation has worsened since the commission's warning. The FBI states, "In 1975, 66 percent of murders of persons (aged 15 to 19) were attributable to guns, while in 1992 the figure rose to 85 percent. This increase supports the theory that today's high-school-aged youths are exposed to an environment that includes guns."[143] The Office of Juvenile Justice reports, "By 1997, the homicide rate for 15- to 24-year-olds was 15.2 per 100,000, which is higher than the combined total homicide rate of eleven industrialized nations," and goes on to point out, "Firearms were the weapons of choice in nearly two-thirds of all murders."[144] And, in 2001, then-President Bush noted, "In America, a teenager today is more likely to die from a gunshot than from all natural causes of death combined."[145]

The Centers for Disease Control report that in 2009, 31,228 deaths resulted from firearms—including suicides and accidents—and "for at least the 40 years prior to 2004, the two leading causes of injury death were MVT [motor vehicle traffic] deaths and firearms."[146] Guns also take a grave and worsening toll among our children. According to a report from the Children's Defense Fund, nearly 100,000 children were killed by guns between 1979 and 2003.[147]

In the face of facts like these—indeed, in the face of his own nearly fatal shooting by a would-be assassin—then-President Reagan refused to support any legislative attempts to control the sale of handguns.[148] His successor, President George H. W. Bush, followed suit.[149] On Thanksgiving Day 1993, Bush's successor, Bill Clinton, signed into law the so-called Brady Bill, which went only so far as imposing a five-day waiting period for gun purchases to enable checks to see whether would-be gun purchasers have criminal records (states that do instant background checks are not required to have a waiting or "cooling off" period). The Brady Law leaves it to the states to enforce the waiting period and to get their police to make a "reasonable effort" to conduct the background checks. However, the bill provided no sanctions for states that did not comply, and it left it effectively up to the states to provide funding for the checks and to determine what is a "reasonable effort."[150] From 1994, when the Brady Law went into effect, until 2003, over 1.1 million applications for firearms have been rejected, but as Blumstein notes, "it is not known how many of those customers eventually bought guns from an unregulated source."[151] Moreover, while the Brady Law prohibits sales of guns to individuals with prior felony convictions, it does not apply to private sellers (only to dealers). And, the sad fact is that, as different studies show, between half and three-quarters of those arrested for crimes involving weapons had *no prior felony conviction*.[152]

Moreover, many states continue to have lax gun laws with predictable effects. A 2008 *Washington Post* report stated that: "States with lax gun laws had higher rates of handgun killings, fatal shootings of police officers, and sales of weapons that were used in crimes in other states, according to a study underwritten by a group of more than 300 U.S. mayors"; and, further, that "[n]early all guns recovered in crimes are initially sold legally."[153] The Supreme Court's decision in *Heller* (interpreting the Second Amendment to confer an individual right to own guns) makes regulation more difficult.[154] But it is unlikely to prohibit universal background checks on gun purchasers or bans on assault weapons (guns that can fire rapidly, and hold large amounts of ammunition). Can we believe that our leaders sincerely want to cut down on violent crime and the injuries it produces when they oppose even as much as *registering* guns or *licensing* gun owners, much less actually restricting the sale and movement of guns as a matter of national policy? (Many people wrongly believe that universal registration and licensing exist, when in fact only a few states require this.)[155]

Can we really believe that if guns were less readily available, violent criminals would simply switch to other weapons to commit the same number of crimes and do the same amount of damage? Is there a weapon other than the handgun that works as quickly, that allows its user so safe a distance, or that makes the criminal's physical strength (or speed or courage, for that matter) irrelevant? Could a bank robber hold a row of tellers at bay with a switchblade? Studies indicate that, if gun users switched to the next deadliest weapon—the knife—and attempted the same number of crimes, we could still expect *two-thirds fewer fatalities* because the fatality rate of the knife is roughly one-third that of the gun. In other words, if guns were eliminated and the number of crimes held steady, we could expect to save as many as two out of every three persons who are now the victims of firearm homicide.

Drugs

The United States has an enormous drug abuse and addiction problem. There is considerable evidence, however, that our attempts to cure it are worse than the disease itself. Most people associate drugs with crime because addicts steal. But addicts steal because the cost of drugs is high. This high cost is related to the drugs being illegal, because everyone in the distribution chain needs to profit enough to compensate for the risk of being caught and locked up. Much of the violence surrounding the drug trade is also related to drugs being illegal, because then the drug trade is in the hands of gangs and organized crime, and their disputes are not resolved through free markets or the legal system. In response, the U.S. has engaged in a Drug War that has cost billions, incarcerated millions, and is responsible for little change in drug usage. Moreover, the criminalization of drugs undercuts public health efforts to deal with drug addiction. Paul Goldstein provides a useful categorization of the relationship between drugs and crime:

- *Pharmacological/psychological consequences:* Criminal activity is caused by the chemical properties of the drug acting on the person's brain.
- *Economic/compulsive crimes:* Criminal activity is caused by drug users committing crimes to get money to support their habit.
- *Systemic crime:* Criminal activity like violence and corruption are a regular part of doing business in the illicit drug trade because there is no regulation and formal dispute-resolution mechanisms are unavailable.[156]

About the pharmacological consequences of drugs, says Alfred Blumstein, the drug "that has the strongest pharmacological effect is alcohol. ... Heroin is a downer, so heroin doesn't do much. And there hasn't been shown to be much pharmacological effect of the other serious drugs on crime, not anything comparable to that of alcohol, which has been shown to be a strong stimulator of violence."[157] PCP tends to be one of the only other drugs to have a pharmacological link to violence. High doses of cocaine and methamphetamine can lead to some psychoses that include paranoia and delusion, which can lead to violence.

Further, many health effects are related less to pharmacology than to the criminalization of drugs. There is little evidence, for example, proving that heroin is a *dangerous* drug. James Q. Wilson, a defender of the prohibition of heroin and other drugs, admits that "there are apparently no specific pathologies—serious illnesses or physiological deterioration—that are known to result from heroin use per se."[158] Prior to 1914, when anyone could go into a drugstore and purchase heroin and other opiates the way we buy aspirin today, hundreds of thousands of upstanding, law-abiding citizens were hooked.[159] But opiate addiction is not in itself a *cause* of crime. If anything, it is a pacifier.[160] There is, writes Arnold Trebach, "nothing in the pharmacology, or physical and psychological impact, of the drug that would propel a user to crime."[161] On the basis of available scientific evidence, there is every reason to suspect that we do our bodies more *irreversible* damage by smoking cigarettes and drinking liquor than by using heroin. Most of the physical damage associated with heroin use is probably attributable to the trauma of withdrawal, a product not so much of heroin as of its occasional unobtainability. Health problems, including HIV/AIDS and hepatitis, are partly related to the criminalization of drugs, which hinders public health efforts like the distribution of clean needles to addicts.

THC, the active ingredient in marijuana, "is a very safe drug" according to *The Science of Marijuana*.[162] The 1988 Surgeon General's Report lists tobacco as a more dangerous drug than marijuana.[163] According to the findings and conclusions of Francis Young, administrative law judge for the Drug Enforcement Administration, "despite [its 5,000-year-] long history of use and the extraordinarily high numbers of social smokers, there are simply no credible medical reports to suggest that consuming marijuana has caused a single death" and no amount of marijuana that a person could possibly eat or smoke would constitute a lethal dose. By contrast, aspirin overdoses cause hundreds of deaths a year.[164] A Police Foundation review in 2000 concluded that: "By any of the major criteria of harm—mortality, morbidity, toxicity, addictiveness and relationship with crime—cannabis is less harmful than any of the other major illicit drugs, or than alcohol or tobacco."[165]

Trebach points out that, although federal authorities documented 2,177 deaths from the most popular illicit drugs in 1985, between 400,000 and 500,000 people died from alcohol and tobacco during the same year.[166] A 2007 study of Florida autopsies found that "cocaine, heroin and all methamphetamines caused 989 deaths, while legal opioids—strong painkillers in brand name drugs like Vicodin and OxyContin—caused 2,328." No deaths were attributed to marijuana.[167] Doug Bandow, a senior advisor to President Reagan and a Cato Institute Fellow, found that all illicit drugs combined accounted for about 5,000 deaths, "most of which" are "caused by the effects of prohibition" rather than the drug's pharmacology.[168]

Some argue that the evil of drugs (especially heroin and crack) is that they are *addicting*, because this is a bad thing even if the addicting substance is not itself harmful. It is hard to deny that the image of a person enslaved to a chemical is ugly and repugnant to our sense, that the dignity of human beings lies in their capacity to control their destinies. More questionable, however, is whether this is, in the case of adults, anybody's business but their own. Even so, suppose we agree that addiction is an evil worthy of prevention. Isn't imprisoning someone as punishment for using a potentially addictive substance an irrational way to express concern about the enslavement of addiction—especially when, instead, we could offer treatment? And, doesn't that make us hypocrites given our inconsistent policies about all our other addictions? What about cigarette smoking, which, unlike heroin, contributes to cancer and heart disease? Nicotine's addictiveness—according to former Surgeon General C. Everett Koop—is similar to that of heroin, and *more addicting than cocaine,* more likely to addict the new user, and more difficult to quit once addicted.[169] What about the roughly 15 million alcoholics in the nation working their way through their livers and into their graves?[170]

Former Washington, D.C., Police Chief Maurice Turner helps explain the economic crimes associated with drugs:

> If you see an addict going through withdrawal, he's in some kind of damn pain. ... When they get pretty well strung out, they have about a $100- to $120-a-day habit. When they get that type of habit, they're going to have to steal approximately six times that much [because fences don't pay list price].[171]

Professor Blumstein agrees that "you need money to buy drugs, so the higher the price of the drug, the greater the incentive to commit the crime."[172] The high price of drugs is due to their being illegal; there is nothing about heroin itself that makes it extremely costly. The heroin for which an addict pays $100 or more a day could be produced legally at a cost of a few cents for a day's supply. However, once sale or possession of heroin is made a serious criminal offense, a number of consequences follow. First, the prices go up because those who supply it face grave penalties, and those who want it, want it bad. Second, because the supply (and the quality) of the drug fluctuates depending on how vigorously the agents of the law try to prevent it, addicts live in constant uncertainty about the next fix, and must devote much of their wit and energy to getting it and to getting enough money to pay for it. They do not, then, fit easily into the routines of a nine-to-five job, even if they could get one that would pay enough to support their habits. Finally, all the difficulties of securing the drug add up to an incentive to be not merely a user but a dealer as well, because this both brings in money and makes one's own supply more certain. Addicts thus have an incentive to find and encourage new addicts, which they would not have if drugs were legally and cheaply available.

If we add to this the fact that overall drug use has remained widespread, and possibly even increased, in spite of all our law enforcement efforts, can we doubt that the cure is a *source* of crime? The result is a recipe for large-scale and continual robbery and burglary, which would not exist if the drugs were available legally. A study by Anglin and Speckart of the relationship between narcotics use and crime concludes that there is "strong evidence that there is a strong causal relationship, at least in the United States, between addiction to narcotics and property crime levels."[173]

Do a little arithmetic. Making some conservative assumptions, suppose that there are half a million addicts with $100-a-day habits. Suppose that they fill their habits only 250 days a year (sometimes they're in jail or in the hospital). Suppose that they have to steal for half their drug needs, and that they must steal three times the dollar value of what they need because they must convert their booty into cash through a fence. (These conservative assumptions are similar to those made in a report of the U.S. Department of Health, Education, and Welfare, titled *Social Cost of Drug Abuse*, estimating the amount of theft in which heroin addicts had to engage to support their habits in 1974.)[174] If you have done your arithmetic, you have seen that our half-million addicts need to steal $18,750,000,000 a year to support their habits. This is more than the $15.7 billion that the FBI estimates as the loss due to property crimes during 2010,[175] and it doesn't even take into consideration theft by those addicted to other drugs, such as crack cocaine.

The Bureau of Justice Statistics reports that, in 2004, roughly one of every six prisoners—17 percent of state inmates, 18 percent of federal inmates—said that they had committed their current offense in order to get money for drugs.[176] With jail inmates, "around a quarter of property and drug offenders said they committed their offense to get money for drugs, compared to under a tenth of violent and public-order offenders."[177] Because heroin doesn't produce crime through its pharmacological effects, and because it is so costly only because it's illegal, it is not the "disease" of heroin addiction but its "cure" that leads to property crime. *It is our steadfast refusal to provide heroin through legal sources that, for a significant number of the hundreds of thousands of heroin addicts in the United States, translates a physical need for a drug into a physical need to steal billions of dollars worth of property a year.*

Against this conclusion, it is sometimes countered that studies show that a large proportion of criminal heroin addicts were criminals before they were addicts. But, Anglin and Speckart state that "while involvement in property crime activities generally precedes the addiction career, after addiction occurs the highly elevated property crime levels demonstrated by addicts appear to be regulated by similarly high narcotics use levels."[178] Thus, even for addicts who already were criminals, heroin addiction increases the amount they need to steal and works to make them virtually immune to attempts to wean them from a life of crime or prostitution. Consequently, even if all heroin addicts were criminals before they were addicts, the illegality of heroin would still be a source of crime because of the increased pressure it places on the addict to steal a lot and to steal often. Much the same reasoning applies to other illegal addictive drugs.

Finally, much of the violence associated with drugs falls under Goldstein's third category: systemic crime. We have already seen the link between the crack trade and the murder epidemic of the late 1980s and early 1990s.[179] The large quantities of cash generated by drug dealers and the relatively low salaries of police officers create temptations for corruption. A *New York Times* report during the height of the crack cocaine's popularity noted that "researchers say there are now more than 100 cases each year in state and Federal courts in which law enforcement officials are charged or implicated in drug corruption."[180] Says William Green, assistant commissioner for internal affairs at the U.S. Customs Service, "The money that's being offered by the drug dealers is so big it is just hard to visualize."[181] The Mollen Commission report on police corruption in New York City found "willful blindness" to corruption throughout the police department, resulting in networks of rogue officers who dealt in drugs and preyed on black and Hispanic neighborhoods.[182]

A General Accounting Office review found that drug-related corruption was more likely to involve multiple officers rather than a lone offender, and their review of "drug-related police corruption found on-duty officers engaged in serious criminal activities, such as (1) conducting unconstitutional searches and seizures; (2) stealing money and/or drugs from drug dealers; (3) selling stolen drugs; (4) protecting drug operations; (5) providing false testimony; and (6) submitting false crime reports."[183] Add to this the corruption of border control agents and some military officials involved in interdiction campaigns.

Having learned nothing from our experience with heroin, we have applied, with predictable results, the same policy to cocaine and crack that failed with heroin. The price per pure gram of cocaine and of heroin has generally gone down between 1980 and the present, which means that for all the hoopla of the war on drugs, not to mention the enormous increase in the number of persons sent to prison for drug offenses, there is a plentiful supply. In spite of three U.S.-led international drug wars since 1971, worldwide illicit opium production rose from 990 tons in 1971 to 4,200 tons in 1989, and a U.N. report states that "in 2007, global opium production reached its highest point since 1990, at 8,800 metric tons."[184] This is evidence of a long history of failure and largely futile attempts to pressure foreign countries to reduce domestic production of narcotic substances. Even when such pressure works, it serves only to push production elsewhere. And when the pressure lets up, it's back to business as usual.

According to the Office of National Drug Control Policy (ONDCP), during the decade of the 1990s, "heroin users consumed 14 metric tons at the beginning and end of the decade," while "cocaine users consumed somewhere between 270 and 450 metric tons of pure cocaine each year." [185] The *Washington Post*, reviewing a 2008 U.N. study, noted that in Colombia, the "amount of land devoted to production of coca, the leaf used to make cocaine, has grown at a dramatic pace" despite an eight-year eradication program costing $5 billion. U.S. production estimates show "nearly as much" acreage in 2006 as when the program started in 2001.[186] U.N. estimates of total world cocaine manufacture increased from 774 metric tons in 1990 to 994 in 2007.[187] Likewise, attempts to use the U.S. Coast Guard and Navy to interdict cocaine coming into the United

States by sea have failed to put a dent in the traffic. After all, America has over 88,000 miles of coastline.[188] In response to the drug czar's claim that we "are disrupting the production and flow of cocaine," a *New York Times* editorial titled "Not Winning the War on Drugs" noted that "while seizures are up, so are shipments."[189] The *Wall Street Journal* reports that a kilogram of cocaine that cost between $55,000 and $65,000 in 1981, cost between $20,000 and $40,000 in 1987.[190] The National Narcotics Intelligence Consumers' Committee reports cocaine prices as low as $10,500 per kilogram in 1994.[191] In a summary of these trends, a 2004 ONDCP report indicated that "powder cocaine prices have declined by roughly 80 percent since 1981," and "purity-adjusted prices were at or near all-time lows in 2003."[192] Although prices have increased from the extreme low point in the last several years, the *New York Times* reports that experts say this is "mostly the result of a strong Euro and fast-growing demand in Europe."[193] All of this testifies to the general failure of our costly "war on drugs" to make these drugs harder to obtain—a conclusion endorsed by the conservative American Enterprise Institute in a 2005 book on drug policy.[194]

In 1988, the *National Law Journal* surveyed 181 chief prosecutors or their top drug deputies throughout the United States and reported that "nearly two-thirds of the country's top state and local prosecutors say they are having little to no impact in the fight against illegal narcotics."[195] The American Enterprise Institute study stated that "on the whole, then, there is now less reason than ever to believe that current policies are an efficient and effective response to the problem of illicit drugs."[196] This failing drug war cost federal, state, and local governments approximately $33 billion in 1999, up nearly $5 billion from 1994.[197] The National Drug Control Budget alone was $25.9 billion for fiscal year 2010.[198]

In sum, we have an antidrug policy that is failing at its own goals and succeeding only in adding to crime. First, there are the heroin and crack addicts, who must steal to support their habits. Then, there are the drug merchants who—due to the illegality of drugs—have fabulous financial incentives to provide illicit substances to a willing body of consumers. This in turn contributes to the high rate of inner-city murders and other violence as drug gangs battle for the enormous sums of money available. Next, there are the law enforcement officials who, after risking their lives for low salaries, are corrupted by irresistible amounts of money. Finally, there are the otherwise law-abiding citizens who are made criminals because they use cocaine, a drug less harmful than tobacco, and those who are made criminals because they use marijuana, a drug that is safer than alcohol and less deadly than aspirin.

Much of the recent dramatic growth in our prison population (documented above) is the result of the hardening of drug enforcement policy starting in the Reagan years and continuing into the present: In 1968 there were 162,000 drug arrests nationwide, the number climbing to more than 1.6 million in 2010, and the Bureau of Justice Statistics reports that half of federal inmates were serving sentences for drug violations in 2010.[199] The absolute numbers are even more striking. In 2010, federal prisons held 97,472 drug offenders, compared to 30,470 in 1990.[200] On the state level, there were less than 20,000 drug offenders in state prisons in 1990, but by 2009, there were 242,200.[201] Because numerous studies show that arrested drug dealers in inner-city neighborhoods are quickly replaced, it was apparent from the start that this policy would have little success in reducing the availability of illicit drugs.[202] What it does succeed in is leaving inner-city youths with criminal records that reduce their chances of getting a legitimate job. All this is occurring at a time when there is increasing evidence that we are wasting money on the "war on drugs" and would be better off decriminalizing drugs, taxing their production and sale, and expanding treatment and public health initiatives. Because that would be far less costly than the "war," this would leave over money to fight a more effective war against muggers and rapists rather than recreational drug users. Evidence from the 11 states that decriminalized marijuana possession in the 1970s suggests that decriminalization does not lead to increased use. President Clinton's former Surgeon General, Joycelyn Elders, recommended that we study seriously the possibility of decriminalizing drugs as a means to reducing violence, noting that "other countries had decriminalized drug use and had reduced their crime rates without increasing the use of narcotics."[203] For example, in 2001 Portugal eliminated criminal penalties for all drugs in amounts for personal use. Possession for personal use can still trigger a hearing before the Commission for the Dissuasion of Drug Addiction, a three-person tribunal that discourages drug use and encourages addicts to get treatment. An evaluation, published in the *British Journal of Criminology*, found reductions in problematic drug use and states that Portugal's experience

> demonstrates that—contrary to some predictions—decriminalization does not inevitably lead to rises in drug use. It can reduce the burden upon the criminal justice system. It can further contribute to social and health benefits. Moreover, such effects can be observed when decriminalizing all illicit drugs. This is important, as decriminalization is commonly restricted to cannabis alone.[204]

Former Baltimore Mayor Kurt Schmoke has called for consideration of decriminalization, and so has Jerry Wilson, former chief of police of Washington, D.C. (where 42 percent of murders were drug-related in 1990).[205] A draft of a report commissioned by the American Medical Association recommended legalization of marijuana and decriminalization of other illicit drugs. The report was shelved when some doctors "expressed outrage at its recommendation."[206] A more recent call for decriminalization is from the Global Commission on Drug Policy, whose members include: the former Presidents of Mexico, Colombia, Brazil, and Switzerland; a former Secretary General of the United Nations, a former U.S. Secretary of State; the Prime Minister of Greece; and a former Chair of the U.S. Federal Reserve and economic advisor to President Obama. They state that "the global war on drugs has failed, with devastating consequences for individuals and societies." They suggest ending the criminalization of drugs, experimenting with models of legal regulation that "undermine the power of organized crime" and "offer health and treatment services to those in need."[207]

Some form of decriminalization of marijuana, heroin, and cocaine would reduce the criminalization of otherwise law-abiding users; it would drive down the price of drugs, which would reduce the need for addicts to steal, and reduce as well the incentives to drug traffickers and smugglers to ply their trades and to find new users; and it would free up personnel and resources for a more effective war against the crimes that people fear most.

In the face of all this, it is hard not to share the frustration expressed by Norval Morris, former dean of the University of Chicago Law School: "It is trite but it remains true that the main causes of crime are social and economic. The question arises whether people really care. The solutions are so obvious. *It's almost as if America wished for a high crime rate.*"[208] If this is so, then *the system's failure is only in the eye of the victim: For those in control, it is a roaring success!*

WHAT WORKS TO REDUCE CRIME

Surveying the programs that might contribute to reducing crime, criminologist Elliot Currie concludes that "four priorities seem especially critical: preventing child abuse and neglect, enhancing children's intellectual and social development, providing support and guidance to vulnerable adolescents, and working extensively with juvenile offenders." About these programs, Currie observes that "the best of them work, and they work remarkably well given how limited and underfunded they usually are."[209] A study titled *Diverting Children from a Life of Crime: Measuring Costs and Benefits*, issued in June 1996 by the Rand Corporation, concluded:

> Programs that try to steer the young from wrongdoing—the training of parents whose children often misbehave, for example, or incentives to graduate from high school—are far more cost-effective in preventing crime over the long term than are mandatory sentences that imprison repeat adult offenders for long periods.[210]

A more recent report from the Rand Corporation, titled *Investing in Our Children: What We Know and Don't Know about the Costs and Benefits of Early Childhood Interventions*, reached a similar conclusion. Evaluating nine programs in which early interventions were targeted at disadvantaged children, the study concludes that such programs lead to decreased criminal activity and save taxpayer dollars at the same time.[211] Similar results were found for Head Start programs: "At age 27, those who participated [in Head Start programs as children] had lower arrest rates, higher education rates, earned more money, [and] were more likely to be homeowners and less likely to receive social services."[212]

The National Treatment Improvement Evaluation Study (NTIES), "the largest study of its kind, which followed more than 5,300 clients in programs funded by the federal Center for Substance Abuse Treatment," concludes that

> drug and alcohol treatment programs significantly reduced substance use, crime, and homelessness. ... Use of most illicit

substances in the year after treatment entry declined about 50 percent compared with the year before. ... Arrest rates fell substantially in the sample—from 48 percent to 17 percent.[213]

And a study by the Rand Corporation Drug Policy Research Center, titled *Controlling Cocaine: Supply versus Demand Programs,* found that "[t]reatment is seven times more cost-effective than domestic drug enforcement in reducing cocaine use and 15 times more cost-effective in reducing the social costs of crime and lost productivity."[214] The study also concluded that "treatment is the most effective way to reduce violent crime."[215]

A review of more than 500 crime-prevention program evaluations yielded a list of what works. Among the programs that appear effective in reducing crime, the report lists family therapy and parent training for delinquent and at-risk adolescents; teaching of social competency skills in schools, and coaching of high-risk youth in "thinking skills"; vocational training for older male ex-offenders; extra police patrols in high-crime hot spots; monitoring of high-risk repeat offenders by specialized police forces as well as incarceration; rehabilitation programs with risk-focused treatments for convicted offenders; and therapeutic community treatment for drug-using offenders in prisons.[216]

In 2007, the journal *Criminology and Public Policy* devoted an entire issue to "taking stock" of the field, "not to offer innovative or new policies," but "a complete issue devoted to noted scholars taking the position that we now have enough knowledge about some aspect of crime and justice that a policy is advised." The titles of some of the published papers include "Build the Capacity of Communities to Address Crime," "Restore Rationality to Sentencing Policy," "Make Rehabilitation Corrections' Guiding Paradigm," "Target Juvenile Needs to Reduce Delinquency," "Save Children From a Life of Crime," and "Protect Individual Punishment Decisions from Mandatory Penalties."[217]

In short, there is a growing body of knowledge showing that early childhood intervention, drug treatment, and numerous other programs can work to reduce crime. As Professor Blumstein observed, "If you intervene early, you not only save the costs of incarceration, you also save the costs of crime and gain the benefits of an individual who is a taxpaying contributor to the economy."[218] But, as Peter Greenwood, author of the Rand Corporation Study, *Diverting Children from a Life of Crime,* says, "The big policy question is, who will act on this?"[219]

FAILING TO REDUCE CRIME: ERIKSON, DURKHEIM, AND FOUCAULT

As the Introduction noted, we contend that the criminal justice system must actually fight crime—or at least some crime—but only enough to keep it from getting out of hand and to keep the struggle against crime vividly and dramatically in the public's view, though never enough to substantially reduce or eliminate crime. We call this way of looking at criminal justice policy the

Pyrrhic defeat theory. A "Pyrrhic victory" is a military victory purchased at such a cost in troops and treasure that it amounts to a defeat. The Pyrrhic defeat theory argues that the failure of the criminal justice system yields such benefits to those in positions of power that it amounts to a victory (see Chapter 4).

Erikson, Durkheim and the Benefits of Deviance

The Pyrrhic defeat theory draws heavily upon Kai T. Erikson's suggestion in his book, *Wayward Puritans*, that societies derive benefit from the existence of crime, and thus there is reason to believe that social institutions work to maintain rather than to eliminate crime. Thus, it will serve to clarify our view if we compare it with Erikson's.

Professor Erikson's theory is based on the view of crime that finds expression in one of the classic works of sociological theory, *The Division of Labor in Society*, by Émile Durkheim. Writing toward the end of the nineteenth century, Durkheim

> had suggested that crime (and by extension other forms of deviation) may actually perform a needed service to society by drawing people together in a common posture of anger and indignation. The deviant individual violates rules of conduct which the rest of the community holds in high respect; and when these people come together to express their outrage over the offense and to bear witness against the offender, they develop a tighter bond of solidarity than existed earlier.[220]

The solidarity that holds a community together, in this view, is a function of the intensity with which the members of the community share a living sense of the group's cultural identity, of the boundary between acceptable and unacceptable behavior that gives the group its distinctive character. It is necessary, then, for the existence of a community as a *community* that its members learn and constantly relearn the location of its "boundaries." Erikson writes that these boundaries are learned in dramatic confrontations with

> policing agents whose special business it is to guard the cultural integrity of the community. Whether these confrontations take the form of criminal trials, excommunication hearings, courts-martial, or even case conferences, they act as boundary-maintaining devices in the sense that they demonstrate to whatever audience is concerned where the line is drawn between behavior that belongs in the special universe of the group and behavior that does not.[221]

In brief, this means not only that a community makes good use of unacceptable behavior *but also that it positively needs unacceptable behavior.* Not only does unacceptable behavior cast in relief the terrain of behavior acceptable to the community; it also reinforces the intensity with which the members of the community identify that terrain as their shared territory. On this view, *deviant behavior is an ingredient in the glue that holds a community together.* "This," Erikson continues,

> raises a delicate theoretical issue. If we grant that human groups often derive benefit from deviant behavior, can we then assume that they are organized in such a way as to promote this resource? Can we assume, in other words, *that forces operate in the social structure to recruit offenders and to commit them to long periods of service in the deviant ranks?* ...
>
> Looking at the matter from a long-range historical perspective, it is fair to conclude that prisons have done a conspicuously poor job of reforming the convicts placed in their custody; but the very consistency of this failure may have a peculiar logic of its own. Perhaps we find it difficult to change the worst of our penal practices because we expect the prison to harden the inmate's commitment to deviant forms of behavior and draw him more deeply into the deviant ranks.[222]

Drawing on Durkheim's recognition that societies benefit from the existence of deviants, Erikson entertains the view that societies have institutions whose unannounced function is to recruit and maintain a reliable supply of deviants. Modified for our purposes, Erikson's view would become the hypothesis that the American criminal justice system fails to reduce crime because a visible criminal population is essential to maintaining the "boundaries" that mark the cultural identity of American society and to maintaining the solidarity among those who share that identity. In other words, in its failure, the criminal justice system succeeds in providing some of the cement necessary to hold American society together as a society.

As we said in the Introduction, this idea is one of several that contribute to the Pyrrhic defeat theory, but the idea is also transformed in the process. Here, then, we aim to acknowledge the debt to the Durkheim–Erikson thesis and to state the difference between it and the view that we will defend. The debt is to the insight that societies may promote behavior that they seem to desire to stamp out, and that failure to eliminate deviance may be a success of some sort.

The difference, on the other hand, is this: Both Durkheim and Erikson jump from the *general* proposition that the failure to eliminate deviance promotes social solidarity to the *specific* conclusion that the form in which this failure occurs in a particular society can be explained by the contribution the failure makes to promoting consensus on shared beliefs and thus feelings of social solidarity. This is a "jump" because it leaves out the important question of how a social group forms its particular consensus around one set of shared beliefs rather than another; that is, Durkheim and Erikson implicitly assume that a consensus already exists (at least virtually) and that deviance is promoted to manifest and reinforce it. This leads to the view that social institutions reflect beliefs already in people's heads, already largely and spontaneously shared by all of them.

In our view, even if it is granted that societies work to strengthen feelings of social solidarity, the set of beliefs about the world around which those feelings will crystallize are by no means already in people's heads and spontaneously shared. A consensus is made, not born, although, again, we do not mean that it is made intentionally. It is created, not just reflected, by social institutions. Thus, the failure to stamp out deviance does not simply reinforce a consensus that already exists; it is part of the process by which a very particular consensus is created.[223] In developing the Pyrrhic defeat theory, we try to show how the failure of criminal justice works to create and reinforce a very particular set of beliefs about the world, about what is dangerous and what is not, and about who is a threat and who is not. This does not merely shore up general feelings of social solidarity; it allows those feelings to be attached to a social order characterized by striking disparities of wealth, power, and privilege, and by considerable injustice.

A Word About Foucault

Michel Foucault is another thinker who has suggested that the failure of the criminal justice system—prisons in particular—serves a function for society. His view of this failure and its function is, at points, close to the one for which we argue here, but there are differences as well. In his book, *Discipline and Punish,* Foucault notes that complaints about the failure of prisons to curb crime, indeed their tendency to increase crime by promoting recidivism, have accompanied the prison throughout its history—so much so that Foucault asks, "Is not the supposed failure part of the functioning of the prison?"[224] In response, Foucault writes that the prison "has succeeded extremely well ... in producing delinquents, in an apparently marginal, but in fact centrally supervised milieu; in producing the delinquent as a pathologized subject."[225] That is, the prison regime transforms the offender from a lawbreaker into a *delinquent in need of correction,* an abnormal individual in need of treatment. And this development licenses a permanent policing of the potentially troublesome classes.

Foucault suggests that the new prison regime that emerged in France in the nineteenth century was a response to a "new threat" posed by peasants and workers against the "new system of the legal exploitation of labour,"[226] by which he means capitalism. This is a class-based explanation of the new prison regime, in which criminality gets identified "almost exclusively [with] a certain social class ... the bottom rank of the social order."[227] Among the advantages produced by this prison regime and the policing that accompanies it are the maintenance of illegality at a sufficiently low level so that it does not pose a general threat to the social order, and the weakening of the poorer classes—from whom both the delinquents and their victims tend to come—by dividing the poor against themselves. Moreover, says Foucault, "[d]elinquency, controlled illegality, is an agent for the illegality of the dominant groups."[228] Here he has in mind the profits to be made from drugs and prostitution, alongside a general toleration of the "delinquency of wealth."[229] This much is generally in accord with the thesis of *The Rich Get Richer,* which argues that the failure of the criminal justice system to significantly reduce crime, as well as the identification of crime with the harmful acts of poor people, serves the interests of the rich and powerful by creating the general belief that the greatest threat to the well-being of ordinary folks comes from the poor rather than from the rich.[230]

But Foucault goes further. He contends that delinquency, "with the generalized policing that it authorizes, constitutes a means of perpetual surveillance of the population: an apparatus that makes it possible to supervise, through the delinquents themselves, the whole social field."[231] For Foucault, then, the prison is part of a "general tactics of subjection" that amount to a system of permanent social surveillance. Stretching from the "Panopticon" model of a prison, in which a single guard can watch a large number of inmates without himself being seen, to the emergence of a "scientific" criminological establishment that observes and studies delinquents, and from there to the modern medical-psychological establishment that keeps records on just about everyone, ubiquitous surveillance works to make people feel observed and thus makes them into the agents of their own normalizing discipline. Thus, the prison spreads out into a "carceral archipelago," a whole system of institutions and practices, including the disciplines such as psychology and medicine, aimed at "normalization."[232] In sum, writes Foucault,

> the normalizing power has spread. Borne along by the omni-
> presence of the mechanisms of discipline, basing itself on all the
> carceral apparatuses, it has become one of the major functions of
> our society. The judges of normality are everywhere. We are in the
> society of the teacher-judge, the doctor-judge, the educator-judge,
> the 'social-worker'-judge; it is on them that the universal reign of
> the normative is based; and each individual, wherever he may find
> himself, subjects to it his body, his gestures, his behaviour, his apti-
> tudes, his achievements.[233]

With this, Foucault has left criminal justice behind and presented a theory of the nature of modern society generally. Also left behind is the class structure of the exercise of power that was present in the origins of the prison system as Foucault described it. Now, power is everywhere, exercised by everyone on him or herself and on everyone else.[234] No doubt, this captures something of the flavor of modern life, in which people at all levels of society are subjected to myriad pressures to be "normal," from the tsk-tsks of teachers and doctors to the self-help books and advice columns that offer to make us better earners and better lovers and better parents. The judges of normality are, indeed, everywhere.

But this account also mystifies the exercise of power. Rather than operating along a class axis that might be eliminated, and to serve interests that might be identified and critiqued, power now seems its own goal, a universal fact of modern life, driven by no particular interest beyond that of discipline—"the policing of normality" as an end in itself.[235] The enemy is everywhere and nowhere in particular, so there is no clear target for resistance. Not only is the class structure of the exercise of power—particularly criminal justice power—flattened out here, the moral status of the exercise is obscured as well. Absent from Foucault's analysis is attention to the difference between those forms of discipline that are necessary for the freedom of each to coexist peacefully with the freedom of the rest and those forms of discipline that simply serve the interests of the rich and powerful.[236] So there is no clear guidance about what should be resisted. The analysis in *The Rich Get Richer* will strive to keep the class nature of the criminal justice system in view, while recognizing the importance of distinguishing between those exercises of power that are necessary for the protection of freedom and those that simply serve the interests of the wealthy.

Summary

This chapter has tried to establish the first part of the Pyrrhic defeat theory, namely, that the war on crime is a failure and an avoidable one: The American criminal justice system—the entire process from lawmaking to law enforcing—has failed to eliminate the high rates of crime that characterize our society and threaten our citizens. Over the last several decades, crime has generally risen, although in recent years it has declined. Numerous causes—economic and social—have contributed to this, such that serious observers agree that criminal justice policy and practice cannot be credited with more than a fraction of the recent declines. At the same time, however, neither should it be thought on this basis that public policy cannot reduce the crime we have. Crime is not a simple and unavoidable consequence of either the number of youngsters in our populace or the degree of urbanization of our society. Moreover, there are a number of policies, we have good reason to believe would succeed in reducing crime—effective gun control, decriminalization of illicit drugs, amelioration of poverty, prevention of child abuse and neglect, and early intervention with at-risk youngsters—that we refuse to implement on any significant scale. The Pyrrhic defeat theory shares with the Durkheim–Erikson view of the functional nature of crime, the idea that societies may promote behavior that they seem to want to eliminate. However, it differs from their view in insisting that the failure to stamp out crime doesn't simply reflect an existing consensus but contributes to creating one, one that is functional for only a certain part of our society. This chapter concluded by discussing Foucault's claim that the failure of the prison is part of a larger structure of disciplinary surveillance that pervades modern society. His account of the beginnings of this regime parallels the class analysis for which we shall argue. However, as he develops his theory, Foucault leaves class structure behind and thus mystifies the nature of the power exercised in the criminal justice system. Readers interested in the relationship between the theory presented in *The Rich Get Richer* and Marxism, should consult Appendix I.

Study Questions

1. What does Zimring mean when he compares crime policy to "a version of 'heads I win, tails you lose'"? What evidence do the authors present to support this view?
2. What are some of the criminal justice factors involved in the declining crime rate, and how much impact did they have?
3. What are the noncriminal justice factors involved in the declining crime rate and how does each contribute?
4. What excuses have been given for our inability to reduce the amount of crime we have? How do you evaluate these excuses?
 5. What causes crime? How, and why, do the authors distinguish a "cause" from a "source" of crime? What do the authors say are sources of crime? Be sure to explain how they link each source with higher crime rates.
6. Do you think we "make the world of violence that surrounds us" as Currie says? If not, why is it beyond our ability to influence? If so, what could we do to reduce the amount of crime? To what extent are these solutions within the criminal justice system, or do noncriminal-justice policies have a greater impact on crime?
7. What does it mean to say that "the criminal justice system is 'designed to fail'" and "crime is functional for a society"? How does the Pyrrhic defeat theory differ on this from the Durkheim–Erikson theory?
8. List the costs and benefits of our current war on drugs. Is it worth it? Do you think that legalizing all or some illicit drugs would reduce crime? If so, would you agree to legalization?

Additional Resources

Jeffrey Reiman & Paul Leighton, eds., *The Rich Get Richer and the Poor Get Prison: A Reader* (Boston: Pearson, 2010). This volume is a collection of accessible articles that were either used as reference material for *The Rich Get Richer* or provide lively complementary examples or analysis. The reader is divided into sections that parallel the chapters of *The Rich Get Richer*, and each section of the reader opens with a substantial introduction, written by the editors, that provides article summaries, context, and linkages to *The Rich Get Richer*.

The authors also maintain a companion website to the text at *http://www.paulsjusticepage. com/reiman.htm*

Notes

1. Joel Dyer, *The Perpetual Prisoner Machine* (Boulder, CO: Westview Press, 2000), p. 2.
2. Lynne Vieraitis, Tomislav Kovandzic, and Thomas Marvell, "The Criminogenic Effects of Imprisonment," *Criminology and Public Policy* 6, no. 3 (2007) (589–622): 590.
3. John Irwin and James Austin, *It's About Time: America's Imprisonment Binge*, 3rd ed. (Belmont, CA: Wadsworth Publishing, 2001); Loïc Wacquant, "Class, Race & Hyperincarceration in Revanchist America," *Daedalus* 139, no. 3 (2010): 74–90; Ernest Drucker, *A Plague of Prisons: The Epidemiology of Mass Incarceration in America* (New York: The New Press, 2011).

4. Katherine Beckett and Theodore Sasson, *The Politics of Injustice: Crime and Punishment in America* (Thousand Oaks, CA: Pine Forge Press, 2000), p. 52.

5. Richard Nixon, State of the Union Address, 1970. *http://www.presidency.ucsb.edu/ws/index.php?pid=2921.*

6. Jimmy Carter, Drug Abuse Message to Congress, 1977. *http://www.presidency.ucsb.edu/ws/index.php?pid=7908.*

7. Franklin Zimring, "The New Politics of Criminal Justice," *Perspectives on Crime and Justice: 1999-2000 Lecture Series,* NCJ 184245, March 2001, p. 3.

8. State of the Union Message, as reported in *The Washington Post,* January 26, 1994, p. A13.

9. Fox Butterfield, "A Large Drop in Violent Crime Is Reported," *The New York Times,* September 18, 1996, p. A14.

10. "Popgun Politics." *U.S. News & World Report,* September 30, 1996, p. 41.

11. David H. Bayley, "The Cop Fallacy," *The New York Times,* August 13, 1993, p. A17.

12. The White House, Office of the Press Secretary, "Radio Address of the President to the Nation," January 11, 1997.

13. State of the Union Address. January 20, 1999, *http://www.washingtonpost.com/wp-srv/politics/special/states/docs/sou99.htm.*

14. President George Bush, "Remarks by the President on Project Safe Neighborhoods," May 14, 2001, *www.presidency.ucsb.edu/ws/index.php?pid=45608.*

15. Private prisons are for-profit companies that build and/or manage prisons. They are part of a larger criminal justice-industrial complex that has a vested interest in crime and discussed more in Chapter 4.

16. "Combat Crime and Drug Abuse," Ch. 9, *A Blueprint for New Beginnings: A Responsible Budget for America's Priorities* (Washington, D.C.: U.S. Government Printing Office, 2001), *www.gpoaccess.gov/usbudget/fy02/pdf/blueprnt.pdf.*

17. Executive Office of the President, "Statement of Administration Policy: H.R. 1279: Gang Deterrence and Community Protection Act of 2005," May 11, 2005, *www.presidency.ucsb.edu/ws/index.php?pid=24850.*

18. Office of Management and Budget, *Fiscal Year 2006: Department of Justice, www.whitehouse.gov/omb/budget/fy2006/justice.html.* The document does find that federal funding to continue support for the 100,000 police was cut because an assessment rated the program as "Results Not Demonstrated."

19. See Senator Barack Obama, "Remarks at Howard University Convocation," September 28, 2007, *http://www.howard.edu/newsroom/news/2007/071001RemarksofSenatorBarackObama.htm.*

20. Federal laws required a mandatory five-year sentence for crimes involving 500 grams (about a pound) of powder cocaine or 5 grams (about one-sixth of an ounce) of crack cocaine. See Chapter 3 for more discussion.

21. Josh Gerstein, President Obama backing off strict crime policy. *Politico,* September 11, 2010, *http://www.politico.com/news/stories/0910/42004.html.*

22. Eric Holder, Statement of Attorney General Eric Holder on the 2011 Preliminary Uniform Crime Report, 2011, *http://www.justice.gov/opa/pr/2011/December/11-ag-1666.html.*

23. General Accounting Office, COPS Grants Were a Modest Contributor to Declines in Crime in the 1990s. Washington D.C.: General Accounting Office. GAO-06-104, 2005, *http://www.gao.gov/new.items/d06104.pdf. P. 1.*

24. See Senator Barack Obama, "Remarks at Howard University Convocation," 2007.

25. Justice Policy Institute. No date. More of the Same: President Obama's budget has too little invested in long-term solutions, and is likely to contribute to rising incarceration rates, p. 1. *http://www.justicepolicy.org/images/upload/09-05_FAC_FY2010%20Budget%20Factsheet_PS.pdf*.

26. Jacob Sullum, Bummer: Barack Obama turns out to be just another drug warrior, *Reason*, October, 2011, *http://reason.com/archives/2011/09/12/bummer*.

27. Ibid.

28. Douglas Berman, New poll reports that large majority of Americans consider "War on Drugs" a failure. *Sentencing Law and Policy Blog*, 2010, *http://sentencing.typepad.com/sentencing_law_and_policy/2010/07/new-poll-reports-that-large-majority-of-americac-see-war-on-drugs-to-be-a-failure.html*.

29. Sullum, Bummer: Barack Obama turns out to be just another drug warrior, 2011.

30. *Sourcebook*, Table 6.28.2009.

31. Elliot Currie, *Crime and Punishment in America* (New York: Metropolitan Books, Henry Holt, 1998), p. 12; BJS, *Correctional Populations in the United States, 2009*, NCJ 123681, December 2010. Table 1, p. 2; and *StatAbst–2011*, Table 12, p.18.

32. BJS, *Criminal Offender Statistics, www.ojp.usdoj.gov/bjs/crimoff.htm* (last revised June 27, 2005).

33. William J. Chambliss, *Power, Politics, and Crime* (Boulder, CO: Westview Press, 1999), p. 127; see also Currie, *Crime and Punishment in America*, pp. 30–36.

34. Keller, Josh. 2010. "Calif. Governor Proposes Amending Constitution to Bolster Higher Education," *Chronicle of Higher Education*, January 6, *http://chronicle.com/article/Calif-Governor-Proposes/63440/*.

35. *Brown v Palta*, No. 09-1233, *http://www.supremecourt.gov/opinions/10pdf/09-1233.pdf*.

36. James Austin, Marino A. Bruce, Leo Carroll, Patricia L. McCall, and Stephen C. Richards "The Use of Incarceration in the United States," *Critical Criminology* 10 (2001): 20.

37. Pew Center on the States, *One in 100: Behind Bars in America 2008* (Washington, D.C.: Pew Charitable Trusts, 2008), *http://www.pewcenteronthestates.org*.

38. *UCR–2010*, Table 1 and *Sourcebook*, Table 3.106.2009.

39. Elliott Currie, "Reflections on Crime and Criminology at the Millennium," *Western Criminology Review* 2, no. 1 (1999), *http://wcr.sonoma.edu/v2n1/currie.html*.

40. Lorraine Adams and David Vise, "Crime Rates Down for 7th Straight Year," *The Washington Post*, October 18, 1999, p. A2 (emphasis in original).

41. David Vise and Lorraine Adams, "Despite Rhetoric, Violent Crime Climbs," *The Washington Post*, December 5, 1999, p. A3.

42. Quoted in ibid.

43. Quoted in ibid.

44. *Sourcebook–1998*, Table 6.48, p. 502; and *Prisoners in 2004*, p. 1. See also Vise and Adams, "Despite Rhetoric, Violent Crime Climbs."

45. John DiIulio, "Rethinking Crime–Again," *Democracy: A Journal of Ideas* 16, (Spring 2010): 46–57. *http://www.democracyjournal.org/16/6739.php*

46. Joan Petersilia, "Community Corrections," in James Q. Wilson and Joan Petersilia (eds) *Crime and Public Policy* (Oxford: Oxford University Press, 2010).

47. William Spelman, "The Limited Importance of Prison Expansion," in Alfred Blumstein and Joel Wallman (ed.) *The Crime Drop in America* (New York: Cambridge University Press, 2000), p. 123.

48. R. Rosenfeld, "Patterns in Adult Homicide: 1980–1995," in Blumstein and Wallman, *The Crime Drop in America*, 130–163.

49. Bruce Western, *Punishment and Inequality in America* (New York: Russell Sage Foundation, 2006), p. 191.
50. Franklin Zimring, *The Great American Crime Decline* (New York: Oxford University Press, 2007), pp. 131, 55.
51. John Conklin, *Why Crime Rates Fell* (Boston: Allyn & Bacon, 2003), p. 200.
52. Vincent Schiraldi, "Spend More Money on Education, Not Prisons," *Newsday*, August 29, 2002, p. A39.
53. Republican Contract With America. Available at *http://www.house.gov/house/Contract/CONTRACT.html*. The contract advocated for the Taking Back Our Streets Act which made "cuts in social spending"—meaning money for community crime prevention—to "fund prison construction and additional law enforcement." See H.R. 4170, Drug Importer Death Penalty Act of 1996. The official summary of the bill states that importing "a controlled substance in an amount the Attorney General has determined is equal to 100 usual dosage amounts to life imprisonment without possibility of release (or, if the defendant has violated such provision on more than one occasion and if certain requirements under the Federal criminal code are met, to death)." *http://www.govtrack.us/congress/bill.xpd?bill=h104-4170*.
54. Newt Gingrich and Pat Nolan, "Prison Reform: A Smart Way for States to Save Money and Lives," *Washington Post*, Jan 7, 2011, *http://www.washingtonpost.com/wp-dyn/content/article/2011/01/06/AR2011010604386.html*.
55. Michael Lynch, *Big Prisons, Big Dreams* (Piscataway, N.J.: Rutgers University Press, 2007).
56. Joan Petersilia, "Beyond the Prison Bubble" *National Institute of Justice Journal*, vol 268 (October 2011). *http://www.nij.gov/nij/journals/268/prison-bubble.htm*.
57. Philip Cook and Jens Ludwig, "Controlling Crime: How To Do More With Less," *The Crime Report*, November 14, 2011, *http://www.thecrimereport.org/news/articles/2011-11-controlling-crime-how-to-do-more-with-less*.
58. Philip Cook, Anthony Braga, and Mark Moore, "Gun Control," in James Q. Wilson and Joan Petersilia (eds) *Crime and Public Policy* (Oxford: Oxford University Press, 2010). Robert Apel and Daniel Nagin, "General Deterrence: A Review of Recent Evidence," 2010, ibid. Richard Rosenfeld, "Changing Crime Rates," 2010, ibid.
59. Conklin, *Why Crime Rates Fell*, p. 69.
60. Eric Pooley, "One Good Apple," *Time*, January 15, 1996, pp. 54–56.
61. Currie, "Reflections on Crime and Criminology at the Millennium."
62. Conklin, *Why Crime Rates Fell*, p. 71.
63. Alfred Blumstein, "Why Is Crime Falling—or Is It?" in National Institute of Justice, *Perspectives on Crime and Justice: 2000–2001 Lecture Series*, p. 16.
64. Blumstein, "Why Is Crime Falling—or Is It?" pp. 19–21.
65. Blumstein, "The Recent Rise and Fall of American Violence," in Blumstein and Wallman, *The Crime Drop in America*, pp. 4–5.
66. Quoted in Pierre Thomas, "In a Reversal, U.S. Homicide Numbers Fall," *The Washington Post*, December 31, 1995, p. A8.
67. "Popgun Politics," *U.S. News & World Report*, September 30, 1996, p. 33.
68. Blumstein, "Why Is Crime Falling—or Is It?" pp. 12, 17–18, 24. An improving economy helped reduce crime rates, but the financial crisis and recession have not caused crime rates to increase because people who are unemployed or have reduced income shift gradually to crime as their economic resources become depleted. Congress has extended unemployment benefits and people have savings

that they draw down before turning to crime. Further, unemployed people "find themselves in routine activities that are more home-based," thus reducing their time spent in public places where they are at higher risk of victimization. The unemployed become "guardians for their residences," which lowers property-based crime victimization. Bushway, Shawn, "Labor Markets and Crime," in James Q. Wilson and Joan Petersilia (eds) *Crime and Public Policy*. (Oxford: Oxford University Press, 2010), p. 191.

70. Jessica Wolpaw Reyes, "Environmental Policy as Social Policy? The Impact of Childhood Lead Exposure on Crime," *The B.E. Journal of Economic Analysis & Policy*. 7, no. 1(2007): 1–43. *http://www.bepress.com/bejeap/vol7/iss1/art51*.

71. Rick Nevin, "Understanding International Crime Trends: The Legacy of Pre-school Lead Exposure," *Environmental Research* 104, no. 3 (2007): 315–36. *http://www.precaution.org/lib/crime_trends_and_preschool_lead_exposure.070501.pdf*

72. Shankar Vedantam, "Research Links Lead Exposure, Criminal Activity," *Washington Post*, July 8, 2007, *http://www.washingtonpost.com/wp-dyn/content/article/2007/07/07/AR2007070701073.html*.

73. David Garland, *Punishment and Modern Society* (Chicago: University of Chicago Press, 1990), pp. 165–66.

74. *Challenge*, p. 35.

75. *Sourcebook 2003*, Table 3.106; and *UCR–2010*, Table 1.

76. BJS, *Justice Expenditures and Employment in the U.S., 2007*, NCJ 231540, September 2010, Tables 1 and 2.

77. BJS, *Justice Expenditures and Employment in the U.S., 2003*, NCJ 212260, April 2006, p. 3.

78. For 1990, expenditure on private security was $52 billion, and the number of people employed in some form of private security work was "more than 1.5 million people, outnumbering police officers by a 2:1 margin. The latest figures show that this ratio is now about 3:1, with more than $100 billion, dwarfing law enforcement expenditures [on police] of around $40 billion." Randall Shelden, *Controlling the Dangerous Classes* (Boston: Allyn & Bacon, 2001), p. 280.

79. On this issue, we have made ample use of the discussion and references in Victor Kappeler, Mark Blumberg, and Gary Potter *The Mythology of Crime and Criminal Justice*, 3rd ed. (Prospect Heights, IL: Waveland, 2000), pp. 257–72.

80. Heather Mason Kiefer, "Public on Justice System: Fair, but Still Too Soft," *Gallup Poll*, February 3, 2004, *http://www.gallup.com/poll/10474/Public-Justice-System-Fair-Still-Too-Soft.aspx*; and Ernest van den Haag, "When Felons Go Free: Worse than a Crime," *National Review*, January 20, 1992, p. 50.

81. James Lynch and William Alex Pridemore, "Crime in International Perspective," in James Q. Wilson and Joan Petersilia (eds) *Crime and Public Policy* (Oxford: Oxford University Press, 2010).

82. International Centre for Prison Studies, *http://www.prisonstudies.org/info/worldbrief/wpb_stats.php*. Figures for the UK are from 2011 and do not include juveniles or those held in Immigration Detention Centers; Germany from 2011; Belgium from 2010; and Canada from 2009.

83. Lynch and Pridemore, "Crime in International Perspective," p. 25.

84. Lynch and Pridemore, "Crime in International Perspective," p. 38.

85. Ibid.

86. Caitlin E. Hughes and Alex Steven, "What Can We Learn From The Portuguese Decriminalization Of Illicit Drugs?" *British Journal of Criminology* 50, no. 6 (2010): 1001.

87. David Montgomery, "Whoa! Canada! Legal Marijuana. Gay Marriage. Peace. What the Heck's Going on Up North, Eh?" *The Washington Post*, July 1, 2003,

p. C01; and DeNeen L. Brown, "A Tolerance for IV Drug Users: Vancouver Seeks to Protect Addicts, Not Punish Them," *The Washington Post*, August 21, 2001, p. A01.

88. *Canada (Attorney General) v. PHS Community Services Society* 2011 SCC 44. *http://www.cbc.ca/news/canada/montreal/story/2011/09/29/bc-insite-supreme-court-ruling-advancer.html*.

89. BJS, *Capital Punishment, 21009—Statistical Tables*, NCJ 236510, December 2011, p. 1.

90. Michael Tonry, "Crime and Human Rights—How Political Paranoia, Protestant Fundamentalism, and Constitutional Obsolescence Combined to Devastate Black America," *Criminology* 46, no. 1 (2008): 6–7. He notes that in Europe, the longest sentence for a single offense, even murder, is 14 years. A German Court struck down life sentences without parole, and Tonry explains their reasoning as being that "hope for the future and belief in the possibility of a better life is a basic human right" so there must be meaningful review of the need for continued incarceration after the passage of not more than 14 years.

91. BJS, *Correctional Populations in the United States, 2010*, NCJ 236319, December 2011, Table 1; *Sourcebook*, Table 6.1.2009; and Pew Center on the States. 2010. *One in 31: The Long Reach of American Corrections. http://www.pewcenteronthestates.org/report_detail.aspx?id=49382*.

92. Elliott Currie, *Confronting Crime: An American Challenge* (New York: Pantheon, 1985), p. 12; cited in Kappeler et al., *The Mythology of Crime and Criminal Justice*, 2nd ed., p. 207.

93. See "Crime Cases Known To The Police, Cases Cleared Up And Arrestees By Type Of Crime (1990–2008)," *Japan Statistical Yearbook 2011*, edited by the Statistical Research and Training Institute, and published by the Statistics Bureau, both under the Ministry of Internal Affairs and Communications, Chart 25-1, p. 775. *http://www.stat.go.jp/english/data/nenkan/index.htm*. Crime totals were based on the sum for homicide, robbery, rape, and "bodily injury" (which translates to aggravated assault) to make them comparable with UCR categories for violent crime. Population for 2008 was 127,692,000 from Chart 2.1 of the yearbook. (Thanks to Satoko Motohara for help clarifying the meanings of the categories.) *UCR–2008*, Table 1.

94. *Japan Statistical Yearbook 2011*, Table 2-3, p. 39 and Table 25-2, p. 776; *UCR–2008*, Table 5.

95. United Nations Office on Drugs and Crime, *International Homicide Statistics*, 2004, pp. 1–10, *http://www.unodc.org/documents/data-and-analysis/IHS-rates-05012009.pdf*. All numbers sited are from the 2004 or 2005 United Nations Survey of Crime Trends and Operations of Criminal Justice Systems.

96. Elliott Currie, "Violence and Social Policy," in Walter DeKeseredy and Molly Dragiewicz (eds) *Routledge Handbook on Critical Criminology* (New York: Routledge, 2012), p. 466.

97. *UCR–2007*, Table 4.

98. Quoted in K. Taylor and F. Soady, eds., *Violence: An Element of American Life* (Boston: Holbrook Press, 1972), p. 49.

99. *UCR–2010*, Table 5 and Table 6.

100. *Time*, June 30, 1975, p. 11.

101. *StatAbst—2011*, Table 8, p. 12; and *UCR–2010*, computed from Table 38.

102. *UCR–1990*, p. 50, Table 1; *UCR–1985*, p. 41, Table 1; and *StatAbst—1992*, p. 14, Table 12.

103. "Serious Crime Rises Again in New York," *The New York Times*, March 22, 1988, pp. B1, B6.

104. Research reviewed by Conklin also notes that in Japan and Scotland, there was no correlation between the proportion of young males and homicide rates between 1901 and 1970. Conklin, *Why Crime Rates Fell*, p. 155.

105. Currie, "Violence and Social Policy," p. 466.

106. See, for example, John Braithwaite, "Poverty, Power, and White-Collar Crime," in Kip Schlegel and David Weisburd (ed.) *White-Collar Crime Reconsidered* (Boston: Northeastern University Press, 1992), pp. 78–107.

107. *StatAbst—2004–5*, Table 672, p. 447; *StatAbst—1972*, Table 528, p. 324; Carmen DeNavas-Walt, Bernadette Proctor, and Jessica Smith, U.S. Census Bureau, *Current Population Reports*, P60-239, *Income, Poverty & Health Insurance Coverage in the United States: 2010* (Washington, D.C.: U.S. Government Printing Office, 2011).

108. *Income, Poverty & Health Insurance Coverage in the United States: 2010*, p. 14; *Income, Poverty & Health Insurance Coverage in the United States: 2010*; National Center for Children in Poverty at Columbia University, "Who Are America's Poor Children?" March 2011, p. 4. *http://www.nccp.org/publications/pdf/text_1001.pdf.*

110. *The Washington Post*, September 6, 1982, p. 2.

111. *The Washington Post*, September 14, 1982, pp. 1, 4.

112. David Kamin and Isaac Shapiro, "Studies Shed New Light on Effects of Administration's Tax Cuts." Center on Budget and Policy Priorities, 2004, *http://www.cbpp. org/cms/index.cfm?fa=view&id=2116.*

113. BLS, "Employment status of the civilian noninstitutional population by race, sex, and age." Figures are for August 2011. *http://www.bls.gov/news.release/empsit.t02. htm.* See also "Racial Gulf: Blacks' Hopes, Raised by '68 Kerner Report, Are Mainly Unfulfilled," *The Wall Street Journal*, February 26, 1988, pp. 1, 9; and "Today's Native Sons," *Time*, December 1, 1986, pp. 26–29.

114. Edward Wolff, *Top Heavy: A Study of the Increasing Inequality of Wealth in America* (New York: Twentieth Century Fund Press, 1995), p. 2.

115. Arthur Kennickell, "Ponds and Streams: Wealth and Income in the U.S., 1989 to 2007," *http://www.federalreserve.gov/econresdata/scf/scf_workingpapers.htm.*

116. David Francis, "The American Dream Gains a Harder Edge," *Christian Science Monitor*, May 23, 2005, *http://www.csmonitor.com/2005/0523/p17s01-cogn.html.* See also, Gregg Barak, Paul Leighton, and Jeanne Flavin, *Class, Race, Gender and Crime*, 3rd ed (Lanham, MD: Rowman and Littlefield, 2010).

117. Janny Scott and David Leonhardt. "Class In America: Shadowy Lines That Still Divide," *New York Times*, May 15, 2005, p. A1.

118. John Rawls, *Justice as Fairness*, p. 146. Note that Rawls is not using the term *underclass* in the technical sense in which it is used in some sociological literature. For him, it simply refers to the economically worst-off group in a society, and emphasizes their likely sense of exclusion.

119. The most comprehensive health examination survey in the United States found that 10 million Americans, including 4 million children, suffer from hunger; see K. Alaimo et al. "Food Insufficiency Exists in the United States: Results from the Third National Health and Nutrition Examination Survey (NHANES III)," *American Journal of Public Health* 88, no. 3 (March 1998): 419–26.

120. Todd R. Clear, "Tougher' Is Dumber," *The New York Times*, December 4, 1993, p. 21.

121. Quoted in Michelle Alexander, *The New Jim Crow* (New York: The New Press, 2011), p. 8.

122. BJS, *Recidivism of Prisoners Released in 1994*, NCJ 193427, June 2002, p. 1.

123. Pew Center on the States. *State of Recidivism: The Revolving Door of America's Prisons* (Washington, DC: The Pew Charitable Trusts, 2011), p. 2.

124. "Warehousing" is a particular style of incarceration. It means putting people in prison only to keep them off the street and without an effort to rehabilitate them. See John Irwin, *The Warehouse Prison* (Oxford: Oxford University Press, 2007).

125. BJS, *Prisoners in 2010*, Appendix Table 23.

126. Struckman-Johnson, Cindy and David Struckman-Johnson. "Sexual Coercion Rates," in Seven Midwestern Prison Facilities for Men. *Prison Journal* 80, no. 4 (2000): 379–390.

127. Robert Johnson and Hans Toch, "Introduction," in Robert Johnson and Hans Toch (ed.) *The Pains of Imprisonment* (Beverly Hills, CA: Sage, 1982), pp. 19–20.

128. Just Detention International, *Prisoner Rape Factsheet. http://justdetention.org/en/fact_sheets.aspx.*

129. Human Rights Watch, "No Escape: Male Rape in U.S. Prisons," *www.hrw.org/reports/2001/prison* (no longer available).

130. Michael Tonry, "Crime and Human Rights," p. 24.

131. Fox Butterfield, "More Blacks in Their 20's Have Trouble with the Law," *The New York Times*, October 5, 1995, p. A18; and Pierre Thomas, "Study Suggests Black Male Prison Rate Impinges on Political Process," *The Washington Post*, January 30, 1997, p. A3. See Jeffrey Reiman, "Liberal and Republican Arguments against the Disenfranchisement of Felons," *Criminal Justice Ethics* 24, no. 1 (Winter–Spring 2005): 3–18.

132. Conklin, *Why Crime Rates Fell*, pp. 83–84; and Todd Clear, *Imprisoning Communities: How Mass Incarceration Makes Disadvantaged Neighborhoods Worse* (New York: Oxford University Press, 2009).

133. The "deprivations of prison" refers to what Sykes described in his book *Society of Captives*: deprivation of freedom (secluded from outside world); deprivation of autonomy (reduced to childlike status because of few decisions); deprivations of goods and services (in a materialistic world, your worth depends on what you have); deprivation of security; and deprivation of heterosexual relations. (Princeton: Princeton University Press, 1958)

134. Justice Policy Institute. 2011. Federal Folly. *http://www.justicepolicy.org/uploads/justicepolicy/documents/fy2012_congressional_budget_factsheet.pdf.*

135. State of the Union Message, January 21, 2004, as provided by the Republican National Committee, *www.gop.com*. Budget estimate from Congressional Budget Office, H.R. 1593–110th Congress (2007): Second Chance Act of 2007. *http://www.govtrack.us/congress/bill.xpd?bill=h110-1593&tab=reports* (accessed October 19, 2008).

136. Cook, Philip, Anthony Braga, and Mark Moore. 2011. "Gun Control," in James Q. Wilson and Joan Petersilia (eds) *Crime and Public Policy*. (Oxford: Oxford University Press), pp. 260–261.

137. Philip J. Cook and Jens Ludwig, *Gun Violence: The Real Costs* (New York: Oxford University Press, 2000), pp. 15, 34, 35.

138. Garen Wintemute, "Guns and Gun Violence," in Blumstein and Wallman, *The Crime Drop in America*, p. 52.

139. Wintemute, "Guns and Gun Violence," pp. 54–57.

140. National Research Council, *Firearms and Violence: A Critical Review*, Committee to Improve Research Information and Data on Firearms, ed. Charles Wellford, John Pepper, and Carol Petrie, Committee on Law and Justice, Division of Behavioral and Social Sciences and Education (Washington, D.C.: National Academies Press, 2005), pp. 57–58.

141. L. Hepburn, M. Miller, D. Azrael, and D. Hemenway, "The US Gun Stock: results from the 2004 national firearms survey," *Injury Prevention* 13 (2007): 15–19. The researchers note they based this estimate on removal of the top 3% of gun owners in their survey, who claimed to own more than 25 guns each.

142. *Challenge*, p. 239.

143. *UCR–1995*, p. 36.

144. Office of Juvenile Justice and Delinquency Prevention, "Fact Sheet," February 1999, no. 93, *http://ojjdp.ncjrs.gov/ojstatbb/offenders/qa03103.asp?qaDate=2006*.

145. Bush, "Remarks by the President on Project Safe Neighborhoods."

146. Kenneth Kochanek et al. "Deaths: Preliminary Data for 2009". *National Vital Statistics Reports* 59, no. 4 (2011): 20. *http://www.cdc.gov/nchs/data/nvsr/nvsr59/nvsr59_04. pdf*. National Center for Health Statistics, "The Three Leading Causes of Injury Mortality in the United States, 1999–2005," May 2008, *http://www.cdc.gov/nchs/ products/pubs/pubd/hestats/injury99-05/injury99-05.htm*.

147. Children's Defense Fund, *Protect Children, Not Guns, 2006, www.childrensdefense. org/child-research-data-publications/data/protect-children-not-guns-report-2006.pdf*.

148. Presidential news conference, June 16, 1981; see also "Reagan Denounces Gun Control Laws," *The Washington Post*, May 7, 1983, p. A8.

149. "Whenever there is a crime involving a firearm, there are various groups, some of them quite persuasive in their logic, that think you can ban certain kinds of guns, and I am not in that mode" (George H. W. Bush, quoted in George Will, "Playing with Guns," *Newsweek*, March 27, 1989, p. 78).

150. Pierre Thomas, "Brady Gun Law Contains No Penalties, Little Money for States," *The Washington Post*, December 3, 1993, p. A3.

151. BJS, *Background Checks for Firearm Transfers*, 2003, NCJ 204428, September 2004, p. 1; and Blumstein, "The Recent Rise and Fall of American Violence," p. 5.

152. Lawrence W. Sherman, "Reducing Gun Violence: What Works, What Doesn't, What's Promising," *NIJ Perspectives on Crime and Justice: 1999–2000 Lecture Series*, NCJ 184245, March, 2001, p. 74.

153. Cheryl W. Thompson, "Report Links State Gun Laws to Rates of Slayings, Trafficking," *The Washington Post*, December 5, 2008, p. A10.

154. *D.C. v Heller*, 554 US 270 (2008).

155. See generally, Legal Community Against Violence. 2011. *Model Laws for a Safer America*. *http://www.lcav.org/publications-briefs/model_laws/Model_Laws_for_a_Safer_America.pdf*

156. Cited in Blumstein, "Why Is Crime Falling—or Is It?" p. 13.

157. "A LEN Interview with Professor Alfred Blumstein of Carnegie Mellon University," *Law Enforcement News* 21, no. 422 (April 30, 1995): 11.

158. Quoted in Doug Bandow, "War on Drugs or War on America?" 3 *Stanford Law and Policy Review* 242 *(Fall 1991)*, p. 246.

159. Troy Duster, *The Legislation of Morality: Law, Drugs, and Moral Judgment* (New York: Free Press, 1970), pp. 3, 7, inter alia.

160. Cf. Philip C. Baridon, *Addiction, Crime, and Social Policy* (Lexington, MA: Lexington Books, 1976), pp. 4–5.

161. Arnold Trebach, *The Heroin Solution*, (New Haven, CT: Yale University Press, 1982), p. 246.

162. Leslie Iverson, *The Science of Marijuana*, 2nd ed. (Oxford: Oxford University Press, 2008), p. 58. Further, "although there have been many rumors that the long-term use of marijuana leads to irreversible damage to higher brain functions, the results of numerous scientific studies have failed to confirm this" p. 167.

163. Marvin D. Miller, National Organization for the Reform of Marijuana Laws, testimony at the Hearings on Proposals to Legalize Drugs held by the House Select Committee on Narcotics Abuse and Control, September 29, 1988, p. 19.

164. U.S. Department of Justice, Drug Enforcement Administration, Opinion and Recommended Ruling, Findings of Fact, Conclusions of Law and Decision of Administrative Law Judge Francis L. Young, in the Matter of MARIJUANA RESCHEDULING PETITION, Docket no. 86-22, September 6, 1988, pp. 56–57. *www.ukcia.org/pollaw/lawlibrary/young.php.*

165. Iverson, *Science of Marijuana*, p. 186.

166. Arnold S. Trebach, Testimony at the Hearings on Proposals to Legalize Drugs Held by the House Select Committee on Narcotics Abuse and Control, September 29, 1988 (Washington, D.C.: U.S. Government Printing Office, 1988), pp. 11–12.

167. Damien Cave, "Legal Drugs Kill Far More Than Illegal, Florida Says," *New York Times*, June 14, 2008, *http://www.nytimes.com/2008/06/14/us/14florida.html.*

168. Bandow, "War on Drugs or War on America?" *Stanford Law & Policy* Review 3 (Fall 1991): 245.

169. Surgeon General C. Everett Koop quoted, and reports on the relative addictiveness of cigarettes and cocaine, in Bandow, *War on Drugs or War on America?* p. 249.

170. "The largest study ever made of drug abuse in this country shows that two widely available legal drugs—alcohol and the tranquilizer Valium—are responsible for the greatest amount of drug-related illness, the government reported yesterday." Stuart Auerbach, "2 Drugs Widely Abused," *The Washington Post*, July 9, 1976, p. A1.

171. Quoted in Doug Bandow, *War on Drugs or War on America?* p. 250.

172. "A LEN interview with Professor Alfred Blumstein of Carnegie Mellon University," p. 11.

173. M. Douglas Anglin and George Speckart, "Narcotics Use and Crime: A Multisample, Multimethod Analysis," *Criminology* 26, no. 2 (1988): 226.

174. U.S. Department of Health, Education, and Welfare, Public Health Service, National Institute on Alcohol Abuse and Alcoholism, Special Action Office for Drug Abuse Prevention, *Social Cost of Drug Abuse* (Washington, D.C.: U.S. Government Printing Office, 1974), pp. 20–21.

175. *UCR–2010, http://www.fbi.gov/about-us/cjis/ucr/crime-in-the-u.s/2010/crime-in-the-u.s.-2010/property-crime.*

176. BJS, *Drug Use and Dependence, State and Federal Prisoners 2004*, NCJ 213530, October 2006, p. 1.

177. BJS, *Substance Dependence, Abuse, and Treatment of Jail Inmates, 2002*, NCJ 209588, July 2005, p. 7.

178. Anglin and Speckart, "Narcotics Use and Crime," p. 197.

179. "Drug Wars Push D.C. to Brink of Homicide Record: Police Efforts Futile as Turf Disputes Raise 1988 Slaying Total to 285," *The Washington Post*, October 26, 1988, p. A1.

180. "Enemy Within: Drug Money Is Corrupting the Enforcers," 1998. pp. A1, A12. *http:///www.nytimes.com/1988/04/11/us/enemy-within-drug-money-is-corrupting-the-enforcers.html.*

181. Ibid.

182. Clifford Krauss, "2-Year Corruption Inquiry Finds a 'Willful Blindness' in New York's Police Dept," *The New York Times*, July 7, 1994, p. A1.

183. General Accounting Office, *Law Enforcement: Information on Drug-Related police Corruption.* (GAO/GGD-98-111). (Washington, D.C.: General Accounting Office, 1998), p. 8.

184. United Nations Office on Drugs and Crime, *Afghanistan Opium Survey 2007 Executive Summary*, p. 8, *http://www.unodc.org/pdf/research/AFG07_ExSum_web.pdf.*

185. Ibid., p. 18.

186. Juan Forero, "Coca Cultivation Rises in Columbia, U.N. Says," *Washington Post,* June 19, 2008, p. A10.

187. Alfred W. McCoy and Alan Block. "U.S. Narcotics Policy: An Anatomy of Failure," in Alfred W. McCoy and Alan A. Block (eds.), *War on Drugs: Studies in the Failure of U.S. Narcotics Policy* (Boulder: Westview Press, 1992), p. 3; United Nations Office on Drugs and Crime, *Coco Cultivation in the Andean Regions,* 2005, p. 9, *www.ncjrs.gov/App/Publications/abstract.aspx?ID=232688;* Forero, p. A10.

188. Bandow, "War on Drugs or War on America?" p. 244; and BJS, *Drugs, Crime, and the Justice System,* December 1992, p. 44.

189. "Not Winning the War on Drugs," *New York Times,* July 2, 2008, *http://www. nytimes.com/2008/07/02/opinion/02wed1.html.*

190. "Cocaine Down: Signs Indicate That America's Cocaine Habit Is Easing," *The Wall Street Journal,* July 20, 1987, p. 21.

191. National Narcotics Intelligence Consumers' Committee, *The NNICC 1994: The Supply of Illegal Drugs to the United States,* DEA-95051 August (Washington, D.C.: NNICC, 1995), p. 1.

192. ONDCP, *The Price and Purity of Illicit Drugs: 1981 through the Second Quarter of 2003,* NCJ 207768, November 2004, pp. v–vi.

193. "Not Winning the War on Drugs," *New York Times,* July 2, 2008, *http://www. nytimes.com/2008/07/02/opinion/02wed1.html.*

194. David Boyum and Peter Reuter, *An Analytic Assessment of U.S. Drug Policy* (Washington, D.C.: AEI Press, 2005). "Yet despite the incarceration of hundreds of thousands of drug dealers and steadfast attempts to stop overseas cultivations and trafficking, drugs have become substantially cheaper, casting doubt on the effectiveness of this strategy" (p. 2).

195. "Prosecutors Admit: No Victory in Sight," *National Law Journal,* August 8, 1988, p. S-2.

196. Boyum and Reuter. *An Analytic Assessment of U.S. Drug Policy,* p. 2.

197. BJS Fact Sheet, *Drug Data Summary,* NCJ-167246, February 1998.

198. ONDCP, *National Drug Control Budget—FY 2012 Funding Highlights. http://www. whitehouse.gov/sites/default/files/ondcp/policy-and-research/fy12highlight_exec_sum. pdf.*

199. Bandow, *War on Drugs or War on America?* p. 243; and McCoy and Block, "U.S. Narcotics Policy," p. 6. UCR 2010, Table 29; and BJS, *Prisoners in 2010,* p. 1.

200. BJS, *Prisoners in 2001,* p. 14; and BJS, *Prisoners in 2010,* Appendix Table 18.

201. BJS, *Prisoners in 2010,* Table 16B.

202. Michael Tonry, "Racial Politics, Racial Disparities, and the War on Crime," *Crime & Delinquency* 40, no. 4 (October 1994): 487.

203. BJS, *Correctional Populations in the U.S., 1992,* p. 31; Surgeon General Joycelyn Elders's statement was reported in *International Herald Tribune,* December 8, 1993, p. 1. She reiterated the suggestion after "reviewing many studies," and even after President Clinton's opposition to the idea was reported. "Elders Reiterates Her Support for Study of Drug Legalization," *The Washington Post,* January 15, 1994, p. A8.

204. Hughes and Stevens, "What Can We Learn From The Portuguese Decriminalization Of Illicit Drugs?" p. 1016.

205. Jerry V. Wilson, "Our Wasteful War on Drugs," *The Washington Post,* January 18, 1994, p. A20.

206. Christopher Wren, "A.M.A. Shelves Disputed Report on Drugs," *The New York Times,* June 23, 1996, p. A22.

207. Global Commission on Drug Policy, *War on Drugs*, 2011, p. 2, *http://www. globalcommissionondrugs.org/*.
208. *Time*, June 30, 1975, p. 17 (emphasis added).
209. Currie, *Crime and Punishment in America*, pp. 81, 98.
210. Fox Butterfield, "Intervening Early Costs Less than '3-Strikes' Laws, Study Says," *The New York Times*, June 23, 1996, p. A24.
211. Peter W. Greenwood, "Costs and Benefits of Early Childhood Intervention," OJJDP Fact Sheet no. 94, February (Washington, D.C.: U.S. Department of Justice, Office of Juvenile Justice and Delinquency Prevention, 1999).
212. Steven Donziger, ed., *The Real War on Crime: The Report of the National Criminal Justice Commission* (New York: HarperPerenniel, 1966), p. 216.
213. "Federally Funded Drug and Alcohol Programs Found Effective in Reducing Drug Use, Crime, Homelessness," *Psychiatric Services* 47, no. 11 (November 1996): 1280.
214. *The National Report on Substance Abuse* 8, no. 15 (July 1, 1994): p. 2.
215. Rand Corporation Press Release, *www.ndsn.org/JULY94/RAND.html*.
216. Lawrence Sherman, et al., "Preventing Crime: What Works, What Doesn't, What's Promising," *NIJ Research in Brief*, NIJ171676, July (Washington, D.C.: National Institute of Justice, 1988).
217. *Criminology and Public Policy* 6, no. 4 (2007).
218. Quoted in Butterfield, "Intervening Early Costs Less than '3-Strikes' Laws," p. A24.
219. Ibid. For an extensive list of promising programs aimed at reducing crime, see Donziger, *The Real War on Crime*, app. B.
220. Kai T. Erikson, *Wayward Puritans* (New York: Wiley, 1966), p. 4. Reprinted by permission of John Wiley & Sons, Inc.
221. Ibid., p. 11.
222. Ibid., pp. 13–15 (emphasis added).
223. Garland suggests that this is true of Erikson's study even if Erikson does not highlight this aspect. Garland writes that Erikson's study

    is a description of the deep social and religious tensions within [Puritan] community. ... In this context, it becomes clear that the exercise of criminal punishments ... was also the forceful imposition of a particular framework of politico-religious authority on a society riven by factions and deep tensions. (Garland, *Punishment and Modern Society*, p. 79)

224. Michel Foucault, *Discipline and Punish: The Birth of the Prison*, trans. Alan Sheridan (London: Allen Lane), p. 271.
225. Ibid., p. 277.
226. Ibid., p. 274.
227. Ibid., p. 275.
228. Ibid., p. 279.
229. Ibid., p. 288.
230. Foucault writes that the system includes an attempt to shape "the common perception of delinquents: to present them as close by, everywhere present and everywhere to be feared" (ibid., p. 286).
231. Ibid., p. 281.
232. Ibid., pp. 296–97.
233. Ibid., p. 304.
234. "Foucault's description of Western liberal democracy as a society of surveillance, disciplined from end to end, is deliberately reminiscent of ... totalitarianism" (Garland, *Punishment and Modern Society*, p. 151).

235. According to Nicos Poulantzas,

Now, for Foucault, the power relation never has any other basis than itself: it becomes a pure 'situation' in which power is always immanent; and the question what power and power to do what appears as a mere obstacle. This leads Foucault into a particular logical impasse from which there is no possible escape. ... For if power is always already there, if every power situation is immanent in itself, why should there ever be resistance? From where would resistance come, and how would it be even possible? (Nicos Poulantzas, State, Power, Socialism, trans. P. Camiller [London: NLB, 1978], p. 149)

236. According to David Garland,

Foucault's vision of power may be a positive conception in the sense that power moulds, trains, builds up, and creates subjects, but it also involves a thoroughly negative evaluation. Foucault writes as someone who is absolutely 'against' power. His critique is not of one form of power in favour of another but is rather an attack upon power itself. ... [However, t]here is an important sense in which discipline can create freedom as well as control. As Foucault's own subsequent work shows, discipline is necessary to the development of self-control. (Garland, Punishment and Modern Society, p. 174)

CHAPTER 2

A Crime by Any Other Name ...

If one individual inflicts a bodily injury upon another which leads to the death of the person attacked we call it manslaughter; on the other hand, if the attacker knows beforehand that the blow will be fatal we call it murder. Murder has also been committed if society places hundreds of workers in such a position that they inevitably come to premature and unnatural ends. Their death is as violent as if they had been stabbed or shot. ... Murder has been committed if society knows perfectly well that thousands of workers cannot avoid being sacrificed so long as these conditions are allowed to continue. Murder of this sort is just as culpable as the murder committed by an individual.

—FREDERICK ENGELS, *The Condition of the Working Class in England*

Based on an examination of the various ways that Americans are harmed, this chapter shows that some of the greatest dangers that we face come from acts that are not labeled crimes. Readers are asked to compare the harms produced by crimes with the harms of noncriminal behavior as a step toward determining if the harsh treatment of those who impose criminal harms, and the gentle treatment of those who impose noncriminal harms, represent intelligent policy. As the response to the Defenders of the Present Legal Order shows, the acts that lead to these noncriminal harms share many elements of criminal conduct—they are harmful acts done knowingly or recklessly. However, they tend to be ignored or minimized by the criminal justice system. The inclusion of certain harmful acts within the criminal law, and the exclusion of other harmful acts, show that the criminal law does not reflect an objective reality about "dangerous crime." The criminal justice system acts as a carnival mirror that distorts reality by magnifying the threat of street crime while minimizing other harmful behaviors. Could it be that the criminal justice system is focusing on the dangerous acts of the poor, and leaving us unprotected against the dangerous acts of the rich?

WHAT'S IN A NAME?

If it takes you an hour to read this chapter, by the time you reach the last page, two of your fellow citizens will have been murdered. *During that same time, more than six Americans will die as a result of unhealthy or unsafe conditions in the workplace!* Although these work-related deaths were due to human actions, they are not called murders. Why not? Doesn't a crime by any other name still cause misery and suffering? What's in a name?

The fact is that the label "crime" is not used in America to name all or the worst of the actions that cause misery and suffering to Americans. It is reserved primarily for the dangerous actions of the poor.

In 1993, an article appeared in the *New York Times* with the headline "Company in Mine Deaths Set to Pay Big Fine." It reported an agreement by the owners of a Kentucky mine to pay a fine for safety misconduct that may have led to "the worst American mining accident in nearly a decade." Ten workers died in a methane explosion, and the company pleaded guilty to "a pattern of safety misconduct" that included falsifying reports of methane levels and requiring miners to work under unsupported roofs. The company was fined $3.75 million. The acting foreman at the mine was the only individual charged by the federal government, and for his cooperation with the investigation, the prosecutors recommended that he receive the minimum sentence: probation to six months in prison. The company's president expressed regret for the tragedy that occurred, and the U.S. attorney said he hoped the case "sent a clear message that violations of Federal safety and health regulations that endanger the lives of our citizens will not be tolerated."[1] Compare this with the story of Colin Ferguson, who prompted an editorial in the *New York Times* that same year, with the headline "Mass Murder on the 5:33."[2] Colin had boarded a commuter train at Pennsylvania Station, and methodically shot passengers with a 9-mm pistol, killing 6 and wounding 19. Colin Ferguson was surely a murderer, maybe a mass murderer. Our question is, why wasn't the death of the miners also murder? Why weren't those responsible for subjecting 10 miners to deadly conditions also "mass murderers"? Why do 10 dead miners amount to an "accident" and a "tragedy," and 6 dead commuters a "mass murder"? "Murder" suggests a murderer, whereas "accident" and "tragedy" suggest the work of impersonal forces. But the charge against the company that owned the mine said that they "repeatedly exposed the mine's work crews to danger and that such conditions were frequently concealed from Federal inspectors responsible for enforcing the Mine Safety Act." And the acting foreman admitted to falsifying records of methane levels only two months before the fatal blast. Someone was responsible for the conditions that led to the death of 10 miners. Is that person not a murderer, perhaps even a *mass murderer?*

These questions are at this point rhetorical. Our aim is not to discuss this case, but rather to point to the blinders we wear when we look at such an "accident." While the question is rhetorical, the answer matters greatly for justice and the lives of hard-working Americans. And the question continues to haunt us. In the 2010 Upper Big Branch mine "disaster" in West Virginia, an explosion killed 29 miners. A Department of Labor report notes that the explosion at the mine was "preventable," and that "unlawful policies and practices implemented by [mine owner] PCC/Massey were the root cause of this tragedy." The investigation uncovered "multiple examples of systematic, intentional, and aggressive efforts by PCC/Massey to avoid compliance with safety and health standards, and to thwart detection of that non-compliance by federal and state regulators."[3] The company paid a $209 million settlement, and one person was convicted of lying to federal investigators and destroying records. No criminal charges were filed against top officials, and a *New York Times* editorial said: "The way to end safety abuses in this dangerous industry is to make management face felony penalties for gross violations instead of allowing executives to pay fines with the company checkbook."[4] Why isn't this happening?

In each case, there was an investigation and one person was held responsible for wrongdoing about record-keeping. The company was fined. But no one was tried for *murder.* No one was thought of as a murderer. *Why not?* Would miners not be safer if such people were treated as murderers? Might the miners at Big Branch not still be alive if executives were being charged as criminals for acts like this? Didn't those miners have a right to be protected by the criminal justice system against the violence that took their lives? *And if not, why not?*

Will a president of the United States address the Yale Law School and recommend mandatory prison sentences for such people? Will he mean these people when he says,

> These relatively few, persistent criminals who cause so much misery and fear are really the core of the problem. The rest of the American people have a right to protection from their violence.[5]

Once we are ready to ask this question seriously, we are in a position to see that the reality of crime—that is, the acts we label crime, the acts we think of as crime, and the actors and actions we treat as criminal—is *created*: It is a reality shaped by decisions as to *what* will be called crime and *who* will be treated as a criminal.

THE CARNIVAL MIRROR

It is sometimes coyly observed that the quickest and cheapest way to eliminate crime would be to throw out all the criminal laws. There is a sliver of truth to this view. Without criminal laws, there would indeed be no "crimes." There would, however, still be dangerous acts. This is why we cannot solve our crime problem quite so simply. The criminal law *labels* some acts "crimes." In doing this, it identifies those acts as so dangerous that we must use the extreme methods of criminal justice to protect ourselves against them. This does not mean that criminal law *creates* crime—it simply "mirrors" real dangers that threaten us. What is true of the criminal law is true of the whole justice system. If police did not arrest or prosecutors charge or juries convict, there would be no "criminals." This does not mean that police or prosecutors or juries create criminals, any more than legislators do. They *react* to real dangers in society. The criminal justice system—from lawmakers to law enforcers—is just a mirror of the real dangers that lurk in our midst. *Or so we are told.*

How accurate is this mirror? We need to answer this in order to know whether or how well the criminal justice system is protecting us against the real threats to our well-being. The more accurate a mirror is, the more the image it shows is created by the reality it reflects. The more misshapen a mirror is, the more the distorted image it shows is created by the mirror, not by the reality reflected. It is in this sense that we will argue that the image of crime is *created*: The American criminal justice system is a mirror that shows a distorted image of the dangers that threaten us—an image created more by the shape of the mirror than by the reality reflected. What do we see when we look in the criminal justice mirror?

In 1975, the *Washington Post* carried an article headlined "Arrest Data Reveal Profile of a Suspect." The article reported the results of a study of crime in Prince George's County, a suburb of Washington, D.C. It read in part as follows:

> The typical suspect in serious crime in Prince George's County is a black male, aged 14 to 19, who lives in the area inside the Capital Beltway where more than half of the county's 64,371 reported crimes were committed in 1974. [The study] presents a picture of persons, basically youths, committing a crime once every eight minutes in Prince George's County.[6]

This report is hardly a surprise. The portrait it paints of "the typical suspect in serious crime" is probably a pretty good rendering of the image lurking in the back of the minds of most Americans who fear crime. The portrait generally fits the national picture presented in the FBI's *Uniform Crime Reports* (*UCR*) for the same year. In Prince George's County, "youths between the ages of 14 and 19 were accused of committing nearly half [45.5 percent] of all 1974 crimes."[7] For the nation in 1974, the FBI reported that persons in this age group accounted for 39.5 percent of arrests for the FBI Index crimes (criminal homicide, forcible rape, robbery, aggravated assault, burglary, larceny, and motor vehicle theft).[8] These youths were male and disproportionately black. In Prince George's County, males "represented three of every four serious crime defendants."[9] In the nation in 1974 more than 80 percent were males.[10] In Prince George's County, where blacks made up approximately 25 percent of the population, "blacks were accused of 58 percent of all serious crimes."[11] In the nation, where blacks made up 11.4 percent of the population in 1974, they accounted for 34.2 percent of arrests for Index crimes.[12]

This was the *Typical Criminal* in 1974; but little has changed since. Let us look more closely at the face in today's criminal justice mirror, and we shall see much the same Typical Criminal.

The person is, first of all, a *he*. Of 13.1 million persons arrested for crimes in 2010, 75 percent were males. Of persons arrested for violent crimes, 81 percent were men. Second, he is *young*. Nearly half (42 percent) of men arrested for all crimes were under the age of 25; and the same is true of violent crimes. Third, he is predominantly *urban*. Cities with populations over 250,000 had a rate of 275 arrests for violent crimes per 100,000 inhabitants, while cities with populations under 10,000 had 146 such arrests per 100,000 inhabitants.[13] "Half of all homicides occur in the 63 largest cities, which house only 16 percent of the population."[14] Fourth, he is disproportionately *black*: Blacks are arrested for violent crimes at a rate more than three times that of their percentage in the national population. In 2010, with blacks representing 13 percent of the nation's population, they made up 38 percent of violent crime arrests and 29 percent of all crime arrests.[15] Finally, he is *poor*. Almost one-third (29 percent) of 2002 jail inmates were unemployed (without full- or part-time work) prior to being arrested, an unemployment rate considerably higher than that of adults in the general population, and almost half (45 percent) reported pre-arrest incomes below $7,200 a year.[16] As the President's Commission reported nearly 40 years ago, "The offender at the end of the road in prison is likely to be a member of the lowest social and economic groups in the country."[17]

This is the Typical Criminal feared by most law-abiding Americans. Poor, young, urban, (disproportionately) black males make up the core of the enemy forces in the crime war. They are seen as a vicious, unorganized guerrilla army, threatening the lives, limbs, and possessions of the law-abiding members of society, necessitating recourse to the ultimate weapons of force and detention in our common defense. This picture is widely shared. In his book, *How to Stop Crime,* retired Police Chief Anthony Bouza writes, "Street crime is mostly a black and poor young man's game."[18] Listen to the sad words of the Reverend Jesse Jackson: "There is nothing more painful to me at this stage of my life than to walk down the street and hear footsteps and start thinking about robbery—and then look around and see someone white and feel relieved."[19] In 2005, William Bennett, President Reagan's secretary of education (1985–88) and the first President Bush's "drug czar" (1989–90), commented, "I do know that it's true that if you wanted to reduce crime, you could—if that were your sole purpose—you could abort every black baby in this country, and your crime rate would go down."[20] In *The Color of Crime,* Kathryn Russell speaks of the "criminalblackman" to highlight the close connection between these words in popular culture.[21] Marjorie Zatz characterizes this notion as follows: "The 'criminalblackman' is a composite of white fears of black men's criminality. It may become so strong and so widespread that it allows for racial hoaxes, in which a white offender blames an African American, usually male, for the offense in question and is readily believed by criminal justice agents and/or the general public."[22]

Where do we get this picture? How do we know who the criminals are who so seriously endanger us that we must stop them with force and lock them in prisons? "From the arrest records, probation reports, and prison statistics," the President's Commission on Law Enforcement and Administration of Justice, authors of *The Challenge of Crime in a Free Society*, tells us, the "'portrait' of the offender emerges."[23] *These sources are not merely objective readings taken at different stages in the criminal justice process: Each of them represents human decisions.* "Prison statistics" and "probation reports" reflect *decisions* of juries on who gets convicted and decisions of judges on who gets probation or prison and for how long. "Arrest records" reflect decisions about which crimes to investigate and which suspects to take into custody. All these decisions rest on the most fundamental of all decisions: The *decisions* of legislators as to which acts shall be labeled "crimes" in the first place.

In short, our picture of crime reflects a reality—criminal acts, arrests, convictions, imprisonment, and so on—but this reality of crime is not a simple objective threat to which the criminal justice system reacts: *It is a reality that takes shape as it is filtered through a series of human decisions running the full gamut of the criminal justice system*—from the lawmakers who determine what behavior shall be in the province of criminal justice to the law enforcers who decide which individuals will be brought within that province. And it doesn't end with the criminal justice system as such, because the media—television, newspapers, and the Internet—contribute as well to the image that people have of crime in our society.[24] Here, too, human decisions are fundamental. The news media do not simply report the facts. There are too many facts out there. A selection must be made. People working in the news media must choose which facts are *news*, and they must choose how to represent those facts.

Note that by emphasizing the role of "human decisions," we do not mean to suggest that the reality of crime is voluntarily and intentionally "created" by individual "decision makers." Their decisions are themselves shaped by the social system, much as a child's decision to become an engineer rather than a samurai warrior is shaped by the social system in which he or she grows up. Thus, to have a full explanation of how the reality of crime is created, we have to understand how our society is structured in a way that leads people to make the decisions they do. In other words, these decisions are part of the social phenomena to be explained, they are not the explanation.

The present discussion, however, emphasizes the role of the decisions themselves for the following reasons: First, they are conspicuous points in the social process, relatively easy to spot and verify empirically. Second, because they are decisions aimed at protecting us from the dangers in our midst, we can compare the decisions with the real dangers and determine whether they are accurately responding to the real dangers. Third, because the reality of crime—the real actions labeled crimes, the real individuals identified as criminals, and the real faces we watch in the news as they travel from arrest to court to prison—results from these decisions, we can determine whether that reality corresponds to the real dangers in our society. Where that reality does correspond to the real dangers, we can say that the reality of crime simply reflects the real dangers in society. Where the reality of crime does not correspond to the real dangers, we can say that it is a reality *created* by those decisions. Then we can investigate the role played by the social system in encouraging, reinforcing, and otherwise shaping those decisions.

To capture this way of looking at the relation between the reality of crime and the real dangers "out there" in society, we refer to the criminal justice system as a "mirror." Whom and what we see in this mirror are functions of the decisions about who and what is criminal. Our poor, young, urban, black male, who is so well represented in arrest records and prison populations, appears not simply because of the threat he poses to the rest of society. As dangerous as he may be, he would not appear in the criminal justice mirror *if* it had not been decided that the acts he performs should be labeled "crimes," *if* it had not been decided that he should be arrested for those crimes, *if* he had had access to a lawyer who could persuade a jury to acquit him and a judge to expunge his arrest record, and *if* it had not been decided that he is the type of individual and his is the type of crime that warrant imprisonment. *The shape of the reality we see in the criminal justice mirror is the outcome of all these decisions.* We want to know how accurately the reality we see in this mirror reflects the real dangers that threaten us in society.

This reality is not created out of nothing. The mugger, the rapist, the murderer, the burglar, and the robber all pose a definite threat to our well-being, and they ought to be dealt with in ways that effectively reduce that threat to the minimum level possible (without making the criminal justice system itself a threat to our lives and liberties). Of central importance, however, is that the threat posed by the Typical Criminal is not the greatest threat to which we are exposed. The acts of the Typical Criminal are not the only acts that endanger us, nor are they the acts that endanger us the most. As this chapter demonstrates, we have a great and sometimes even a greater chance of being killed or disabled by an occupational injury or disease, by unnecessary surgery, or by shoddy medical services, than by aggravated assault or even homicide! Yet even though these threats to our well-being are graver than that posed by our poor young criminals, they do not show up in the FBI's *UCR* as serious crimes. The individuals responsible for them do not turn up in arrest records or prison statistics. *They never become part of the reality reflected in the criminal justice mirror, although the danger they pose is at least as great as, and often greater than, the danger posed by those who do!*

Similarly, the general public loses more money *by far* (as shown in Chapter 3) from tax cheating and fraud and from consumer deception and embezzlement than from all the property crimes reported by the FBI. Yet these far more costly acts are either not criminal, or if technically criminal, not prosecuted, or if prosecuted, not punished, or if punished, only mildly. In any event, although the individuals responsible for these acts take more money out of the ordinary citizen's pocket than our Typical Criminal, they rarely show up in arrest statistics and almost never in prison populations. *Their faces rarely appear in the criminal justice mirror, although the danger they pose is at least as great as, and often greater than, that of those who do.*

The inescapable conclusion is that the criminal justice system does not simply *reflect* the reality of crime; it has a hand in *creating* the reality we see.

It magnifies the real threat of street crime while minimizing the real harms of corporate misbehavior.

The criminal justice system is like a mirror in which society can see the face of the evil in its midst. Because the system deals with some evils and not with others, because it treats some minor evils as grave and treats some of the gravest evils as minor, the image it throws back is distorted, like the image in a carnival mirror. Thus, the image cast back is false, not because it is invented out of thin air, but because the proportions of the real are distorted: Large becomes small, and small large; grave becomes minor, and minor grave. Like a carnival mirror, although nothing is reflected that does not exist in the world, the image is more a creation of the mirror than a picture of the world.

If criminal justice really gives us a carnival-mirror image of "crime," we are doubly deceived. First, we are led to believe that the criminal justice system is protecting us against the gravest threats to our well-being when, in fact, the system is protecting us against only some threats and not necessarily the gravest ones. We are deceived about how much protection we are receiving, and thus are left vulnerable. The second deception is just the other side of this one. If people believe that the carnival mirror is a true mirror—that is, if they believe the criminal justice system simply reacts to the gravest threats to their well-being—they come to believe that whatever is the target of the criminal justice system must be the greatest threat to their well-being. In other words, if people believe that the most drastic of society's weapons are wielded by the criminal justice system *in reaction to* the gravest dangers to society, they will believe the reverse as well: that those actions that call forth the most drastic of society's weapons *must be* those that pose the gravest dangers to society.

A strange alchemy takes place when people accept uncritically the legitimacy of their institutions: What *needs* justification becomes *proof* of justification. People come to believe that prisoners must be criminals *because* they are in prison and that the inmates of insane asylums must be *crazy* because they are in insane asylums.[25] The criminal justice system's use of extreme measures—such as force and imprisonment—is thought to be justified by the extreme gravity of the dangers it combats. By this alchemy, these extreme measures become *proof* of the extreme gravity of those dangers, and the first deception, which merely misleads the public about how much protection the criminal justice system is actually providing, is transformed into the second, which deceives the public into believing that the acts and actors that are the targets of the criminal justice system pose the gravest threats to its well-being. Thus, the system may not only fail to protect us from dangers as great as or greater than those listed in the FBI's *UCR*; it may also do still greater damage by creating the false security of the belief that only the acts treated as serious in the FBI's *UCR* really threaten us and require control.

The following discussion describes how and why the criminal justice carnival mirror distorts the image it creates.

CRIMINAL JUSTICE AS CREATIVE ART

The Pyrrhic defeat explanation for the "failure" of criminal justice in America holds that criminal justice *fails* (that is, it does little to reduce our high crime rates) in order to project a particular *image* of crime. Chapter 1 described the failure to adopt policies that could eliminate our high crime rates. It is the task of this chapter and the next to prove that the reality of crime is *created* and that it is created in a way that promotes a particular *image* of crime: *The image that serious crime—and, therefore, the greatest danger to society—is the work of the poor.*

The notion that the reality of crime is created is derived from Richard Quinney's theory of the *social reality of crime.*[26] Here as elsewhere, however, an idea that contributes to the Pyrrhic defeat theory is transformed along the way, so it will help in presenting our view to compare it with Quinney's.

Quinney maintains that crime has a "social reality" rather than an objective reality. What he means can be explained with an example. Wherein lies the reality of money? Certainly not in the "objective" characteristics of green printed paper. It exists rather in the "social" meaning attributed to that paper and the pattern of "social" behavior that is a consequence of that meaning. If people did not act as if that green printed paper had value, it would be just green paper, not real money.[27] The reality of a crime as *a crime* does not lie simply in the objective characteristics of an action. It lies in the "social" meaning attached to that action and the pattern of "social" behavior—particularly the behavior of criminal justice officials—that is a product of that meaning. Quinney is right in this. When we speak of the reality of crime, we are referring to much more than physical actions, such as stabbing or shooting. We mean as well the reality that a society gives those physical actions by labeling them and treating them as criminal.

Quinney further maintains that this reality of crime is *created*. By this, he means that crime is a definition of behavior applied by lawmakers and other criminal justice decision makers. "Crime," Quinney writes,

> is a definition of behavior that is conferred on some persons by others. Agents of the law (legislators, police, prosecutors, and judges), representing segments of a politically organized society, are responsible for formulating and administering criminal laws. Persons and behaviors, therefore, become criminal because of the formulation and application of criminal definitions. Thus, crime is created.[28]

This is *not* what we have in mind when we say that the reality of crime is created. Quinney's position amounts to this: Crimes are established by the criminal law, and the criminal law is a human creation; therefore, crime is created. This is true, but it does not take us very far. After all, who can deny that crime is created *in this sense?* Only someone who has been hypnotized into forgetting that law books are written by human beings could deny that "crime" is a label that human beings apply to certain actions.

What *is* controversial, however, is whether the label is applied appropriately. "Crime," after all, is not merely a sound—it is a word with a generally accepted meaning. Speaking generally, it means at least "an intentional action that is harmful to society." Of course, "crime" also has a narrower technical definition, namely, "an act prohibited by a criminal law." The point of prohibiting an act by the criminal law is to protect society from an injurious or dangerous act. Thus, though any act prohibited by criminal law is a crime in the narrow technical sense, not every act so prohibited is rightly prohibited, and thus not every act labeled "crime" is labeled appropriately. To determine whether the label "crime" is applied appropriately, we must use the more general definition. The label of crime is applied appropriately when it is used to identify all, or at least the worst, acts that are harmful to society. The label is applied inappropriately when it is attached to harmless acts or when it is not attached to seriously harmful acts. When we argue that the reality of crime is created, we point to the ways in which the label "crime" has not been applied appropriately. It is, of course, appropriate to label muggings and rapes as crimes. What is inappropriate is to fail to label equally or even more harmful intentional acts as crimes. What is inappropriate is to use the criminal justice system to convey the image that the greatest danger we face lies in the harmful acts of the poor.

One might ask why the inappropriate use of the label "crime" is a reason for saying that crime is created. The answer is this: By calling something *created,* we call attention to the fact that human actors are responsible for it. Calling crime created points to human actors *rather than objective dangers* as determining the shape that the reality of crime takes in our society. If the label "crime" is applied consistently to the most dangerous or harmful acts, then it is misleading to point to the fact that human decision makers are responsible for how the label is applied because their decisions are dictated by compelling objective reasons. Rather than creating a reality, their decisions trace a reality that already exists. On the other hand, if the label is not applied appropriately, it is sensible to assume that it is applied for reasons that lie with the decision makers and not in the realm of objective dangers. This means that when the label "crime" is applied inappropriately, it is essential to call attention to the fact that human actors are responsible for it. Thus, it is precisely when the label "crime" is applied inappropriately that it is important to point out that the reality of crime is *created.*

By calling crime created, we want to emphasize the human responsibility for the shape of crime, not in the trivial sense that humans write the criminal law, *but rather to call attention to the fact that decisions as to what to label and treat as crime are not compelled by objective dangers, and thus that, to understand the reality of crime, we must look to the social processes that shape those decisions.*

By calling crime created, we suggest that our picture of crime—the portrait that emerges from arrest statistics, prison populations, politicians' speeches, news media, and fictionalized presentations, the portrait that in turn influences lawmakers and criminal justice policy makers—is not a photograph of the real dangers that threaten us. Its features are not simply traced from the real dangers in the social world. Instead, it is a piece of creative art. It is a picture in which some dangers are portrayed, and others omitted. Because it cannot be explained as a straight reflection of real dangers, we must look elsewhere to understand the shape it takes.

This argument, which will occupy us in this chapter and the next, leads to *five hypotheses* about the way in which the public's image of crime is created. That image reflects a reality to be sure; but that reality is itself created by the decisions made at critical points in the criminal justice process. To demonstrate that the reality of crime is created, and that the criminal justice system is a carnival mirror that shows us a distorted image of the dangers that threaten us, we will try to prove that, at each of the crucial decision-making points in criminal justice, the decisions made do not appropriately reflect the real and most serious dangers we face. The five hypotheses are as follows.

1. *Of the decisions of legislators:* The definitions of crime in the criminal law do not reflect the only or the most dangerous of antisocial behaviors
2. *Of the decisions of police and prosecutors:* The decisions on whom to arrest or charge do not reflect the only or the most dangerous behaviors legally defined as "criminal"
3. *Of the decisions of juries and judges:* Criminal convictions do not reflect the only or the most dangerous individuals among those arrested and charged
4. *Of the decisions of sentencing judges:* Sentencing decisions do not reflect the goal of protecting society from only or the most dangerous of those convicted by meting out punishments proportionate to the harmfulness of the crime committed
5. *Of all these decisions taken together:* What criminal justice policy decisions (in hypotheses 1 through 4) do reflect is the implicit identification of crime with the dangerous acts of the poor, an identification amplified by media representations of crime

The Pyrrhic defeat theory is composed of these five hypotheses, *plus* the proposition that the criminal justice system is failing in avoidable ways to eliminate our high crime rates (argued in Chapter 1), *plus* the *historical inertia* explanation of how this failure is generated and left uncorrected because of the ideological benefits it produces (argued in Chapter 4). Note that the fifth hypothesis goes beyond the criminal justice system to point to the role of the media. That is, while the structure of criminal justice practice enables it to create an image of crime as the work of the poor, the media serve as the conveyor of that image to the wider public. Moreover, this conveyor adds a twist of its own, not merely conveying an accurate picture of the whole of criminal justice practice with its biases, but actually magnifying those biases. So, we shall see that the media portray crime—in reality and in fiction—in ways that overrepresent the *types* of crimes committed by poor people (even when committed by rich folks on TV), and that obscure the social factors that lead to crime in reality (argued in this chapter and in Chapter 4). Finally, we tie this theory of how and why the criminal justice system functions as it does together with the *historical inertia* explanation. That is, we will try to show how the decisions that create the biased image of crime reflect a traditional understanding of crime and are left unchanged because the particular distribution of costs and benefits to which those decisions give rise serves to make the system self-reinforcing.

A CRIME BY ANY OTHER NAME …

Think of a crime, any crime. Picture the first crime that comes into your mind. What do you see? The odds are you are not imagining a mining company executive sitting at his desk, calculating the costs of proper safety precautions, and deciding not to invest in them. Probably what you do see with your mind's eye is one person attacking another physically or robbing something from another via the threat of physical attack. Look more closely. What does the attacker look like? It's a safe bet he (and it is a *he*, of course) is not wearing a suit and tie. In fact, you—like us, like almost anyone else in America—picture a young, tough, lower-class male when the thought of crime first pops into your head. You (we) picture someone like the Typical Criminal described earlier. The crime itself is one in which the Typical Criminal sets out to attack or rob some specific person.

This last point is important. It indicates that we have a mental image not only of the Typical Criminal, but also of the *Typical Crime*. If the Typical Criminal is a young, lower-class male, the Typical Crime is *one-on-one harm*—where "harm" means physical injury, loss of something valuable, or both. If you have any doubts that this is the Typical Crime, look at any random sample of police or private eye shows on television. How often do you see the officers on the TV show *COPS* investigate consumer fraud or failure to remove occupational hazards? When *Law & Order* detectives happen to track down a well-heeled criminal, it is almost always for violent crimes such as murder. A study of TV crime shows indicated that, while the fictional criminals portrayed on television are on average both older and wealthier than the real criminals who figure in the FBI's *UCR*, "TV crimes are almost 12 times as likely to be violent as crimes committed in the real world."[29] A review of several decades of research confirms that violent crimes are overrepresented on TV news and fictional crime shows, and that "young people, black people, and people of low socioeconomic status are underrepresented as offenders or victims in television programs"—exactly opposite from the real world, in which nonviolent property crimes far outnumber violent crimes, and young, poor, and black folks predominate as offenders and victims.[30]

Notice, then, that TV crime shows focus on the crimes typically committed by poor people, but they do not present these as uniquely committed by poor people. Rather than contradict the Pyrrhic defeat theory, this combination confirms it in a powerful way. The result of this combination is that TV crime shows broadcast the double-edged message that the one-on-one crimes of the poor are the typical crimes that rich and poor criminals alike commit—thus, they are not caused uniquely by the pressures of poverty; *and* that the criminal justice system pursues both rich and poor criminals—thus, when the criminal justice system happens mainly to pounce on the poor in real life, it is not from any class bias.[31] In other words, what is most important about the televised portrayals of crime is the *kinds* of crimes that are shown, not *who* is typically shown to be guilty. By overrepresenting violent one-on-one crimes, television confirms the commonsense view that these are the crimes that threaten us. Then, since in the real world those crimes are disproportionately committed by poor people, it is enough to create the image that it is the poor who pose the greatest danger to law-abiding Americans.

In addition to the steady diet of fictionalized TV violence and crime, there has been an increase in the graphic display of crime on many TV news programs. Crimes reported on TV news are also far more frequently violent than real crimes are.[32] An article in the *Washingtonian* says that the word around two prominent local TV news programs is "If it bleeds, it leads."[33] The Center for Media and Public Affairs reports a dramatic increase in homicide coverage on evening news programs starting in 1993, just as homicide rates were falling significantly. Other researchers found that news programs were highly selective in the homicides they reported. The murders that were chosen for coverage tended to be committed by strangers in neighborhoods where average household income was over $25,000 a year, while we know that most murders occur between people known to each other and take place in low-income neighborhoods. The effect is to magnify the risk of lower-class crime to middle-class individuals. Is it any wonder that fear of crime has persisted even as crime rates have gone down?[34]

What's more, a new breed of nonfictional "tabloid" TV show has appeared in which viewers are shown films of actual violent crimes—blood, screams, and all—or reenactments of actual violent crimes, sometimes using the actual victims playing themselves! Among these are *COPS* and *America's Most Wanted*. The *Wall Street Journal,* reporting on the phenomenon of tabloid TV, informs us, "Television has gone tabloid. The seamy underside of life is being bared in a new rash of true-crime ... shows."[35] Here, too, the focus is on crimes of one-on-one violence.

It is important to identify this model of the Typical Crime because it functions like a set of blinders. It keeps us from calling a mine "disaster" a mass murder even if 10 men are killed, even if someone is responsible for the unsafe conditions in which they worked and died. One study of newspaper reporting of a food-processing plant fire, in which 25 workers were killed and criminal charges were ultimately brought, concludes that "the newspapers showed little consciousness that corporate violence might be seen as a crime."[36] More recently, the *Washington Post* reported that the Peanut Corporation of America "knowingly shipped out contaminated peanut butter 12 times in the past two years." The company's salmonella-tainted peanuts were linked to 9 deaths and over 700 cases of illness, many requiring hospitalization.[37] Media covered the recall of more than four thousand peanut-based products, but made no mention of "mass-murder" or even "crime," although federal law makes it a felony to place adulterated food into commerce. A press conference, at which the victims called for criminal charges, received no attention from mainstream

disregard is considered
(or should be) criminal

media.[38] This is due to our fixation on the model of the Typical Crime. This particular piece of mental furniture so blocks our view that it keeps us from using the criminal justice system to protect ourselves from the greatest threats to our bodies and possessions.

What keeps a mine "disaster" from being a mass murder in our eyes is that it is not a one-on-one harm. What is important in one-on-one harm is not the numbers, but the *desire of someone (or ones) to harm someone (or ones) else.* An attack by a gang on one or more persons or an attack by one individual on several, fits the model of one-on-one harm; that is, for each person harmed, there is at least one individual who wanted to harm that person. Once he selects his victim, the rapist, the mugger, or the murderer all want that person to suffer. A mine executive, on the other hand, does not want his employees to be harmed. He would truly prefer that there be no accident, and no injured or dead miners. What he does want is something legitimate. It is what he has been hired to get: maximum profits at minimum costs. If he cuts corners to save a buck, he is just doing his job. If 10 or 29 men die because he cut corners on safety, we may think him crude or callous, but not a murderer. He is, at most, responsible for *indirect harm,* not one-on-one harm. For this, he may even be criminally indictable for violating safety regulations, but not for murder. The men are dead as an unwanted consequence of his (perhaps overzealous or undercautious) pursuit of a legitimate goal. So, unlike the Typical Criminal, he has not committed the Typical Crime, or so we generally believe. As a result, men are dead who might be alive now if cutting corners of the kind that leads to loss of life, whether suffering is specifically aimed at or not, were treated as murder.

This is our point. Because we accept the belief—encouraged by our politicians' statements about crime and by the media's portrayal of crime—that the model for crime is one person specifically and directly trying to harm another, we accept a legal system that leaves us unprotected against much greater dangers to our lives and well-being than those threatened by the Typical Criminal. Before developing this point further, let us anticipate and deal with some likely objections. Defenders of the present legal order are likely to respond to our argument at this point with irritation. Because this will surely turn to outrage in a few pages, let's talk to them now, while the possibility of rational communication still exists.

The "Defenders of the Present Legal Order" (we'll call them "the Defenders" for short) are neither foolish nor evil people. They are not racists, nor are they oblivious to the need for reform in the criminal justice system to make it more even-handed, and for reform in the larger society to make equal opportunity a reality for all Americans. Their response to our argument at this point is that the criminal justice system *should* occupy itself with one-on-one harm. Harms of the sort exemplified in the "mine tragedy" are really *not* murders and are better dealt with through stricter government enforcement of safety regulations. The Defenders admit that this enforcement has been rather lax and recommend that it be improved. Basically, though, they think this division of labor is right because it fits our ordinary moral sensibilities.

The Defenders maintain that, according to our common moral notions, someone who tries to do another harm is really more evil than someone who jeopardizes others while pursuing legitimate goals but doesn't aim to harm anyone. The one who jeopardizes others in this way doesn't want to hurt them. He or she doesn't have the goal of hurting someone in the way that a mugger or a rapist does. Moreover, being directly and purposely harmed by another person, the Defenders believe, is terrifying in a way that being harmed indirectly and impersonally, say, by a safety hazard, is not, even if the resultant injury is the same in both cases. And we should be tolerant of the one responsible for lax safety measures because he or she is pursuing a legitimate goal—that is, his or her dangerous action occurs as part of a productive activity, something that ultimately adds to social wealth and thus benefits everyone—whereas doers of one-on-one harm benefit no one but themselves. Thus, the latter are rightfully in the province of the criminal justice system with its drastic weapons, and the former are appropriately dealt with by the milder forms of regulation (or, perhaps, treated legally as responsible for civil *torts*, rather than for criminal acts).[39] Further, the Defenders insist, the crimes targeted by the criminal justice system are imposed on their victims totally against their will, whereas the victims of occupational hazards chose to accept their risky jobs and thus have, in some degree, consented to subject themselves to the dangers. Where dangers are consented to, the appropriate response is not blame but improved safety, and this is most efficiently done by regulation rather than with the guilt-seeking methods of criminal justice.

In sum, the Defenders make four objections: (1) Someone who purposely tries to harm another is really more evil than someone who harms another without aiming to, even if the degree of harm is the same; (2) being harmed directly by another person is more terrifying than being harmed indirectly and impersonally, as by a safety hazard, even if the degree of harm is the same; (3) someone who harms another in the course of an illegitimate and purely self-interested action is more evil than someone who harms another as a consequence of a legitimate and socially productive endeavor; (4) the harms of typical crimes are imposed on their victims against their wills, whereas harms such as those due to occupational hazards are consented to by workers when they agree to a job.

All four of these objections are said to reflect our common moral beliefs, which are a fair standard for a legal system to match. Together they are said to show that the Typical Criminal does something worse than the one responsible for an occupational hazard and thus deserves the special treatment provided by the criminal justice system. Some or all of these objections may have already occurred to the reader. Thus, it is important to respond to the Defenders. In doing so, we will show that neither our common moral beliefs nor our traditional legal notions justify treating indirect harms as regulatory matters rather than serious crimes.

1. DEFENDERS' FIRST OBJECTION Someone who purposely tries to harm another is really more evil than someone who harms another without aiming to, even if the degree of harm is the same. Thus, the Typical Criminal is rightly subject to criminal justice, while the cost-cutting executive who endangers his workers is rightly subject to noncriminal safety regulations.

Response.   The Defenders' first objection confuses intention with aim or purpose, and it is intention that brings us properly within the reach of the criminal law. It is true that a mugger aims to harm his victim in a way that a corporate executive who maintains an unsafe workplace does not. But the corporate executive acts knowingly, recklessly, or negligently nonetheless, and these are all ways of acting *intentionally*—which makes his actions appropriately subject to criminal law. What we intend is not just what we want to make happen, but what we do on purpose knowing what is likely to happen as the normal result of what we have done. As criminal law theorist Hyman Gross points out, "What really matters here is whether conduct of a particular degree of dangerousness was done intentionally."[40] Whether the actor wants or aims for that conduct to harm someone is a different matter, which is relevant to the actor's *degree* of culpability (not to whether he or she is culpable at all).

Here's an example (adapted from one given by Gross) to help understand the legally recognized degrees of culpability: Suppose a construction worker digs a trench in a neighborhood where children regularly play, and leaves the trench uncovered. One rainy day, children are killed while playing in the trench when its walls cave in on them. If the construction worker dug the trench and left it uncovered in order to kill the children, then their deaths were caused *purposely*. But suppose that the trench was dug and left uncovered not in order to harm the children, but merely knowing that children played in the area. Then, their deaths were brought about *knowingly*. If digging the ditch and leaving it uncovered were done without knowledge that children played in the area, but without making sure that they did not, then their deaths were brought about *recklessly*. Finally, if the trench was dug and left uncovered without knowledge that children played in the area and some, but inadequate, precautions were taken to make sure no children were there, then their deaths were brought about *negligently*.[41]

What's important here is that all these ways of causing death count for the law as intentional, and thus as criminally culpable. The difference between purposely, knowingly, recklessly, or negligently causing death is a difference within the range of intentional action. Second, culpability decreases as we go from purposely to knowingly to recklessly to negligently killing because, according to Gross, the outcome is increasingly due to chance and not to the actor; that is, the one who kills on purpose leaves less to chance that the killing will occur than the one who kills knowingly (the one who kills on purpose will take precautions against the failure of his killing, while the one who kills knowingly won't), and likewise the one who kills recklessly leaves wholly to chance whether there is a victim at all. The one who kills negligently reduces this chance, but insufficiently.

The kernel of truth in the Defenders' first objection is that the common street mugger harms on purpose, while the executive harms only knowingly or recklessly or negligently. But both act intentionally. We have criminal laws against reckless or negligent harming. Thus, refusal to treat those responsible for occupational hazards and the like as criminals is not justified by our ordinary moral sensibilities, as the Defenders claim. Moreover, don't be confused into thinking that, because all workplaces have some safety measures, all workplace deaths are at most due to negligence. To the extent that precautions are not taken against particular dangers (such as leaking methane), deaths due to those dangers are—by Gross's standard—caused recklessly or even knowingly (because the executive knows that potential victims are in harm's way from the danger he fails to reduce). More than 70 percent of the Occupational Safety and Health Administration's (OSHA) citations are for violations they deem "serious," that is, where "there is a substantial probability that death or serious physical harm could result and the employer knew, or should have known, of the hazard."[42] Nancy Frank concludes from a review of state homicide statutes that "a large number of states recognize unintended deaths caused by extreme recklessness as murder."[43]

There is more to be said. Remember that Gross attributes the difference in degrees of culpability to the greater role left to chance as we descend from purposely to knowingly to recklessly to negligently harming. In this light, it is important to note that the executive (say, the mine owner) imposes danger on a larger number of individuals than the Typical Criminal typically does. So, while the Typical Criminal purposely harms a particular individual, the executive knowingly subjects a large number of workers to a risk of harm. As the risk becomes greater and the number of workers increases, it becomes increasingly likely that one or more workers will be harmed. This means that the gap between the executive and the Typical Criminal shrinks. By not harming workers purposely, the executive leaves more to chance; but by subjecting large numbers to risk, he leaves it less and less to chance that *someone* will be harmed, and, thus, he rolls back his moral advantage over the Typical Criminal. If you keep your workers in mines or factories with high levels of toxic gases or chemicals, you start to approach 100 percent likelihood that at least one of them will be harmed as a result. That means that the culpability of the executive approaches that of the Typical Criminal.

A different way to make the Defenders' first objection is to say that the executive has failed to protect his workers, while the Typical Criminal has acted positively to harm his victim. In general, people think it is worse to harm someone than to fail to prevent their being harmed (perhaps you should feed starving people on the other side of town or of the world, but few people will think you are a murderer if you don't and the starving die). But people are normally held responsible for the effects of inaction when they have a special obligation to aid people. This applies to the parent who causes his child's death by failing to feed him, the doctor who causes her patient's death by failing to care for her, and the coal mine owner who causes his employees' death by failing to take legally mandated safety precautions. It may also cover the society that fails to rectify harm-producing injustices in its midst. This is another way in which the moral difference between the safety-cutting executive and the Typical Criminal shrinks away.

Further, the Defenders overestimate the importance of specifically trying to do evil in our moral estimate of people. The mugger who aims to hurt someone is no doubt an ugly character, but so too is the well-heeled executive who calmly and callously chooses to put others at risk. Most murders, we know, are committed in the heat of some passion, such as rage or jealousy, and/or under the influence of drugs or alcohol. Two lovers or neighbors or relatives find themselves in a heated argument. One (often it is a matter of chance *which* one) picks up a weapon and strikes the other a fatal blow. Such a person is clearly a murderer and rightly subject to punishment by the criminal justice system. Is this person more evil than the executive who, knowing the risks, calmly makes a calculation that profits for owners are more important than mandated safety equipment for workers?

The one who kills in a heated argument kills from passion. What she does she probably would not do in a moment of calm. She is likely to feel "she was not herself." The one she killed was someone she knew, a specific person who at the time seemed to her to be the embodiment of all that frustrated her, someone whose very existence made life unbearable. We do not suggest that this is true of all killers, although there is reason to believe that it is true of many. Nor do we suggest that such a state of mind justifies murder. What it does do, however, is suggest that the killer's action, arising out of anger at a particular individual, does not show general disdain for the lives of others. Here is where she is different from our mine executive. Our mine executive wanted to harm no one in particular, but *he knew his acts were likely to harm someone.* Once someone is harmed, the victim is someone in particular. Nor can our executive claim that "he was not himself." His act is done not out of passion, but out of cool reckoning. It is here that his evil shows. In his willingness to jeopardize the lives of unspecified others (workers, consumers, neighboring communities) who pose him no real threat, in order to make a few dollars, he shows his general disdain for all his fellow human beings. Can it really be said that he is less evil than one who kills from passion? The Model Penal Code includes within the definition of murder any death caused by "extreme indifference to human life."[44] Is our executive not a murderer by this definition?

It's worth noting that, in answering the Defenders here, we have portrayed harms from occupational hazards in their best light. They are not, however, all just matters of well-intentioned, but excessive risk taking. Consider, for example, the Manville (formerly Johns Manville) asbestos case. It is predicted that 240,000 Americans working now or who previously worked with asbestos will die from asbestos-related cancer over a period of 30 years. But documents made public during congressional hearings in 1979 show "that Manville and other companies within the asbestos industry covered up and failed to warn millions of Americans of the dangers associated with the fireproof, indestructible insulating fiber."[45] An article in the *American Journal of Public Health* attributes thousands of deaths to the cover-up.[46] Later in this chapter we document similar intentional cover-ups, such as the falsification of reports on coal-dust levels in mines, which leads to crippling and often fatal black lung disease. Surely someone who knowingly subjects others to risks and tries to hide those risks from them is culpable in a high degree.

2. DEFENDERS' SECOND OBJECTION   Being harmed directly by another person is more terrifying than being harmed indirectly and impersonally, as by a safety hazard, even if the degree of harm is the same.

> **Response.**   The Defenders are largely right in believing that direct personal assault is terrifying in a way that indirect impersonal harm is not. We say "largely right" here because deaths from some occupational hazards—slowly suffocating to death in a collapsed mine, or living in fear of an occupational cancer's spreading and becoming fatal—may well be as or more terrifying than some direct personal assaults. Nonetheless, even granting the Defenders their general point that direct assault is usually more terrifying than indirect harm, it does not follow that indirect harms should be treated as noncriminal regulatory matters. This difference in terrifyingness is no stranger to the criminal justice system. Prosecutors, judges, and juries constantly have to consider how terrifying an attack is in determining what to charge and what to convict offenders for. This is why we allow gradations in charges of homicide or assault and allow particularly grave sentences for particularly grave attacks. In short, the difference the Defenders are pointing to here might justify treating a one-on-one murder as graver than murder due to lax safety measures, but it doesn't justify treating one as a grave crime and the other as a mere regulatory (or very minor criminal) matter. After all, although it is worse to be injured with terror than without, it is still the injury that constitutes the worst part of violent crime. If that is so, then the worst part of violent crime is still shared by the indirect harms that the Defenders would relegate to regulation.
>
> As with the first objection, we should keep in mind that indirect harms can have a large number of victims. Pollution, unsafe work places, hazardous products, and tainted food can have a widespread impact. The financial fraud of Enron and other companies (discussed in Chapter 3) affected tens of thousands of people who lost more money than they would have in a mugging. Judge Miles Lord noted this issue in a speech from the bench to executives of the A.H. Robbins Company, which made a birth control device called the Dalkon Shield. The device was not just ineffective, but its design caused many women to get pelvic infections, which led to 18 deaths and 350,000 claims of injury. Judge Lord said, "If one poor young man were, by some act of his—without authority or consent—to inflict such damage upon one woman, he would be jailed for a good portion of the rest of his life. And yet your company without warning to women invaded their bodies by the millions and caused them injuries by the thousands."[47]

3. DEFENDERS' THIRD OBJECTION   Someone who harms another in the course of an illegitimate and purely self-interested action is more evil than someone who harms another as a consequence of a legitimate and socially productive endeavor.

Response. There is also something to the Defenders' claim that indirect harms, such as ones that result from lax safety measures, are part of legitimate productive activities, whereas one-on-one crimes generally are not. No doubt, we must tolerate the risks that are necessary ingredients of productive activity (unless those risks are so great as to outweigh the gains of the productive activity). But this doesn't imply we shouldn't identify the risks that are excessive and use the law to protect innocent people from them. If those risks are great enough, the fact that they may further a productive or otherwise legitimate activity is no reason against making them crimes if that's what's necessary to protect workers, consumers, and communities. A person can commit a crime to further an otherwise legitimate endeavor and it is still a crime. If a manager threatens to assault his workers if they don't work faster, the fact that getting them to work faster is a legitimate goal for a manager doesn't make the manager's act any less criminal. Using child labor may help legitimate businesses reap higher profits, but the law wisely prohibits this exploitation. By the same logic, the fact that leaving mine roofs unsupported, or failing to monitor explosive gasses in the mine, may serve the legitimate purpose of cutting costs, but it is no reason against treating such dangerous acts as crimes. If acts that endanger others ought to be crimes, then the fact that the acts are means to legitimate aims doesn't change the fact that they ought to be crimes.

4. DEFENDERS' FOURTH OBJECTION   The harms of typical crimes are imposed on their victims against their wills, whereas harms such as those due to occupational hazards are consented to by workers when they agree to a job.

Response. Cases like the Manville asbestos show that the Defenders overestimate the reality of the "free consent" with which workers take on the risks of their jobs. You can consent to a risk only if you know about it, and often the risks are concealed. Moreover, the Defenders overestimate generally the degree to which workers freely consent to the conditions of their jobs. Managers at Upper Big Branch threatened miners with being fired if they complained about safety risks.[48] More generally, although no one is forced at gunpoint to accept a particular job, virtually everyone is forced by the requirements of necessity to take some job. Moreover, workers can choose jobs only where there are openings, which means they cannot simply pick their place of employment at will. At best, workers can choose among the dangers present at various worksites, but rarely can they choose to face no danger at all.

For nonwhites and women, the choices are further narrowed by discriminatory hiring and long-standing occupational segregation (funneling women into nursing or food-processing jobs and blacks into janitorial and other menial occupations), not to mention subtle and not-so-subtle practices that keep nonwhites and women from advancing within their occupations. Consequently, for all intents and purposes, most workers *must* face the dangers of the jobs that are available to them. What's more, remember that, while here we have been focusing on harms due to occupational hazards, much of the indirect harm that we shall document in what follows is done not to workers but, for example, to hospital patients (subjected to careless medical care), to neighbors of industrial sites (breathing dangerous concentrations of pollutants), and to consumers of unsafe food and dangerous products. And these victims surely don't consent to these risks.

Finally, recall that the basis of all of the Defenders' objections is that the idea that one-on-one harms are more evil than indirect harms is part of our common moral beliefs. Though it is fair to judge criminal justice practices in light of ordinary moral beliefs, it is also important not to overlook the role of legal institutions in shaping our ordinary moral beliefs about right and wrong. The great historian of English law, Sir James Fitzjames Stephens, held that a

> great part of the general detestation of crime which happily prevails amongst the decent part of the community in all civilized countries arises from the fact that the commission of offences is associated in all such communities with the solemn and deliberate infliction of punishment wherever crime is proved.[49]

One cannot simply appeal to ordinary moral beliefs to defend the criminal law because the criminal law has already had a hand in shaping ordinary moral beliefs. At least one observer has argued that making narcotics use a crime at the beginning of the twentieth century *caused* a change in the public's ordinary moral notions about drug addiction, which prior to that time had been viewed as a medical problem.[50] It is probably safe to say that, in our own time, antidiscrimination legislation has sharpened the public's moral condemnation of racial and gender discrimination. Hence, we might speculate that if the criminal justice system began to prosecute—and if the media began to portray—those who inflict *indirect harm* as serious criminals, our ordinary moral notions would change on this point as well.

We are left with the conclusion that there is no moral basis for treating *one-on-one harm* as criminal and *indirect harm* as merely a regulatory affair (or only as a tort). What matters, then, is whether the purpose of the criminal justice system will be served by including, in the category of serious crime, actions that are predictably likely to produce serious harm, yet that are done in pursuit of otherwise legitimate goals and without the desire to harm anyone.

What is the purpose of the criminal justice system? No esoteric answer is required. Norval Morris and Gordon Hawkins write that "the prime function of the criminal law is to protect our persons and our property."[51] *The Challenge of Crime in a Free Society*, the report of the President's Commission on Law Enforcement and Administration of Justice, tells us that "any criminal justice system is an apparatus society uses to enforce the standards of conduct necessary to protect individuals and the community."[52] Whatever else we think a criminal justice system should accomplish, we doubt if anyone would deny that its central purpose is to protect us against the most serious threats to our well-being. *This purpose is seriously undermined by taking one-on-one harm as the model of crime.* It prevents the criminal justice system from protecting our persons and our property from dangers at least as great as those posed by one-on-one harm. This is so because, as we will show, a large number of actions that are not labeled *criminal* lead to loss of life, limb, and possessions on a scale comparable to those actions that are represented in the FBI Crime Index. A crime by any other name still causes misery and suffering.

* * *

The remainder of this chapter identifies some acts that are *crimes by other names:* acts that cause harm and suffering comparable to that caused by acts called crimes. Our purpose is to confirm the first hypothesis: that the definitions of crime in the criminal law do not reflect the only or the most dangerous behaviors in our society. To do this, we will need some measure of the harm and suffering caused by crimes with which we can compare the harm and suffering caused by noncrimes. Our measure need not be too refined because the point can be made by showing that there are some acts that we do not treat as crimes, but that cause harm roughly comparable to that caused by acts we do treat as crimes. Because the harms caused by noncriminal acts fall into the categories of death, bodily injury (including the disabling effects of disease), and property loss, we will compare the harms done by noncriminal acts with the injuries caused by the crimes of murder, aggravated assault, and theft. In order to compare the harms produced by both criminal and noncriminal acts, we will generally use the most recent year for which there are ample statistics from both categories.

According to the FBI's *UCR,* in 2010 there were 14,748 murders and non-negligent manslaughters and 778,901 aggravated assaults. "Murder and non-negligent manslaughter" includes all "willful (nonnegligent) killing of one human being by another." "Aggravated assault" is defined as an "attack by one person on another for the purpose of inflicting severe or aggravated bodily injury."[53] Thus, as measures of the harm done by crimes in 2010, we can say that serious crimes led to roughly 14,700 deaths and 780,000 instances of serious bodily injury short of death that year. As a measure of monetary loss due to property crime, we can use $15.7 billion, the figure the FBI estimates to be the total loss due to property crime in 2010.[54] Whatever the shortcomings of these reported crime statistics, they are the statistics on which public policy has traditionally been based.[55] Thus, we will consider any actions that lead to loss of life, physical harm, and property loss, comparable to the figures in the FBI's *UCR,* as actions that pose grave dangers to the community comparable to the threats posed by crimes. They are surely precisely the kinds of harmful actions from which a criminal justice system whose purpose is to protect our persons and property ought to protect us. *They are crimes by other names.*

In making this case, the following sections review a number of research reports, both historical and contemporary. The continued inclusion of older reports—sometimes seen as "outdated"—is meant to underscore that these harms are neither new nor recently discovered. The harms are not transient, but ongoing, and the inclusion of findings reported over several decades should bolster confidence in the validity of sometimes scarce contemporary research.

Work May Be Dangerous to Your Health

When the *President's Report on Occupational Safety and Health*[56] was published in 1972, the government estimated the number of job-related illnesses at

390,000 per year and the number of annual deaths from industrial disease at 100,000. Since that time, numerous studies have documented the alarmingly high incidence of disease, injury, and death due to hazards in the workplace *and* the fact that much or most of this carnage is the consequence of the refusal of management to pay for safety measures, of government to enforce safety standards, and sometimes of management's willful defiance of existing law.[57]

For 2010, the U.S. Department of Labor's Bureau of Labor Statistics (BLS) reports 3.1 million workplace injuries and illnesses, about half of which (1.6 million) resulted in lost workdays, job transfer or restricted duties at work. BLS also reports 212,800 cases of nonfatal occupational illness.[58] BLS notes that "some conditions (for example, long-term latent illnesses caused by exposure to carcinogens) often are difficult to relate to the workplace and are not adequately recognized and reported. These long-term latent illnesses are believed to be understated in the survey's illness measures."[59]

Complete data are also difficult to come by because of disincentives that discourage workers from reporting and employers from recording illnesses and injuries. A General Accounting Office report notes that

> workers may not report a work-related injury or illness because they fear job loss or other disciplinary action, or fear jeopardizing rewards based on having low injury and illness rates. In addition, employers may not record injuries or illnesses because they are afraid of increasing their workers' compensation costs or jeopardizing their chances of winning contract bids for new work.[60]

A study by the National Institute for Occupational Safety and Health concludes that "there may be several thousand more workplace deaths each year than employers report."[61] In spite of these known problems, OSHA made several changes that worsened the problem of underreporting. In 1995, OSHA changed its data collection system so that companies are now under an "honor system" to report accurate injury and death numbers to the government. Several public health researchers noted "that the cessation of on-site data collection appears to have exacerbated the underreporting by employers." In 2002, OSHA changed the record keeping standard so "fewer injuries and illnesses were required to be recorded."[62]

For these reasons, we must look elsewhere for accurate figures. In his testimony before the Senate Committee on Labor and Human Resources, Dr. Philip Landrigan, director of the Division of Environmental and Occupational Medicine at the Mount Sinai School of Medicine in New York City, stated,

> data indicate that occupationally related exposures are responsible each year in New York State for 5,000 to 7,000 deaths and for 35,000 new cases of illness (not including work-related injuries). These deaths due to occupational disease include 3,700 deaths from cancer. ...
>
> Crude national estimates of the burden of occupational disease in the United States may be developed by multiplying the New York State data by a factor of 10. New York State contains slightly less than 10 percent of the nation's workforce, and it in-

cludes a broad mix of employment in the manufacturing, service and agricultural sectors. Thus, it may be calculated that occupational disease is responsible each year in the United States for 50,000 to 70,000 deaths, and for approximately 350,000 new cases of illness.[63]

Landrigan's estimates of deaths from occupational disease are corroborated by a National Safe Workplace Institute study, which estimates that the number of occupational disease deaths is between 47,377 and 95,479. Mark Cullen, director of the occupational medicine program at the Yale University School of Medicine, praised this study as "a very balanced, very comprehensive overview of occupational health."[64] In a 1997 article in the American Medical Association (AMA) journal *Archives of Internal Medicine*, researchers at San Jose State University in California aggregated many national and large regional data sets and came up with an estimate, for 1992, of 60,300 deaths from occupational illness.[65]

Dr. Samuel Epstein, professor emeritus of environmental and occupational medicine at the University of Illinois School of Public Health, and then-chairman of the Cancer Prevention Coalition, states, "Over 10 percent of adult cancer deaths result from occupational exposures, which are also a recognized cause of cancer in children: parents exposed to carcinogens on the job often expose their unborn children to the same cancer-causing chemicals."[66] With current estimates of annual cancer deaths running above 570,000, this translates into approximately 57,000 adult deaths a year from occupationally caused cancer alone. A 1999 report estimates approximately 55,000 annual deaths from occupational disease, though noting that the number may be as high as 94,000.[67]

In light of these various estimates, we can hardly be overestimating the actual death toll if we take the conservative route and set it at 50,000 deaths a year resulting from occupational disease.

As for nonfatal occupational illness, BLS reports 212,800 cases for 2010, and the San Jose State University researchers estimate 862,200 cases (based on data from 1992). These illnesses are of varying severity. Because we want to compare these occupational harms with those resulting from aggravated assault, we shall stay on the conservative side here, too, as with deaths from occupational diseases, and say that there are annually, in the United States, approximately 200,000 job-related serious illnesses. This is a conservative figure in light of the San Jose State University researchers' estimate of 862,200 cases, as well as the likelihood of underreporting. Note also that these figures don't include the effects of workers' exposure to occupational illnesses on the health of their families.[68] Taken together with 50,000 deaths from occupational diseases, how does this compare with the threat posed by crime?

Before jumping to any conclusions, note that the risk of occupational disease and death falls only on members of the labor force, whereas the risk of crime falls on the whole population, from infants to the elderly. Because the civilian labor force is about half of the total population (154 million in 2009 out of a total civilian population of 307 million),[69] to get a true picture of the *relative* threat posed by occupational diseases compared with that posed by crimes, we should multiply the crime statistics by half (0.5) when comparing them with the figures for occupational disease and death. Using the crime figures for 2010 (cited earlier in this chapter), we note that the *comparable* figures would be:

	Occupational Disease	Crime (x 0.5)
Death	50,000	7,350
Other physical harm	200,000	390,000

Those who believe that this paints an inaccurate picture because so many crimes go unreported, should consider that homicides are by far the most completely reported of crimes. For obvious reasons, the general underreporting of crimes is not equal. It is easier to avoid reporting a rape or a mugging than a corpse. Second, although not the best, aggravated assaults are among the better-reported crimes. Estimates from the Justice Department's National Crime Victimization Survey indicate that 62 percent of aggravated assaults were reported to the police in 2008, compared with 34 percent of thefts.[70] On the other hand, we should expect more, not less, underreporting of industrial than criminal victims because diseases and deaths are likely to cost firms money in the form of workdays lost and insurance premiums raised; occupational diseases are frequently first seen by company physicians who have an incentive to diagnose complaints as either malingering or not job related, and many occupationally caused diseases do not show symptoms or lead to death until after the employee has left the job. Most independent contractors and self-employed workers are not included in BLS reports.

In sum, both occupational and criminal harms are underreported, though there is reason to believe that the underreporting is worse for occupational than for criminal harms. Bear in mind, also, that we have accepted the statistics on criminal harms as reported, while we have reduced substantially the reported estimates for occupational harms. However one may quibble with figures presented here, it is fair to say that, if anything, they understate the extent of occupational harm compared with criminal harm.

Note further that the estimates in the last chart are *only* for occupational *diseases* and deaths from those diseases. They do not include death and disability from work-related injuries. Here, too, the statistics are gruesome. BLS's *National Census of Fatal Occupational Injuries* reports 4,041 workplace fatalities in 2010 (not counting work-related homicides).[71] Added to the previous figure, this brings the number of occupation-related deaths to 54,041 a year.

The BLS reported that, in 2010, there were 3.1 million recordable cases of nonfatal injuries and illnesses. A recordable case involves days away from work, medical treatment other than first aid, loss of consciousness, restriction of work or motion, transfer to another job, or "cancer, chronic irreversible disease, a fracture or cracked bone, or a punctured eardrum."[72] Of these, BLS says that 1.6 million entailed days away from work, restricted activity or job transfer. To make sure that we are counting more serious harms, we will use this figure of 1.6 million. Note that this figure includes physical harms from both disease and injury. Thus, it replaces our previous figure of 200,000. This is an especially conservative estimate given that another national database of occupational injuries and illnesses that result in treatment in an *emergency* department of a hospital recorded 3.4 million visits for 2003, a level fairly constant since 1982.[73]

If, on the basis of these additional figures, we recalculated our table comparing occupational harms from both disease and injury with criminal harms, it would look like this:

	Occupational Disease and Injury	Crime (x 0.5)
Death	54,041	7,350
Other physical harm	1,600,000	390,000

Can there be any doubt that workers are more likely to stay alive and healthy in the face of the danger from the underworld than from the work world? Secretary of Labor Hilda Solis noted:

> Every day in America, 12 people go to work and never come home. Every year in America, 3.3 million people suffer a workplace injury from which they may never recover. These are preventable tragedies that disable our workers, devastate our families, and damage our economy.[74]

To say that some of these workers died from accidents due to their own carelessness is about as helpful as saying that some of those who died at the hands of murderers deserved it. It overlooks the fact that when workers are careless, it is not because they love to live dangerously. They have production quotas to meet, quotas that they themselves do not set. If quotas were set with an eye to keeping work at a safe pace rather than keeping the production-to-wages ratio as high as possible, it might be more reasonable to expect workers to take the time to be careful. Beyond this, we should bear in mind that the vast majority of occupational deaths result from disease, not accident, and disease is generally a function of conditions outside a worker's control. Examples of such conditions are:

- **the level of coal dust in the air:** "260,000 miners receive benefits for [black lung] disease, and perhaps as many as 4,000 retired miners die from the illness or its complications each year"; about 10,000 working miners "have X-ray evidence of the beginnings of the crippling and often fatal disease."[75]

- *textile dust:* some 100,000 American cotton textile workers suffer breathing impairments caused by acute byssinosis, or brown lung, and another 35,000 former mill workers are totally disabled with chronic brown lung.[76]
- *asbestos fibers:* it has been estimated that, under the lenient asbestos standard promulgated by OSHA in 1972, anywhere from 18,400 and 598,000 deaths from lung cancer would result from exposure to asbestos.[77]
- *coal tars:* "workers who had been employed five or more years in the coke ovens died of lung cancer at a rate three and a half times that for all steelworkers"; coke oven workers develop cancer of the scrotum at a rate five times that of the general population.[78]
- *repetitive motion:* according to the National Academy of Sciences, there are more than 1 million repetitive motion injuries annually.[79] Repetitive strain disease reportedly afflicts "keyboard operators, assembly-line workers, meat processors, grocery check-out clerks, secretaries and other employees everyday. ... OSHA officials argue that ... carpal tunnel problems lead the list in average time lost from work (at a median of 30 days per case), well above amputations (24 days) and fractures (20)."[80]

To blame the workers for occupational disabilities and deaths is to ignore the history of governmental attempts to compel industrial firms to meet safety standards that would keep dangers (such as chemicals or fibers or dust particles in the air), that are outside the worker's control, down to a safe level. This has been a continual struggle, with firms using everything from their own "independent" research institutes to more direct and often questionable forms of political pressure to influence government in the direction of loose standards and lax enforcement. So far, industry has been winning because OSHA has been given neither the personnel nor the mandate to fulfill its purpose. Between 1990 and 2007, the number of OSHA inspectors declined from 1,300 to 1,100 and "it is estimated that OSHA actively regulates [the work conditions of] only about 20% of the American workforce."[81] Dr. David Michaels, Assistant Secretary of Labor for Occupational Safety and Health, noted that federal OSHA has 1,200 inspectors and "state plans have around the same, so there are less than 2,500 inspectors to cover 7.5 million workplaces employing more than 130 million workers."[82]

The problem does not lie with OSHA alone, but starts with the legislators who decided in 1970 that causing the death of an employee by willfully violating safety laws was a misdemeanor. As noted by a *New York Times* investigation: "The maximum sentence, six months in jail, is half the maximum for harassing a wild burro on federal lands." Although Congress has rarely voted down tougher sentences for street crime, it has rejected every attempt to get tougher with those who willfully (and sometimes repeatedly) violate safety laws, in spite of evidence that stricter laws could save lives. On top of lax laws, OSHA discourages prosecutions and criminal referrals to such an extent that a 1988 congressional report noted, "A company official who willfully and recklessly violates federal OSHA laws stands a greater chance of winning a state lottery than being criminally charged."[83]

Likewise, the level of fines was increased only once (in 1990) from the levels set in 1970, and thus have not kept pace with inflation. In Congressional testimony on the Protecting America's Workers Act (which did not become law), Assistant Secretary Michaels noted how the current penalties do not provide deterrence: "Currently, serious violations—those that pose a substantial probability of death or serious physical harm to workers—are subject to a maximum civil penalty of only $7,000." Further, "Willful and repeated violations carry a maximum penalty of only $70,000." Worse still, those are maximum penalties and in 2007, the median initial penalty for cases involving the death of a worker was $5,900; the median final penalty after settlement was $3,675.[84] Elsewhere, Michaels noted that in 2010, the average penalty for a serious violation was $1,000, and that was after some administrative adjustments to the schedule of fines to make it tougher.[85]

Is a person who kills another in a bar brawl a greater threat to society than a business executive who refuses to cut into his profits to make his plant a safe place to work? By any measure of death and suffering, the latter is by far a greater danger than the former. However, because he wishes his workers no harm, and because he is only indirectly responsible for death and disability while pursuing legitimate economic goals, his acts are not labeled "crimes." Once we free our imagination from the blinders of the one-on-one model of crime, can there be any doubt that the criminal justice system does *not* protect us from the gravest threats to life and limb? It seeks to protect us when danger comes from a young, lower-class male in the inner city. When a threat comes from an upper-class business executive in an office, the criminal justice system looks the other way. This is in the face of growing evidence that for every American citizen murdered by thugs, more than three American workers are killed by the recklessness of their bosses and the indifference of their government.

indifference vs intent?

Health Care May Be Dangerous to Your Health

An article in the *Journal of the American Medical Association* (*JAMA*) estimates that there are 225,000 deaths a year due to medical treatment, making it "the third leading cause of death in the United States, after deaths from heart disease and cancer."[86] Between 1.7 and 2 million people in the United States acquired health-care-associated infections, which resulted in 88,000 to 100,000 deaths according to the Centers for Disease Control and other studies published in *JAMA*.[87] This is more than five times the number of deaths due to homicides, and they are deaths that could have been prevented by following established hygiene protocols.[88] And this is only the beginning.

On July 15, 1975, Dr. Sidney Wolfe, of Ralph Nader's Public Interest Health Research Group, testified before the House Commerce Oversight and Investigations Subcommittee that there "were 3.2 million cases of unnecessary surgery performed each year in the United States." These unneeded operations, Wolfe added, "cost close to $5 billion a year and kill as many as 16,000 Americans."[89] Wolfe's estimates of unnecessary surgery were based on studies comparing the operations performed and surgery recommended by doctors who are paid for the operations they do with those performed and recommended by salaried doctors who receive no extra income from surgery.

The figure accepted by Dr. George A. Silver, professor of public health at the Yale University School of Medicine, is 15,000 deaths a year "attributable to unnecessary surgery."[90] Silver places the annual cost of excess surgery at $4.8 billion.[91] In an article on an experimental program by Blue Cross and Blue Shield aimed at curbing unnecessary surgery, *Newsweek* reported that

> a Congressional committee earlier this year [1976] estimated that more than 2 million of the elective operations performed in 1974 were not only unnecessary—but also killed about 12,000 patients and cost nearly $4 billion.[92]

Because the number of surgical operations performed in the United States rose from 16.7 million in 1975 to 28.7 million in 2008,[93] there is reason to believe that at least somewhere between (the congressional committee's estimate of) 12,000 and (Dr. Wolfe's estimate of) 16,000 people a year still die from unnecessary surgery. In 2010, the FBI reported that 1,704 murders (in which the weapon is known) were committed with a "cutting or stabbing instrument."[94] Obviously, the FBI does not include the scalpel as a cutting or stabbing instrument. If it did, it would have had to report that between 13,704 and 17,704 persons were killed by "cutting or stabbing" in 2010, depending on whether you take Congress's figure or Wolfe's. No matter how you slice it, the scalpel is more dangerous than the switchblade.

This is only a fraction of the problem. A report issued in 1999 by the National Academy of Sciences' Institute of Medicine (IOM) stated that up to "98,000 hospitalized Americans die every year and 1 million more are injured as a result of preventable medical errors that cost the nation an estimated $29 billion a year."[95] (Bear in mind as well that "[t]he IOM considered only errors committed in hospitals, and not in other medical settings where they undoubtedly abound: clinics, outpatient surgery centers and doctors' offices.")[96] The report goes on to predict that, if a "centralized system for keeping tabs on medical errors" were put in place, "the number of deaths from medical mistakes could be cut in half within five years."[97] However, due to resistance by doctors and hospitals to mandatory reporting of errors and to other recommendations in the IOM report, no significant progress has been made. "As a result, experts contend, it's doubtful that patients checking into most of America's 5,200 hospitals [in 2002] are any less likely to be killed or injured than they were on November 29, 1999, when the report was issued."[98] Indeed, things may be worse. "Operations on the wrong body part or the wrong patient have increased according to the Joint Commission on the Accreditation of Healthcare Organizations, which inspects hospitals."[99]

A report in *JAMA*, titled "Five Years After *To Err is Human*: What Have We Learned?" asserts that efforts to reduce errors "are affecting safety at the margin, [but] their overall impact is hard to see in national statistics." The article notes many barriers, including an insurance system that rewards hospitals for errors by paying additional sums for the treatment of problems caused by mistakes. The IOM called for reducing preventable injuries by 90 percent, and the authors write that "such a commitment has yet to emerge; indeed, it is not in sight."[100] The article lists a number of interventions that dramatically reduce adverse events, including those proposed by Dr. Peter Pronovost of Johns Hopkins, who has created medical safety checklists and works on ways to enforce their use. When implemented to reduce infection in a number of Intensive Care Units in Michigan, in the "first eighteen months, the hospitals saved … more than fifteen hundred lives. The successes have been sustained for almost four years—all because of a stupid little checklist."[101]

The results of large-scale research published in 2010 by the *New England Journal of Medicine* confirm that little progress has occurred. A review of the research appeared in the *New York Times* under the headline, "Study Finds No Progress in Safety at Hospitals." It noted that "about 18 percent of patients were harmed by medical care, some more than once, and 63.1 percent of the injuries were judged to be preventable." In almost 3 percent of the cases patients suffered a permanent injury, and another 2.4 percent of the injuries caused or contributed to the death of a patient. "[M]any of the problems were caused by the hospitals' failure to use measures that had been proved to avert mistakes."[102]

Recall the example of digging a trench: "Suppose that the trench was dug and left uncovered, knowing that children played in the area. Then, their deaths were brought about *knowingly*." *Knowingly* was the second degree of culpability, right below *purposely*—and is more culpable than *recklessly* or *negligently*. Suppose that preventable and deadly potential hospital errors were identified but left unprevented, knowing that vulnerable patients would be in the area. Didn't the doctors and hospital officials who resisted correcting previously identified dangerous practices bring about 98,000 deaths *knowingly*?

The FBI also should add the hypodermic needle and the prescription drug to the list of potential murder weapons. Silver points out that these are also death-dealing instruments:

> Of the 6 billion doses of antibiotic medicines administered each year by injection or prescription, it is estimated that 22 percent are unnecessary. Of the doses given, 10,000 result in fatal or near-fatal reactions. Somewhere between 2,000 and 10,000 deaths probably would not have occurred if the drugs, meant for the patient's benefit, had not been given.[103]

These estimates are supported by the Harvard Medical Practice Study. Its authors write that, of the 1.3 million medical injuries (which they estimated on the basis of hospital records for 1984), 19 percent (247,000) were related to medications, and 14 percent of these (34,580) resulted in permanent injury or death.[104] Another report estimates that, in part due to faulty warning labels on prescription drugs, "100,000 hospital patients die [annually] of adverse reactions to medication and 2.2 million are injured."[105] Further, "experts have estimated that more than one million serious drug errors occur annually in hospitals alone."

TABLE 2.1   How Americans Are Murdered, 2010

Total Murders Where Weapon Is Known	Firearms	Knife or Other Cutting Instrument	Other Weapon: Blunt Objects, Arson, Strangulation, Poison, etc.	Personal Weapons: Hands, Fists, etc.
12,996*	8,775	1,704	1,772	745

*This figure is lower than the number of murders and nonnegligent manslaughters used elsewhere in the text, due to the fact that the FBI lacks data on the weapons used in roughly one-sixth of the homicides it reports. "Other Weapon" represents all the other categories that are not reported separately here, including the category "Other Weapon/Not Stated."
Source: UCR–2010, Expanded Homicide Data Table 8.

If someone had the temerity to publish a *UCR* that really portrayed the way Americans are murdered, the FBI's statistics on the *type* of weapon used in murder would have to be changed from those shown in Table 2.1 to something like those shown in Table 2.2. The figures shown in Table 2.2 would give American citizens a much more honest picture of what threatens them. Nonetheless, we are not likely to see such a table published by the criminal justice system, perhaps because it would also give American citizens a more honest picture of *who* threatens them.

Finally, aside from the other losses it imposes, unnecessary surgery was estimated to have cost between $4 and $5 billion in 1974. The price of medical care has increased about eightfold between 1974 and 2010. Thus, assuming that the same number of unneeded operations was performed in 2010, the cost of unnecessary surgery would be between $32 and $40 billion. To this we

TABLE 2.2   How Americans Are *Really* Murdered, 2010

Total Murders Where Weapon Is Known	Occupational Hazard or Disease	Firearms	Knife or Other Cutting Instrument, Including Scalpel	Other Weapon: Blunt Objects, Poison, Strangulation, Prescription Drug, Other Medical Treatment, etc.	Personal Weapons: Hands, Fists, etc.
168,320*	55,324	8,775	13,704	89,772	745

*The figures in this row represent the relevant figures in Table 2.1 plus the most conservative figures for the relevant categories discussed in the text. Note in particular that, under the category "Other Weapon," we have included the low estimate of the number of people who die from unnecessary prescription drugs (2,000) according to Dr. Silver, plus 86,000 (the 98,000 hospital deaths due to error that the IOM predicted could have been prevented within five years of their report minus 12,000, the lower estimate of deaths due to unnecessary surgery).

should add the unnecessary 22 percent of the 6 billion doses of medication administered. Even at an extremely conservative estimate of $3 a dose, this adds about $4 billion.[106] In short, assuming that earlier trends have continued, there is reason to believe that unnecessary surgery and medication cost the public between $36 and $44 billion annually, far outstripping the $16 billion taken by the thieves that concern the FBI.[107] This gives us yet another way in which we are robbed of more money by practices that are not treated as criminal than by practices that are.

Waging Chemical Warfare Against America

Nearly half of Americans can expect to contract cancer during their lifetimes. The American Cancer Society (ACS) estimated that 420,000 Americans would die of cancer in 1981. The Society's estimate for 2011 was 571,950 deaths from cancer, with more than 1.6 million new cases diagnosed.[108] A recent report from the President's Cancer Panel stated that "approximately 41 percent of people in the U.S. will be diagnosed with cancer at some point in their lives, and about 21 percent of Americans will die from cancer."[109] While scientific discoveries about cells and genes grab the headlines, "a 1978 report issued by the President's Council on Environmental Quality unequivocally states that 'most researchers agree that 70 to 90 percent of cancers are caused by environmental influences and are hence theoretically preventable'."[110] An editorial in the *New England Journal of Medicine* in 2000 notes a "widely accepted estimate that 80 to 90 percent of human cancer is due to environmental factors."[111]

This means that a concerted national effort could result in saving 400,000 or more lives a year and reducing each individual's chances of getting cancer in his or her lifetime from nearly 1 in 2 to 1 in 12, or less. If you think this would require a massive effort in terms of money and personnel, you are right. How much of an effort, though, would the nation make to stop a foreign invader who was killing 1,500 people a day and bent on slaughtering one-fifth of the present population? And how has the "cancer establishment"—the publicly funded National Cancer Institute (NCI) and the private ACS—responded? The President's Cancer Panel indicates that in 2008 "no more than 14 percent of NCI's nearly $4.83 billion budget" went to occupational and environmental cancer issues; and that year the ACS spent less than $4 million on environmental cancer.[112] An earlier group of experts stated that NCI spent 2.5 percent of its budget on prevention and ASC spent 0.1 percent of revenue on environmental research. "The cancer establishment's funding for primary prevention is trivial," they wrote, adding that there is "minimal research on avoidable exposures to a wide range of occupational and environmental industrial carcinogens, including nationwide cancer clusters in the vicinity of nuclear power plants, petrochemical industries, and Superfund hazardous waste sites that are disproportionately located in ethnic and low-socioeconomic communities."[113]

Not only are we losing the chemical war on all fronts, but it also looks as if we do not even have the will to fight. A 2002 article in the *Washington*

Post reports that "the Bush administration has begun a broad restructuring of the scientific advisory committees that guide federal policy in areas such as patient rights and public health, eliminating some committees that were coming to conclusions at odds with the president's views." One committee, "which had been assessing the effects of environmental chemicals on human health[,] has been told that nearly all of its members will be replaced—in several instances by people with links to the industries that make those chemicals. One new member is a California scientist who helped defend Pacific Gas and Electric Co. against the real-life Erin Brockovich."[114]

While the Bush administration may have been a low point, the enduring problem is noted by the President's Cancer Panel: "With nearly 80,000 chemicals on the market in the United States, many of which are used by millions of Americans in their daily lives and are un- or understudied and largely unregulated, exposure to potential environmental carcinogens is widespread."[115] The main legislation in this area is the 1976 Toxic Substances Control Act (TSCA), which does not require industry or government to confirm the safety of new chemicals. In fact, because chemical companies are required to report information about known health hazards caused by their products, they generally do not conduct tests that might reveal such problems.[116] A bill to update and fix the TSCA, the Kid Safe Chemicals Act of 2008, died in the 110th Congress, and has not been reintroduced even though an American Public Health Association policy statement notes that a large number of independent studies "have concluded that TSCA has fallen short of its objectives and has not served as an effective vehicle for the public, industry, or government to assess the hazards of chemicals in commerce or control those of greatest concern."[117]

Chemical warfare is being waged against us on three fronts:

- pollution
- cigarette smoking
- food additives

Pollution includes air pollution, toxic waste and environmental pollution from chemicals. The World Health Organization estimates suggest that in the U.S., 13 percent of preventable deaths and preventable disability-adjusted life years (years of life lost due to premature death) were caused by these forms of pollution.[118] In a study published in *Environmental Health Perspectives* in 2002, five medical experts on children's health estimated the total economic costs of four childhood diseases and disabilities caused by environmental pollution. Included in this total are increased costs of medical care as well as the costs of decreased productivity and lifetime earnings due to sickness and decreased I.Q. The authors "estimate that the annual costs of environmentally attributable diseases in American children total $54.9 billion ..."[119] A study published in 2005 estimates the cost in economic productivity due to lowered intelligence caused by exposure of fetuses to methyl mercury of American origin at $3.1 billion annually. This study was published two months after the U.S. Environmental Protection Agency (EPA) issued a rule reversing "strict controls on emissions of mercury from coal-fired power plants."[120]

The evidence linking *air pollution* and cancer, as well as other serious and often fatal diseases, has been accumulating rapidly in recent years. In 1993, *JAMA* reported research that found "'robust' associations between premature mortality and air pollution levels."[121] A later study published in *JAMA* states that "air pollution accounts for the majority (60%) of mortality related to toxic agents," and causes 22,000 to 52,000 deaths a year.[122] That estimate is consistent with the 40,600 deaths in the U.S. that the World Health Organization attributes to outdoor air pollution, and is lower than an EPA estimate of 63,000 to 88,000.[123] In 2002, *JAMA* published a study that concludes "that people living in the most heavily polluted metropolitan areas have a 12 percent higher risk of dying of lung cancer than people in the least polluted areas."[124]

Another study by two NCI researchers found that in *all* U.S. counties with smelters, the incidence of lung cancer is above the national average. "The researchers found high lung cancer death rates not only in men—who are often exposed to arsenic on their jobs inside smelters—but also among women, who generally never went inside smelters and were not previously believed to have been exposed to arsenic." Explanation: "neighborhood air pollution from industrial sources of inorganic arsenic."[125] New Jersey, however, took the prize for having the highest cancer death rate in the nation. NCI investigators found that "19 of New Jersey's 21 counties rank in the top 10 percent of all counties in the nation for cancer death rates." Salem County, home of E. I. Du Pont de Nemours and Company's Chambers Works, which has been manufacturing chemicals since 1919, "has the highest bladder cancer death rate in the nation—8.7 deaths per 100,000 persons."[126] During 1975, the epidemiological branch of the NCI did a massive county-by-county analysis of cancer in the United States, mapping the "cancer hotspots" in the nation. The result was summed up by Dr. Glenn Paulson, Assistant Commissioner of Science in the New Jersey Department of Environmental Protection: "If you know where the chemical industry is, you know where the cancer hotspots are."[127] What distinguishes these findings from the material on occupational hazards discussed above is that NCI investigators found higher death rates for all those living in the cancer hotspots, not just the workers in the offending plants.

NCI has identified as carcinogens, or suspected carcinogens, 23 of the chemicals commonly found in our drinking water.[128] Moreover, according to one observer, we are now facing a "new plague—toxic exposure." Of the extent of contamination, he says that

> this country generates between 255 million and 275 million metric tons of hazardous waste annually, of which as much as 90 percent is improperly disposed of. ... The Office of Technology Assessment estimates that there are some 600,000 contaminated sites in the country, of which 888 sites have been designated or proposed by the Environmental Protection Agency for priority cleanup under the Superfund program.[129]

Studies have borne out the correlation between nearness to toxic wastes and above-average cancer mortality rates, as well as the positive correlation between residential poverty and nearness to toxic wastes.[130] Other studies indicate that race is an even more important determinant of the location of toxic waste dumps. Writes Robert Bullard,

> Toxic time bombs are not randomly scattered across the urban landscape. ... The Commission for Racial Justice's landmark study, *Toxic Wastes and Race in the United States,* found race to be the most important factor (i.e., more important than income, home ownership rate, and property values) in the location of abandoned toxic waste sites. ... [T]hree out of five African Americans live in communities with abandoned toxic waste sites.[131]

As it did with OSHA, the Reagan administration instituted a general slowing down of enforcement of EPA regulations. Reagan tried to cut the EPA's enforcement budget by 45 percent during his first two years in office.[132] President Bush Sr. followed suit. The EPA's research and development staff, whose work provides the scientific basis for such regulations, was reduced by nearly 25 percent between 1981 and 1992.[133] The EPA Superfund spearheads cleanups of large-scale toxic waste with money collected from polluters and from taxes on certain businesses. But increasingly, companies that have toxic waste responsibilities use bankruptcy to escape them, and the "polluters pay"-based taxes expired in 1995.[134] In addition, the EPA recently *lowered* the value it places on each life when doing cost-benefit analysis of regulations. The *Washington Post* notes this could set a "scary precedent, making it seem that lifesaving pollution reductions are not worth the cost."[135]

So the chemical war goes on. No one can deny that we know the enemy. No one can deny that we know the toll it is taking. Indeed, we can compute the number of deaths that result every day that we refuse to mount an offensive. Yet we still refuse. Thus, for the time being, the only advice we can offer someone who values his or her life is "if you must breathe our air, don't inhale."

The evidence linking *cigarette smoking* and cancer is overwhelming and need not be repeated here. The ACS simply notes, "Smoking remains the most preventable cause of death in our society."[136] Cigarettes are widely estimated to cause 30 percent of all cancer deaths, and 87 percent of lung cancers, which translates into "an estimated 443,000 premature deaths each year between 2000 and 2004. In addition, an estimated 8.6 million people suffer from chronic conditions related to smoking."[137] These deaths and conditions result in medical expenses over $80 billion, and productivity loss estimated at nearly $97 billion.[138] According to the NCI, current and former smokers are responsible over their lifetimes for half a trillion dollars in excess health care costs. Tobacco use costs Medicare $10 billion annually and Medicaid about $13 billion.[139]

This is enough to expose the hypocrisy of running a full-scale war against marijuana and heroin (which produce no degenerative disease), while allowing cigarette sales and advertising to flourish. It also should be enough to underscore the point that, once again, there are threats to our lives much greater than criminal homicide. Indeed, not only does our government fail to protect us against this threat, but it also promotes it! The government provided a price-support program for the tobacco industry (making up the difference when market price fell below a target price) from 1933 to 1982, and in 1986 it wrote off $1.1 billion in loans that it had made to tobacco farmers.[140] The U.S. Congress has turned down more than 1,000 proposed tobacco control bills since 1964, the year of the first Surgeon General's Report on the dangers of tobacco. This may be related to the enormous generosity of the tobacco industry. Common Cause reports that, from 1995 to 2000, "tobacco interests have given more than $32 million in political donations to state and federal candidates and political parties." The Phillip Morris Companies alone gave over $10,000,000 between 1995 and 2000. Common Cause adds, "analysis of recent tobacco-related votes in Congress shows a strong correlation between the amount that Members received and how they voted."[141]

If you think that tobacco harms only people who knowingly decide to take the risk, consider the following. In 1995, *JAMA* devoted a special issue to several thousand pages of internal documents from the Brown and Williamson Tobacco Corporation and BAT Industries (formerly British American Tobacco Company). Brown and Williamson (B&W) is the third-largest cigarette maker in the United States and a wholly owned subsidiary of BAT, the world's second-largest private producer of cigarettes. An editorial in this issue states that "[t]he documents show ... that executives at B&W knew early on that tobacco use was harmful and that nicotine was addictive ... that the industry decided to conceal the truth from the public ... that despite their knowledge to the contrary, the industry's public position was (and continues to be) that the link between smoking and ill health was not proven ... and that nicotine was not addictive." The editorial concludes that "the evidence is unequivocal—the U.S. public has been duped by the tobacco industry."[142]

Moreover, the cigarette industry intentionally targets young people—who are not always capable of assessing the consequences of their choices—with its ads, and it is successful. Some 2.6 million youngsters between the ages of 12 and 18 are smokers.[143]

In addition, the EPA has released data on the dangers of "secondhand" tobacco smoke (which nonsmokers breathe when smoking is going on around them). They report that each year, secondhand smoke causes 3,000 lung cancer deaths, contributes to 150,000 to 300,000 respiratory infections in babies, exacerbates the asthmatic symptoms of 400,000 to 1,000,000 children with the disease, and triggers 8,000 to 26,000 new cases of asthma in children who don't yet have the disease.[144] A 1993 issue of *JAMA* reported that tobacco contributes to 10 percent of infant deaths.[145]

Let's be clear: We do not advocate making cigarette smoking illegal on the model of our failed attempts to make drugs like heroin illegal. Restrictions on advertising aimed at youngsters, more substantial and pointed warnings on tobacco packaging, measures to protect nonsmokers from secondhand smoke, and perhaps higher insurance premiums for those who choose to smoke, seem reasonable.

Research from the early 1980s found that the average American consumes *one pound* of chemical *food additives* per year.[146] Speaking on the floor of the U.S. Senate in 1972, Senator Gaylord Nelson said,

> People are finally waking up to the fact that the average American daily diet is substantially adulterated with unnecessary and poisonous chemicals and frequently filled with neutral, nonnutritious substances. We are being chemically medicated against our will and cheated of food value by low nutrition foods.[147]

A hard look at the chemicals we eat and at the federal agency empowered to protect us against eating dangerous chemicals reveals the recklessness with which we are being "medicated against our will." Thirty years ago, Beatrice Hunter wrote *The Mirage of Safety,* a catalog of the dangers in the foods people ate. It also described how the Food and Drug Administration, through a combination of lax enforcement and uncritical acceptance of the results of the food industry's own "scientific" research, had allowed the American public to be a guinea pig for nearly 3,000 food additives. As a result, we were—and are—subjected to chemicals strongly suspected of producing cancer, gallbladder ailments, hyperkinesis (now called attention deficit and hyperactivity) in children; in others they "may adversely affect the rate of DNA, RNA, and protein synthesis"; and to still others suspected of causing birth defects.[148]

Today, the problem is worse. Americans consume more than 15 million pounds of artificial food dyes. There is enough research linking certain petroleum-derived food dyes with hyperactivity that "the British government told the food and restaurant industries to eliminate the dyes" in 2009, and the European Union requires foods and beverages containing any of six dyes to carry "a warning on the label that the colour 'may have effects on activity and attention in children'."[149] Because of this warning, many multinational corporations reformulate food to be dye free for Europe while leaving them for U.S. consumers. For example, in England, McDonald's strawberry sundaes use no artificial dye; but in the U.S., artificial dye Red 40 is used in the product.

The food additives are, of course, only some of the dangerous chemicals that we eat. During the late 1990s, American farmers applied about 1.1 billion pounds of more than 600 different types of pesticide.[150] Dr. Landrigan of the Mount Sinai School of Medicine, in a 1992 issue of the *American Journal of Public Health,* points to

> recent data from the US Environmental Protection Agency (EPA) showing that infants and young children are permitted to have dietary exposures to potentially carcinogenic and neurotoxic pesticides that exceed published standards by a factor of more than 1000.[151]

Landrigan also estimates that between 3 and 4 million American preschool children have dangerously elevated blood-lead levels, which could result in long-term neuropsychological impairment.

To call government and industry practices reckless is mild in view of the fact that, in spite of the growth in knowledge about the prevention and cure of cancer, the number of American who contract and die from cancer continues to rise. Based on the knowledge we have, there can be no doubt that air pollution, tobacco, and food additives amount to a chemical war that makes the crime wave look like a football scrimmage. Even with the most conservative estimates, it is clear that *the death toll in this war is far higher than the number of people killed by criminal homicide!*

Poverty Kills

We are long past the day when we could believe that poverty was caused by forces outside human control. Poverty is "caused" by lack of money, which means that once a society reaches a level of prosperity at which many enjoy a relatively high standard of living, then poverty can be eliminated or at least reduced significantly by transferring some of what the "haves" have to the "have-nots." In other words, regardless of what caused poverty in the past, what causes it to continue in the present is the refusal of those who have more to share with those who have less. Now you may think these remarks as trite or naïve. They are not offered as an argument for redistribution of income, although we believe that such redistribution is long overdue. These remarks are presented to make a much simpler point, which is that poverty exists in a wealthy society like ours *because we allow it to exist.* Therefore, we[152] share responsibility for poverty and for its consequences.

The poverty for which we are responsible "remains," in the words of *Business Week* in 1992, "stubbornly high."[153] The problem has persisted and was made worse by financial crisis of 2008. Moreover, it has particularly nasty features. For example, it affects blacks and children at a rate higher than the national average. In 2010, 9.9 percent of white (non-Hispanic) Americans and 27.4 percent of black Americans were below the poverty level.[154] Among children, in 2009, about 17 percent of white children and about 35 percent of black children lived in poverty.[155] A study published by the Urban Institute ranked the United States highest in child poverty among the eight industrialized nations studied. Moreover, the Urban Institute estimates that 2.3 million Americans experience homelessness each year, including 1 million children who are also exposed to interruptions in, or lack of, education each year.[156] Of the homeless, some 29 to 46 percent work, which means that at least half a million working Americans cannot afford shelter.[157]

We are prone to think that the consequences of poverty are fairly straightforward: Less money means fewer things. So poor people have fewer clothes or cars or appliances, go to the theater less often, and live in smaller homes with less or cheaper furniture. This is true and sad, but perhaps not intolerable. In addition, however, one of the things poor people have less of is *good health.* Less money means less nutritious food, less heat in winter, worse air quality in summer, less distance from other sick people or from unhealthy work or toxic waste dumping sites, less knowledge about illness or medicine, fewer doctor visits and childhood immunizations, fewer dental visits, less preventive health care, and (in the United States at least) less first-quality medical attention when all these other deprivations take their toll and a poor person finds him- or herself seriously ill. The result is that the poor suffer more from poor health and die earlier than those who are well-off. Poverty robs them of their days while they are alive and kills them before their time. A prosperous society that allows poverty in its midst is a party to murder.

A review of more than 30 historical and contemporary studies of the relationship of economic class to life expectancy affirms the conclusion that "class influences one's chances of staying alive. Almost without exception, the evidence shows that classes differ on mortality rates."[158] An article in *JAMA* in 1993 confirms the existence of this cost of poverty:

> People who are poor have higher mortality rates for heart disease, diabetes mellitus, high blood pressure, lung cancer, neural tube defects, injuries, and low birth weight, as well as lower survival rates from breast cancer and heart attacks.[159]

A 1998 news release from the U.S. Department of Health and Human Services confirms the continued "strong relationship between socioeconomic status and health in the United States for every race and ethnic group studied."[160] A 2005 *Washington Post* article headlined "Race Gap Persists in Health Care, Three Studies Say" reports on a study by a Harvard School of Public Health researcher published in the *New England Journal of Medicine*. The researcher is quoted as commenting, "We have known for 20 years that we have a problem in our health care system: blacks and whites do not receive equal care. We hoped all the attention paid to this topic would result in some improvement. What we found is that we have not made much progress."[161]

An article in a 2011 issue of the *American Journal of Public Health* reported the results of an analysis of 50 studies of deaths attributable to "social factors." The authors found that in 2000, 133,000 deaths were attributable to individual-level poverty, 119,000 to income inequality, and 39,000 to area-level poverty—and another 176,000 to racial segregation. Their results are consistent with the findings of earlier studies done with different methodologies.[162] For example, a 2004 study found that almost 900,000 deaths could have been prevented during the decade of the 1990s, if African Americans received the same care as whites did.[163] Numerous other studies have suggested that allocation of health services is marked by racial bias.[164]

A comparison of the health and mortality of blacks and whites in America yields further insight into the relationship of health and mortality to economic class. In 2010, one of every four blacks lived below the poverty line, as compared with one of every 10 whites. In 2007, black infant mortality (during the first year of life) was 13.2 per 1,000 live births, compared with 5.6 per 1,000 for whites.[165] In short, black mothers lost their babies within the first year of life more than twice as often as white mothers did. In the face of this persistent disparity, the Reagan administration reduced funding for maternal and child health programs by more than 25 percent and attempted to reduce support for immunization programs for American children.[166]

Cancer survival statistics show a similar picture. Between 2001 and 2007, 59.4 percent of blacks diagnosed with cancer were still alive five years after the diagnosis, compared with 68.6 percent of whites.[167] This disparity has been noted since at least the early 1970s. One important cause of this difference is that "white patients tended to have higher percentages of cancers diagnosed while localized,"[168] that is, earlier in their development. This means, at a minimum, that at least some of the difference turns out to be due to such things as better access to medical care, higher levels of education about the early-warning signs of cancer, and so on, all of which correlate strongly with higher income levels. Data reported in the journal *Science* suggest that "blacks get more cancer not because they're black, but because they're poor."[169] A study of the stage at which women had breast cancer diagnosed, found that white and black women living in areas characterized by lower average income and educational attainment were diagnosed later than those in areas marked by higher income and educational attainment. Within the same areas, black women were diagnosed later than whites, except in the areas of highest income and education, where the black disadvantage disappeared.[170] "And while black women show a lower incidence of breast cancer than white women, they nevertheless die from it more often."[171]

Life expectancy figures paint the most tragic picture of all. For 2007, life expectancy among blacks born that year was 73.6 years, whereas among whites it was 78.4 years.[172] That this difference cannot be attributed wholly to genetic factors is borne out by a "study of the relative contribution of various risk factors and income levels to mortality among blacks" reported in *JAMA*. The study "estimated that 38 percent of excess [of black over white] mortality could be accounted for by family income."[173] A stronger conclusion is reached by a study reported in a 1992 issue of the *American Journal of Public Health,* whose authors concluded, "In no instance were Black–White differences in all-cause or coronary mortality significantly different when socioeconomic status was controlled."[174]

A report from the Pew Environmental Health Commission says: "Our analysis shows that the burden of asthma falls most heavily on those below the poverty line. ... This is most likely due to higher risks among those in poverty for poor indoor air quality, air pollution, infections, poor nutrition, lack of breast feeding of babies, and other factors known to be associated with asthma development and/or exacerbation. This gap has been constant for at least 20 years."[175]

The number of poor Americans continues to grow each year. By 2010 it was 46.2 million, up from 30.1 million in 1990 and from 25.2 million in 1980.[176] In 2010, the Census Department records 49.9 million people without health insurance coverage (and that doesn't include those who are inadequately covered).[177] The percentage of the poor covered by Medicaid has gone from 65 percent to less than 40 percent. Hardest hit have been poor women and their children, many of whom have been removed from Medicaid coverage because income eligibility rules have not kept up with inflation. "In 1986, the average state income cutoff for Medicaid was 48 percent of the federal poverty level, compared to 71 percent in 1975."[178] Estimates indicate that only one-third of those who lose Medicaid benefits get private insurance; the rest do without. Moreover, the percent of nonelderly Americans doing without has grown in the past decade: It was 14.8 percent of the population in 1987 and 17.2 percent in 2005.[179] According to the National Academy of Sciences, lack of health insurance results in some 18,000 premature deaths a year because people without insurance don't get the health care they need.[180] Sadly, inadequate health insurance also often leads to poverty because "the leading cause of personal bankruptcy in the United States is unpaid medical bills."[181]

The World Health Organization and various human rights statutes recognize a right to health that is fundamental to enjoying other rights. Not every disease is a violation of human rights, but public health researchers note a category of health inequities that raise ethical concerns because they are avoidable and associated with social disadvantage and discrimination.[182] Such inequities are identified by comparing the health levels of the socially disadvantaged with those of the most privileged groups. Those levels are clearly attainable and provide "minimum standards for what should be possible for everyone in that society."[183] Needless to say, we are nowhere near providing these levels of health to poor Americans.

In short, *poverty hurts, injures, and kills—just like crime.* A society that could remedy its poverty but does not is an accomplice in crime.

Summary

The criminal justice system does not protect us against the gravest threats to life, limb, or possessions. Its definitions of crime are not simply a reflection of the objective dangers that threaten us. The workplace, the medical profession, the air we breathe, and the poverty we refuse to rectify lead to far more human suffering, result in far more death and disability, and take far more dollars from our pockets than the murders, aggravated assaults, and thefts reported annually by the FBI. What is more, this human suffering is preventable. The government could treat many of these harmful behaviors as criminal, and turn the massive powers of the state against their perpetrators in the way that they are turned against the perpetrators of the so-called common crimes. But it does not. A government really intent on protecting us would strengthen and enforce work safety regulations, police the medical profession, require that clean-air standards be met, be more attentive to the massive chemical exposure faced by the public, and devote sufficient resources to the poor to alleviate the major disabilities of poverty. But it does not. Instead we hear a lot of cant about law and order and a lot of rant about crime in the streets. It is as if our leaders were not only refusing to protect us from the major threats to our well-being, but also trying to cover up this refusal by diverting our attention to crime, as if it were the only real threat.

As we have seen, the criminal justice system is a carnival mirror that presents a distorted image of what threatens us. The distortions do not end with the definitions of crime. As we will see in what follows, new distortions enter at every level of the system, so that, in the end, when we look in our prisons to see who really threatens us, virtually all we see are poor people. By that time, most of the well-to-do people who endanger us have been discreetly weeded out of the system. As we watch this process unfold in the next chapter, bear in mind the conclusion of the present chapter: All the mechanisms by which the criminal justice system comes down more frequently and more harshly on the poor criminal than on the well-off criminal take place *after most of the dangerous acts of the well-to-do have been excluded from the definition of crime itself.* The bias against the poor within the criminal justice system is all the more striking when we recognize that the door to that system is shaped in a way that excludes in advance the most dangerous acts of the well-to-do. Demonstrating this has been the purpose of the present chapter.

Note that the question of what should be defined as crimes is a philosophical question that requires us to reflect on the proper aims of a criminal justice system. In this chapter, we have pointed out the important consequences for criminal justice and public well-being of how "crime" is defined. In Appendix II, Jeffrey Reiman argues that the social science of criminology needs a similar philosophical reflection on the proper definition of crime "in order to establish its intellectual independence of the state, which … is equivalent to declaring its status as a social science rather than an agency of social control, as critical rather than servile, as illumination rather than propaganda."

Study Questions

1. What should be our definition of the term "crime"? Why does it matter what we call things? Should there be an overlap between the acts we label crimes and the acts we think are morally wrong?
2. Quickly—without thinking about it—picture to yourself a criminal. Describe what you see. Where did this picture come from? Are there people in our society who pose a greater danger to you than the individual you pictured? Why or why not?
3. What is meant by likening the criminal justice system to a "carnival mirror"?
4. Do you believe the criminal law as it stands is correct in what it labels as a crime? In answering, be sure to review the objections made by the Defenders of the Present Legal Order, and the authors' responses.
5. Do you think a business executive who refuses to invest in safety precautions with the result that several workers die is morally better than, equal to, or worse than a mugger who kills his victim after robbing him? What if the executive knowingly violated a safety regulation? What if the mugger was high on drugs? Explain your response.
6. What is meant by speaking of criminal justice as "creative art"? How does the view presented here differ from that of Quinney?
7. Give examples of social practices that are more dangerous to your well-being than common crime. How should these practices be dealt with?

Additional Resources

Jeffrey Reiman and Paul Leighton, *The Rich Get Richer and Poor Get Prison: A Reader* (Boston: Pearson, 2010). This volume is a collection of accessible articles that were either used as reference material for *The Rich Get Richer* or provide lively complementary examples or analysis. The reader is divided into sections that parallel the chapters of *The Rich Get Richer*, and each section of the reader opens with a substantial introduction, written by the editors, that provides article summaries, context, and linkages to *The Rich Get Richer*.

The authors also maintain a companion website to the text at *http://www.paulsjusticepage.com/reiman.htm*

Notes

1. "Company in Mine Deaths Set to Pay Big Fine," *The New York Times*, February 21, 1993, p. A19.
2. "Mass Murder on the 5:33," *The New York Times*, December 10, 1993, p. A34.
3. Alvin Brown. No date. Fatal Underground Mine Explosion April 5, 2010: Upper Big Branch Mine-South, Performance Coal Company Montcoal, Raleigh County, West Virginia, ID No. 46-08436, p. 2. Washington, D.C.: U.S. Department of Labor, Mine Safety and Health Administration. *http://www.msha.gov/Fatals/2010/UBB/PerformanceCoalUBB.asp*.
4. Editorial. 2011. "Unsettled Justice at Upper Big Branch," *New York Times*, Dec 7. *http://www.nytimes.com/2011/12/08/opinion/unsettled-justice-at-upper-big-branch.html?*
5. Gerald R. Ford, "To Insure Domestic Tranquility: Mandatory Sentence for Convicted Felons," speech delivered at the Yale Law School Sesquicentennial Convocation, New Haven, CT, April 25, 1975, in *Vital Speeches of the Day* 41, no. 15 (May 15, 1975): 451.
6. "Arrest Data Reveal Profile of Suspect," *The Washington Post*, September 16, 1975, p. C1.
7. Ibid.; see also Maryland–National Capital Parks and Planning Commission, *Crime Analysis 1975: Prince George's County* (August 1975), p. 86.
8. *UCR–1974*, p. 186.
9. Maryland–National Capital Parks and Planning Commission, *Crime Analysis 1975*, p. 3.
10. See *UCR–1974*, p. 190.
11. "Arrest Data Reveal Profile of Suspect," p. C1; and Maryland–National Capital Parks and Planning Commission, *Crime Analysis 1975*, p. 86.
12. *UCR–1974*, p. 190.
13. *UCR–2010*, Table 31 and 42.
14. Lawrence W. Sherman, "Reducing Gun Violence: What Works, What Doesn't, What's Promising," NIJ, *Perspectives on Crime and Justice: 1999–2000 Lecture Series*, March 2001, NCJ 184245, p. 75.
15. *UCR–2010*, Table 43A; and calculations from *StatAbst–2011*, Table 6, p. 10. New census procedures allow for counting of multiple races, so those who identify as black only are 12.9 percent (39,641,000 out of a total population of 299,398,000); those who identify as black and some other race are 13.6 percent (41,804,000 out of a total population of 299,398,000).

16. BJS, *Profile of Jail Inmates 2002*, July 2004, NCJ 201932.

17. *Challenge*, p. 44; see also p. 160.

18. Anthony Bouza, *How to Stop Crime* (New York: Plenum, 1993), p. 57.

19. Quoted in George Will, "A Measure of Morality," *The Washington Post*, December 16, 1993, p. A25.

20. Brian Faler, "Bennett under Fire for Remark on Crime and Black Abortions," *The Washington Post*, September 30, 2005, A05.

21. Kathryn Russell, *The Color of Crime: Racial Hoaxes, White Fear, Black Protectionism, Police Harassment, and Other Macroaggressions* (New York: New York University Press, 1998), p. 3; cited in Marjorie S. Zatz, "The Convergence of Ethnicity, Gender, and Class on Court Decisionmaking: Looking toward the 21st Century," in NIJ, *Criminal Justice 2000, volume 3: Policies, Processes, and Decisions of the Criminal Justice System*, NCJ 182410, p. 507.

22. Zatz, "The Convergence of Ethnicity, Gender, and Class on Court Decisionmaking," p. 509.

23. Ibid.

24. "Mass news representations in the 'information age' have become the most significant communication by which the average person comes to know the world outside his or her immediate experience"; Gregg Barak, *Media, Process and the Social Construction of Crime* (New York: Garland, 1994), p. 3.

25. This transformation has been noted by Erving Goffman in his sensitive description of total institutions, *Asylums* (Garden City, N.Y.: Doubleday, 1961):

    > The interpretative scheme of the total institution automatically begins to operate as soon as the inmate enters, the staff having the notion that entrance is prima facie evidence that one must be the kind of person the institution was set up to handle. A man in a political prison must be traitorous; a man in a prison must be a law-breaker; a man in a mental hospital must be sick. If not traitorous, criminal, or sick, why else would he be here? (p. 84)

    So, too, a person who calls forth the society's most drastic weapons of defense must pose the gravest danger to its well-being. Why else the reaction? The point is put well and tersely by D. Chapman: "There is a circular pattern in thinking: we are hostile to wicked people, wicked people are punished, punished people are wicked, we are hostile to punished people because they are wicked." ("The Stereotype of the Criminal and the Social Consequences," *International Journal of Criminology and Penology* 1 [1973]: 16).

26. Richard Quinney, *The Social Reality of Crime* (Boston: Little, Brown, 1970). In his later work, for example, *Critique of Legal Order: Crime Control in Capitalist Society* (Boston: Little, Brown, 1973), and *Class, State & Crime* (New York: McKay, 1977), Quinney moves clearly into a Marxist problematic and his conclusions dovetail with many in this book. In our view, however, Quinney has not yet accomplished a satisfactory synthesis between the "social reality" theory and his later Marxism. Elsewhere, Reiman has examined Quinney's theory from the standpoint of moral philosophy. See Jeffrey H. Reiman, "Doing Justice to Criminology: Reflections on the Implications for Criminology of Recent Developments in the Philosophy of Justice," in Marc Riedel and Duncan Chappell (ed.) *Issues in Criminal Justice: Planning and Evaluation* (New York: Praeger, 1976), pp. 134–42.

27. Discussions of monetary policy often use the term "fiat currency" to convey that dollars do not have value because they are linked to a gold standard or other extrinsic source of value. Fiat currencies have value because the government

declares them to have value and people then believe and behave as if the paper and coins have value.

28. Quinney, *The Social Reality of Crime*, p. 15.

29. *The Washington Post*, January 11, 1983, p. C10.

30. Lydia Voigt et al., *Criminology and Justice* (New York: McGraw-Hill, 1994), pp. 11–15; the quotation is on p. 15.

31. This answers Graeme Newman, who observes that most criminals on TV are white and wonders what the "ruling class" or conservatives "have to gain by denying the criminality of Blacks." Graeme R. Newman, "Popular Culture and Criminal Justice: A Preliminary Analysis," *Journal of Criminal Justice* 18 (1990): 261–74.

32. Newman, "Popular Culture and Criminal Justice," pp. 263–64.

33. Barbara Matusow, "If It Bleeds, It Leads," *Washingtonian*, January 1988, p. 102.

34. Victor Kappeler, Mark Blumberg, and Gary Potter, *Mythology of Crime and Criminal Justice*, 3rd ed. (Prospect Heights, IL: Waveland, 2000), pp. 41–42.

35. "Titillating Channels: TV Is Going Tabloid as Shows Seek Sleaze and Find Profits, Too," *The Wall Street Journal* (May 18, 1988): 1.

36. John P. Wright, Francis T. Cullen, and Michael B. Blankenship, "The Social Construction of Corporate Violence: Media Coverage of the Imperial Food Products Fire," *Crime & Delinquency* 41, no. 1 (January 1995): 32. We discuss this case in Chapter 3.

37. Lyndsey Layton, "Peanut Processor Ignored Salmonella Tests, Knowingly Sold Tainted Products." *Washington Post*, January 28, 2009. *http://www.washingtonpost. com/wp-dyn/content/article/2009/01/27/AR2009012702992.html?hpid=topnews*.

38. See Government Accountability Project. 2011. Salmonella victims to call for criminal charges against former peanut corp. CEO. *http://www.whistleblower. org/press/press-release-archive/2011/989-salmonella-victims-to-call-for-criminal-charges-against-former-peanut-corp-ceo*. A Google search for "peanut corporation salmonella victims" turned up no hits for coverage of the news conference in the first 50 results.

39. Another way to put the Defenders' claim here is that one-on-one harms are appropriately "crimes," while indirect harms are appropriately "torts." *Torts* are noncriminal harms that justify civil suits for damages, but not criminal prosecution and punishment. Since our dispute with the Defenders is about whether indirect harms *should* be crimes, these legal labels cannot resolve our dispute. They may, however, give readers familiar with legal terminology a different way of understanding what is at stake: The Defenders think that indirect harms are rightly treated as torts, while we think that many of them should count as crimes, and serious ones at that.

40. Hyman Gross, *A Theory of Criminal Justice* (New York: Oxford University Press, 1979), p. 78. See generally Chapter 3, "Culpability, Intention, Motive," which we have drawn on in making the argument of this and the following two paragraphs.

41. We owe this example, modeled on one by Hyman Gross, to Andrew W. Austin of the University of Wisconsin–Green Bay.

42. Occupational Safety and Health Administration, OSHA Facts, August 2007, *http://www.bls.gov/iif/*.

43. Nancy Frank, "Unintended Murder and Corporate Risk-Taking: Defining the Concept of Justifiability," *Journal of Criminal Justice* 16 (1988): 18.

44. *Model Penal Code*, final draft (Philadelphia: American Law Institute, 1962).

45. Russell Mokhiber, *Corporate Crime and Violence: Big Business Power and the Abuse of Public Trust* (San Francisco: Sierra Club, 1988), pp. 278, 285.

46. David E. Lilienfeld, "The Silence: The Asbestos Industry and Early Occupational Cancer Research—A Case Study," *American Journal of Public Health* 81, no. 6 (June 1991): 791. This article shows how early the industry knew of the link between asbestos and cancer and how hard they tried to suppress this information. See also Paul Brodeur, *Outrageous Misconduct: The Asbestos Industry on Trial* (New York: Pantheon, 1985).

47. Morton Mintz, "A Crime Against Women: A. H. Robbins and the Dalkon Shield," *Multinational Monitor* 7, no. 1 (January 15, 1986), *http://multinational-monitor.org/hyper/issues/1986/0115/index.html* .

48. Editorial, "Unsettled Justice at Upper Big Branch," *New York Times*.

49. Sir James Fitzjames Stephen, from his *History of the Criminal Law of England 2* (1883), excerpted in *Crime, Law and Society*, eds. Abraham S. Goldstein and Joseph Goldstein (New York: Free Press, 1971), p. 21.

50. Troy Duster, *The Legislation of Morality: Law, Drugs and Moral Judgment* (New York: Free Press, 1970), pp. 3–76.

51. Norval Morris and Gordon Hawkins, *The Honest Politician's Guide to Crime Control* (Chicago: University of Chicago Press, 1970), p. 2.

52. *Challenge*, p. 7.

53. *UCR–2010*, Table 1; definitions available at *http://www.fbi.gov/about-us/cjis/ucr/crime-in-the-u.s/2010/crime-in-the-u.s.-2010/violent-crime/murdermain* and *http://www.fbi.gov/about-us/cjis/ucr/crime-in-the-u.s/2010/crime-in-the-u.s.-2010/violent-crime/aggravatedassaultmain*.

54. *UCR–2010*, Property Crime Overview.

55. See Willard Oliver, "The Power to Persuade: Presidential Influence over Congress on Crime Control Policy," *Criminal Justice Review* 28, no. 1 (2003). The author finds *UCR* reported crime "to have the most impact on congressional committees and subcommittees initiating hearings on crime and drugs" (p. 125), and this factor remains significant across several variations in model specifications.

56. White House, *President's Report on Occupational Safety and Health* (Washington, D.C.: U.S. Government Printing Office, 1972).

57. "James Messerschmidt, in a comprehensive review of research studies on job-related accidents, determined that somewhere between 35 and 57 percent of those accidents occurred because of direct safety violations by the employer. Laura Shill Schraeger and James Short Jr. found 30 percent of industrial accidents resulted from safety violations and another 20 percent resulted from unsafe working conditions." Kappeler et al., *Mythology of Crime and Criminal Justice*, p. 104. See James Messerschmidt, *Capitalism, Patriarchy, and Crime: Toward a Socialist Feminist Criminology* (Totowa, NJ: Rowman & Littlefield, 1986); and Laura Shill Schraeger and James Short, "Toward a Sociology of Organizational Crime," *Social Problems* 25 (April 1978): 407–19. See also Joseph A. Page and Mary-Win O'Brien, *Bitter Wages: Ralph Nader's Study Group Report on Disease and Injury on the Job* (New York: Grossman, 1973); Rachel Scott, *Muscle and Blood* (New York: Dutton, 1974); Jeanne M. Stellman and Susan M. Daum, *Work Is Dangerous to Your Health* (New York: Vintage, 1973); and Joel Swartz, "Silent Killers at Work," *Crime and Social Justice* 3 (Summer 1975): 15–20.

58. BLS, "Workplace Injury and Illness–2010" October 20, 2010, pp. 1, 2, and Table 6A, Updated information is available from *http://www.bls.gov/news.release/pdf/osh.pdf*. Note that this survey "excludes farms with fewer than 11 employees."

59. BLS "Workplace Injury and Illness in 2006," October 16, 2007, p. 6.
60. General Accounting Office, "Enhancing OSHA's Records Audit Process Could Improve the Accuracy of Worker Injury and Illness Data," 2009, p. 1. GAO-10-10. *http://www.gao.gov/new.items/d1010.pdf.*
61. "Is OSHA Falling Down on the Job?" *The New York Times*, August 2, 1987, pp. A1, A6.
62. Lee Friedman and Linda Forst, "The Impact of OSHA Recordkeeping Regulation Changes on Occupational Injury and Illness Trends in the US," *Occupational and Environmental Medicine* 64 (2007): 454–60; quote from p. 459.
63. Philip Landrigan, testimony before the Senate Committee on Labor and Human Resources, April 18, 1988, p. 2. For cancer deaths, see *StatAbst–1988*, Table 117, p. 77 and Table 120, p. 80.
64. "Safety Group Cites Fatalities Linked to Work," *The Wall Street Journal* (August 31, 1990): B8; and Sally Squires, "Study Traces More Deaths to Working than Driving," *The Washington Post*, August 31, 1990, p. A7.
65. J. P. Leigh, S. B. Markowitz, M. Fahs, C. Shin, and P. J. Landrigan, "Occupational Injury and Illness in the United States: Estimates of Costs, and Morbidity, and Mortality," *Archives of Internal Medicine* 157, no. 14 (July 1997): 1557–68.
66. Cancer Prevention Coalition, "U.S. National Cancer Institute," *www.preventcancer.com/losing/nci/why_prevent.htm.*
67. J. Paul Leigh and John Robbins, "Occupational Disease and Workers, Compensation: Coverage, Costs and Consequences," *The Milbank Quarterly* 82, no. 4 (2004): 694.
68. NIOSH, "Worker Health Chartbook, 2000: Nonfatal Illness," April 2002. See also NIOSH, "Protecting Workers' Families: A Research Agenda," May 2002.
69. *StatAbst—2011*, Table 2, p. 8, Table 584, p. 377.
70. *Sourcebook Online*, Table 3.33.2008 (figures rounded to nearest whole percentage point).
71. BLS, "Fatal Workplace Injuries in 2010 (Preliminary Results)," *http://www.bls.gov/news.release/pdf/cfoi.pdf.* (BLS reports a total of 4,547 workplace fatalities, of which 506 are homicides.)
72. BJS, "Occupational Health and Safety Definitions," *http://www.bls.gov/iif/oshdef.htm.*
73. Friedman and Forst, p. 459, citing the National Electronic Injury Surveillance System.
74. Hilda Solis, "One Is Too Many," 2011. *http://social.dol.gov/blog/one-is-too-many/*
75. Philip J. Hilts, "U.S. Fines Mine Companies for False Air Tests," *The New York Times*, April 5, 1991, p. A12. The fines, by the way, amounted to a total of $5 million distributed among 500 mining companies found to have tampered with the coal-dust samples used to test for the risk of black lung disease.
76. Joan Claybrook and the Staff of Public Citizen, *Retreat from Safety: Reagan's Attack on America's Health* (New York: Pantheon, 1984), p. 83. Chronic brown lung is a severely disabling occupational respiratory disease. See also Page and O'Brien, *Bitter Wages*, p. 18.
77. Claybrook, *Retreat from Safety*, p. 97. See also Page and O'Brien, *Bitter Wages*, p. 23; and Scott, *Muscle and Blood*, p. 196.
78. Scott, *Muscle and Blood*, pp. 45–46; cf. Page and O'Brien, *Bitter Wages*, p. 25.
79. Cindy Skrzycki, "Alarm over a Sheepish Non-rule," *The Washington Post*, October 29, 2002, p. E1.

80. Curt Suplee, "House to Consider 'Ergo Rider' Restraints on OSHA," *The Washington Post*, July 11, 1996, p. A4. In 2010, carpal tunnel required a median of 27 days to recuperate. BLS, "Nonfatal Occupational Injuries and Illnesses Requiring Days Away From Work," 2010. *http://www.bls.gov/news.release/osh2.nr0.htm*.

81. Friedman and Forst, p. 459.

82. David Michaels, Speech to Public Citizen, January 18, 2011. *http://osha.gov/pls/oshaweb/owadisp.show_document?p_table=SPEECHES&p_id=2380*.

83. David Barstow, "When Workers Die: U.S. Rarely Seeks Charges for Deaths in Workplace," *The New York Times*, December 22, 2003, p. A1, *http://www.nytimes.com/2003/12/22/national/22OSHA.html*. Barstow found 1,242 cases of deaths related to willful violations between 1982 and 2002, but OSHA declined prosecution in 93 percent of the cases. Recently, "OSHA began to accede to employer demands that it replace the word 'willful' with 'unclassified' in citations involving workplace deaths."

84. David Michaels, Testimony before the Subcommittee On Workforce Protections, Committee On Education and Labor, U.S. House Of Representatives, March 16, 2010. *http://www.osha.gov/pls/oshaweb/owadisp.show_document?p_table=TESTIMONIES&p_id=1062*; AFL-CIO. 2011. *Death on the Job. http://www.aflcio.org/issues/safety/memorial/upload/dotj_2011.pdf*, p. 21 (citing an April 2008 report on OSHA enforcement in fatality cases prepared by the majority staff of the Senate Committee on Health, Education, Labor and Pensions). Protecting America's Workers Act proposed to increase penalties for cases involving willful or repeat violations that result in a fatality to $250,000—"the level where they will have the same value, accounting for inflation, as they had in 1990." PAWA died in Congress and has not even been reintroduced.

85. David Michaels,Testimony before the Committee On Education and The Workforce, Subcommittee On Workforce Protections, U.S. House Of Representatives, October 5, 2011. *http://osha.gov/pls/oshaweb/owadisp.show_document?p_table=TESTIMONIES&p_id=1482*.

86. Barbara Starfield, MD, MPH, "Is US Health Really the Best in the World?" *Journal of the American Medical Association* 284, no. 4 p. 483 (July 26, 2000), *http://jama.jamanetwork.com/article.aspx?articleid=192908*.

87. Centers for Disease Control and Prevention, "Estimating Health Care-Associated Infections and Deaths in U.S. Hospitals, 2002," *http://www.cdc.gov/ncidod/dhqp/pdf/hicpac/infections_deaths.pdf*; D. Diekama and M. Climo, "Preventing MRSA Infections: Finding it is Not Enough," *JAMA* 299, no. 10 (2008): 1190–92; and "Publication of Guidance on Public Reporting of Healthcare-Associated Infections," *JAMA* 294 (2005): 896, *http://jama.ama-assn.org/cgi/content/full/294/8/896*. See also *http://hospitalinfectionrates.org*; and "Coming Clean," *The New York Times*, June 6, 2005, p. A19.

88. See, for example, the work of Dr. Peter Pronovost discussed in the text accompanying note 104.

89. *The Washington Post*, July 16, 1975, p. A3.

90. George A. Silver, "The Medical Insurance Disease," *Nation* 222, no. 12 (March 27, 1976): 369.

91. Ibid., p. 371.

92. *Newsweek*, March 29, 1976, p. 67. Lest anyone think this is a new problem, compare this passage written in a popular magazine over 40 years ago:

> *Unnecessary operations on women, stemming from the combination of a trusting patient and a split fee, have been so deplored by honest doctors that the phrase "rape of the pelvis"*

has been used to describe them. The American College of Surgeons, impassioned foe of fee-splitting, has denounced unnecessary hysterectomies, uterine suspensions, Caesarian sections. (Howard Whitman, "Why Some Doctors Should Be in Jail," *Colliers* [October 30, 1953]: 24).

93. *StatAbst–2011*, Table 171, p. 118.

94. *UCR–2010*, Expanded Homicide Data Table 8.

95. Sandra G. Boodman, "No End to Errors," *The Washington Post Health*, December 3, 2002, p. F1. The original report was L. Kohn, J. Corrigan, and M. Donaldson, eds., *To Err Is Human: Building a Safer Health System* (Washington, D.C.: National Academy Press, 1999).

96. Ibid., p. F6.

97. Rick Weiss, "Medical Errors Blamed for Many Deaths: As Many as 98,000 a Year in U.S. Linked to Mistakes," *The Washington Post*, November 30, 1999, p. A1.

98. Boodman, "No End to Errors," p. F1.

99. Ibid., p. F6.

100. Lucien Leape and Donald Berwick, "Five Years After *To Err Is Human*: What Have We Learned?" *Journal of the American Medical Association* 293, no. 19 (2005): 2384–90.

101. Atul Gawande, "The Checklist," *The New Yorker*, December 10, 2007, *http://www.newyorker.com/reporting/2007/12/10/071210fa_fact_gawande*. See also Peter Pronovost et al., "An Intervention to Decrease Catheter-Related Bloodstream Infections in the ICU," *New England Journal of Medicine* 356, no. 25 (2007): 2660, *http://www.nejm.org/doi/pdf/10.1056/NEJMoa061115*. An interview with Pronovost discusses the larger implications, including the problem of getting his projects funded, *http://histalk2.com/2008/02/11/histalk-interviews-peter-pronovost-md-phd-johns-hopkins-university/*.

102. Denise Grady, "Study Finds No Progress in Safety at Hospitals," *New York Times*, November 24, 2010. *http://www.nytimes.com/2010/11/25/health/research/25patient.html?_r=1&hpw*.

103. Silver, "The Medical Insurance Disease," p. 369. Silver's estimates are extremely conservative. Some studies suggest that between 30,000 and 160,000 individuals die as a result of drugs prescribed by their doctors. See Boyce Rensberger, "Thousands a Year Killed by Faulty Prescriptions," *The New York Times*, January 28, 1976, pp. A1, A17. If we assume with Silver that at least 20 percent are unnecessary, this puts the annual death toll from unnecessary prescriptions at between 6,000 and 32,000 persons. For an in-depth look at the recklessness with which prescription drugs are put on the market and the laxness with which the Food and Drug Administration exercises its mandate to protect the public, see the series of eight articles by Morton Mintz, "The Medicine Business," *The Washington Post*, June 27–30, July 1–4, 1976.

104. Paul Weiler, Howard Hiatt, Joseph Newhouse, William Johnson, Troyen Brennan, and Lucian Leape, *A Measure of Malpractice: Medical Injury, Malpractice Litigation and Patient Compensation* (Cambridge, MA: Harvard University Press, 1993), p. 54. The data given here come from the Harvard Medical Practice Study. See also Christine Russell, "Human Error: Avoidable Mistakes Kill 100,000 Patients a Year," *The Washington Post Health*, February 18, 1992, p. 7.

105. Sheryl Gay Stohlberg, "Faulty Warning Labels Add to Risk in Prescription Drugs," *The New York Times*, June 4, 1999, p. A27.

106. In 2009, total prescription drug expenditures were $250 billion. A conservative estimate that 10 percent of the dollars expended were unnecessary would be $25 billion. *StatAbst–2011*, Table 141, p. 104.

107. The rate of increase of medical costs is calculated from *StatAbst—1995*, Table 167, p. 117, which lists the medical care index at 47.5 for 1975 and *StatAbst—2011*, Table 142, p. 105, which lists the index at 388.4. Note that the assumption that the *number* of unnecessary operations and prescriptions has remained the same between 1974 and 2003 is a conservative assumption in that it effectively assumes that the rate of these practices relative to the population has declined because population has increased in the period.

108. American Cancer Society, "Cancer Facts & Figures 2011," p. 1. *http://www. cancer.org/Research/CancerFactsFigures/CancerFactsFigures/cancer-facts-figures-2011*.

109. President's Cancer Panel. 2010. *Reducing Environmental Cancer* (2008–2009 Annual Report). Washington, D.C.: U.S. Department of Health and Human Services, p. 1. *http://deainfo.nci.nih.gov/advisory/pcp/annualReports/index.htm*.

110. Lewis Regenstein, *America the Poisoned* (Washington, D.C.: Acropolis Books, 1982), pp. 246–47.

111. Editorial, "Cancer—Nature, Nurture, or Both," *New England Journal of Medicine* 343, no. 2 (July 13, 2000): 135.

112. President's Cancer Panel. 2010, pp. 5–6.

113. Samuel S. Epstein, Nicholas A. Ashford, Brent Blackwelder, Barry Castleman, Gary Cohen, Edward Goldsmith, Anthony Mazzocchi, and Quentin D. Young, "The Crisis in U.S. and International Cancer Policy," *International Journal of Health Services* 32, no. 4 (2002): 693.

114. Rick Weiss, "HHS Seeks Science Advice to Match Bush Views," *The Washington Post*, September 17, 2002, p. A1. Erin Brokovitch sued the utility company PG&E for the contamination of a community's drinking water and won $300 million in 1993. A story that was later made into a popular Hollywood film, *Erin Brokovitch*.

115. President's Cancer Panel. *Reducing Environmental Cancer*, transmittal letter (page not numbered).

116. President's Cancer Panel. *Reducing Environmental Cancer*, p. 19.

117. American Public Health Association. 2007. "Calling on the US Congress to Restructure the Toxic Substances Control Act of 1976," *http://www.apha.org/advocacy/ policy/policysearch/default.htm?id=1350*. The groups include the National Academy of Sciences, the US General Accounting Office, the Congressional Office of Technology Assessment, Environmental Defense, the US Environmental Protection Agency (EPA), former EPA officials, the US Government Accountability Office, and the University of California. Citations and links are available from the URL above.

118. Bob Weinhold, "Assessing the Global Composite Impact of Chemicals on Health," *Environmental Health Perspectives*, 2011, 119: a162–a163.

119. Phillip J. Landrigan, Clyde B. Schechter, Jeffrey M. Lipton, Marianne C. Fahs, and Joel Schwartz, "Environmental Pollutants and Disease in American Children: Estimates of Morbidity, Mortality, and Costs for Lead Poisoning, Asthma, Cancer and Developmental Disabilities," *Environmental Health Perspectives* 110, no. 7 (July 2002): 726.

120. Leonardo Trasande, Phillip J. Landrigan, and Clyde B. Schechter, "Public Health and Economic Consequences of Methyl Mercury Toxicity to the Developing Brain," *Environmental Health Perspectives* 113, no. 5 (May 2005): 591, 593, 594. The EPA ruling was issued on March 15, 2005. The authors attribute approximately half the economic cost ($1.3 billion) to emissions from American coal-fired power plants.

121. Paul Cotton, "'Best Data Yet' Say Air Pollution Kills below Levels Currently Considered Safe," *Journal of the American Medical Association* 269, no. 24 (June 23–30, 1993): 3087. See also Michelle Bell et al., "Ozone and Short-Term Mortality in 95 US Urban Communities, 1987–2000," *JAMA* 292, no. 19 (2004): 2372–78.

122. Ali Mokdad, James Marks, Donna Stroup, and Julie Gerberding, "Actual Causes of Death in the United States: 2000," *JAMA* 291, no. 10 (2004): 1238–45.

123. Weinhold, Assessing the Global Composite Impact of Chemicals on Health.

124. Cited in Eric Pianin, "Study Ties Pollution, Risk of Lung Cancer," *The Washington Post*, March 6, 2002, p. A1.

125. Bill Richards, "Arsenic: A Dark Cloud over 'Big Sky Country,'" *The Washington Post*, February 3, 1976, pp. A1, A5.

126. Quotations in this paragraph are from Auerbach, "N.J.'s Chemical Belt Takes Its Toll," p. A1.

127. Quoted in Stuart Auerbach, "N.J.'s Chemical Belt Takes Its Toll: $4 Billion Industry Tied to Nation's Highest Cancer Death Rate," *The Washington Post*, February 8, 1976, p. A1.

128. Toxic Substances Strategy Committee, Council on Environmental Quality, *Toxic Chemicals and Public Protection: A Report to the President*, Washington, D.C., May 1980, p. 6; quoted by Regenstein, *America the Poisoned*, p. 184. See also p. 170 in Regenstein.

129. Michael Edelstein, *Contaminated Communities: The Social and Psychological Impacts of Residential Toxic Exposure* (Boulder, CO: Westview Press, 1988), p. 3.

130. Jay M. Gould, *Quality of Life in American Neighborhoods: Levels of Affluence, Toxic Waste, and Cancer Mortality in Residential Zip Code Areas* (Boulder, CO: Westview Press, 1986), pp. 22, 28.

131. Robert Bullard, "Environmental Justice for All," in Robert Bullard (ed.) *Unequal Protection: Environmental Justice and Communities of Color* (San Francisco: Sierra Club Books, 1994), p. 17.

132. Joan Claybrook, *Retreat from Safety*, pp. 117–29.

133. Walter A. Rosenbaum, "The Clenched Fist and the Open Hand: Into the 1990s at EPA," in N. Vig and M. Kraft (ed.) *Environmental Policy in the 1990s: Toward a New Agenda* (Washington, D.C.: CQ Press, a division of Congressional Quarterly Inc., 1994), p. 132.

134. Juliet Eilperin, "Lack of Funds Delaying Toxic Waste Cleanups," *The Washington Post*, July 28, 2004, p. A6.

135. David Fahrenthold, "Cosmic Markdown: EPA Says Life is Worth Less," *The Washington Post*, July 19, 2008, p. A1.

136. American Cancer Society, "Cancer Facts and Figures 2005," p. 40.

137. American Cancer Society, "Cancer Facts & Figures 2011" p. 35.

138. G. E. Guindon et al., *The Cost Attributable to Tobacco Use: A Critical Review of the Literature* (Geneva: World Health Organization, 2006); and Centers for Disease Control, *Smoking-Attributable Mortality, Years of Potential Life Lost, and Productivity Losses—United States, 2000–2004*.

139. *Scientific Priorities for Cancer Research: NCI's Extraordinary Opportunities: Research on Tobacco and Tobacco-Related Cancers*, http://web.archive.org/web/20021111135403/http://2001.cancer.gov/tobacco.htm.

140. "The Price of Tobacco: The Basics," *The New York Times*, March 23, 1993, p. A14.

141. Common Cause, the Campaign for Tobacco-Free Kids, the American Heart Association, and the American Lung Association, "Buying Influence, Selling Death: How Big Tobacco's Campaign Contributions Harm Public Health," March 14,

2001, pp. 1, 2, *www.commoncause.org*. The report is no longer available but updated information is available at *http://tobaccofreeaction.org/contributions/*.

142. Dr. James S. Todd et al., "The Brown and Williamson Documents: Where Do We Go From Here?" *Journal of the American Medical Association* 274, no. 3 (July 19, 1995): 256, 258.

143. "U.S. Urged to Escalate Tobacco War," *The Washington Post*, January 12, 2002, p. A17.

144. Geoffrey Cowley, "Poison at Home and at Work: A New Report Calls Second-hand Smoke a Killer," *Newsweek*, June 29, 1992, p. 55.

145. J.M. McGinnis and W.H. Foege, "Actual Causes of Death in the United States," p. 2208. *Journal of the American Medical Association*, 1993 Nov 10; 270(18): 2207–12.

146. Beatrice Hunter, *The Mirage of Safety* (New York: Penguin, 1982), p. 4.

147. Quoted in ibid., p. 2.

148. Hunter, *The Mirage of Safety* .

149. Sarah Kobylewski and Michael F. Jacobson, *Food Dyes: A Rainbow of Risks* (Washington, D.C.: Center for Science in the Public Interest, 2010), p. 4. *http://cspinet.org/new/pdf/food-dyes-rainbow-of-risks.pdf*. Food Standards Agency (UK). Compulsory warnings on colours in food and drink. *http://www.food.gov.uk/news/newsarchive/2010/jul/eucolourswarn*.

150. David Pimentel, "Environmental and Economic Costs of the Application of Pesticides Primarily in the United States," *Environment, Development, and Sustainability* 7 (2005): 229–52.

151. Philip Landrigan, "Commentary: Environmental Disease—A Preventable Epidemic," *American Journal of Public Health* 82, no. 7 (July 1992): 942.

152. At the very least, "we" includes all the households that earn considerably above the median income for the nation (around $49,445 for a household in 2010) and who resist, or who vote for candidates who resist, moves to redistribute income significantly.

153. Karen Pennar, "The Rich Are Richer—and America May Be the Poorer," *Business Week*, November 18, 1991, pp. 85–88

154. Carmen DeNavas-Walt, Bernadette Proctor, and Jessica Smith, U.S. Census Bureau, Income, Poverty & Health Insurance Coverage in the United States: 2010, Current Population Reports, P60-239 (Washington, D.C.: U.S. Government Printing Office, 2011), p. 15

155. *StatAbst—2012*, Table 712, p. 465.

156. The Urban Institute, *A New Look at Homelessness in America*, February 1, 2000, *www.urban.org/url.cfm?ID=900302*.

157. Urban Institute. 1999. "HOMELESSNESS: Programs and the People They Serve," p. 29. *http://www.urban.org/uploadedpdf/homelessness.pdf*.

158. Aaron Antonovsky, "Class and the Chance for Life," in Lee Rainwater (ed.) *Inequality and Justice* (Chicago: Aldine, 1974), p. 177.

159. McGinnis and Foege, "Actual Causes of Death in the United States," p. 2211.

160. *HHS News*, "Health in America Tied to Income and Education," July 30, 1998, *www.cdc.gov/nchs/pressroom/98news/huspr98.htm*. See also R. Wilkinson, *Unhealthy Societies: The Afflictions of Inequality* (London: Routledge, 1996).

161. Rob Stein, "Race Gap Persists in Health Care, Three Studies Say," *The Washington Post*, August 18, 2005, p. A1.

162. Sandro, Galea, Melissa Tracy, Katherine J. Hoggatt, Charles DiMaggio, and Adam Karpati, "Estimated Deaths Attributable to Social Factors in the United States," *American Journal of Public Health* 101, no. 8 (2011): 1456–65.

163. January Payne, "Dying for Basic Care," *The Washington Post,* December 21, 2004, p. HE1. The report itself notes that "socioeconomic conditions represent a more pertinent cause of disparities than race."

164. Jane Perkins, "Race Discrimination in America's Health Care System," Clearinghouse Review 27, no. 4 (1993): 371. Sonia Nazario, "Curing Doctors of Bedside Bias," *International Herald Tribune,* December 23, 1993, p. 8. Alan M. Gittelsohn et al., "Income, Race, and Surgery in Maryland," *American Journal of Public Health* 81, no. 11 (November 1991): 1435.

165. *Income, Poverty & Health Insurance Coverage in the United States,* 2007, p.13; and *StatAbst—2008,* Table 108, p. 81.

166. Robbins, "Can Reagan Be Indicted?" pp. 12–13. See also "Infant Mortality Down; Race Disparity Widens," *The Washington Post,* March 12, 1993, p. A11.

167. *StatAbst—2012,* Table 182, p. 124.

168. National Institutes of Health, *Cancer Patient Survival Experience,* June 1980, pp. 4–5.

169. Ann Gibbons, "Does War on Cancer Equal War on Poverty?" *Science* 253 (July 19, 1991): 260.

170. Barbara L. Wells and John W. Horm, "Stage at Diagnosis in Breast Cancer: Race and Socioeconomic Factors," *American Journal of Public Health* 82, no. 10 (October 1992): 1383.

171. Gibbons, "Does War on Cancer Equal War on Poverty?" p. 260.

172. *StatAbst—2012,* Table 104, p. 77. Richard Allen Williams reports that "there is no reason why the life span of the White should differ from that of the Black," in his *Textbook of Black-Related Diseases* (New York: McGraw-Hill, 1975), p. 2.

173. McGinnis and Foege, "Actual Causes of Death in the United States," p. 2211.

174. Julian E. Keil et al., "Does Equal Socioeconomic Status in Black and White Men Mean Equal Risk of Mortality?" *American Journal of Public Health* 82, no. 8 (August 1992): 1133.

175. Pew Environmental Health Commission. No date. "Attack Asthma: Why America Needs A Public Health Defense System To Battle Environmental Threats," p. 10.

176. *Income, Poverty & Health Insurance Coverage in the United States: 2010,* p. 14; *StatAbst—1996,* Table 49, p. 48.

177. *Income, Poverty & Health Insurance Coverage in the United States: 2010,* p. 23.

178. David Stipp, "The Tattered Safety Net"; see also Dan Goodgame, "Ready to Operate," *Time,* September 20, 1993, p. 55.

179. *StatAbs—2008,* Calculated from Table 148, p. 108.

180. Ceci Connolly, "Study: Uninsured Don't Get Needed Health Care: Delayed Diagnoses, Premature Deaths Result," *The Washington Post,* May 22, 2002, p. A3.

181. Malcolm Gladwell, "The Moral-Hazard Myth: The Bad Idea Behind Our Failed Health Care System," *The New Yorker,* August 29, 2005, *http://newyorker.com/archive/2005/08/29/050829fa_fact.*

182. P. Braveman and S. Gruskin, "Defining Equity in Health," *Journal of Epidemiology and Community Health* 57, no. 4 (2003): 254–58. Centers for Disease Control and Prevention. 2011. "CDC Health Disparities and Inequalities Report—United States, 2011," *Morbidity and Mortality Weekly Report,* January 14. Supplement, vol. 60. *http://www.cdc.gov/mmwr/pdf/other/su6001.pdf.*

183. Braveman and Gruskin, "Defining Equity in Health," p. 255.

CHAPTER **3**

... And the Poor Get Prison

When we come to make an intelligent study of the prison
at first hand ... we are bound to conclude that after all it
is not so much crime in its general sense that is penalized,
but that it is poverty which is punished.

Take a census of the average prison and you will find that a large
majority of people are there not so much because of the particular
crime they are alleged to have committed, but for the reason that they
are poor and ... lacked the money to engage the services of first class
and influential lawyers.

—EUGENE V. DEBS, *Walls and Bars*

Laws are like spiders' webs: they catch the weak and the small,
but the strong and the powerful break through them.

—SCYTHIAN, *one of the Seven Wise Men of Ancient Greece*

Chapter 3 of *The Rich Get Richer* examines the processes by which our prisons
and jails come to be occupied predominately by those from the lowest social
and economic classes. Having argued in Chapter 2 that the criminal law does
not treat as crimes many serious harmful acts done by the well-off, Chapter 3
now argues that, among the acts that are treated as crimes, the criminal justice
system "weeds out the wealthy." For similar crimes, the poor are more likely
to be arrested, more likely to be charged, more likely to be convicted, and
more likely to be sentenced to longer prison sentences, than members of
middle and upper classes.

WEEDING OUT THE WEALTHY

The offender at the end of the road in prison is likely to be a member of the lowest social and economic groups in the country.[1]

This statement in the *Report of the President's Commission on Law Enforcement*
and Administration of Justice is as true today as it was over four decades ago

when it was written. Our prisons are indeed, as Ronald Goldfarb has called them, the "national poorhouse."[2] To most citizens, this comes as no surprise—recall the Typical Criminal and the Typical Crime. Dangerous crimes, they think, are committed mainly by poor people. Seeing that prison populations are made up primarily of the poor only makes them surer of this. They think, in other words, that the criminal justice system gives a true reflection of the dangers that threaten them.

In our view, it also comes as no surprise that our prisons and jails predominantly confine the poor. This is not because these are the individuals who most threaten us. It is because the criminal justice system effectively weeds out the well-to-do, so that *at the end of the road in prison,* the vast majority of those we find there come from the lower classes. This weeding-out process starts before the agents of law enforcement go into action. Chapter 2 argued that our very definition of crime *excludes* a wide variety of actions at least as dangerous as those included and often worse. Is it any accident that the kinds of dangerous actions excluded are the kinds most likely to be performed by the affluent in America? Even before we mobilize our troops in the war on crime, we have already guaranteed that large numbers of upper-class individuals will never come within their sights.

This process does not stop at the definition of crime. It continues throughout each level of the criminal justice system. At each step, from arresting to sentencing, the likelihood of being ignored or released or treated lightly by the system is greater the better off one is economically. As the late U.S. Senator Philip Hart wrote,

> Justice has two transmission belts, one for the rich and one for the poor. The low-income transmission belt is easier to ride without falling off and it gets to prison in shorter order. The transmission belt for the affluent is a little slower and it passes innumerable stations where exits are temptingly convenient.[3]

This means that the criminal justice system functions from start to finish in a way that makes certain that "the offender at the end of the road in prison is likely to be a member of the lowest social and economic groups in the country." *For the same criminal behavior,* the poor are more likely to be arrested; if arrested, they are more likely to be charged; if charged, more likely to be convicted; if convicted, more likely to be sentenced to prison; and if sentenced, more likely to be given longer prison terms than members of the middle and upper classes.[4] In other words, the image of the criminal population one sees in our nation's jails and prisons is distorted by the shape of the criminal justice system itself. It is the face of evil reflected in a carnival mirror, but it is no laughing matter.

The face in the criminal justice carnival mirror is also, as we have already noted, very frequently a black face. Although blacks do not make up the majority of the inmates in our jails and prisons, they make up a proportion that far outstrips their proportion in the population. Here, too, the image we see is distorted by the processes of the criminal justice system itself—a distortion that has been going on for decades. Edwin Sutherland and Donald Cressey wrote, in the 1974 edition of their widely used textbook *Criminology,* that

> numerous studies have shown that African-Americans are more likely to be arrested, indicted, convicted, and committed to an institution than are whites who commit the same offenses, and many other studies have shown that blacks have a poorer chance than whites to receive probation, a suspended sentence, parole, commutation of a death sentence, or pardon.[5]

The latest edition of this classic says much the same, adding only that blacks are not arrested or convicted more in those cases where a black victimizes a black—suggesting that bias against black victims works together with bias against black offenders.[6]

Many still believe that blacks are overrepresented in prison *only* because they commit more than their share of crimes. But, in 2008, respondents to the *National Crime Victimization Survey (NCVS)* reported that approximately 23 percent of their assailants in violent victimizations (rape, robbery, and simple and aggravated assault) were perceived to be black. That same year, the FBI indicated that 32 percent of the arrests for rape were of blacks, along with 56 percent of robbery arrests, 34 percent of aggravated assault arrests, and 32 percent of arrests for other assaults. These figures suggest that police are arresting blacks much more frequently than the occurrence of their perceived offenses.[7] Because arrest determines the pool from which charged, convicted, and imprisoned individuals are selected, this means that deep bias persists throughout the criminal justice system.

There are various problems with comparing *UCR* and *NCVS* statistics, and various possible explanations for the divergence of black–white arrest rates from the rates at which blacks and whites are perceived offenders. Thus, we do not claim that the results just presented prove definitively the presence of racism. Nonetheless, the results are consistent with studies that examine disproportionate minority contact (DMC) with the criminal justice system while controlling for differential rates of criminal activity. In research based on extensive data in three cities, researchers concluded that: "The often stated reason for DMC—that it simply reflects the difference in offending rates among different racial/ethnic groups— cannot be supported by the information provided by these three studies, and we suspect that it is simply incorrect in general."[8] Thus, we follow the majority of researchers in holding that the criminal justice system is widely marked by racial discrimination as well as by economic bias.[9] For example, Cassia Spohn reviewed 40 "recent and methodologically sophisticated studies investigating the linkages between race/ethnicity and sentence severity," and found that

> these studies suggest that race and ethnicity do play an important role in contemporary sentencing decisions. Black and Hispanic offenders—and particularly those who are young, male, or unemployed—are more likely than their white counterparts to be sentenced to prison; in some jurisdictions, they also receive longer sentences ... than do similarly situated white offenders.[10]

Spohn and others like Marvin Free note that studies concluding that racial discrimination was negligible often had many methodological short-comings, especially ignoring *indirect* and *interaction* effects. For example, some studies have shown that black defendants are less likely than whites to be released on bail prior to trial. Because pretrial detention increases the likelihood of eventual incarceration, discrimination at the bail decision will *indirectly* produce greater likelihoods of prison sentences for blacks than whites.[11] Moreover, blacks who victimize whites receive harsher sentences than whites who victimize whites, and blacks who victimize blacks receive the lightest sentences. Thus, race of victim *interacts* with offender race to produce biased sentences. This will be so even if, overall, sentences for black criminals are no worse than those for white criminals due to the fact that harshness for black-on-white crimes and leniency for black-on-black crimes may cancel each other out. Such facts have led Spohn to conclude that the question should no longer be "'does race make a difference?' but, rather '*when* does race make a difference—under what conditions, for what types of offenders, and in interaction with what other factors?'"[12]

Interestingly, statistics on differential treatment of races are available in abundance while statistics on differential treatment of economic classes are rare and getting rarer. Although the FBI tabulates arrest rates by race (as well as by sex, age, and geographic area), it omits class or income. The *Sourcebook of Criminal Justice Statistics* shows household income categories only for crime victims. Both independent and government data gatherers are more willing to own up to America's racism than to its class bias. Writes Majorie Zatz, "Class is one of the paramount sociological variables, yet our measures of it in criminal justice data are abysmal." She continues, "There is general recognition among scholars that some of the race effects that have been found [in research on sentencing] may be due in part to class effects."[13]

We will take advantage of this last hint and use race as a rough proxy for class. Certainly racism is a distinct, resilient, and powerful form of bias in our system, and it often targets well-off blacks. Racism has a long, inglorious history in American society, in which the massive imprisonment of young black men in the last decades is but the latest in a series of policies controlling and isolating blacks that spans slavery, Jim Crow,[14] and northern ghettoization.[15] In emphasizing class, we do not wish to minimize the importance of race. Our goal is to provide much-needed discussion about the reality of economic discrimination. As sociologist William Julius Wilson wrote, in *The Declining Significance of Race*, the point is not to deny the reality of racism, but to highlight the importance of class structure for blacks.[16]

Michelle Alexander's important book *New Jim Crow* argues that illegal discrimination against blacks has been replaced by legal discrimination against black criminals. That is, once blacks are labeled as "criminals," then whites can "engage in all the discriminatory practices we supposedly left behind." Blacks with criminal records are subject to "legalized discrimination in employment, housing, education, public benefits and jury service, just as their parents, grandparents and great-grandparents once were."[17] But calling this phenomenon a "new Jim Crow" suggests that class is not important, because the old Jim Crow treated rich and poor blacks similarly—neither could use the "whites only" drinking fountain. Today's mass incarceration, by contrast, is reserved primarily for poor blacks (and whites). We focus, then, on class bias because our criminal justice system now weeds out wealthy blacks as well as wealthy whites.

Though we use data on economic class where it is available, we will supplement this by using evidence of differential treatment of blacks—and of Hispanics—as evidence for differential treatment of members of the lower classes. Here are five reasons that support this strategy.

1. First and foremost, black Americans are disproportionately poor. In 2010, 9.9 percent of white non-Hispanic Americans lived below the poverty line compared to 27.4 percent of black Americans.[18] The picture is even worse when we shift from income to wealth (property such as a home, stocks, and savings). On average, blacks in America own one-fifth to one-sixth of the wealth that white non-Hispanics do.[19] Ownership of business is another important measure of economic power, and in 2010, 15.6 percent of white non-Hispanic families had business equity compared to only 8.3 percent of non-white or Hispanic families; the median value, though, was $97,200 for whites and $43,000 for nonwhites and Hispanics.[20] Unemployment figures give a similarly dismal picture. In 2010, 8.7 percent of white workers and 16 percent of black workers were unemployed. Among those in the crime-prone ages of 16 to 19, about 23 percent of white youngsters and 43 percent of black youngsters—almost one of every two!—were jobless.[21]

2. The factors most likely to keep one out of trouble with the law and out of prison—such as a suburban living room instead of a tenement alley to gamble in or legal counsel able to devote time to one's case instead of an overburdened public defender—are the kinds of things that money can buy regardless of one's race, creed, or national origin. Zatz states, "[S]ome of the racial differences found in processing and sanctioning decisions may be attributable to class differences in access to resources."[22] Moreover, as we shall see, arrests of blacks for illicit drug possession or dealing have skyrocketed, rising way out of proportion to drug arrests for whites, though research shows no greater drug use among blacks than among whites. However, drug arrests are most easily made in "disorganized inner-city" areas, where drug sales are more likely to take place out-of-doors, and dealers are more willing to sell to strangers. Blacks and Hispanics are more likely than whites to live in such inner-city areas and thus more likely than whites to be arrested on drug charges.[23] And, though racism surely plays a major role here, one very important reason that blacks and Hispanics are more likely than whites to live in disorganized inner-city areas is that a greater percentage of blacks and Hispanics are poor and unemployed. What might at first look like a straightforward racial disparity turns out to reflect lower economic status as well.

3. Blacks who travel the full route of the criminal justice system and end up in jail or prison are close in economic condition to whites who travel the same path. In 1978, 53 percent of black jail inmates had prearrest incomes below $3,000, compared with 44 percent of whites.[24] In 1983, the median pre-arrest income of black jail inmates was $4,067 and that of white jail inmates was $6,312. About half of blacks in jail were unemployed before arrest, while 44 percent of whites were.[25] In 1991, 30 percent of whites in the prison population and 38 percent of blacks reported no full- or part-time employment during the month before their arrest.[26]

4. Some studies suggest that race works to heighten the effects of economic conditions on criminal justice outcomes, so that "being unemployed *and* black substantially increase[s] the chances of incarceration over those associated with being either unemployed or black."[27] This means that racism will produce a kind of selective economic bias, making a certain segment of the unemployed even more likely to end up behind bars.

5. Finally, in light of the relatively high incidence of poverty and/or unemployment among blacks and Hispanics, both racially biased criminal justice policies and economically biased criminal justice policies will result in poor people being disproportionately arrested and imprisoned. We are more concerned with this consequence than with the intention behind it.

For all these reasons, while racism is clearly a distinct and powerful phenomenon in America, we will treat it here as a kind of economic bias or a tool that achieves the same end.

The remainder of this chapter shows how the criminal justice system functions to *weed out the wealthy* (meaning both middle- and upper-class offenders) at each stage of the process and, thus, produces a distorted image of the crime problem. Before entering into this discussion, however, three points are worth noting.

First, it is not our view that the poor are all innocent victims persecuted by the evil rich. The poor do commit crimes, and the vast majority of the poor who are confined in our prisons are probably guilty of the crimes for which they were sentenced. In addition, there is good evidence that the poor do commit a greater portion of the crimes against persons and property listed in the FBI Index than the middle and upper classes do, relative to their numbers in the national population. What we have already tried to prove is that the crimes in the FBI Index are not the only acts that threaten us, nor are they the acts that threaten us the most. What this chapter proves is that the poor are arrested and punished by the criminal justice system much more frequently than their contribution to the crime problem warrants.

Second, the following discussion has been divided into three sections that correspond to the major criminal justice decision points and that also correspond to hypotheses 2, 3, and 4 stated on page 75 in Chapter 2. As always, such classifications are a bit neater than reality, and so they should not be taken as rigid compartments. Many of the distorting processes operate at all criminal justice decision points. The section in which a given issue is treated is a reflection of the point in the criminal justice process at which the disparities are the most striking.

Third, the movement from arrest to sentencing is a funneling process, so that discrimination that occurs at any early stage shapes the population that reaches later stages. Thus, for example, some studies find little economic bias in sentence length for people convicted of similar crimes. When reading such studies, remember that the population that reaches the point of sentencing has already been subject to whatever discrimination exists at earlier stages. If, for example, among people with similar offenses and records, poor people are more likely to be charged and more likely to be convicted, then, even if the sentencing of convicted criminals is evenhanded, it will reproduce the discrimination that occurred before.

Arrest and Charging

Most official records of who commits crime are really statistics on who gets arrested and convicted. If, as we will show, the police are more likely to arrest some people than others, these official statistics may tell us more about police behavior than about criminals. In any event, they give us little reliable data about those who commit crimes and do not get caught. Some social scientists, suspicious of the bias built into official records, have tried to devise other methods of determining who has committed a crime. Most often, these methods involve an interview or questionnaire in which the respondent is assured of anonymity and asked to reveal whether he or she has committed any offenses for which he or she could be arrested and convicted. Techniques to check the reliability of these self-reports also have been devised; however, if their reliability is still in doubt, common sense dictates that they would understate rather than overstate the amount of crime that never comes to official notice. In light of this, the conclusions of these studies are rather astounding. It seems that crime is the national pastime.

The President's Crime Commission conducted a survey of 10,000 households and discovered that "91 percent of all Americans have violated laws that could have subjected them to a term of imprisonment at one time in their lives."[28] A number of other studies, some dating back to the 1940s, support the conclusion that serious criminal behavior is widespread among middle- and upper-class individuals, although these individuals are rarely, if ever, arrested.[29] The authors of a 1990 review of literature on class and delinquency conclude, "Research published since 1978, using both official and self-reported data suggests...that there is no pervasive relationship between SES [socioeconomic status] and delinquency."[30] Crime is widely distributed among the different classes. Other studies suggest that some forms of serious crime—forms usually associated with lower-class youth—show up *more frequently* among higher-class persons than among lower-class ones.[31] For instance, Empey and Erickson interviewed 180 white males aged 15 to 17 who were drawn from different economic strata. They found that "virtually all respondents reported having committed not one but a variety of different offenses." Although youngsters from the middle classes constituted 55 percent of the group interviewed, they admitted to 67 percent of the instances of breaking and entering,

70 percent of the instances of property destruction, and an astounding 87 percent of all the armed robberies admitted to by the entire sample.[32]

Even those who conclude that "lower status youngsters commit delinquent acts more frequently than do higher status youngsters"[33] also recognize that lower-class youth are significantly overrepresented in official records. Gold writes that "about five times more lowest than highest status boys appear in the official records; if records were complete and unselective, we estimate that the ratio would be closer to 1.5:1."[34] The simple fact is that for the same offense, poor people are more likely to come to the attention of the police. Once apprehended, *a poor person is more likely to be arrested and, if arrested, charged than a middle- or upper-class person.*[35] Gold writes that

> boys who live in poorer parts of town and are apprehended by police for delinquency are four to five times more likely to appear in some official record than boys from wealthier sections who commit the same kinds of offenses. These same data show that, at each stage in the legal process from charging a boy with an offense to some sort of disposition in court, boys from different socioeconomic backgrounds are treated differently, so that those eventually incarcerated in public institutions, that site of most of the research on delinquency, are selectively poorer boys.[36]

When individuals were apprehended, "if the offender came from a higher status family, police were more likely to handle the matter themselves without referring it to the court."[37]

Terence Thornberry reached a similar conclusion in his study of 3,475 delinquent boys in Philadelphia. Thornberry found that among boys arrested *for equally serious offenses* and who had *similar prior offense records,* police were more likely to refer the lower-class youths than the more affluent ones to juvenile court. The police generally dealt with the wealthier youngsters informally, for example, by holding them in the station house until their parents came rather than instituting formal procedures. Of those referred to juvenile court, Thornberry found further that, for *equally serious offenses* and with *similar prior records,* the poorer youngsters were more likely to be institutionalized than were the affluent ones. The wealthier youths were more likely to receive probation than the poorer ones. As might be expected, Thornberry found the same relationships when comparing the treatment of black and white youths apprehended for equally serious offenses.[38]

Later studies continue to show similar effects. For example, Sampson found that, for the same crimes, juveniles in lower-class neighborhoods were more likely to have some police record than those in better-off neighborhoods.[39] A study of youth in Seattle, Washington, also found that "regardless of race and self-reported criminal behavior, youth from poorer families are more likely to be arrested."[40] In some studies, "court officials acknowledge that they consciously and affirmatively take steps to direct low-income families into the juvenile justice system, because they believe that the court will 'help' the youth and 'facilitate the services, accountability, and discipline' needed to become a productive adult."[41] (Although, in fact, "such hopes all too often fail to be realized.")[42]If you think these differences are not so important because they are true only of young offenders, remember that this group accounts for much of the crime problem. Moreover, other studies not limited to the young tend to show the same economic bias. McCarthy found that, in metropolitan areas, for similar suspected crimes, unemployed people were more likely to be arrested than employed people.[43]

As indicated earlier, we take racial bias as either a form of bias against the poor or a proxy for it, and blacks are more likely to be suspected or arrested than whites. A 1988 *Harvard Law Review* overview of studies on race and the criminal process concludes that "most studies ... reveal what many police officers freely admit: that police use race as an independently significant, if not determinative, factor in deciding whom to follow, detain, search, or arrest."[44] Furthermore, according to Jerome Miller, "A 1994 study of juvenile detention decisions found that African American and Hispanic youths were more likely to be detained at each decision point, even after controlling for the influence of offense seriousness and social factors (e.g., single-parent home). Decisions by both police and the courts to detain a youngster were highly influenced by race."[45] The study states that "[n]ot only were there direct effects of race, but indirectly, socioeconomic status was related to detention, thus putting youth of color again at risk for differential treatment."[46] And there is some evidence that charges against blacks are thrown out more frequently than charges against whites because blacks are arrested on the basis of less evidence.[47]

In a 2007 research report, criminologists first reviewed recent high-quality research on disproportionate minority contact with the juvenile justice system. They conclude that: "Minority youth are more likely to have contact with the system and to penetrate further into it than non-minority youth." The same researchers then analyzed their own data from three U.S. cities and found that "for most offenses, African Americans have somewhat higher prevalence rates of delinquent behavior than Whites, but their contact/referral rates far exceed those of Whites."[48] Specifically,

> In Pittsburgh, 38.1% of White offenders (individuals who committed an offense) were apprehended and referred to court, but 66.3% of African American offenders were apprehended and referred to court. In Rochester, 19.2% of White offenders and 51.3% of African American offenders were contacted/arrested, and, in Seattle, 33.2% of White offenders were apprehended and referred to court, while 64.4% of African American offenders were apprehended and referred to court.[49]

This analysis is based on the number of offenders and thus already controls for the higher amount of crime committed by blacks. Further, 32 of 44 states that have studied DMC found "evidence of ethnic or racial differences in juvenile justice system decision-making that was unaccounted for by differential criminal activity."[50]

There is also the disturbing finding that many black people are arrested for the crime of "driving while black." John Lamberth of Temple University set out to study whether the police arrest black drivers on the New Jersey Turnpike out of proportion to their percentage in the driving population and to their rate of committing traffic violations. Lamberth and his team "recorded data on more than forty-two thousand cars." They found that "blacks and whites violated the traffic laws at almost exactly the same rate" but "73.2 percent of those stopped and arrested were black, while only 13.5 percent of the cars on the road had a black driver or passenger." Lamberth notes that the disparity between these two numbers is "statistically vast."[51] Similar studies, with similar results, were carried out in Maryland and Ohio.

For reasons mentioned earlier, a disproportionately large percentage of the casualties in the recent war on drugs are poor inner-city minority males. In contrast, the authors of *Dorm Room Dealers* report on the "anti-targets" of the drug war—a network of affluent, mostly white, college students in Southern California who had $80,000 to $160,000 a month in drug sales. Almost all the dealers were from "middle-upper class to affluent/upper class" and "had parents of considerable economic standing"—mayors, businesspeople, and doctors.[52] Because of their class status, they operated with relative impunity despite "the near absent or, perhaps more accurately, pathetic risk-minimization strategies."[53] The authors, while fully aware of class biases in the criminal justice system, "were still taken aback by the lack of criminal justice and university administration attention paid these dealers, despite the brazenness, incompetence, and general dearth of street smarts that tended to characterize the dealers' daily practices."[54]

In contrast, Victor Rios' research in Oakland, California, describes a "youth control complex," in which a range of criminal justice, community, media, and business institutions "treat young people's everyday behaviors as criminal activity."[55] Rios testifies to a citation for "not wearing a properly fitted bicycle helmet," and describes how "talking back" or "looking at them crazy" can lead to a citation for disorderly conduct.[56] This "hypercriminalization" steered the boys deeper into the system because missed court dates would lead to arrest warrants, and inability to pay their fines lead to probation, which entailed more intense police scrutiny.[57]

More generally, the "War on Drugs" disproportionately targets racial minorities, even though surveys dating back to the 1990s show blacks do not use drugs more than whites, and more recent studies show whites are more likely than nonwhites to have dealt drugs.[58] A study conducted by the Sentencing Project, based mainly on Justice Department statistics, indicates that "Blacks make up 12 percent of the United States' population and constitute 13 percent of all monthly drug users … but represent 35 percent of those arrested for drug possession, 55 percent of those convicted of drug possession and 74 percent of those sentenced to prison for drug possession."[59]

Any number of reasons can be offered to account for the differences in police treatment of poor versus well-off citizens. Some argue that they reflect that the poor have less privacy.[60] What others can do in their living rooms or backyards, the poor do on the street. Others argue that a police officer's decision to book a poor youth and release a middle-class youth reflects either the officer's judgment that the higher-class youngster's family will be more likely and more able to discipline him or her than the lower-class youngster's, or differences in the degree to which poor and middle-class complainants demand arrest. Many argue that police training and police work condition the officers to be suspicious of certain kinds of people, such as lower-class youth, blacks, Hispanics, and so on,[61] and thus more likely to detect their criminality. Still others hold that police mainly arrest those with the least political clout,[62] those who are least able to focus public attention on police practices or bring political influence to bear, and these happen to be the members of the lowest social and economic classes.

Regardless of which view one takes, and probably all have some truth in them, one conclusion is inescapable: One of the reasons the offender "at the end of the road in prison is likely to be a member of the lowest social and economic groups in the country" is that the police officers who guard the access to the road to prison make sure that more poor people make the trip than well-to-do people.

Likewise for prosecutors. The *Harvard Law Review* overview of studies on race and the criminal process asserts, "studies indicate that prosecutors are more likely to pursue full prosecution, file more severe charges, and seek more stringent penalties in cases involving minority defendants than in cases involving nonminority defendants."[63] One study of whites, blacks, and Hispanics arrested in Los Angeles on suspicion of having committed a felony found that, *among defendants with equally serious charges and prior records,* 59 percent of whites had their charges dropped at the initial screening, compared with 40 percent of blacks and 37 percent of Hispanics.[64]

The *weeding out of the wealthy* starts at the very entrance to the criminal justice system: The decision about whom to investigate, arrest, or charge is not made simply on the basis of the offense committed or the danger posed. It is a decision distorted by a systematic economic bias that works to the disadvantage of the poor.

This economic bias is a two-edged sword. Not only are the poor arrested and charged out of proportion to their numbers for the kinds of crimes poor people generally commit—burglary, robbery, assault, and so forth—but also, when we reach the kinds of crimes poor people almost never have the opportunity to commit, such as antitrust violations, industrial safety violations, embezzlement, and large-scale tax evasion, the criminal justice system shows an increasingly benign and merciful face. When it comes to crime in the streets, where the perpetrator is apt to be poor, he or she is even more likely to be arrested and formally charged. When it comes to crime in the suites, where the offender is apt to be affluent, the system is most likely to deal with the crime noncriminally, that is, by civil litigation or informal settlement. When it does choose to proceed criminally, as we will see in the section on sentencing, it rarely goes beyond a slap on the wrist. Not only is the main entry to the road to prison held wide open to the poor, but the access routes for the wealthy are largely sealed off. Once again, we should not be surprised at whom we find in our prisons.

Many writers have commented on the extent and seriousness of "white-collar crime," but, for those of us trying to understand how the image of crime is created, four points should be noted.

1. White-collar crime is costly; it takes far more dollars from our pockets than all the FBI Index crimes combined.
2. White-collar crime is more widespread than the crimes of the poor.
3. White-collar criminals are rarely arrested or charged; the system has developed kindlier ways of dealing with the more delicate sensibilities of its higher-class clientele.
4. When white-collar criminals are prosecuted and convicted, their sentences tend to be lenient when judged by the cost their crimes have imposed on society.

The first three points will be discussed here, and the fourth will be presented in the sections that follow.

Everyone agrees that the cost of white-collar crime is enormous. In 1985, *U.S. News & World Report* reported, "Experts estimate that white-collar criminals rake in a minimum of $200 billion annually."[65] Marshall Clinard also cites the $200 billion estimate in his book, *Corporate Corruption: The Abuse of Corporate Power*.[66] That $200 billion in 1985 dollars is equivalent to $428 billion in 2011 dollars.[67] Nonetheless, it underestimates the cost. Some experts placed the cost of white-collar crime for firms doing business in the government sector alone at $500 billion a year during the 1990s.[68] A 2004 study by the Association of Certified Fraud Examiners has found that "the typical organization loses six percent of its annual revenues to occupational fraud, the same result ... obtained from ... studies in 1996 and 2002."[69] A more recent study by them found a 7 percent loss is typical, and if that percentage were applied to the estimated 2010 U.S. Gross Domestic Product, we could project a loss of just over a trillion dollars.[70] A survey of more than 1,000 U.S. households conducted by the National White Collar Crime Center in 1999 found that one in three American households had been the victim of white-collar crime in the previous year. A 2005 replication of the survey found almost half of households had been victimized.[71]

We need a rough estimate of the cost of white-collar crime so that we can compare its impact with that of the crimes reported on by the FBI. For this purpose, we can start with the conservative estimates in the U.S. Chamber of Commerce's *A Handbook on White-Collar Crime*.[72] Because the *Handbook* was issued in 1974, we will have to adjust its figures to take into account both inflation and growth in population to compare these figures with losses reported for 2010 by the FBI. (In light of the avalanche of statistics the government puts out on street crimes, it's worth wondering why the Chamber has not seen fit to revise its more than 35-year-old figures, and why no other private or public institution—neither the FBI nor the U.S. Department of Commerce—keeps up-to-date statistics on the overall cost of white-collar crime.) In some categories, we modify the Chamber's figures in light of more recent estimates. As usual, we use conservative estimates when there is a choice. The result will be a rough estimate of the costs of different categories of white-collar crime, as well as of the overall total. To the extent possible, numbers reflect direct losses—not indirect costs like prevention, remediation, or lost opportunities—to make it comparable with losses from property crime reported by the FBI.

First, the modifications: As might be expected, the cost of computer crime is far beyond the $1 billion estimated by the Chamber in 1974. In its *2005 FBI Computer Crime Survey*, the FBI generalized from its survey findings to the nation as a whole and calculated the cost of computer crimes to be $67.2 billion for U.S. businesses. They note: "While these are rough approximations, they are very conservative."[73] Since then, online crime "has taken off as a serious industry."[74] A 2011 survey by Norton (widely known creator of antivirus software) found $32 billion in annual cash losses for U.S. families due to cybercrime.[75] According to the Congressional Research Service, "the FBI estimates that all types of computer crime in the U.S. now costs industry about $400 billion."[76] We will use this "very conservative" FBI figure of $67 billion for business and add Norton's figure of $32 billion to families for a total of $99 billion.

Telemarketing fraud is said to cost consumers $40 billion a year.[77] We will use this figure as a conservative estimate for the cost of fraud against consumers, though it represents only one among many forms that consumer fraud can take.[78] As for business victims of consumer fraud, illegal competition, and deceptive practices, "figures ranging between $50 and $240 billion have been posited as the amounts 'lost' in the United States through industrial espionage."[79] We will use the low estimate of $50 billion here, noting again that it covers only one form of illegal competition, and updating it to $65 billion based on inflation since the estimate was made.[80]

Government revenue loss has also outstripped the Chamber's estimate of $12 billion annually. An article in *U.S. News & World Report* maintains that "25 percent of Americans admit to tax cheating which costs $100 billion annually."[81] To that should be added another $70 billion in offshore tax evasion related to "tax haven" nations that has largely arisen since the *U.S. News* article.[82] That $170 billion is a conservative estimate because this doesn't include payroll tax fraud or defense and other procurement fraud.

Credit card fraud has also exceeded the Chamber's expectations, amounting to $8.6 billion in 2008.[83] This is a conservative number that represents bank and merchant losses, but not consumer costs from inappropriate credit card fees imposed by financial institutions. Check fraud losses add another $5.5 to $20 billion.[84] We will add the $8.6 billion from credit card fraud to the $5.5 billion lower estimate of check fraud for a total of $14.1 billion, which is again conservative given that the loss from identity fraud (credit card, check, and loans) is estimated to be $50 billion.[85]

The cost of pilferage has increased as well, with the National White Collar Crime Center estimating it to range between $20 and $90 billion.[86]

The FBI claims that *organized* retail theft costs between $30 and $37 billion a year.[87] These estimates do not include intellectual property thefts in the form of counterfeit goods, which result in losses to corporations of $200 to $250 billion.[88] We will use $40 billion for the cost of pilferage, which is conservative given that it is below the midpoint of the Center's estimate and because organized retail theft does not include employee theft or theft by government workers.

Insurance fraud has also gone far beyond the Chamber's 1974 estimates. The Coalition Against Insurance Fraud estimates that insurance fraud costs more than $80 billion a year—a figure endorsed by the FBI in their 2009 financial crimes report.[89] We will use the $80 billion figure, which is surely an underestimate in light of the rock-bottom estimates for health care fraud of $80 billion, and which doesn't include the costs of other types of insurance fraud, like the $30 billion cost of auto insurance to consumers to cover fraud.[90]

Further, security thefts and frauds have far outstripped the Chamber's 1974 estimate of $4 billion, with the FBI's Economic Crimes Unit estimating the cost of securities and commodities fraud at $40 billion in 2006.[91] This is the same amount found in a 2000 survey by the North American Securities Administrators Association.[92] We will use $40 billion, which is a conservative estimate in light of the continued rapid growth of financial services and the number of Americans with investments. Outbreaks of fraud like those that occurred in the savings and loan industry in the 1980s, the corporate scandals starting with Enron in 2001, or the financial crisis of 2008 (all of which we look at later in this chapter) are not included in these statistics either.

And there is now a new category, not even dreamt of by the Chamber in 1974: theft of cellular phone services, estimated to cost $1 billion a year.[93] We will use the $1 billion as a conservative estimate of all telecommunications service theft.

For the remainder of the Chamber's figures, we will assume that the rate of white-collar crime relative to the population remained constant from 1974 to 2010 and that its real dollar value remained constant as well (two conservative assumptions in light of the evidence just cited, which shows considerable growth in many white-collar crimes). Thus, we will simply adjust these figures to reflect the growth in population and inflation since 1974. Between 1974 and 2010, the population of the United States increased by 44.3 percent, and the Consumer Price Index by 342 percent[94] (i.e., 2010s population is 144.3 percent of 1974's, and 2010's prices are 442 percent of 1974's). Thus, we can bring the Chamber of Commerce's figures up-to-date by multiplying them by 6.38 (1.443 × 4.42). This, taken together with the modifications indicated in the previous paragraphs, gives us an estimated total cost of white-collar crime in 2010 of *about $610 billion*. (See Table 3.1 for the total cost and the breakdown into costs per category of white-collar crime.) The $610 billion figure jibes with the estimates quoted earlier, but it is surely on the conservative side. Nonetheless, it is *nearly forty times larger than* the $15.7 billion that is the total amount stolen in all reported property crimes for 2010, according to the FBI.

TABLE 3.1 The Cost of White-Collar Crime, 2010		
		$ (in billions)
Bankruptcy fraud		0.5
Bribery, kickbacks, and payoffs		19.2
Computer- and Internet-related crime		99.0
Consumer fraud, illegal competition, and deceptive practices		190.0
Consumer victims	40.0	
Business victims	65.0	
Government revenue loss	170.0	
Credit card and check fraud		14.1
Credit card	8.6	
Check	5.5	
Embezzlement and pilferage		59.2
Embezzlement (cash, goods, and services)	19.2	
Pilferage	40.0	
Insurance fraud		80.0
Receiving stolen property		22.3
Securities thefts and frauds		40.0
Cellular phone fraud		1.0
Total (billions)		**$610.3**

Source: Chamber of Commerce of the United States, *Handbook on White-Collar Crime, 1974* (Washington, D.C.: Chamber of Commerce of the United States, 1974); figures adjusted for inflation and population growth through 2010, and supplemented from other sources documented in the text.

In addition to the standard forms of white-collar crime by individuals, corporate crime is also rampant. Sutherland, in a classic 1949 study, analyzed the behavior of 70 of the 200 largest U.S. corporations over a period of some 40 years:

> The records reveal that every one of the seventy corporations had violated one or more of the laws, with an average of about thirteen adverse decisions per corporation and a range of from one to fifty adverse decisions per corporation. ... Thus, generally, the official records reveal that these corporations violated the trade regulations with great frequency. The 'habitual criminal' laws of some states impose severe penalties on criminals convicted the third or fourth time. If this criterion were used here, about 90 percent of the large corporations studied would be considered habitual white-collar criminals.[95]

Nevertheless, corporate executives rarely end up in jail, where they would find themselves sharing cells with poorer persons who had stolen less from their fellow citizens. What Sutherland found in 1949 continues up to the present. In his 1990 book, *Corporate Corruption: The Abuse of Power*, Marshall Clinard writes,

> Many government investigations, both federal and state, have revealed extensive law violations in such industries as oil, autos, and pharmaceuticals. ... [O]ver one two-year period, the federal government charged nearly two-thirds of the *Fortune 500* corporations with law violations; half were charged with a serious violation. ... According to a 1982 *U.S. News & World Report* study, more than one out of five of the *Fortune 500* companies had been convicted of at least one major crime or had paid civil penalties for serious illegal behavior between 1970 and 1979.[96]

As for the treatment of these repeat offenders, Clinard says "a large-scale study of sanctions imposed for corporate law violations found that administrative [that is, noncriminal] penalties were employed in two-thirds of serious corporate law violations, and that slightly more than two-fifths of the sanctions ... consisted simply of a warning to the corporation not to commit the offense again."[97]

The continued prevalence of these practices is confirmed in a study of white-collar crime prosecutions by Susan Shapiro, titled "The Road Not Taken: The Elusive Path to Criminal Prosecution for White-Collar Offenders." Focusing on the enforcement practices of the Securities and Exchange Commission (SEC), Shapiro writes that

> while criminal dispositions are often appropriate, they are rarely pursued to the sentencing stage. Out of every 100 suspects investigated by the SEC, 93 have committed securities violations that carry criminal penalties. Legal action is taken against 46 of them, but only 11 are selected for criminal treatment. Six of these are indicted; 5 will be convicted and 3 sentenced to prison. Thus, for Securities and Exchange Commission enforcement, criminal prosecution most often represents the road not taken. Of those found to have engaged in securities fraud, 88 percent never have to contend with the criminal justice system at all.[98]

We shall see later that a large number of potential criminal cases arising out of the savings and loan scandals were dismissed by federal law enforcement agencies because they lacked the personnel to pursue them, even as thousands of new police officers were being hired to fight street crime. With upper-class lawbreakers, the authorities prefer to sue in civil court for damages or for an injunction rather than treat the wealthy as common criminals. Judges have, on occasion, stated in open court that they would not make criminals of reputable businessmen. One would think it would be up to the businessmen to make criminals of themselves by their actions, but, alas, this privilege is reserved for the lower classes.

After 2000, the Department of Justice (DOJ) increased its use of Non-Prosecution Agreements (NPAs) and Deferred Prosecution Agreements

(DPAs), which provide that DOJ will not prosecute if the company agrees to implement certain reforms. According to the General Accounting Office, "DOJ intends for these agreements to promote corporate reform; however, DOJ does not have performance measures in place to assess whether this goal has been met. Therefore, it could be difficult for DOJ to justify its increasing use of these tools."[99]

The clientele of the criminal justice system forms an exclusive club. Entry is largely a privilege of the poor. The crimes they commit are the crimes that qualify one for admission, and they are admitted in greater proportion than their share of those crimes. Curiously enough, the crimes the affluent commit are not the kind that easily qualify one for membership in the club.

And as we have seen, the reluctance to use the full force of the criminal justice system in pursuit of white-collar criminals is matched by a striking reluctance to use the full force of current public and private research organizations to provide up-to-date estimates of its cost. This coincidence is worth pondering by anyone interested in how criminal justice policy gets made and how research and statistics function in the process.

Adjudication and Conviction

Between arrest and imprisonment lies the crucial process that determines guilt or innocence. Studies of individuals accused of similar offenses and with similar prior records show that the poor defendant is more likely to be adjudicated guilty than is the wealthier defendant.[100] In the adjudication process the only thing that *should* count is whether the accused is guilty and whether the prosecution can prove it beyond a reasonable doubt. Unfortunately, at least two other factors that are irrelevant to the question of guilt or innocence significantly affect the outcome: One is the ability of the accused to be free on bail prior to trial, and the second is access to legal counsel able to devote adequate time and energy to the case. Because both bail and high-quality legal counsel cost money, it should come as no surprise that here, as elsewhere, the poor do poorly.

Being released on bail is important in several respects. First and foremost is that those who are not released on bail are kept in jail like individuals who have been found guilty. They are thus punished while they are still legally innocent. The Bureau of Justice Statistics reported that local jails held 748,728 inmates at midyear 2010, and 62 percent of inmates had not been convicted, up from 56 percent in 2000.[101] Beyond the obvious ugliness of punishing people before they are found guilty, confined defendants cannot actively aid in their own defense by seeking out witnesses and evidence. Several studies have shown that among defendants accused of the same offenses, those who make bail are more likely to be acquitted than those who do not.[102] In a study of unemployment and punishment, Chiricos and Bales found that "after the effects of other factors [seriousness of crime, prior record, etc.] were controlled, an unemployed defendant was 3.2 times more likely to be incarcerated before trial than his employed counterpart."[103]

Marvin Free reports on 12 studies that show racial disparities in bail and pretrial release decisions even when legally relevant variables (prior record, etc.) were held constant. Some studies showed interaction effects, such that "being lower class [is] a greater disadvantage for African Americans than for whites." Another such study revealed that "while overall African American defendants were 1.6 times more likely than white defendants to be detained prior to trial…, young, unemployed African American males were six times more likely than their white counterparts to be detained."[104]

Furthermore, because the time spent in jail prior to adjudication of guilt may count as part of the sentence, the accused are often placed in a ticklish position. Suppose you are innocent and have been in the slammer for two months awaiting trial. The prosecutor offers a deal: If you plead guilty to such-and-such (usually a lesser offense than has been charged, say, possession of burglar's tools instead of burglary), the prosecutor promises to ask the judge to sentence you to two months. In other words, plead guilty and walk out of jail today (free, but with a criminal record that will make finding a job hard and ensure a stiffer sentence next time around), or maintain your innocence, stay in jail until trial, and then be tried for the full charge instead of the lesser offense! Not only does the prosecutor threaten to prosecute for the full charge, but they may also threaten to press for the most severe penalty as well—for taking up the court's time.

Plea bargaining such as this is an everyday occurrence in the criminal justice system. Contrary to the image conveyed by dramatic courtroom arguments in televised crime dramas, between 85 and 95 percent of convictions are the result of a negotiated plea.[105] There's no trial, just a bargain in which the accused agrees to plead guilty (usually to a lesser offense than he or she is charged with, or to one offense out of many he or she is charged with) in return for a promise of leniency from the prosecutor with the consent of the judge. If you were the jailed defendant offered a deal like this, how would you choose? Suppose you were a poor black man not likely to be able to retain a high-profile private attorney?

The advantages of access to adequate legal counsel during the adjudicative process are obvious, but still worthy of mention. In 1963, the U.S. Supreme Court handed down the landmark *Gideon* v. *Wainwright* decision, holding that the states must provide legal counsel to the indigent in all felony cases. As a result, no person accused of a serious crime need face his or her accuser without a lawyer. However, the Supreme Court has set the standard for ineffective assistance of counsel so low that even sleepy, drunk, and bad lawyers are acceptable. The problem of adequate legal representation is particularly acute in death penalty cases. According to Robert Johnson, "Most attorneys in capital cases are provided by the state. Defendants, as good capitalists, routinely assume that they will get what they pay for: next to nothing." Their perceptions, he concludes, "may not be far from right."[106] Indeed, Stephen Gettinger maintains that an inadequate defense was "the single outstanding characteristic" of the condemned persons he studied.[107]

A *Time* magazine article on this topic noted, "Because the majority of murder defendants are ... broke ... many of them get court-appointed lawyers who lack the resources, experience or inclination to do their utmost. … Some people go to traffic court with better prepared lawyers than many murder defendants get."[108] A 2011 study of Pennsylvania's death penalty cases found similar problems: lawyers "often spend little time preparing their cases and put on only the barest defense. They neglect basic steps, such as interviewing defendants, seeking out witnesses, and investigating a defendant's background." It found that court-appointed lawyers for death penalty cases "get $2,000 for trial preparation and $400 a day in court to handle cases that a veteran defense attorney said required a minimum outlay of $35,000 to $40,000."[109]

In 2004, Johnny Lee Bell was convicted of second degree murder and "received an automatic mandatory sentence of life in prison, despite his public defender's admission that she had spent only 11 minutes preparing for his trial." The National Association of Criminal Defense Lawyers notes that the "case is egregious, but not unsymptomatic given the trend of substandard legal representation that has become common in many states."[110]

The upper-class campus drug dealers studied in *Dorm Room Dealers* had substantially better attorneys than people facing the death penalty. While authorities generally turned a "collective blind eye" to "brazen" illegality, a few dealers did end up in the criminal justice system.[111] One dealer was caught with over 100 marijuana plants and $30,000 in growing equipment, but his parents hired a "high-profile private defense attorney" and horticultural and biological sciences experts plus "various psychiatrists." He ended up with an 18 month "diversion program" that resulted in no jail time, and all records were expunged when he successfully completed the program, so someone running a criminal history check would find nothing about this incident.[112]

Needless to say, the distinct legal advantages that money can buy become even more salient when we enter the realm of corporate and other white-collar crime. Indeed, it is often precisely the time and cost involved in bringing to court a large corporation with its army of legal eagles that is offered as an excuse for the less formal and more genteel treatment accorded to corporate crooks. This excuse is, of course, not equitably distributed to all economic classes, any more than quality legal service is. This means that, regardless of actual innocence or guilt, one's chances of beating the rap increase as one's income increases.

Sentencing

On June 28, 1990, the House Subcommittee on Financial Institutions Supervision, Regulation, and Insurance met in the Rayburn House Office Building to hold hearings on the prosecution of savings and loan (S&L) criminals. The chairman of the subcommittee, Congressman Frank Annunzio, called the meeting to order and said,

> The American people are furious with the slow pace of prosecutions involving savings and loan criminals. These crooks are responsible for 1/3, 1/2, or maybe even more, of the savings and

loan cost. The American taxpayer will be forced to pay $500 billion or more over the next 40 years, largely because of these crooks. For many Americans, this bill will not be paid until their grandchildren are old enough to retire.

We are here to get an answer to one question: "When are the S&L crooks going to jail?"

The answer from the administration seems to be: "probably never."

Frankly, I don't think the administration has the interest in pursuing Gucci-clad, white-collar criminals. These are hard and complicated cases, and the defendants often were rich, successful prominent members of their upper-class communities. It is far easier putting away a sneaker-clad high school dropout who tries to rob a bank of a thousand dollars with a stick-up note, than a smooth talking S&L executive who steals a million dollars with a fraudulent note.

Later in the hearing, Chairman Annunzio questioned the administration's representative:

You cited, Mr. Dennis, several examples in your testimony of successful convictions with stiff sentences, but the average sentence so far is actually about 2 years, compared to an average sentence of about 9 years for bank robbery. Why do we throw the book at people who rob a bank in broad daylight but we coddle people who… rob the bank secretly?[113]

Twelve years later, on July 11, 2002, at a hearing of the Crime and Drugs Subcommittee of the Senate Judiciary Committee on the subject of "Penalties for White Collar Crimes: Are We Really Getting Tough on Crime?" Senator Joseph Biden Jr. said,

Under federal law, if … you steal a car out of my driveway and you drive it across [the state line] into Pennsylvania, ten years. Ten years, federal guideline. You take a pension by violating ERISA, the federal system to safeguard pensions, misdemeanor, maximum one year. The pension may be worth $1,800,000. My car may be worth $2,000.[114]

The simple fact is that the criminal justice system reserves its harshest penalties for its lower-class clients and puts on kid gloves when confronted with a better class of crook.

We will come back to the soft treatment of the S&L crooks shortly. For the moment, note that the tendency to treat higher-class criminals more leniently than lower-class criminals has been with us for a long time. In 1972, the *New York Times* did a study on sentencing in state and federal courts. The *Times* stated that "crimes that tend to be committed by the poor get tougher sentences than those committed by the well-to-do," that federal "defendants who could not afford private counsel were sentenced nearly twice as severely as defendants with private counsel," and that a "study by the Vera Institute of Justice of courts in the Bronx indicates a similar pattern in the state courts."[115]

D'Alessio and Stolzenberg studied a random sample of 2,760 offenders committed to the custody of the Florida Department of Corrections during 1985. They found that poor offenders received longer sentences for violent crimes, such as manslaughter, and for morals offenses, such as narcotics possession. Sentencing guidelines have not reduced this disparity.[116] A study of individuals convicted of drunk driving found that increased education (an indicator of higher economic status) "increase[d] the rate of movement from case filing to probation and decrease[d] the rate of movement to prison."[117]

Chiricos and Bales found that, for individuals guilty of similar offenses and with similar prior records, unemployed defendants were more than twice as likely as their employed counterparts to be incarcerated if found guilty.[118] McCarthy noted a similar link between unemployment and greater likelihood of incarceration.[119] In his study of 28,315 felony defendants in Tennessee, Virginia, and Kentucky, Champion also found that offenders who could afford private counsel had a greater likelihood of probation, and received shorter sentences when incarceration was imposed.[120] A study of the effects of implementing Minnesota's determinate sentencing program shows that socioeconomic bias is "more subtle, but no less real" than before the new program.[121]

Tillman and Pontell examined the sentences received by individuals convicted of Medicaid-provider fraud in California. Because such offenders normally have no prior arrests and are charged with grand theft, their sentences were compared with the sentences of other offenders convicted of grand theft who also had no prior records. While 37.7 percent of the Medicaid defrauders were sentenced to some jail or prison time, 79.2 percent of the others convicted of grand theft were sentenced to jail or prison. This was so even though the median dollar loss due to the Medicaid frauds was $13,000, more than 10 times the median loss due to the other grand thefts ($1,149). Tillman and Pontell point out that most of the Medicaid defrauders were health professionals, while most of the others convicted of grand theft had low-level jobs or were unemployed. They conclude that "differences in the sentences imposed on the two samples are indeed the result of the different social statuses of their members."[122]

As usual, data on racial discrimination in sentencing tell the same story of the treatment of those who cannot afford the going price of justice. A study of offender processing in New York State counties found that for offenders with the same arrest charge and the same prior criminal records, minorities were incarcerated more often than comparably situated whites.[123] A study of 9,690 males who entered Florida prisons in 1992 and 1993, and who were legally eligible for stricter sentencing under the habitual offender statute, shows that for similar prior records and seriousness of crime, race had a "significant and substantial" effect: Black defendants were particularly disadvantaged "for drug offenses and for property crimes."[124] After reviewing 22 recent studies estimating sentencing severity based on federal-level data,

Spohn concluded that "more than two-thirds (15 of 22) of the estimates reveal that blacks [and Hispanics] were sentenced more harshly than whites." Based on a total of 40 recent studies of both federal and state data, Spohn concludes that "Black and Hispanic offenders—particularly those who are young, male, or unemployed—are more likely than their white counterparts to be sentenced to prison; they also may receive longer sentences than similarly situated white offenders."[125] Most striking perhaps is that, in 2010, 42.8 percent of inmates in state and federal prisons were black and 37.8 percent of inmates of jails were black, whereas the FBI reports that blacks make up only 28 percent of all those arrested that year.[126]

Here a mention must be made of the notorious "100-to-1" disparity between sentences for possession of cocaine in powder form (popular in the affluent suburbs) and in crack form (popular in poor inner-city neighborhoods). From 1986 until 2010, federal laws required a mandatory five-year sentence for crimes involving 500 grams (about a pound) of powder cocaine or 5 grams (about one-sixth of an ounce) of crack cocaine. This yields a sentence for first-time crack offenders (with no aggravating factors, such as possession of a weapon) that is longer than the sentence for kidnapping, and only slightly shorter than the sentence for attempted murder![127] About 82 percent of those convicted of federal crack offenses are black; about 8 percent are white.[128] In 1995, 1997, and 2002, the U. S. Sentencing Commission recommended ending the 100-to-1 disparity between powder and crack penalties, and in an unusual display of bipartisanship, Congress rejected their recommendation and kept the law.[129] In his 2007 testimony to Congress, the Chair of the Sentencing Commission stated: "The Commission believes that there is no justification for the current statutory penalty scheme" and it "remains committed" to its 2002 recommendation that any ratio "be no more than 20 to 1." As a candidate, Barack Obama said "let's not make the punishment for crack cocaine that much more severe than the punishment for powder cocaine when the real difference between the two is the skin color of the people using them."[130] The Fair Sentencing Act of 2010 did not eliminate the disparity, but reduced the 100:1 disparity to 18:1. Says sociologist Nikki Jones: "What the Act suggests is that it's better for our criminal justice system to be somewhat racist rather than very racist."[131]

Sentencing disparities between the races are, of course, not new. An extensive study, by the *Boston Globe*, of 4,500 cases of armed robbery, aggravated assault, and rape found that "blacks convicted in the superior courts of Massachusetts receive harsher penalties than whites for the same crimes."[132] A study of criminal justice systems in California, Michigan, and Texas by Petersilia confirms the continuation of this trend. "Controlling for the factors most likely to influence sentencing and parole decisions," she writes, "the analysis still found that blacks and Hispanics are less likely to be given probation, more likely to receive *prison* sentences, more likely to receive longer sentences, and more likely to serve a greater portion of their original time."[133]

The federal government has introduced sentencing guidelines and mandatory minimum sentences that might be expected to eliminate discrimination, and many states have followed suit. The effect of this, however, has been not to eliminate discretion, but to transfer it from those who sentence to those who decide what to charge—that is, from judges to prosecutors. Prosecutors can charge in a way that makes it likely that the offender will get less than the mandatory minimum sentence. Says U.S. District Judge J. Lawrence Irving of San Diego, "[T]he system is run by the U.S. attorneys. When they decide how to indict, they fix the sentence."[134] And discrimination persists. Barbara Meierhoefer studied 267,178 offenders sentenced in federal courts from January 1984 to June 1990. She found that whites were consistently more likely than blacks to be sentenced to less than the minimum sentence. The disparity varied from year to year, reaching a high point in 1988, when blacks were 30 percent more likely than whites to receive at least the minimum sentence. Hispanics fared even worse than blacks. Meierhoefer concludes,

> [D]espite the laws' emphasis on offense behavior, sentences still vary by offender characteristics. ... Further, both black and Hispanic offenders now receive notably more severe sentences than their white counterparts.
>
> The latter trend suggests that there may be questions to be considered concerning the impact of shifting discretion affecting sentencing from the court to the prosecutor's office.[135]

A number of judges have spoken out against the system of sentencing guidelines and mandatory minimum sentences. According to U.S. District Judge Terry Hatter, "[T]he toughest sentences are now strictly 'applied to basically one group of people: poor minority people.'" Appellate Judge Gerald W. Heaney conducted his own study "and found that young black men got longer sentences than their white counterparts for similar crimes. Using 1989 data, he compared sentences under the new system with those under the old. The average sentence for black males was 40 months longer, he found, while the average sentence for white males was 19 months longer."[136] Although many mandatory sentences are still in place, the Supreme Court has ruled that the sentencing guidelines are only advisory. It remains to be seen how much discretion this will actually return to judges, and how that discretion will be exercised. White-collar offenders find ways to manipulate programs in the federal system that reduce their sentences, according to an article in *Forbes* titled "How Corporate Crooks Cut Their Jail Time." It notes that offenders who participate in the Residential Drug Abuse Program are eligible for up to a year off their sentences, and it's "funny how many suddenly discover they have substance abuse problems." Enron executives actually "joked from the witness stand about getting early release for a rehab stint despite being only a 'social drinker'."[137]

There is considerable evidence that *double discrimination*—by race of the victim and of the offender—affects death penalty sentencing. In Florida, for example, blacks "who kill whites are nearly forty times more likely to be sentenced to death than those who kill blacks." Moreover, among "killers of whites, blacks are five times more likely than whites to be sentenced to death." This pattern of double discrimination was also evidenced, though less pronouncedly, in Texas, Ohio, and Georgia, the other states surveyed.[138] Together, these four states account for the vast majority of American death sentences. It was on the basis of such research that what may have been the last major constitutional challenge to the death penalty in our era was raised and rejected. In the 1987 case of *McCleskey* v. *Kemp,* evidence of discrimination on the basis of the victim's race was provided by a study by Professor David Baldus, who examined 2,484 Georgia homicide cases that occurred between 1973 (when the current capital murder law was enacted) and 1979 (a year after McCleskey received his death sentence).[139] After controlling for all legitimate nonracial factors—such as severity of crime and the presence of aggravating factors—Baldus found that "murderers of white victims are still being sentenced to death 4.3 times more often than murderers of black victims."[140] The justices of the Supreme Court acknowledged the systemic disparities, but a majority held that the disparities would not invalidate death penalty convictions unless discrimination could be shown in the individual case at hand.

A 2003 study by criminologists at the University of Maryland looked at some 6,000 homicides committed between 1978 and 1999 in the state of Maryland and concluded the following:

- Black offenders who kill whites are *twice as likely* to get a death sentence as whites who kill whites.
- Black offenders who kill whites are *four times as likely* to get a death sentence as blacks who kill blacks.[141]

Note that all these discriminatory sentences were rendered under statutes that had passed constitutional muster and were, therefore, presumed free of the biases that led the Supreme Court to invalidate all American death penalty statutes in *Furman* v. *Georgia* in 1972.

Another study has shown that whites on death row were more likely to have their sentences commuted than blacks. Also, blacks or whites who have private counsel are more likely to have their executions commuted than condemned persons defended by court-appointed attorneys.[142] A study appearing in the American Bar Association's *Criminal Justice* magazine examined 107 cases of people on death row who were wrongfully convicted. Of these exonerated inmates, 45 percent were black and another 13 percent were other minorities. In short, 58 percent of wrongful convictions were of minority defendants.[143]

As this chapter has already pointed out, justice is increasingly tempered with mercy as we deal with a better class of crime. The Sherman Antitrust Act is a criminal law. It recognizes that a free enterprise economy depends on competition to drive consumer prices down, so agreements by competing firms to refrain from price competition is the equivalent of stealing money from the consumer's pocket. Nevertheless, although such conspiracies cost consumers far more than lower-class theft, price fixing was a misdemeanor until 1974.[144] In the historic *Electrical Equipment* cases in the early 1960s, executives of several major firms met secretly to fix prices on electrical equipment to a degree that is estimated to have cost the buying public well over $1 billion. The executives involved knew they were violating the law. They used plain envelopes for their communications, called their meetings "choir practice," and referred to the list of executives in attendance as the "Christmas card list." This case is rare and famous because it was an early case in which the criminal sanction was actually imposed. Seven executives received and served jail sentences. In light of the amount of money they had stolen from the American public, however, their sentences were more an indictment of the government than of themselves: *thirty days in jail!*

Since then, progress in making sentences reflect the degree of harm done by white collar crimes has followed a slow and zigzagging course. Studies have shown that, even though corporate and white-collar lawbreakers are being more frequently brought to justice and more frequently sanctioned, they still receive more lenient sentences than do those who are sentenced for common property crimes.[145] Hagan and Palloni studied the treatment of white-collar offenders before and after Watergate (a major political scandal that occurred in the 1970s in which President Nixon as well as numerous of his political underlings were implicated in an attempt to compromise the integrity of the electoral process). They conclude that "relative to less-educated common criminals, white-collar offenders were more likely to be imprisoned after Watergate than before, but for shorter periods."[146]

Even after the heightened public awareness of white-collar crime that came in the wake of Watergate and the S&L scandals, it remains the case that the crimes of the poor lead to stiffer sentences than the crimes of the well-to-do (see Table 3.2). Keep in mind while looking at the figures in Table 3.2 that *each* of the "crimes of the affluent" costs the public more than *all* of the "crimes of the poor" put together.

TABLE 3.2   Federal Sentences Served for Different Classes of Crimes, 2009

	Percentage of Convicted Offenders Sentenced to Prison	Average Time Served in Months
Crimes of the Poor		
Robbery	96	80
Burglary	86	31
Auto theft	74	19
Crimes of the Affluent		
Fraud	64	18
Tax law violation and tax fraud	68	16
Embezzlement	47	17

Source: Federal Justice Statistics 2009—Statistical Tables (December 2011, NCJ 233464). Calculated from Tables 5.2 and 7.11 and rounded off.

There has been some toughening of the treatment of white-collar offenders in recent years. But, this toughening has been relatively mild when compared with the treatment dealt out to lower-class offenders. For example, in September 1991, a fire destroyed a chicken-processing plant in Hamlet, North Carolina. When the 100 employees in the plant tried to escape, they found that the company executives had ordered the doors locked "to keep out insects and to keep employees from going outside for coffee breaks, or stealing chickens." Twenty-five workers died in the fire; some were found burned to death at the doors they clawed at, but couldn't open. Another 50 people were injured. The owner of the company and two plant managers were charged with involuntary manslaughter. The outcome: The owner pleaded guilty and was sentenced to 19 years and 6 months in prison. You may or may not think this is severe as a punishment for someone responsible for 25 very painful deaths, but note three revealing facts. First, the sentence was "believed to be the harshest judgment ever handed out for a workplace safety violation." Second, as part of the plea agreement, the involuntary manslaughter cases against the two plant managers were dismissed, though they surely knew that the doors were locked and what the risks were. And third, the owner eventually served a little more than four years in prison and was released.[147]

FINANCIAL FRAUDS   In this section, we present several recent examples of major financial fraud that can serve as case studies for the economic bias that the previous sections reviewed. During the 1980s, the savings and loan scandal occurred, costing taxpayers $500 *billion*. The major portion of this amount was attributed to fraud at financial institutions. In December of 2001, Enron filed the largest corporate bankruptcy in U.S. history to that point, and was followed by revelations of significant fraud in a large number of companies that cost shareholders hundreds of billions of dollars in losses. Then, in 2008, the United States saw a financial meltdown so severe that President Bush announced that "our entire economy is in danger,"[148] and urged Congress to quickly pass a $700 billion bailout on top of *trillions* committed by the Federal Reserve. A final accounting is still in the works, but ordinary people will directly and indirectly pay a substantial "Wall Street incompetence tax."[149] The current financial meltdown is not a natural disaster; it was caused by human beings who are responsible for the harms that resulted from their actions.

The savings and loan scandal.   The federally insured system of savings and loan banks (S&Ls, also known as "thrifts") was created in the 1930s to promote the building and sale of new homes during the Great Depression. The system had built into it important restrictions on the kinds of loans that could be made and was subject to federal supervision to prevent the bank failures that came in the wake of the Depression of 1929. Starting in the 1970s and speeding up in the early 1980s, this entire system of regulation and supervision was first loosened, and then essentially dismantled, as part of the

Reagan administration's policy of deregulation. Although S&Ls could now make riskier investments, their deposits were still insured by the Federal Savings and Loan Insurance Corporation (FSLIC). Translation: The S&Ls could make risky investments shooting for windfall profits, with the taxpayers paying for losses. This combination proved to be financial dynamite. The thrifts made high-risk investments, and many failed in ways that left executives, their friends, family, and business partners substantially richer. By 1982, the bill to the FSLIC for bailing out insolvent thrifts was over $2.4 billion. By 1986, the FSLIC was itself insolvent![150] In 1996, a Government Accounting Office report put the total cost to the American taxpayer of the S&L bailout at $480.9 billion![151]

Not all these losses are due to crime, but fraud was a central factor in 70 to 80 percent of the S&L failures.[152] Much of this fraud took the form of looting of bank funds for the personal gain of bank officers at the expense of the institution. The commissioner of the California Department of Savings and Loans is quoted as saying in 1987, "The best way to rob a bank is to own one."[153] Says *Fortune* magazine, "Though yet perceived only in hazy outline, today's S&L fraud dwarfs every previous carnival of white-collar crime in America."[154]

In response to the enormity of this scandal, American public opinion hardened toward white-collar crime, and federal law enforcement agencies were prosecuting, fining, and even jailing offenders at unprecedented rates. Nonetheless, considering the size of the scandal and the far-reaching damage it did to the American economy and public trust in the banking system, the treatment is still light-handed compared with that of even nonviolent "common" crimes. According to one study, "The average prison term for savings and loan offenders sentenced between 1988 and 1992 was 36 months, compared to 56 months for burglars and 38 months for those convicted of motor vehicle theft." The study goes on to point out that S&L offenders were given lengthier sentences than first-time property crime offenders (who received an average sentence of 26 months), but, lest we think that this shows a new severity, the average loss in an S&L case was $500,000.[155] The average loss per property offense in 1995 was $1,251.[156]

These sentenced S&L offenders represent just a small fraction of the crooks involved in the S&L looting: "from 1987 to 1992, Federal bank and thrift regulators filed a staggering 95,045 criminal referrals with the FBI. The volume was so large that more than 75 percent of these referrals have been dropped without prosecution."[157] At the same time, the Justice Department advised against funding for 425 new agents requested by the FBI and 231 new assistant U.S. attorneys, and the administration recommended against increasing funds authorized by Congress for the S&L investigations from $50 million to $75 million.[158] But, soon after, we find the President and the Congress ready to spend $23 billion on criminal justice and hire thousands of new police officers to keep our streets safe!

To give you a concrete idea of what some of the S&L crooks did and the treatment they received, Table 3.3 presents a roughly representative "rogues gallery." In looking at these rogues, their acts, and their punishments, keep in mind the treatment meted out to the Typical Criminal when he steals a fraction of what they did. Also, soon after the S&L crisis, Congress went on what the authors of *Big Money Crime* describe as a wave of "cavalier" financial deregulation, creating a "paradox of increasing financial deregulation coming on the heels of the most catastrophic experiment with deregulation in history"[159] (up to that point in time).

TABLE 3.3	The Savings and Loan Roster	
Michael Hellerman aka Michael Rapp	Defrauded Flushing Federal S&L (New York) of $8.4 million and Florida Center Bank of $7.5 million.	Received 15 years and a fine of $100,000. Released on parole after serving 5½ years; has not paid any fine, but lawyer claims $100 a month is being deducted from Hellerman/Rapp's salary.
Charles Bazarian	Convicted for "swindling $20 million from two California S&Ls and skimming at least $100,000 from a low-income H.U.D. project." Also convicted with Rapp in Florida case.	Served less than two years for cooperating with authorities, and has paid $18,000 of $110,000 in fines.
Mario Renda	As partner in a brokerage business, he stole about $16 million.	Sentenced to two years in prison and five years probation after pleading guilty to two counts of wire fraud; ordered to pay $9.9 million in restitution and $125,000 in criminal fines; was given early parole after serving 21 months. As of his release from prison, he has paid only a small fraction of the required restitution.
Herman Beebe	Involved in widespread loan fraud involving more than $30 million.	Pleaded guilty to two counts under a bargain in which he received a sentence of one year and one day. Served 10 months and is immune from prosecution for fraud charges in Louisiana and Texas.
Richard Mariucci	As branch manager of Gibraltar Federal (California), stole $3.4 million.	Sentenced to two years and three months.
Arthur Kick	President of North Chicago Federal S&L; stole $1.2 million by misappropriating loans.	Required to make full restitution, and sentenced to three years of probation.

(Continued)

TABLE 3.3	**(continued)**	
Edward Jolly Jr.	Assistant regional vice president and consumer loan manager at First Federal Savings and Loan (South Carolina); stole $4.5 million through fictitious loan applications.	Sentenced to two years and nine months.
Ted Musacchio	President of Columbus Marin S&L (California); stole $9.3 million and lied about it on federal disclosure forms.	Sentenced in January 1990 to five years of probation and required to make immediate restitution of $9.3 million, but had only paid $1,000 by the time of his death in 1993.

Source: Stephen Pizzo and Paul Muolo, "Take the Money and Run: A Rogues Gallery of Some Lucky S&L Thieves," *The New York Times Magazine,* May 9, 1993; Alan Fomhan, "S&L Felons," *Fortune,* November 5, 1990, p. 93; "Former Columbus President Guilty of Misapplying Funds," *American Banker,* December 26, 1989; and "Why S&L Crooks Have Failed to Pay Millions of Dollars in Court-Ordered Restitution: Nineteen Case Studies," in *A Staff Report for the Subcommittee on Financial Institutions Supervision, Regulation and Insurance of the Committee on Banking, Finance and Urban Affairs, House of Representatives,* 102nd Congress, 2nd session, April (Washington, D.C.: U.S. Government Printing Office, 1992).

Enron and a year of corporate financial scandals. In 2001–2002, corporate financial shenanigans caused corporate bankruptcies, unemployment, economic turmoil, and a significant drop in stock market prices. Although the economic losses were widespread, *Fortune* magazine notes, "The not-so-secret dirty secret of the crash is that even as investors were losing 70 percent, 90 percent, even in some cases *all* of their holdings, top officials of many of the companies that have crashed the hardest were getting immensely, extraordinarily, obscenely wealthy."[160]

At center stage was Enron, a multibillion-dollar energy-rights trading company, which declared one of the largest bankruptcies in history on December 2, 2001, with debts of over $31 billion! Enron was subsequently accused of having perpetrated a massive "disinformation" campaign, hiding the degree of its indebtedness from investors by treating loans as revenue, and hiding company losses by creating "special purpose vehicles"[161] with company capital and then attributing losses to them rather than Enron. As Enron shares were tanking, the then-CEO Ken Lay was emailing concerned employees, advising them to hold their shares and buy new ones. Meanwhile, he himself cashed in $103 million of his own shares in the company. Enron executives unloaded nearly a *billion dollars* worth of stock. Employees, however, were locked out of selling the holdings in their pensions during much of the period in which the company's stock fell from $80 a share to $0.30. Enron investors collectively lost about $60 billion, which included many large pension plans and the retirement savings of nearly 20,000 employees.[162]

Enron turned out not to be an isolated incident, and the list of companies touched by financial scandal soon included Tyco, Global Crossing, Qwest, WorldCom, Xerox, Adelphia, MicroStrategy, AOL-Time Warner, K-Mart, and some major banks, such as Citigroup and J. P. Morgan Chase. "About one-tenth of publicly traded companies announced at least one restatement," according to a working paper by the National Bureau of Economic Research, and "companies that had to restate earnings in 2000 and 2001 axed anywhere from 250,000 to 600,000 jobs in 2001 and 2002."[163]

The so-called questionable bookkeeping and misstatements that Enron and others engaged in were not mere technical rule violations without real victims. One important consequence of this corporate crime and financial trickery is the elimination of many people's retirement nest eggs, forcing many older people to put off retirement and many retirees to go back to work: "In this age of the 401(k), when the retirement dreams of middle-class America are tied to the integrity of the stock market, crooks in the corner office are everybody's problem."[164] Other families had college tuition money tied up in stocks, along with their dreams of a more comfortable and secure future.

The scams perpetrated by executives and companies during 2002 are a diverse collection. Some, like those of Adelphia Communications, involve relatively straightforward looting by the founding family, which used the company as its personal bank to enrich themselves. Others, like Enron's, involve complicated financial transactions to inflate earnings, and thus stock prices, artificially. The SEC charged Adelphia with fraudulently excluding $2.3 billion in debt from its earnings report. AES, AOL-Time Warner, Cedent, Halliburton, K-Mart, Lucent Technologies, MicroStrategy, Rite Aid, and Waste Management are all said to have, in different ways, misstated revenues of more than $100 million in each case.

Arthur Andersen accountants served as auditors for Enron while taking in hundreds of millions of dollars from consulting deals with the company. This dual role of auditor and consultant created an obvious conflict of interest. Andersen auditors would surely be reluctant to reveal the full extent of Enron's losses, or to question the propriety of work Andersen consultants had been paid hundreds of millions of dollars for by Enron. Andersen is, of course, quite experienced at this sort of thing, having audited such other corporate suspects as Global Crossing, Halliburton Oil, Qwest, Waste Management, and WorldCom, and, before that, Charles Keating's Lincoln Savings and Loan, "which became a symbol of the nation's savings-and-loan crisis when it failed in 1989 at an eventual cost to taxpayers of $2.9 billion."[165]

Financial service firms like J. P. Morgan Chase and Citigroup earned substantial fees for loaning money to corporations and helping them to hide their level of indebtedness. A *Wall Street Journal* editorial called the banks "Enron Enablers," and *Fortune* added: "They appear to have behaved in a guileful way and helped their corporate clients undertake unsavory practices. And they appear to have had an entire division that, among other things, helped corporations avoid taxes and manipulate their balance sheets through something called structured finance, which is a huge profit center for each bank."[166] In addition, brokerage firms came under fire because their high-profile analysts enthusiastically endorsed stocks publicly that they were disparaging privately, all because their firms derived underwriting fees or other business from the troubled companies.[167] Merrill Lynch analyst Henry Blodgett privately described some stocks as a "piece of shit" while recommending them publicly to small investors.[168]

A summary of the most serious examples of alleged (and sometimes admitted) corporate wrongdoing is provided in Table 3.4, "Scoundrel Capitalism, 2005." Because of the large amount of such wrongdoing, the table focuses on the most harmful incidents and highlights the multiple dimensions of corporate misbehavior. Thus, the sentences given out reported there tend to be the most severe and are not necessarily representative of how "tough" the criminal justice system was on corporate criminals.

TABLE 3.4   Scoundrel Capitalism, 2005*

Name/Company	Alleged Wrongdoing
Adelphia	
The sixth-largest cable company declared bankruptcy after announcing that the founding Rigas family conspired to hide $2.3 billion in debt, some of it improperly used by the Rigas family for personal expenses. Investors lost $60 billion in value when stock fell to $0.15 from a high of $66.00; the company filed for bankruptcy and restated earnings for several years.	The founding Rigas family used the company as their personal bank, improperly took money and loans, created sham transactions and forged financial documents to cover it up, and lied to investors about the company's overall financial condition. A Securities and Exchange Commission (SEC) official describes this as "one of the most extensive financial frauds ever to take place at a public company." They found "rampant self-dealing," including the use of $252 million in Adelphia funds to repay stock market losses; other company money was used to purchase a $12.8 million golf club, the Buffalo Sabres hockey team ($150 million), and luxury condominiums for the Rigas family. The family also used, without reimbursement, airplanes owned by Adelphia, including one for an African safari vacation. Timothy Rigas grew concerned about his father John's "unacceptably large" spending of company money and put him on a $1 million a month allowance.
	John and Timothy were convicted on 18 felony counts each. The judge sentenced Timothy (former Chief Financial Officer) to 20 years and John (founder) to 15 years. John received a lesser sentence because of health problems, but the judge said the sentence was "substantial," "appropriate" for the "egregious" conduct and would send a clear message to other corporate executives. Michael Rigas received 10 months of home confinement after pleading guilty to making a false entry in a company record.

Name/Company	Alleged Wrongdoing

Arthur Andersen

Andersen audited many companies that had to restate earnings. They settled with the SEC in numerous other cases: Enron, WorldCom ($8 billion restatement), Global Crossing, Qwest Communications, Baptist Foundation of Arizona ($217 million settlement), Sunbeam ($110 million settlement), and Colonial Realty ($90 million settlement). The Waste Management case ($1 billion overstated earnings) led to a $229 million shareholder settlement, and an SEC "cease and desist" order on misleading accounting.

Andersen officials ordered the shredding of important Enron documents under the guise of reminding employees about the company's document retention policy. To help dispose of 30 boxes of documents, Andersen called a company named Shred-It, whose motto is "Your secrets are safe with us." Some two tons of documents were destroyed after Andersen executives acknowledged an SEC investigation into Enron's accounting practices was "highly probable" but before the SEC formally started. In argument before the Supreme Court, the Deputy Solicitor General said, "It is the equivalent of sending someone to a crime scene, and wiping up the evidence before police get there with the yellow tape." Andersen also deleted large numbers of emails relating to its internal debates on Enron's financial problems.

Arthur Andersen's conviction for obstruction of justice ended the company as an accounting firm. The conviction was later unanimously overturned by the Supreme Court because the jury instruction about the term "corruptly persuading" the withholding of evidence "failed to convey the requisite consciousness of wrongdoing." The Court's opinion did not suggest that Andersen was innocent and noted an incident where the head of the "engagement team" for Enron "picked up a document with the words 'smoking gun' written on it and began to destroy it, adding 'we don't need this.'"

Enron

Described by executive Jeffrey Skilling as "the world's coolest company," Enron declared the largest corporate bankruptcy in history on December 2, 2001. It restated its earnings and assets downward by

A special committee of Enron's board (the Powers Committee) concluded that partnership arrangements allowed Enron executives to hide the company's losses and liabilities, while earning tens of millions of dollars in fees for themselves. The report was based on a three-month review without subpoena power and limited access to documents. Nevertheless, it "found a systematic and pervasive attempt by Enron's Management to misrepresent the Company's financial condition," and found that Enron employees involved in the partnerships received "tens of millions of dollars they should never have received." Investigators concluded that Enron manipulated the California power crisis for financial gain, entered into transactions

(Continued)

TABLE 3.4 (continued)

Name/Company	Alleged Wrongdoing
$1.5 billion, wiping out 4,200 jobs and $60 billion in market value lost to shareholders.	presenting conflicts of interest, engaged in fraudulent transactions to book revenue, and punished whistleblowers.

Enron executives and directors sold $1 billion worth of shares in the three years before the company collapsed. Just before the bankruptcy announcement, employees were locked out of selling their shares because of "administrative changes" to the stock plan. During this period, when Enron stock lost 28 percent of its value, Ken Lay took $19 million in cash advances that he repaid with Enron stock that was rapidly losing value.

A jury found Skilling guilty on 19 counts, including conspiracy, fraud, false statements, and insider trading. He was sentenced to 24 years, although he could have received more than 30 years based on sentencing guidelines. Lay was convicted of six counts of conspiracy and fraud, plus another four counts of fraud and false statements at a separate trial. He died of a heart attack before his appeal was final, so his conviction was voided and cannot be used against him in civil suits to recover money from his estate.

Chief Financial Officer Andrew Fastow was originally charged with 109 felonies. He plead guilty to two counts of conspiracy in exchange for a 10-year maximum sentence and his promise to cooperate and testify against his bosses. A judge sentenced him to six years; he was released in late 2011.

Kenneth Rice, head of Enron's broadband unit, sold more than $76 million in shares while he knew the company was failing. He faced more than 40 counts and 10 years in prison, but accepted a plea bargain for 27 months and testimony against his bosses.

Global Crossing

Optical fiber company filed the fourth-largest bankruptcy ever, with $12 billion in debt. This company is chartered in Bermuda to avoid U.S. corporate taxes, even though it is headquartered and run out of the United States, and enjoys all the

Allegedly engaged in capacity swaps with Qwest Communications (see next company) to improperly book revenue in order to inflate stock price. In one congressional hearing, Rep. Billy Tauzin (R-LA) said executives "pursued sham transactions to put revenue on the books, to mislead investors, and to prevent further drops in their stock prices." Many of these transactions were done in the last few days, sometimes the last minutes, of the financial quarter to help meet earnings expectations.

No criminal charges were filed against any Global Crossing executives. Three executives agreed to pay a civil fine of $100,000 each in an SEC settlement, but they were not required to admit any wrongdoing. The SEC enforcement division recommended a fine against Chairman Gary Winnick

Name/Company	Alleged Wrongdoing

rights and access to government contracts that U.S. corporations enjoy.

(who worked out of a replica of the Oval Office), but SEC commissioners rejected the idea. The expected $1 million fine was small compared to the $730 million he made in stock sales before the company filed for bankruptcy.

Qwest Communications

The dominant local telephone company in 14 states. Shares dropped to $1 each, from a high of $66.00, losing $90 billion in value for investors. Qwest restated $2.5 billion in revenue.

Alleged to have improperly engaged in hollow trades and capacity swaps with Global Crossing and other telecoms to boost revenue and meet earnings expectations. The SEC charged that CEO Joseph Nacchio and other executives knew of revenue shortfalls, but "fraudulently and materially misrepresented Qwest's performance and growth to the investing public." Rep. James Greenwood (R-PA), who chaired a congressional investigating committee, said: "Investors in Global Crossing and Qwest lost billions of dollars when the truth came out about these companies' finances, while insiders walked away with billions of dollars."

On several occasions, executives asked that the details of the swaps not be put in writing to avoid scrutiny. A memo by Chief Financial Officer (CFO) Robin Szeliga indicated Qwest would penalize anyone who questioned the company's handling of swaps and followed through by blocking business to Morgan Stanley, which publicly questioned Qwest's reliance on swaps. Qwest blames Arthur Andersen, which it says approved the accounting related to the capacity swaps.

Nacchio was convicted on 19 of 42 counts of insider trading and sentenced to six years in prison in what has been called the largest insider trading case in history.

CFO Robin Szeliga was sentenced to two years probation for one count of insider trading in exchange for her testimony against Nacchio.

Qwest paid a $250 million penalty to the SEC.

Tyco

This large conglomerate is chartered in Bermuda to avoid U.S. corporate taxes, even though it is headquartered and run out of the United States, and enjoys all the rights and

Former CEO Dennis Kozlowski and former CFO Mark Swartz looted the company and shareholders of $600 million, $150 million of which was directly stolen through improper loans and unauthorized bonuses, with the rest related to bonuses based on financial misstatements and selling stock at prices artificially inflated by their financial misstatements.

The two men used the money to buy houses, art, and luxury items for themselves, including the infamous $6,000 shower curtain that hung in Kozlowski's $31 million

(Continued)

TABLE 3.4 (continued)	
Name/Company	**Alleged Wrongdoing**
access to government contracts that U.S. corporations enjoy.	apartment, and a $2 million birthday party for Kozlowski's wife on the Italian island of Sardinia that included an ice sculpture of Michelangelo's David with vodka pouring from his genitals.
	Kozlowski also allegedly improperly bought valuable paintings by Renoir and Monet worth $13.2 million and he evaded $1.1 million in New York State sales tax.
	Kozlowski and Swartz were convicted of 22 counts of grand larceny, conspiracy, securities fraud, and falsifying business records. The prosecutor described it as the largest larceny ever prosecuted in New York. They were both sentenced to eight years and four months to 25 years in prison, less than the maximum term of 15 to 30 years. The two men are potentially eligible for parole in 2012. Kozlowski settled the sales tax issue relating to the art and income tax liabilities for $21.2 million.
WorldCom (now MCI)	
Telecommunications giant announced a series of restatements totaling about $11 billion, and its $107 billion bankruptcy displaced Enron as the largest bankruptcy filing in U.S. history. The stock price fell from $64.00 to $0.09, reducing total shareholder value by $180 billion; 17,000 employees have been laid off. The New York State pension plan lost $300 million because of WorldCom investments. The large-scale fraud earned it the name "WorldCon."	The Deputy U.S. Attorney General said CFO Scott Sullivan and Controller David Myers "systematically flouted rules of accounting and lied outright to investors to perpetuate the false image that WorldCom was succeeding." With business deteriorating, executives put pressure on numerous others to, in Myers's words, engage in accounting adjustments for which "there was no justification or documentation and [that] were not in accordance with generally accepted accounting principles." WorldCom executives pressured whistleblowers to remain quiet, and Myers warned employees who had questions not to discuss their concerns with outside auditors.
	CEO Bernard Ebbers was removed from his position when WorldCom declared bankruptcy, but he negotiated a severance package worth $1.5 million a year for life.
	Ebbers received a 25-year sentence after being convicted of securities fraud, conspiracy, and false-statement charges. He faced 30 years to life, based on the amount of loss, the number of victims, for leading a criminal activity involving five or more participants and abusing a position of public trust. The Court of Appeals upheld the sentence as "harsh but not unreasonable," noting that the securities fraud here was "not puffery or cheerleading or even a misguided effort to protect the company" but "were specifically intended to create a false picture of profitability even for professional analysts, which, in Ebbers's case, was motivated by his personal financial circumstances."
	Sullivan faced 25 years because he had directed subordinates to inflate revenues, but received only five years because of his cooperation in convicting Ebbers. The sentencing judge

Name/Company	Alleged Wrongdoing
	described Sullivan as the "day-to-day manager of the scheme at WorldCom." As part of plea bargains that included requirements of cooperation with the government, Myers received one year; accounting director Yates received one year; and director of management reporting Vinson received five months in jail and five months home detention.

* The title comes from a phrase used by Simon Schama in "The Dead and the Guilty," *The Guardian*, September 11, 2002, *www.guardian.co.uk/september11/oneyearon/story/0,12361,789978,00.html*.

Sources: Devin Leonard, "The Adelphia Story," *Fortune*, August 12, 2002, *www.fortune.com/indexw.jhtml?channel=artcol.jhtml&doc_id=208825;CNNMoney*, "Rigas and Sons Arrested," July 25, 2002, *http://money.cnn.com/2002/07/24/news/rigas/* [currently unavailable]; George Mannes, "Adelphia Charges Up the Ante," The Street.com, July 24, 2002, *www.thestreet.com/_yahoo/tech/georgemannes/10033900.html*; Carrie Johnson and Christopher Stern, "Adelphia Founder, Sons Charged," *The Washington Post*, July 25, 2002, p. A1; "Swartz Got Rich Severance Deal," *Boston Globe*, September 26, 2002, *www.boston.com/dailyglobe2/269/business/Swartz_got_rich_severance_deal+.shtml*; Peter Behr and Dan Eggen, "Enron Is Target of Criminal Probe," *The Washington Post*, January 10, 2002, p. A1; Peter Behr and April Witt, "Visionary's Dream Led to Risky Business," *The Washington Post*, July 28, 2002, p. A1; Jonathan Krim, "Fast and Loose at WorldCom: Lack of Controls, Pressure to Grow Set Stage for Financial Deceptions," *The Washington Post*, August 29, 2002, p. A1; Jonathan Krim, "WorldCom Staff Told Not to Talk to Auditor, E-Mails Show," *The Washington Post*, August 27, 2002, p. E3; David M. Ewalt and John Kreiser, "Sidgmore Steps Down as WorldCom CEO; Ebbers May Lose Golden Parachute," *InformationWeek.com*, September 10, 2002, *www.informationweek.com/story/IWK20020910S0007*; Motley Fool, "The Motley Fool Take on Wednesday, Feb. 27, 2002," *www.fool.com/news/take/2002/take020227.htm*; Motley Fool, "The Motley Fool Take on Wednesday, June 5, 2002," *www.fool.com/news/take/2002/take020605.htm*; Robert O' Harrow, "Tyco Executives Free on Bond of $15 Million," *The Washington Post*, September 28, 2002, p. E1; Carrie Johnson and Ben White, "WorldCom Arrests Made," *The Washington Post*, August 2, 2002, p. A1; Ben White, "WorldCom Officer Pleads Guilty to Fraud," *The Washington Post*, October 8, 2002, p. E1; and Citizen Works, "Corporate Crookbook: Corporate Scandal Sheet," *http://citizenworks.org/enron/corp-scandal.php*; Mark Gimein, "You Bought: They Sold," *Fortune*, September 2, 2002, pp. 64–65; "Adelphia's John Rigas and Son Report to Prison in N.C.," *USA Today*, August 13, 2007, *http://www.usatoday.com/money/media/2007-08-13-rigas-prison-nc_N.htm*; "Adelphia founder sentenced to 15 years," *CNN Money*, June 20, 2005, *http://money.cnn.com/2005/06/20/news/newsmakers/rigas_sentencing/*; Arthur Andersen, LLP v. United States 544 U.S. 696 (2005), note 6; Associated Press, "Former Enron exec gets 27 month sentence," *http://www.msnbc.msn.com/id/19293341/*; Kristen Hays, "Ex-Enron CFO Fastow sentenced to 6 years in prison," *Houston Chronicle*, September 26, 2006, *http://www.chron.com/disp/story.mpl/front/4215426.html*; Carrie Johnson, "Felling 'Slap in the Face' After Fastow's Sentence," *The Washington Post*, October 3, 2006, p. D1; Stephen Taub, "No Charges for Global Crossing's Winnick," *CFO.com*, December 14, 2004, *http://www.cfo.com/article.cfm/3493060*; "3 ex-officials of Global Crossing are fined in SEC settlement," *International Herald Tribune*, April 13, 2005, *http://www.iht.com/articles/2005/04/12/business/global.php*; Dan Frosch, "Court Considers New Trial for Former Chief of Quest," *The New York Times*, September 25, 2008, *http://www.nytimes.com/2008/09/26/technology/26qwest.html*; Dan Frosch, "Ex-Quest Chief Gets 6-year Sentence," *The New York Times*, July 28, 2007; U.S. Dept of Justice, "Former Qwest Chief Financial Officer Sentenced for Insider Trading," July 28, 2006, *http://www.usdoj.gov/usao/co/press_releases/archive/2006/July06/7_28_06.html*; Ben White, "Ex-Tyco Executives Convicted," *The Washington Post*, June 18, 2005, A1; Ben White, "Ex-Tyco Executives Sentenced," *The Washington Post*, September 20, 2005, p. D1; Anthony Lin, "Former Tyco Executives Sentenced to Up to 25 years in prison," *Law.com*, September 20, 2005, *http://www.law.com/jsp/article.jsp?id=1127133338846*; Anemona Hartocollis, "ex-Tyco Chief to Settle Tax Evasion Charges," *The New York Times*, May 13, 2006, *http://www.nytimes.com/2006/05/13/business/13tyco.html*; Associated Press, "Conviction of Ex-Worldcom Chief Is Upheld," *The New York Times*, July 29, 2006, *http://www.nytimes.com/2006/07/29/business/29ebbers.html*; Paul Leighton, "Ebbers' 25 year Sentence for WorldCom Fraud Upheld. Good," *PaulsJusticeBlog.com*, August 4, 2006, *http://www.paulsjusticeblog.com/2006/08/ebbers_25_year_sentence_for_worldcom_fraud.php*; Jennifer Bayot and Roben Farzad, "Ex-WorldCom Officer Sentenced to 5 Years in Accounting Fraud," *The New York Times*, August 12, 2005, *http://www.nytimes.com/2005/08/12/business/12worldcom.html*."

In an article on the origins of this crisis, the *New York Times* said: "Here we go again. In an eerie flashback to the savings and loan scandal a decade ago, it turns out that of the lawmakers and regulators investigating some of the causes behind the Enron-Arthur Andersen scandal—Democrats and Republicans alike—may need to look no further than a mirror." The 1995 Private Securities Litigation Reform Act—lobbied heavily for by Arthur Andersen—helped shield companies and their accountants from liability. Five years later, lawmakers "succeeded in forcing regulators to dilute proposed restrictions on accountants. The group includes the [then] current chairman of the Securities and Exchange Commission [Harvey Pitt] and three House and Senate committee chairmen now involved in the cleanup who have been among the accounting industry's largest campaign [contribution] recipients."[169]

The Sarbanes-Oxley Act was signed into law in 2002 to deal with this problem. It created a new board to oversee the accounting and auditing of publicly traded companies, limited the ability of accounting firms to be both auditors and consultants of the same firms, gave shareholders five rather than three years to sue companies that mislead them, and increased possible fines and jail sentences for those who violate new and existing corporate laws. Much of the law is a step in the right direction. However, political compromises in Congress led to changing the standard for holding executives liable for fraud from "reckless" to "knowing," which makes the case more difficult for prosecutors. Congress also limited *disgorgement* (the repayment of money taken by fraud) only to those directly involved, not company officers and directors who only knew about misconduct.[170]

As soon as the ink was dry on the legislation, the *Washington Post* reported, "Members of Congress from both parties accused the administration of undermining or narrowing the scope of provisions covering securities fraud, whistleblower protection and punishment for shredding documents." Critics, including the bill's authors, charged that the Justice Department drew up interpretations and prosecution guidelines that contradicted the legislative intent of the reform measure.[171]

Following up on Sarbanes-Oxley, the U.S. Sentencing Commission increased the penalties for some white-collar crimes. However, "the Justice Department promptly complained that the new guidelines do not go far enough, because the panel failed to crack down harder on lower-level offenders and failed to make it more difficult for white-collar criminals to avoid prison ...."[172] An article in the *Washington Post* reports,

> The Securities and Exchange Commission's staff, over objections from investor and consumer groups, is recommending that the commission back off from several auditing reforms it was considering in response to scandals at Enron Corp. and other companies...
> Said Lynn E. Turner, chief accountant at the SEC in the Clinton administration, 'How can you go through Enron, how can you go through Tyco, how can you go through WorldCom and still have an SEC that is putting accountants before investors?'[173]

[handwritten marginal note: when there's $ involved, they are willing to work w/ them]

In March 2002, after the disclosure of Enron's bankruptcy, but before a wave of other frauds was revealed, *Fortune* magazine observed, "The double standard in criminal justice in this country is starker and more embedded than many realize. Bob Dylan was right: Steal a little, and they put you in jail. Steal a lot, and you're likely to walk away with a lecture and a court-ordered promise not to do it again."[174] As a case in point, Enron's Chief Financial Officer Andy Fastow was charged with 109 felony counts including conspiracy, wire fraud, securities fraud, falsifying books, obstruction of justice, money laundering, insider trading, and filing false income tax returns. He agreed to a plea bargain with a maximum of 10 years in prison and was released late in 2011 after serving six years. However, at the same time, Leandro Andrade received a sentence of 50 years for two counts of stealing videocassettes from K-Mart—a sentence upheld by the Supreme Court as not an unreasonable application of a three-strikes law.[175] A poor guy who steals less than $200 worth of goods to support his drug addiction ends up in jail for life, and a rich guy who masterminds a scam that results in billions of dollars in losses ultimately gets a much smaller sentence and a year off for participating in the prison's substance abuse program because of his dependence on anti-anxiety medication.[176]

Some of the sentences handed down to corporate executives who went to trial have been harsher than what Fastow received, and attention has focused disproportionately on a relatively small number of sentences that are in the range of 15 to 30 years. These are harsh and sometimes taken as evidence that the pendulum has swung to the point of unreasonably harsh sentences. However, such a conclusion ignores the scale of these crimes. These were not run-of-the-mill white-collar crimes, but systemic and widespread frauds that undermined the public's faith in the financial system, and caused extensive harm to employees, communities, and shareholders. The judge sentencing Enron's executive Jeffrey Skilling noted that he had "imposed on hundreds if not thousands of people a life sentence of poverty."[177] Further, focusing on the extreme cases gives a distorted sense of the overall picture of sentencing. An article in the *Federal Sentencing Reporter* tracked 440 of the highest profile cases of corporate fraud and found that the harsh sentences were reserved for those who went to trial and lost, although "the largest concentration of white-collar criminals convicted at trial received five-to-ten-year sentences." Guilty pleas accounted for 57 percent of the cases, and only two of those defendants received sentences of more than 15 years: "the vast majority of those who plead received sentences of fewer than five years—the beneficiaries of sentencing guidelines that reward cooperation."[178]

So, for all the rhetoric about how tough we are on white-collar offenders, a substantial number of those involved in the biggest financial scandal ended up with less than five years, which is equivalent to the mandatory sentence that existed at the same time for possession of five grams of crack cocaine. Those who were found guilty at trial did receive longer sentences, although a final assessment needs to wait until we see how much actual time they serve because of reductions for good time and participation in rehabilitation programs. Also, remember from Chapter 2 that willful violations of health and safety laws that result in a death are still punishable by six months in prison—half the penalty for harassing a wild burro on federal land—so there is only a limited range of crimes of the well-off toward which we can claim to have gotten tougher.

The Financial Meltdown of 2008: "the "best 18 months of grifting this country has ever seen."[179]   Just as the final chapters of the Enron saga were being written, the United States started experiencing its worst financial crisis since the Great Depression. At its source are complex securities based on "subprime" mortgages, which may never be repaid because lax underwriting standards encouraged lenders to give mortgages to borrowers without resources to repay them. These subprime mortgages were in great demand by investment banks that made large profits pooling and reselling them. Credit ratings agencies like Standard & Poor's and Moody's, who are paid by the investment banks, gave the securities higher credit ratings than the borrowers' underlying assets would justify. The Federal Reserve had power to regulate mortgage underwriters, but failed to do so. A six-month investigation by the Associated Press concluded that "federal regulators charged with protecting consumers have thus far made a conscious decision not to act."[180]

To make matters worse, in 2004, the SEC waived its leverage rules for five big Wall Street firms, which allowed them to borrow larger amounts of money and take on more risk (the five firms are Goldman Sachs, Lehman Brothers, Bear Stearns, Merrill Lynch, and Morgan Stanley. Merrill Lynch was sold to Bank of America in January 2009, and Lehman and Bear Sterns are no longer in business.) Previously, the permitted debt-to-capital ratio was 12 to 1, but after the SEC deregulated, firms increased their leveraging to 30 to 1 and even 40 to 1, essentially borrowing $30 and even $40 for each dollar of assets.[181] Further, many companies were involved in buying or selling "credit default swaps," which function like insurance against a company's inability to pay its debt. But unlike insurance, there is no federal or state regulation of the swaps, and thus no centralized clearinghouse to keep track of what parties have sold how much protection and whether they have the assets to cover their bets. Thus, as Wall Street firms started to run into financial trouble, no one knew which ones would have problems due to exposure to the credit default swaps. This lack of transparency caused a lack of trust that helped to freeze up the credit system because no one wanted to lend money in case the borrower turned out to be in deep financial trouble.

Barry Ritholtz, CEO of a financial research firm and author of *Bailout Nation*, stated that a consistent element of the problem has been "an abdication of responsibility from the various entities assigned to supervise and regulate" our financial system.[182] He suggests that we wouldn't allow the Super Bowl to be played without referees because "we *know* that players would give in to their worst impulses,"[183] and the financial system is the same. As investigations were starting "government officials with experience investigating corporate fraud say some of the patterns they are detecting—lying to investors, shifting debt off corporate balance sheets—are familiar." A former member of the Enron Task Force said, "The more things change, the more things stay the same."[184]

That makes part of the story frustratingly familiar. So does the fact that while investors have lost billions, many of those "who drove the financial ship of state aground" raked in hundreds of millions in pay, severance, and stock sales before the collapse. The CEO of Lehman Brothers, Richard Fuld, Jr. sold $490 million in stocks, and had a $34 million annual salary before the 158-year-old firm filed for a record bankruptcy and shares lost 94 percent of their value. During the previous year, Lehman paid out $5.7 billion in bonuses. Angelo Mozilo, CEO and founder of Countrywide Financial, cashed in over $400 million in stock before his company, which had been at the forefront of originating problematic subprime mortgages, was sued by several state attorneys general.[185]

But by 2008, memories of Enron seem to have faded. The *New York Times* reported that "in 1995, bank regulators referred 1,837 cases to the Justice Department;" more recently, however, in "a period encompassing the worst of the crisis, an average of only 72 [cases] a year have been referred for criminal prosecution."[186] Any strengthening of enforcement because of Enron has disappeared. "Legal and financial experts say that a loosening of enforcement measures, cutbacks in staffing at the Securities and Exchange Commission, and a shift in resources toward terrorism at the FBI have combined to make the federal government something of a paper tiger in investigating securities crimes."[187] Then SEC Chairman Christopher Cox said, "We've done everything we can during the last several years in the agency to make sure people understand there's a strong market cop on the beat," but he required staff to get approval of many actions from SEC commissioners. According to former SEC Chairman Arthur Levitt, Jr., this has effectively "handcuffed" the inspection and enforcement division.[188] Further, "the commission delayed settlements while commissioners negotiated to impose smaller penalties than the companies had agreed to pay."[189]

More enforcement problems came to light when Judge Jed Rakoff rejected a proposed settlement in a case in which the SEC claimed Citicorp sold investors a product it was betting would lose value and did not disclose that information, causing investors $700 million in losses. In the settlement, Citigroup did not admit guilt, but agreed to pay $285 million and said it would not violate this provision of the law again. The judge noted that the penalty was "pocket change" to Citigroup, and would have no deterrent effect or make up for investor losses. Further, the promise not to violate the law in the future was the kind of relief that "Citigroup (a recidivist) knew that the S.E.C. had not sought to enforce against any financial institution for at least the last 10 years."[190] Indeed, a *New York Times* investigation found that Citigroup "agreed not to violate the very same antifraud statute in July 2010. And in May 2006. Also as far as back as March 2005 and April 2000." They found 19 companies were repeat offenders who had promised not to do it again.

The FBI has been conspicuously absent from the current situation, even though FBI officials in 2004 said that mortgage-related problems had "the potential to be an epidemic."[191] The FBI is devoting so few resources to white-collar crime that companies are turning to private investigators to prepare "courtroom-ready prosecutions" that they can take to the FBI because they are unable to get the agency's attention otherwise.[192] As a result, the former lead prosecutor of Enron's Lay and Skilling commented that "most sitting U.S. Attorneys now staring at the subprime crisis find scant resources available to pursue sophisticated financial crimes."[193] While the FBI belatedly tried to find additional agents to look into mortgage fraud and investigate firms at the center of the financial crisis, then-Attorney General Michael Mukasey repeatedly rejected calls for an equivalent of the Enron Task Force that was used to prosecute earlier widespread complex financial crime.[194] William Black, a senior regulator who helped oversee savings and loan prosecutions, noted: "If you don't investigate, you don't find."[195] If you don't find evidence, you can't refer cases for prosecution and convict people. And that's just what happened.

The cases against executives and big financial firms have been civil suits, not criminal trials. Goldman Sachs settled in 2010 a SEC suit for $550 million for misleading investors about a subprime mortgage product called Abacus. Another firm, Countrywide, grew quickly to become one of the largest mortgage lenders by steering people into expensive subprime loans. Angelo Mozilo, its CEO, settled with the SEC for $67.5 million for assuring investors "that Countrywide was primarily a prime quality mortgage lender that had avoided the excesses of its competitors" just before the firm was spared bankruptcy by being sold to Bank of America.[196]

Nobel Prize winning economist Joseph Stiglitz puts these cases into the larger perspective: "Yeah, we fine them, and what is the big lesson? ... you're still sitting home pretty with your several hundred million dollars that you have left over after paying fines that look very large by ordinary standards but look small compared to the amount that you've been able to cash in." Ultimately, "the fine is just a cost of doing business," and "we ought to go do what we did in the S&L [crisis] and actually put many of these guys in prison."[197]

While not all the actions that lead to the financial crisis involved a crime, Stiglitz comments that "a considerable amount of what was done should have been illegal if it wasn't."[198] But even under existing law, legal experts noted areas where investigation should have been targeted, but was not: the extent of disclosure by executives about risk due to various mortgage products, the representations they made to investors about questionable loans that were bundled and sold, excessively optimistic estimates of the value of mortgage assets that created illusory profits for which executives received bonuses, cashing in shares based on inside information about looming problems, even misleading statements to boards and regulators about such problems.[199]

As the crisis has progressed, rampant fraud is now evident in mortgage servicing and especially in the paperwork filed with courts to certify facts necessary for a bank to foreclose on people unable to pay. To deal with the rising number of foreclosures, mortgage servicers for major financial institutions hired "robosigners" who quickly signed documents to be filed with the court without checking the accuracy of any of the information. Thomas Cox, a retired lawyer and banker, characterized the testimony of one of the robosigners as follows:

When Stephan says in an affidavit that he has personal knowledge of the facts stated in his affidavits, he doesn't. When he says that he has custody and control of the loan documents, he doesn't. When he says that he is attaching 'a true and accurate' copy of a note or a mortgage, he has no idea if that is so, because he does not look at the exhibits. When he makes any other statement of fact, he has no idea if it is true. When the notary says that Stephan appeared before him or her, he didn't.[200]

The result has been due process violations that resulted in wrongful foreclosures, including violations of additional rights granted to military personnel fighting abroad. At stake here is the protection of property rights (if the banks cannot prove they own the loans, they should not be able to claim the property) and the rule of law (that rich and poor should not be allowed to lie to the court).[201]

The financial crisis did produce sweeping legislation—the Dodd-Frank Wall Street Reform and Consumer Protection Act of 2010. It is too early to assess the impact of this legislation because it is a "framework" that calls for almost one hundred studies, and for agencies to write hundreds of rules. But the co-author, Congressman Barney Frank, says the bill is "facing a death through a thousand cuts" because of lobbying.[202] Such lobbying aims both at putting loopholes in new rules, and reducing the budgets of enforcement agencies. Congress has cut the proposed SEC budget for 2012 to the same level it had for 2011, even though Dodd-Frank gave the agency more responsibilities. The smaller budget does not save taxpayers anything because the SEC is funded by fees paid by the firms it regulates, so financial institutions pay less to government and have a weaker watchdog on the beat.[203] Ritholtz rightly calls this keeping the SEC "defective by design."[204] Former SEC chairman Harvey Pitt agrees: "It's almost as if the commission is being set up to fail."[205]

With the 2008 financial crisis, there have been no criminal prosecutions of top-level executives or major financial institutions at all! The clear trend is that as criminal sentences for corporate crime have increased, there have been fewer prosecutions even though each episode of financial fraud involves larger losses and greater economic turmoil. Notes Stiglitz: "When you say the Pledge of Allegiance you say, with 'justice for all.' People aren't sure that we have justice for all. Somebody is caught for a minor drug offense, they are sent to prison for a very long time. And yet, for these so-called white-collar crimes, which are not victimless, almost none of these guys, almost none of them, go to prison."[206]

More generally, we have seen in this chapter, and the one before, that the criminal justice system is triply biased against the poor. First, there is the economic class bias *among harmful acts* as to which get labeled crimes and which are treated as regulatory matters, as we saw in Chapter 2. Second, there is economic class bias *among crimes* that we have seen in this chapter. The crimes that poor people are likely to commit carry harsher sentences than the "crimes in the suites" committed by well-to-do people. Third, there is economic class bias *among defendants convicted of the same crimes.* Among such defendants, the poor receive less probation and more years of confinement than well-off defendants, assuring us once again that the vast majority of those put behind bars are from the lowest social and economic classes in the nation. On either side of the law, the rich get richer...

... AND THE POOR GET PRISON

At 9:05 a.m. on the morning of September 9, 1971, a group of inmates forced their way through a gate at the center of the prison, fatally injured a guard and took 50 hostages. The Attica prison uprising had begun. It lasted four days, until corrections officers and state troopers stormed the prison and killed 29 inmates and 10 hostages.[207] During those four days the nation saw the faces of its captives on television—the hard black faces of young men who had grown up on the streets of Harlem and other urban ghettos. Theirs were the faces of crime in America. The television viewers who saw them were not surprised. These were the faces of dangerous men who should be locked up. Nor were people outraged when the state launched its murderous attack on the prison, killing many more inmates and guards than the prisoners had. Maybe they were shocked—but not outraged. Neither were they outraged when two grand juries refused to indict any of the attackers, nor when the mastermind of the attack, New York Governor Nelson Rockefeller, was named vice president of the United States three years after the massacre.[208]

They were not outraged because the faces they saw on the TV screens fit and confirmed their beliefs about who is a deadly threat to American society—and a deadly threat must be met with deadly force. How did those men get to Attica? How did Americans get their beliefs about who is a dangerous person? These questions are interwoven. People get their notions about who is a criminal at least in part from the occasional television or newspaper picture of who is inside our prisons. The individuals they see there have been put in prison because people believe certain kinds of individuals are dangerous and should be locked up.

This is not a simple process of selecting the dangerous and the criminal from among the peace-loving and the law-abiding. It is also a process of *weeding out the wealthy* at every stage, so that the final picture—a picture like the one that appeared on the TV screen on September 9, 1971 (and that continues in contemporary TV broadcasts about crime)—is not a true reflection of the real dangers in our society, but a distorted image, the kind reflected in a carnival mirror.

We do not claim that the inmates in Attica were innocent of the crimes that sent them there. They, and most of the individuals in prisons in America, are probably guilty of the crime for which they were sentenced, and maybe more. Rather, the point is that people who are equally or more dangerous, equally or more criminal, are not there; that the criminal justice system works systematically not to punish and confine the dangerous and the criminal, *but to punish and confine the poor who are dangerous and criminal.*

It is successful at all levels. In 1973, there were 204,211 individuals in state and federal prisons, or 96 prisoners for every 100,000 individuals (of all ages) in the general population. By year-end 2010, there were a total of 1,518,104 persons in state and federal prisons, or 489 per 100,000 Americans. Add in the 748,728 in local jails, and the result is 2,266,832 people locked up, a staggering 731 for every 100,000 in the population. One in 137 U.S. residents (of all ages and both sexes) was behind bars at year-end 2010.[209] However, as the nonpartisan Pew Public Safety Performance Project noted, "for the first time, more than one in every 100 *adults* is now confined in an American jail or prison," and for men over 18 years old, one in 54 is incarcerated. This enormous number of prisoners is predominantly from the bottom of society and includes one in every 15 black men over 18 years old.[210]

Of the estimated 1.2 million people in state prisons in 1998, one-third were not employed at all (full- or part-time) prior to their arrests. Nearly half were without full-time employment prior to arrest.[211] Among jail inmates in 2002, 29 percent were not employed prior to arrest—15 percent were looking for work, and 14 percent were not. Approximately 45 percent of jail inmates reported pre-arrest incomes below $7,200 a year.[212] (The Department of Justice has not done surveys to update these figures, another case of missing information on class and criminal justice.) To get an idea of what part of society is in prison, we should compare these figures with comparable figures for the general population. Because more than 90 percent of inmates are adult males, we can look at employment and income figures for adult males in the general population.

In 2002, 5.9 percent of males, 16 years old and above, in the labor force were unemployed and looking for work. That same year, 19.6 percent of jail inmates were unemployed (and looking for work) in the year prior to their arrest. Prisoners were unemployed at a rate more than three times that of their counterparts in the general population.[213] In 2002, about half the adult males in the general population who had any income at all were earning $29,238 or less.[214] Compare this to jail inmates, about half of whom earned $12,000 a year or less in the year before they were arrested. Since this figure includes only jail inmates with income, and 20 percent did not have income before they were arrested, we can say that 70 percent of inmates earned less than half the median income for American males with income![215]

Our prisoners are not a cross-section of America. They are considerably poorer and considerably less likely to be employed than the rest of Americans. Moreover, they are also less educated, which is to say less in possession of the means to improve their sorry situations. As of 1999, 41 percent of U.S. prison inmates had not graduated from high school, compared to 20 percent of the U.S. adult population.[216] In 2002, 44 percent of jail inmates were not high school graduates compared to 16 percent of the general population.[217]

The criminal justice system is sometimes thought of as a kind of sieve in which the innocent are progressively sifted out from the guilty, who end up behind bars. We have tried to show that the sieve works another way as well. It sifts the affluent out from the poor, so it is not merely the guilty who end up behind bars, but the *guilty poor*.

With this information, we have proven the hypotheses set forth in Chapter 2, in the section titled "Criminal Justice as Creative Art." The criminal justice system does not simply weed the peace-loving from the dangerous, the law-abiding from the criminal. At every stage, starting with the very definitions of crime and progressing through the stages of investigation, arrest, charging, conviction, and sentencing, the system *weeds out the wealthy.* It refuses to define as "crimes" or as serious crimes the dangerous and predatory acts of the well-to-do—acts that, as we have seen, result in the loss of thousands of lives and billions of dollars. Instead, the system focuses its attention on those crimes likely to be committed by members of the lower classes. Thus, it is no surprise to find that so many of the people behind bars are from the lower classes. The people we see in our jails and prisons are no doubt dangerous to society, but they are not *the* danger to society, not *the gravest danger* to society. Individuals who pose equal or greater threats to our well-being walk the streets with impunity.

Chapter 1 argued that the society fails to institute policies that have a good chance of reducing crime. Chapter 2 argued that the criminal justice system works to make crime appear to be the monopoly of the poor by restricting the label "crime" to the dangerous acts of the poor and rarely applying it to the dangerous acts of the well-off. Chapter 3 argued that the society does this by more actively pursuing and prosecuting the poor rather than the well-off for the acts that are labeled crime. *The joint effect of all these phenomena is to maintain a real threat of crime that the vast majority of Americans believes is a threat from the poor.* The criminal justice system is a carnival mirror that throws back a distorted image of the dangers that lurk in our midst—and conveys the impression that those dangers are the work of the poor. Chapter 4 suggests who benefits from this illusion and how.

Summary

This chapter has mainly tried to document that, *even among those dangerous acts that our criminal justice system labels as crimes,* the system works to make it more likely that those who end up in jail or prison will be from the bottom of society. This works in two broad ways:

1. *For the same crime,* the system is more likely to investigate and detect, arrest and charge, convict and sentence, and sentence to prison (and for a longer time) a lower-class individual than a middle- or upper-class individual. To support this, we reviewed a large number of studies performed over a long period of time comparing the treatment of high- and low-socioeconomic status offenders and of white and nonwhite offenders, from arrest through sentencing for the same crimes.

2. *Between crimes that are characteristically committed by poor people (street crimes) and those characteristically committed by the well-off (white-collar and corporate crimes),* the system treats the former much more harshly

than the latter, even when the crimes of the well-off take far more money from the public or cause far more death and injury than the crimes of the poor. To support this, we compared the sentences meted out for street crimes with the treatment of those responsible for death and destruction in the workplace as well as those responsible for the S&L scandal and the recent financial cheating at Enron and other major corporations.

And remember, both of these processes only affect those acts that have been labeled crimes, which, as we saw in Chapter 2, largely excludes the harmful acts of the well-off. Taken together, these facts show why it should come as no surprise that our prisons are filled with poor people.

Study Questions

1. Who is in our jails and prisons? How do the people behind bars in America compare with the general population in employment, wealth, and level of education?
2. What is meant by "white-collar crime"? How costly is it compared with the crimes on the FBI's Index?
3. What factors make it likelier that a poor person who commits a crime such as shoplifting or nonaggravated assault will be arrested than a middle-class person who commits the same crime?
4. What factors make it likelier that a middle- or upper-class person charged with a crime will be acquitted than a lower-class person charged with the same crime?
5. Are the people responsible for white-collar crime, including crimes that result in serious injury, more or less blameworthy than muggers? Do we punish white-collar criminals justly?
6. Is the criminal justice system racist? What evidence would establish or refute your view?
7. If killers of whites are more likely to be sentenced to death than killers of blacks, what should we do? Should we abolish the death penalty? Do you agree with the Supreme Court's decision in *McCleskey* v. *Kemp*? Why?
8. What do you see as the key factors behind the three large-scale outbreaks of financial fraud discussed in this chapter? What would help prevent them?

Additional Resources

Jeffrey Reiman and Paul Leighton, eds., *The Rich Get Richer and Poor Get Prison: A Reader* (Boston: Pearson, 2010). This volume is a collection of accessible articles that were either used as reference material for *The Rich Get Richer* or provide lively complementary examples or analysis. The reader is divided into sections that parallel the chapters of *The Rich Get Richer*, and each section of the reader opens with a substantial introduction, written by the editors, that provides article summaries, context, and linkages to *The Rich Get Richer*.

The authors also maintain a companion website to the text at *http://www.paulsjusticepage.com/reiman.htm*

Notes

1. *Challenge*, p. 44.
2. Ronald Goldfarb, "Prisons: The National Poorhouse," *New Republic*, November 1, 1969, pp. 15–17.
3. Philip A. Hart, "Swindling and Knavery, Inc.," *Playboy*, August 1972, p. 158.
4. Compare the statement, written more than half a century ago, by Professor Edwin H. Sutherland, one of the major luminaries of twentieth-century criminology:

    First, the administrative processes are more favorable to persons in economic comfort than to those in poverty, so that if two persons on different economic levels are equally guilty of the same offense, the one on the lower level is more likely to be arrested, convicted, and committed to an institution. Second, the laws are written, administered, and implemented primarily with reference to the types of crimes committed by people of lower economic levels. (E. H. Sutherland, *Principles of Criminology* [Philadelphia: Lippincott, 1939], p. 179)

5. Edwin H. Sutherland and Donald R. Cressey, *Criminology*, 9th ed. (Philadelphia: Lippincott, 1974), p. 133.
6. Edwin Sutherland, Donald Cressey, and David Luckenbill, *Principles of Criminology*, 11th ed. (Dix Hills, New York.: General Hall, 1992), pp. 165 and 306.
7. *Sourcebook*, Table 3.29.2008; *UCR–2008*, Table 43.
8. David Huizinga, Terence Thornberry, Kelly Knight, and Peter Lovegrove, *Disproportionate Minority Contact in the Juvenile Justice System: A Study of Differential Minority Arrest/Referral to Court in Three Cities*, National Institute of Justice, September 2007, Document number 219743, p. 41, *http://www.ncjrs.gov/pdffiles1/ojjdp/grants/219743.pdf*.
9. See Thomas J. Dolan, "The Case for Double Jeopardy: Black and Poor," *International Journal of Criminology and Penology* 1 (1973): 129–50.
10. Cassia C. Spohn, "Thirty Years of Sentencing Reform: The Quest for a Racially Neutral Sentencing Process," in NIJ, *Criminal Justice 2000, vol. 3: Policies, Processes, and Decisions of the Criminal Justice System*, pp. 427–28.
11. Ibid., pp. 435, 466; Marvin D. Free Jr., "Racial Bias and the American Criminal Justice System: Race and Presentencing Revisited," *Critical Criminology* 10 (2001): 198.
12. Spohn, "Thirty Years of Sentencing Reform," p. 480.
13. Marjorie S. Zatz, "The Convergence of Ethnicity, Gender, and Class on Court Decision-Making: Looking toward the 21st Century," in NIJ, *Criminal Justice 2000, vol. 3: Policies, Processes, and Decisions of the Criminal Justice System*, NCJ 182410, p. 515.
14. Jim Crow—named after a popular racist song of the 1800s—describes the system of laws that allowed for the discrimination and segregation of African Americans in the United States from just after the Civil War (1876) to the Civil Right Legislation of 1964.
15. See, for example, Loic Wacquant, "Deadly Symbiosis: When Ghetto and Prison Meet and Mesh," in David Garland (ed.) *Mass Imprisonment in the United States: Social Causes and Consequences* (London: Sage, 2001), pp. 82–120.
16. William Julius Wilson, *The Declining Significance of Race*, 2nd ed. (Chicago: University of Chicago Press, 1980).
17. Michelle Alexander, *The New Jim Crow.* (New York: The New Press, 2011), pp. 1–2.

18. Carmen DeNavas-Walt, Bernadette Proctor, and Jessica Smith, U.S. Census Bureau, *Current Population Reports*, P60-239, *Income, Poverty & Health Insurance Coverage in the United States: 2010* (Washington, D.C.: U.S. Government Printing Office, 2011), Table 4.

19. Arthur Kennickell, "A Rolling Tide: Changes in the Distribution of Wealth in the U.S., 1989–2001," Federal Reserve Board, 2003, p. 34, *www.federalreserve.gov/pubs/oss/oss2/papers/concentration.2001.10.pdf*.

20. Jesse Bricker, et al, "Changes in U.S. Family Finances from 2007 to 2010," *Federal Reserve Bulletin* 98, no. 2 (2012), Table 9 p. 48 and 50.

21. Bureau of Labor Statistics, Current Population Survey, Annual Average Data (complete set of tables), Table 5. *http://www.bls.gov/cps/cpsa2010.pdf*.

22. Zatz, "The Convergence of Ethnicity, Gender, and Class on Court Decision-Making," p. 511.

23. Michael Tonry, "Racial Politics, Racial Disparities, and the War on Crime," *Crime & Delinquency* 40, no. 4 (October 1994): 483, 485–86.

24. *Sourcebook—1981*, p. 463.

25. *StatAbst—1988*, Table 304, p. 175.

26. BJS, *Profile of Inmates in the United States and in England and Wales, 1991*, October 1994, NCJ-145863, p. 13.

27. Theodore Chiricos and William Bales, "Unemployment and Punishment: An Empirical Assessment," *Criminology* 29, no. 4 (1991): 718.

28. Isidore Silver, "Introduction," in President's Crime Commission, *The Challenge of Crime in a Free Society* (New York: Avon, 1968), p. 31.

29. This is the conclusion of Austin L. Porterfield, *Youth in Trouble* (Fort Worth, TX: Leo Potishman Foundation, 1946); Fred J. Murphy, M. Shirley, and H. L. Witmer, "The Incidence of Hidden Delinquency," *American Journal of Orthopsychiatry* 16 (October 1946): 686–96; James F. Short Jr., "A Report on the Incidence of Criminal Behavior, Arrests, and Convictions in Selected Groups," in *Proceedings of the Pacific Sociological Society* (1954): 110–18; F. Ivan Nye, James F. Short Jr., and Virgil J. Olson, "Socioeconomic Status and Delinquent Behavior," *American Journal of Sociology* 63 (January 1958): 381–89; Maynard L. Erickson and Lamar T. Empey, "Class Position, Peers and Delinquency," *Sociology and Social Research* 49 (April 1965): 268–82; William J. Chambliss and Richard H. Nagasawa, "On the Validity of Official Statistics; A Comparative Study of White, Black, and Japanese High-School Boys," *Journal of Research in Crime and Delinquency* 6 (January 1969): 71–77; Eugene Doleschal, "Hidden Crime," *Crime and Delinquency Literature* 2, no. 5 (October 1970): 546–72; Nanci Koser Wilson, *Risk Ratios in Juvenile Delinquency* (Ann Arbor, MI: University Microfilms, 1972); and Maynard L. Erikson, "Group Violations, Socioeconomic Status, and Official Delinquency," *Social Forces* 52, no. 1 (September 1973): 41–52.

30. Charles R. Tittle and Robert F. Meier, "Specifying the SES/Delinquency Relationship," *Criminology* 28, no. 2 (1990): 292. See also R. Gregory Dunaway, Francis Cullen, Velmer Burton Jr., and David Evans, "The Myth of Social Class and Crime Revisited: An Examination of Adult and Class Criminality," *Criminology* 38, no. 2 (2002): 600.

31. Cf. Larry Karacki and Jackson Toby, "The Uncommitted Adolescent: Candidate for Gang Socialization," *Sociological Inquiry* 32 (1962): 203–15; William R. Arnold, "Continuities in Research: Scaling Delinquent Behavior," *Social Problems* 13, no. 1 (1965): 59–66; Harwin L. Voss, "Socio-economic Status and Reported Delinquent Behavior," *Social Problems* 13, no. 3 (1966): 314–24; LaMar Empey and Maynard L.

Erikson, "Hidden Delinquency and Social Status," *Social Forces* 44, no. 4 (1966): 546–54; Fred J. Shanley, "Middle-Class Delinquency as a Social Problem," *Sociology and Social Research* 51 (1967): 185–98; and Jay R. Williams and Martin Gold, "From Delinquent Behavior to Official Delinquency," *Social Problems* 20, no. 2 (1972): 209–29.

32. Empey and Erikson, "Hidden Delinquency and Social Status," pp. 549, 551. Nye, Short, and Olson also found destruction of property to be committed most frequently by upper-class boys and girls; see their "Socioeconomic Status and Delinquent Behavior," p. 385.

33. Martin Gold, "Undetected Delinquent Behavior," *Journal of Research in Crime and Delinquency* 3, no. 1 (1966): 27–46, p. 37; Sutherland and Cressey, *Criminology*, pp. 137, 220.

34. Ibid., p. 44.

35. Comparing socioeconomic status categories, "scant evidence is found that would support the contention that group delinquency is more characteristic of the lower-status levels than other socioeconomic status levels. In fact, only arrests seem to be more characteristic of the low-status category than the other categories." Erikson, "Group Violations, Socioeconomic Status and Official Delinquency," p. 15.

36. Gold, "Undetected Delinquent Behavior," p. 28 (emphasis added).

37. Ibid., p. 38.

38. Terence P. Thornberry, "Race, Socioeconomic Status and Sentencing in the Juvenile Justice System," *Journal of Criminal Law and Criminology* 64, no. 1 (1973): 90–98.

39. Robert Sampson, "Effects of Socioeconomic Context on Official Reaction to Juvenile Delinquency," *American Sociological Review* 51 (December 1986): 876–85.

40. Robert D. Crutchfield, Martie Skinner, Kevin Haggerty, Anne McGlynn, and Richard Catalano, "Racial Disparities in Early Criminal Justice Involvement," *Race and Social Problems*, 1, no. 4 (2009): 228.

41. Tamar Birckhead, "Delinquent by Reason of Indigency (draft)," *Washington University Journal of Law and Policy*, v38 (2012): 5. *http://papers.ssrn.com/sol3/papers.cfm?abstract_id=1918331.*

42. Ibid.

43. Belinda R. McCarthy, "Social Structure, Crime, and Social Control: An Examination of Factors Influencing Rates and Probabilities of Arrest," *Journal of Criminal Justice* 19 (1991): 19–29.

44. Note, "Developments in the Law: Race and the Criminal Process," *Harvard Law Review* 101 (1988): 1496.

45. Jerome Miller, *Search and Destroy: African-American Males in the Criminal Justice System* (New York: Cambridge University Press, 1996), p. 76. The study reported is by M. Wordes, T. Bynum, and C. Corley, "Locking Up Youth: The Impact of Race on Detention Decisions," *Journal of Research in Crime and Delinquency* 31, no. 2 (May 1994).

46. Wordes, Bynum, and Corley, "Locking Up Youth," p. 164; quoted in Miller, *Search and Destroy*, pp. 76–77.

47. Free, "Racial Bias and the American Criminal Justice System," p. 209.

48. Ibid, p. 26.

49. Ibid, pp. 26–27.

50. Birckhead, Delinquent by reason of indigency (draft), p.4.

51. Cited in David A. Harris, "The Stories, the Statistics, and the Law: Why 'Driving while Black' Matters," *Minnesota Law Review* 84 (1999): 265–326,

http://academic.udayton.edu/race/03justice/dwb01.htm. See also Eric Lichtblau, "Profiling Report Leads to a Demotion," The New York Times, August 24, 2005, *http://www.nytimes.com/2005/08/24/politics/24profiling.html.*

52. A. Rafik Mohamed and Erik Fritsvold, *Dorm Room Dealers* (Bolder: Lynne Rienner, 2010), pp. 11–12.

53. Mohamed and Fritsvold, *Dorm Room Dealers*, p. 6.

54. Mohamed and Fritsvold, *Dorm Room Dealers*, p. 7.

55. Victor Rios, *Punished: Policing the Lives of Black and Latino Boys* (New York: New York University Press, 2011), pp. xiv and 40.

56. Rios, *Punished*, p. 44.

57. Rios, *Punished*, pp. xiv and 158–9.

58. Michelle Alexander, "The New Jim Crow," *Ohio State Journal of Criminal Law* 9, no. 1 (2011): 13, notes 21 and 25; Michael Tonry, "Racial Politics, Racial Disparities, and the War on Crime," *Crime & Delinquency* 40, no. 4 (October 1994): 483.

59. Fox Butterfield, "More Blacks in Their 20's Have Trouble with the Law," *The New York Times*, October 5, 1995, p. A8.

60. See, for example, D. Chapman, "The Stereotype of the Criminal and the Social Consequences," *International Journal of Criminology and Penology* 1 (1973): 24.

61. This view is widely held, although the degree to which it functions as a self-fulfilling prophecy is less widely recognized. Versions of this view can be seen in *Challenge*, p. 79; Jerome Skolnick, *Justice without Trial* (New York: Wiley, 1966), pp. 45–48, 217–18; and Jessica Mitford, *Kind and Usual Punishment*, p. 53. Piliavin and Briar write in "Police Encounters with Juveniles,"

    Compared to other youths, Negroes and boys whose appearance matched the delinquent stereotype were more frequently stopped and interrogated by patrolmen—often even in the absence of evidence that an offense had been committed—[and] usually were given more severe dispositions for the same violations. Our data suggest, however, that these selective apprehension and disposition practices resulted not only from the intrusion of long-held prejudices of individual police officers but also from certain job-related experiences of law-enforcement personnel. First, the tendency of police to give more severe dispositions to Negroes and to youths whose appearance correspond to that which police associated with delinquents partly reflected the fact, observed in this study, that these youths also were much more likely than were other types of boys to exhibit the sort of recalcitrant demeanor which police construed as a sign of the confirmed delinquent. Further, officers assumed, partly on the basis of departmental statistics, that Negroes and juveniles who "look tough" (e.g., who wear chinos, leather jackets, boots, etc.) commit crimes more frequently than do other types of youths. (p. 212)

    Cf. Albert Reiss, *The Police and the Public* (New Haven, CT: Yale University Press, 1971). Reiss attributes the differences to the differences in the actions of complainants.

62. Richard J. Lundman, for example, found higher arrest rates to be associated with "offender powerlessness." Richard J. Lundman, "Routine Police Arrest Practices: A Commonwealth Perspective," *Social Problems* 22, no. 1 (October 1974): 127–41.

63. Note, "Developments in the Law" *Harvard Law Review* 101 (1988): 1520; William Bales, "Race and Class Effects on Criminal Justice Prosecution and Punishment Decisions" (Ph.D. diss., Florida State University, Tallahassee, 1987).

64. Cassia Spohn, John Gruhl, and Susan Welch, "The Impact of the Ethnicity and Gender of Defendants on the Decision to Reject or Dismiss Felony Charges," *Criminology* 25 (1987): 175, 180, 185.

65. "Stealing $200 Billion the Respectable Way," *U.S. News & World Report*, May 20, 1985, p. 83.

66. Marshall B. Clinard, *Corporate Corruption: The Abuse of Corporate Power* (New York: Praeger, 1990), p. 15.

67. The Bureau of Labor Statistics, 2012. Consumer Price Index, All Urban Consumers, U.S. City Average. All items was at 105.5 for January 1985 and 226 for November 2011, *http://www.bls.gov/ro5/cpiushistorical.pdf*.

68. August Bequai, "High-Tech Security and the Failings of President Clinton's Commission on Critical Infrastructure Protection," *Computers and Security* 17 (1998): 19–21.

69. Association of Certified Fraud Examiners, "2004 Report to the Nation" p. 8, *www.acfe.com/documents/2004RttN.pdf*.

70. Association of Certified Fraud Examiners, 2008. *Report to the Nation on Occupational Fraud and Abuse*, p. 8, *http://www.acfe.com/uploadedFiles/ACFE_Website/Content/documents/2008-rttn.pdf*; StatAbst–2012, Table 667, p. 435.

71. David Friedrichs, *Trusted Criminals* 4th ed. (Belmont: Wadsworth/Cengage, 2010), p. 47.

72. Chamber of Commerce of the United States, *A Handbook on White Collar Crime* (Washington, D.C.: Chamber of Commerce of the United States, 1974), p. 6. Copyright © 1974 by the Chamber of Commerce of the United States. Table reprinted by permission of the Chamber of Commerce of the United States.

73. Federal Bureau of Investigation, 2005. *FBI Computer Crime Survey*, p. 10, *http://www.digitalriver.com/v2.0-img/operations/naievigi/site/media/pdf/FBIccs2005.pdf*. Specifically, they assume "that non-survey respondents were only one third as likely to have experienced a financial loss" as survey respondents. Further, "these figures did not include much of the staff, technology, time, and software employed to prevent such incidents. These figures also do not begin to address the losses of individuals who are victims of computer crime (intrusions, identity theft, etc.)."

74. Tyler Moore, Richard Clayton, and Ross Anderson, "The Economics of Online Crime," *Journal of Economic Prespectives* 23, no. 3 (2009): 3.

75. Norton, 2011. *Cybercrime Report 2011*. *http://us.norton.com/content/en/us/home_homeoffice/html/cybercrimereport/*.

76. Clay Wilson, *Botnets, Cybercrime and Cyberterrorism: Vulnerabilities and Policy Issues for Congress* (Washington, D.C. Congressional Research Service, 2008), p. 28, *http://www.fas.org/sgp/crs/terror/RL32114.pdf*.

77. Neal Shover and Glenn Coffey, "Telemarketing Predators: Finally, We've Got Their Number," *National Institute of Justice Journal*, no. 252 (July 2005), *http://www.ncjrs.gov/pdffiles1/jr000252d.pdf*.

78. It is essential to be conservative in estimating costs of various white-collar crimes due to the possibility of overlap in the estimates. For example, telemarketing fraud might count some credit card or computer fraud, and vice versa. Nonetheless, working with such partial numbers as we have, we can be quite confident that we are far from overestimating the actual costs—indeed.

79. Peter Grabosky, Russell Smith, and Gillian Dempsey, *Electronic Theft: Unlawful Acquisition in Cyberspace* (Cambridge: Cambridge University Press, 2001), p. 143.

80. The estimate came from a book copyrighted in 2001 using data from the 1990s. To produce a conservative estimate of inflation, we will use the CPI for June 2000 [172.4] and June 2011 [225.7]. *http://www.bls.gov/ro5/cpiushistorical.pdf*.

81. Harrison Rainies, "The State of Greed," *U.S. News & World Report*, June 17, 1996, p. 64.

82. Carl Levin, 2007. Levin, Coleman, Obama Introduce Stop Tax Haven Abuse Act. "Experts have estimated that the total loss to the Treasury from offshore tax evasion alone approaches $100 billion per year, including $40 to $70 billion from individuals and another $30 billion from corporations engaging in offshore tax evasion. Abusive tax shelters add tens of billions of dollars more." We use the lower amount of $40 billion for individuals and the $30 billion from corporations to arrive at the $70 billion figure in the text. *http://levin.senate.gov/newsroom/press/release/?id=6413b85a-2bb4-41b8-8adc-d7e574f6d84a.*

83. Oracle Financial Services, 2010. U.S. Card Fraud. *http://www.oracle.com/us/industries/financial-services/internal/aite-us-card-fraud-wp-165586.pdf.*

84. National White Collar Crime Center. 2009. Check Fraud ($5.5 to $10 billion). *www.nw3c.org/research/site_files/cfm?mode=w;*King Brett. 2011. *Lack of US innovation costing Billions in preventable fraud* ($20 billion). *http://www.finextra.com/community/fullblog.aspx?blogid=5630.*

85. Privacy Rights Clearinghouse, "How Many Identity Theft Victims Are There?" (citing Javelin Strategy & Research Survey, February 2007), *http://www.privacyrights.org/ar/idtheftsurveys.htm.*

86. National White Collar Crime Center. 2002. Embezzlement/Employee Theft. *http://www.nw3c.org/research/site_files.cfm?mode=w.*

87. Federal Bureau of Investigation, 2007. *Organized Retail Theft: New Initiative to Tackle the Problem, http://www.fbi.gov/news/stories/2007/april/retail040607.*

88. National White Collar Crime Center. 2010. Intellectual Property Theft, p. 1–2. *http://www.nw3c.org/research/site_files.cfm?mode=w.*

89. Coalition Against Insurance Fraud, No-Class of 2010 Dishonored For Fraud Hall of Shame, *http://www.insurancefraud.org/article.lasso?RecID=1820*; Federal Bureau of Investigation, 2009. Financial Crimes Report, *http://www.fbi.gov/stats-services/publications/financial-crimes-report-2009.*

90. FBI, Health Care Fraud, *http://www.fbi.gov/publications/financial/fcs_report2006/financial_crime_2006.htm#Health*; National White Collar Crime Center, "Health Care Fraud: January 2007," *http://www.nw3c.org/research/site_files.cfm?mode=w*; and Nicholas Stein, "Inside Operation," *Fortune*, December 8, 2003, p. 130.

91. Federal Bureau of Investigation, "Securities and Commodities Fraud." *http://www.fbi.gov/stats-services/publications/fcs_report2006/financial-crimes-report-to-the-public-fiscal-year-2006#Securities.*

92. Cited in National White Collar Crime Center. 2007. Securities/Investment Fraud, p 4. *http://www.nw3c.org/research/site_files.cfm?mode=w.*

93. "Numbers Game: A High-Tech Arrest Gives Unusual Glimpse of Cell-Phone Fraud," *The Wall Street Journal*, April 29, 1996, p. A16.

94. Population figures from *StatAbst—2012*, Table 1, p. 8 and Table 2, p. 8. CPI calculations: 1974 = 49.3 and 2010 (June) = 218; *StatAbst—1995*, Table 761, p. 492; and The Bureau of Labor Statistics Consumer Price Index (All Urban Consumers) *http://www.bls.gov/ro5/cpiushistorical.pdf.*

95. Sutherland and Cressey, *Criminology*, p. 41 (emphasis added).

96. Clinard, *Corporate Corruption*, p. 15.

97. Clinard, *Corporate Corruption*, p. 15.

98. Susan Shapiro, "The Road Not Taken: The Elusive Path to Criminal Prosecution for White-Collar Offenders," *Law and Society Review* 19, no. 2 (1985): 182.

99. General Accounting Office. 2009. DOJ Has Taken Steps to Better Track Its Use of Deferred and Non-Prosecution Agreements, but Should Evaluate Effectiveness, p. 20. GAO-10-110. *http://www.gao.gov/assets/300/299781.pdf.*

100. See, for example, Theodore G. Chiricos, Philip D. Jackson, and Gordon P. Waldo, "Inequality in the Imposition of a Criminal Label," *Social Problems* 19, no. 4 (Spring 1972): 553–72.

101. BJS, Jail Inmates at Midyear 2010—Statistical Tables, April 2011 (revised 6-28-2011), NCJ 233431, Table 1 and 7; *Jail Inmates at Midyear 2007*, June 2008, NCJ221945, pp. 1 and 5.

102. See, for example, C. E. Ares, A. Rankin, and J. H. Sturz, "The Manhattan Bail Project: An Interim Report on the Use of Pre-trial Parole," *NYU Law Review* 38 (1963): 67; C. Foote, "Compelling Appearances in Court-Administration of Bail in Philadelphia," *University of Pennsylvania Law Review* 102 (1954): 1031–79; and C. Foote, "A Study of the Administration of Bail in New York City," *University of Pennsylvania Law Review* 106 (1958): 693. For statistics on persons held in jail awaiting trial, see U.S. Bureau of the Census, *The Social and Economic Status of the Black Population in the U.S., 1974* (Washington, D.C.: U.S. Government Printing Office, 1975), p. 171; and USLEAA, *Survey of Inmates in Local Jails 1972: Advance Report* (Washington, D.C.: U.S. Government Printing Office, 1974), pp. 5, 8.

103. Chiricos and Bales, "Unemployment and Punishment," p. 712.

104. Free, "Racial Bias and the American Criminal Justice System," p. 203.

105. Blumberg, *Criminal Justice*, pp. 28–29; *Challenge*, p. 134.

106. Robert Johnson, *Condemned to Die: Life under Sentence of Death* (New York: Elsevier, 1981), p. 138.

107. Stephen Gettinger, *Sentenced to Die: The People, the Crimes, and the Controversy* (New York: Macmillan, 1979), p. 261.

108. Richard Lacayo, "You Don't Always Get Perry Mason," *Time*, June 1, 1992, pp. 38–39. Perry Mason was a 1957-66 TV series about a masterful lawyer.

109. Nancy Phillips, In life and death cases, costly mistakes. *Philadelphia Inquirer*, October 23, 2011, *http://articles.philly.com/2011-10-23/news/30313341_1_lawyers-in-capital-cases-death-penalty-appeals-death-penalty.*

110. National Association of Criminal Defense Lawyers, "Getting What They Pay For: The Fallacy of Quality Indigent Defense," *Indigent Defense* (May–June 2004), *www.nacdl.org/public.nsf/DefenseUpdates/Louisiana029.*

111. A. Rafik Mohamed and Erik Fritsvold, *Dorm Room Dealers* (Boulder: Lynne Rienner, 2010), p. 173.

112. Mohamed and Fritsvold, *Dorm Room Dealers*, pp. 161, 167.

113. "When Are the Savings and Loan Crooks Going to Jail?" Hearing before the Subcommittee on Financial Institutions Supervision, Regulation and Insurance of the Committee on Banking, Finance, and Urban Affairs, House of Representatives, 101st Congress, 2nd Session, June 28, 1990 (Washington, D.C.: U.S. Government Printing Office, 1990), pp. 1, 21.

114. "Penalties for White Collar Offenses: Are We Really Getting Tough on Crime?" Hearing of the Crime and Drugs Subcommittee of the Judiciary Committee, U.S. Senate, 107th Congress, 2nd session, July 11, 2002 (Washington, D.C.: U.S. Government Printing Office, 2002).

115. Lesley Oelsner, "Wide Disparities Mark Sentences Here," *The New York Times*, September 27, 1972, p. 1.

116. Stewart J. D'Alessio and Lisa Stolzenberg, "Socioeconomic Status and the Sentencing of the Traditional Offender," *Journal of Criminal Justice* 21 (1993): 71–74.

117. Barbara C. Nienstedt, Marjorie Zatz, and Thomas Epperlein, "Court Processing and Sentencing of Drinking Drivers," *Journal of Quantitative Criminology* 4, no. 1 (1988): 39–59.
118. Theodore Chiricos and William Bales, "Unemployment and Punishment: An Empirical Assessment," *Criminology* 29, no. 4 (1991): 701–24.
119. Belinda R. McCarthy, "A Micro-Level Analysis of Social Control: Intrastate Use of Jail and Prison Confinement," *Justice Quarterly* 7, no. 2 (June 1990): 334–35.
120. Dean J. Champion, "Private Counsels and Public Defenders: A Look at Weak Cases, Prior Records, and Leniency in Plea Bargaining," *Journal of Criminal Justice* 17, no. 4 (1989): 143.
121. T. Miethe and C. Moore, "Socioeconomic Disparities under Determinate Sentencing Systems: A Comparison of Preguideline and Postguideline Practices in Minnesota," *Criminology* 23, no. 2 (1985): 358.
122. Robert Tillman and Henry Pontell, "Is Justice 'Collar-Blind'? Punishing Medicaid Provider Fraud," *Criminology* 30, no. 4 (1992): 547–73, quote on p. 560.
123. James F. Nelson, "Hidden Disparities in Case Processing: New York State, 1985–1986," *Journal of Criminal Justice* 20 (1992): 181–200.
124. C. Crawford, T. Chiricos, and G. Kleck, "Race, Racial Threat, and Sentencing of Habitual Offenders," *Criminology* 36, no. 3 (1998): 481–511.
125. Cassia C. Spohn, "Thirty Years of Sentencing Reform," pp. 455, 481.
126. BJS, *Jail Inmates at Midyear 2010—Statistical Tables* (April 2011, NCJ 233431), Table 7; BJS, *Prisoners in 2010*, (December 2011, NCJ 236096), calculated from Table 16A (584,800 black out of 1,365,400 total inmates); *UCR–2010*, Table 43.
127. *Criminal Justice Newsletter*, March 1, 1995, p. 3; and *Criminal Justice Newsletter*, April 17, 1995, p. 5.
128. BJS, *Federal Drug Offenders, 1999, with Trends 1984–1999*, November 2001, NCJ 187285, Table 8, p. 11.
129. Ronald Smothers, "Wave of Prison Uprisings Provokes Debate on Crack," *The New York Times*, October 24, 1995, p. A12. Statement of Ricardo Hinjosa, Chair United States Sentencing Commission Before the Senate Judiciary Committee, February 12, 2008, *http://www.ussc.gov/testimony/Hinososa_Testimony_021208.pdf.*
130. Senator Barack Obama, "Remarks at Howard University Convocation," September 28, 2007, *http://www.barackobama.com/2007/09/28/remarks_of_senator_barack_obam_26.php.*
131. Nikki Jones, 2011 "Something Smells Like Pig, You Say?" *http://thepublicintellectual. org/2011/05/02/if-it-smells-like-a-pig/*. She puts the sentencing of crack cocaine in the context of post-Civil War "Pig Laws," which "took a crime more likely to be committed by black people and made the penalty for that infraction harsher."
132. "Blacks Receive Stiffer Sentences," *Boston Globe*, April 4, 1979, pp. 1, 50ff.
133. J. Petersilia, "Racial Disparities in the Criminal Justice System: A Summary," *Crime & Delinquency* 31, no. 1 (1985): 28. See also G. Bridges and R. Crutchfield, "Law, Social Standing and Racial Disparities in Imprisonment," *Social Forces* 66, no. 3 (1988): 699–724.
134. Mary Pat Flaherty and Joan Biskupic, "Rules Often Impose Toughest Penalties on Poor, Minorities," *The Washington Post*, October 9, 1996, p. A26.
135. Barbara S. Meierhoefer, *The General Effect of Mandatory Minimum Prison Terms: A Longitudinal Study of Federal Sentences Imposed* (Washington, D.C.: Federal Judicial Center, 1992), esp. pp. 1, 20, 25. Between October 1989 and 1990, 46 percent of whites received federal sentences below the mandatory minimum, but 32 percent of blacks did; *Sourcebook—1991*, Table 5.43, p. 542.

136. Flaherty and Biskupic, "Rules Often Impose Toughest Penalties on Poor, Minorities," p. A26.

137. Kai Falkenberg, "How Business Crooks Cut Their Jail Time," *Forbes*, January 12, 2009, *http://www.forbes.com/forbes/2009/0112/064.html*.

138. William J. Bowers and Glenn L. Pierce, "Racial Discrimination and Criminal Homicide under Post-Furman Capital Statutes," in *The Death Penalty in America*, ed. H. A. Bedau (New York: Oxford University Press, 1982), pp. 206–24.

139. *McCleskey v. Kemp*, 107 S. Ct. 1756 (1987). The research central to this case was that of David Baldus, reported in D. Baldus, C. Pulaski, and G. Woodworth, "Comparative Review of Death Sentences: An Empirical Study of the Georgia Experience," *Journal of Criminal Law and Criminology* 74 (1983): 661–725. See also R. Paternoster, "Race of Victim and Location of Crime: The Decision to Seek the Death Penalty in South Carolina," *Journal of Criminal Law and Criminology* 74, no. 3 (1983): 754–88; R. Paternoster, "Prosecutorial Discretion in Requesting the Death Penalty: A Case of Victim-Based Racial Discrimination," *Law and Society Review* 18 (1984): 437–78; S. Gross and R. Mauro, "Patterns of Death: An Analysis of Racial Disparities in Capital Sentencing and Homicide Victimization," *Stanford Law Review* 37 (1984): 27–120; and Michael L. Radelet and Glenn L. Pierce, "Race and Prosecutorial Discretion in Homicide Cases," *Law and Society Review* 19 (1985): 587, 615–19.

140. Anthony G. Amsterdam, "Race and the Death Penalty," in S. Gold (ed.) *Moral Controversies* (Belmont, CA: Wadsworth, 1993), pp. 268–69.

141. Susan Levine and Lori Montgomery, "Large Racial Disparity Found by Study of Md. Death Penalty," *The Washington Post*, January 8, 2003, pp. A1, A8. See also U.S. General Accounting Office, *Death Penalty Sentencing: Research Indicates Pattern of Racial Disparities*, Report to the Senate and House Committees on the Judiciary, February (Washington, D.C.: U.S. General Accounting Office, 1990), esp. p. 5.

142. Marvin E. Wolfgang, Arlene Kelly, and Hans C. Nolde, "Comparison of the Executed and the Commuted among Admissions to Death Row," in Richard Quinney (ed.) *Crime and Justice in Society* (Boston: Little, Brown, 1969), pp. 508, 513.

143. Karen Parker, Mari DeWees, and Michael Radelet, "Race, the Death Penalty and Wrongful Convictions," *Criminal Justice* 18, no. 1 (2003), *www.abanet.org/crimjust/spring2003/death_penalty.html*.

144. "Antitrust: Kauper's Last Stand," *Newsweek*, June 21, 1976, p. 70. On December 21, 1974, the Antitrust Procedures and Penalty Act was passed, striking out the language of the Sherman Antitrust Act, which made price fixing a misdemeanor punishable by a maximum sentence of one year in prison. According to the new law, price fixing is a felony punishable by up to three years in prison. Because prison sentences were a rarity under the old law and usually involved only 30 days in jail when actually imposed, there is little reason to believe the new law will strike fear in the hearts of corporate crooks.

145. K. Johnson, "Federal Court Processing of Corporate, White Collar, and Common Crime Economic Offenders over the Past Three Decades," *Mid-American Review of Sociology* 11, no. 1 (1986): 25–44.

146. J. Hagan and A. Palloni, "'Club Fed' and the Sentencing of White-Collar Offenders before and after Watergate," *Criminology* 24, no. 4 (1986): 616–17. See also J. Hagan and P. Parker, "White-Collar Crime and Punishment: The Class Structure and Legal Sanctioning of Securities Violations," *American Sociological Review* 50 (1985): 302–16.

147. John P. Wright, Francis T. Cullen, and Michael B. Blankenship, "The Social Construction of Corporate Violence: Media Coverage of the Imperial Food Products Fire," *Crime & Delinquency* 41, no. 1 (January 1995): 23–24; Laurie Grossman,

"Owner Sentenced to Nearly 20 Years over Plant Fire," *The Wall Street Journal*, September 15, 1992, p. A10; and Wil Haygood, "Still Burning: After a Deadly Fire, a Town's Losses Were Just Beginning," *The Washington Post*, November 10, 2002, p. F4.

148. Sheryl Stolberg and David Herszenhorn, "Bush and Candidates to Meet on Bailout," *The New York Times*, September 24, 2008, *http://www.nytimes.com/2008/09/25/business/economy/25bush.html?_r=1.*

149. The phrase "Wall St Incompetence Tax" is from financial blogger Barry Ritholtz, who in September 2008 estimated it to be $5,000 to 10,000 for every man, woman and child in the U.S., *http://bigpicture.typepad.com/comments/2008/09/ceo-clawback-pr.html.*

150. This summary of the history leading up to the S&L debacle is based on Henry Pontell and Kitty Calavita, "White-Collar Crime in the Savings and Loan Scandal," *Annals of the American Academy of Political and Social Science* 525 (January 1993): 31–45.

151. "Indirect Costs Raise Total for S&L Bailout to $480.9 Billion," *The Wall Street Journal*, July 15, 1996, p. B8A.

152. Pontell and Calavita, "White-Collar Crime in the Savings and Loan Scandal," p. 32, citing U.S. General Accounting Office, "Failed Thrifts: Internal Control Weaknesses Create an Environment Conducive to Fraud, Insider Abuse and Related Unsafe Practices," Statement of Frederick D. Wolf, Assistant Comptroller General, before the Subcommittee on Criminal Justice, Committee on the Judiciary, House of Representatives, March 22, 1989; and U.S. Congress, House, Committee on Government Operations, "Combating Fraud, Abuse and Misconduct in the Nation's Financial Institutions," 72nd report by the Committee on Government Operations, October 13, 1989.

153. Pontell and Calavita, "White-Collar Crime in the Savings and Loan Scandal," p. 37.

154. Alan Fornham, "S&L Felons," *Fortune*, November 5, 1990, p. 92.

155. *Criminal Justice Newsletter*, December 15, 1994, p. 5.

156. *UCR–1995*, p. 36.

157. Stephen Pizzo and Paul Muolo, "Take the Money and Run: A Rogues' Gallery of Some Lucky S&L Thieves," *The New York Times Magazine*, May 9, 1993, p. 26.

158. "When Are the Savings and Loans Crooks Going to Jail?" Hearing before the Subcommittee on Financial Institutions Supervision, Regulation and Insurance of the Committee on Banking, Finance, and Urban Affairs, House of Representatives, 101st Congress, 2nd Session, June 28, 1990 (Washington, D.C.: U.S. Government Printing Office, 1990), p. 2.

159. Kitty Calavita, Henry Pontell, and Robert Tillman, *Big Money Crime: Fraud and Politics in the Savings and Loan Crisis* (Berkeley: University of California Press, 1997), p. 131.

160. Mark Gimein, "You Bought: They Sold," *Fortune*, September 2, 2002, pp. 64–65.

161. Under the rules of special purpose vehicles (SPVs) ("independent" off-balance sheet entities), if 3 percent of the money comes from outside and is "at risk" then it is considered independent. Because the Enron deals were so large, they had a difficult time finding people to put up the other 3 percent. Enron ended up guaranteeing people substantial returns for being part of the deal, meaning the money of the outside individual was not truly at risk.

162. Allan Sloan, "Free Lessons on Corporate Hubris, Courtesy of Enron," *The Washington Post*, December 4, 2001, p. E3; see also Gimein, "You Bought: They Sold," passim.

163. Daniel Gross, "The Crime: Slow Job Growth. A Suspect: Enron," *The New York Times*, September 11, 2005, *http://www.nytimes.com/2005/09/11/business/11view.html?_r=2.*

164. Clifton Leaf, "White-Collar Criminals: Enough Is Enough," *Fortune Magazine*, March 2, 2002, p. 64.

165. David Hilzenrath, "Two Failures with a Familiar Ring: Arthur Andersen Audited Foundation, S&L That Collapsed," *The Washington Post*, December 6, 2001, p. A21.

166. Julie Creswell, "Banks on the Hot Seat," *Fortune*, September 2, 2002, p. 80.

167. In one case, the National Association of Securities Dealers fined the Salomon Smith Barney Unit of Citigroup $5 million for "materially misleading research reports" on Winstar Communications. Analysts kept a $50 target price and a "buy" rating on the company until the price of a share hit $0.14. An article for TheStreet.com notes, Salomon made $24 million in fees from Winstar. "[T]he NASD trumpets that this settlement is the third largest in NASD's history. Well, if we were the NASD and we wanted to strike fear in the hearts of brokerage firms, we would keep that little statistic a secret." George Mannes, "The Five Dumbest Things on Wall Street This Week," *TheStreet.com*, September 27, 2002, *www.thestreet.com/story/10065679/the-five-dumbest-things-on-wall-street-this-week.html.*

168. David Teather, "The Whores of Wall Street," *Guardian*, October 2, 2002, *www.guardian.co.uk/usa/story/0,12271,802926,00.html.*

169. Stephen Labaton, "Now Who, Exactly, Got Us Into This?" *The New York Times*, February 3, 2002, *http://query.nytimes.com/gst/fullpage.html?res=9F0DE3DC143DF930A35751C0A9649C8B63.*

170. The particulars of the legislations and some of its limitations are from Citizen Works, *http://citizenworks.org/enron/accountinglaw.php.*

171. Jonathan Weisman, "Some See Cracks IN Reform Law," *The Washington Post*, August 7, 2002, p. E1.

172. Carrie Johnson, "Panel Boosts Penalties for White-Collar Offenses," *The Washington Post*, January 9, 2003, p. E1.

173. Kathleen Day, "SEC Staff Urges Limit to Reforms: Vote Planned Today on Auditing Rules," *The Washington Post*, January 22, 2003, p. E1.

174. Leaf, "White-Collar Criminals: Enough Is Enough," p. 63.

175. "3 strikes" is one form of the "tough on crime" movement. Borrowing from baseball games, the law imposes mandatory sentences of 25 years to life in prison for a third felony conviction (anything with a sentence greater than one year). Its original intention was to lock up repeat violent offenders, but the popularity of "tough on crime" lead politicians to expand its application to "repeat and violent offender," which included many nonviolent offenders who filled the prisons.

176. Jeffrey Reiman and Paul Leighton, *A Tale of Two Criminals: We're Tougher on Corporate Criminals, but They Still Don't Get What They Deserve* (Boston: Allyn & Bacon, 2005), *www.paulsjusticepage.com/RichGetRicher/fraud2004.htm.* See also *http://www.paulsjusticeblog.com/2008/02/getting_tough_on_corporate_crime.php.*

177. Carrie Johnson, "Skilling gets 24 Years for Fraud at Enron," *The Washington Post*, October 24, 2006, p. A1.

178. Emily Barker, Brian Boxter, Alison Frankel, and Nate Raymond, "Progress Report," *Federal Sentencing Reporter* 20, no. 3 (February 2008): 206–10.

179. Matt Taibbi, "Wall Street's Bailout Hustle," *Rolling Stone*, February 17, 2010, *http://www.rollingstone.com/politics/news/wall-streets-bailout-hustle-20100217.*

180. Quoted in Barry Ritholtz, "Nonfeasance in Financial Oversight," *The Big Picture Blog*, August 18, 2008, *http://bigpicture.typepad.com/comments/2008/08/weak-rules-crip.html.*

181. Barry Ritholtz, "A Memo Found in the Street," *Barrons*, September 29, 2008, *http://online.barrons.com/article/SB122246742997580395.html*.

182. Ritholtz, "Nonfeasance in Financial Oversight."

183. Barry Ritholtz, "Where's the Ref?" *Forbes*, September 12, 2008, *http://www.forbes.com/home/2008/09/12/lehman-greenspan-regulation-opinions-cx_br_0912ritholtz.html*.

184. Carrie Johnson, "Prosecutors Expected to Spare Wall St Firms," *The Washington Post*, October 3, 2008, p. D1.

185. Barry Ritholtz, "CEO Clawback Provisions in Bailout?" *The Big Picture Blog*, September 24, 2008, *http://www.ritholtz.com/blog/2008/09/ceo-clawback-provisions-in-the-bailout/l*; Yalman Onaran and Christopher Scinta, "Lehman Files Biggest Bankruptcy After Suitors Balk (Update 1)," *Bloomberg*, September 15, 2008, *http://noir.bloomberg.com/apps/news?pid=newsarchives&sid=a6cDDYU5QYyw*.

186. Gretchen Morgenson and Louise Story, "In Financial Crisis, No Prosecutions of Top Figures," *New York Times*, April 14, 2011. *http://www.nytimes.com/2011/04/14/business/14prosecute.html*.

187. Eric Lichtblau, "Federal Cases of Stock Fraud Drop Sharply," *The New York Times*, December 24, 2008, *http://www.nytimes.com/2008/12/25/business/25fraud.html?_r=1*.

188. Amit Paley and David Hilzenrath, "SEC Chief Defends His Restraint," *The Washington Post*, December 24, 2008, p. A1.

189. Floyd Norris, "Can Mary Schapiro Save the SEC?" *The New York Times*, December 17, 2008, *http://norris.blogs.nytimes.com/2008/12/17/can-she-save-the-sec/*.

190. *U.S. Securities and Exchange Commission v Citigroup Global Markets* 11-cv-07387-JSR (11/28/2011), p 11.

191. Richard Schmitt, "FBI Saw Threat of Loan Crisis," *Los Angeles Times*, August 25, 2008, p. A1.

192. Eric Lichtblau, David Johnson, and Ron Nixon, "FBI Struggles to Handle Financial Fraud Cases," *The New York Times*, October 18, 2008, *http://www.nytimes.com/2008/10/19/washington/19fbi.html*.

193. Schmitt, "FBI Saw Threat of Loan Crisis."

194. Lichtblau, Johnson, and Nixon, "FBI Struggles to Handle Financial Fraud Cases."

195. William Black (Bill), "Bill Black: The High Price of Ignorance," 2011, *http://www.nakedcapitalism.com/2011/11/bill-black-the-high-price-of-ignorance.html*.

196. Securities and Exchange Commission, Former Countrywide CEO Angelo Mozilo to Pay SEC's Largest-Ever Financial Penalty Against a Public Company's Senior Executive, 2011, *http://www.sec.gov/news/press/2010/2010-197.htm*.

197. Sam Gustin, "Joseph Stiglitz Interview Transcript," Oct. 20, 2010, *http://www.dailyfinance.com/2010/10/22/joseph-stiglitz-interview-transcript/*.

198. Gustin, "Joseph Stiglitz Interview Transcript," 2010.

199. Morgenson and Story, In Financial Crisis, No Prosecutions of Top Figures.

200. David Streitfeld, "From a Maine House, a National Foreclosure Freeze," *New York Times*, October 14, 2010, *http://www.nytimes.com/2010/10/15/business/15maine.html?_r=1*.

201. See Congressman Alan Greyson's letter to FBI Director Mueller, available at *http://www.ritholtz.com/blog/2010/10/grayson-to-fbi-prosecute-the-frauds/*. See also Barry Ritholtz, "Why Foreclosure Fraud Is So Dangerous to Property Rights," *http://www.ritholtz.com/blog/2010/10/why-foreclosure-fraud-is-so-dangerous-to-property-rights/*

202. Gary Rivlin, "The Billion-Dollar Bank Heist: How the Financial Industry Is Buying off Washington—and Killing Reform," *Newsweek*, July 11, 2011, *http://www.thedailybeast.com/newsweek/2011/07/10/the-billion-dollar-bank-heist.html.*

203. James Stewart, "As a Watchdog Starves, Wall Street Is Tossed a Bone," *New York Times*, July 15, 2011. *http://www.nytimes.com/2011/07/16/business/budget-cuts-to-sec-reduce-its-effectiveness.html?_r=3&ref=business.*

204. Barry Ritholtz, 2010. "SEC: Defective by Design?" Big Picture Blog, *http://www.ritholtz.com/blog/2010/03/sec-defective-by-design/.*

205. Edward Wyatt, S.E.C. "Hurt by Disarray in Its Books," *New York Times*, February 2, 2011, *http://www.nytimes.com/2011/02/03/business/03sec.html?_r=1&hpw.*

206. Sam Gustin, "Joseph Stiglitz Interview Transcript," 2010.

207. Tom Wicker, *A Time to Die* (New York: Quadrangle, 1975), pp. 311, 314.

208. Ibid., p. 310.

209. *Sourcebook—1987*, p. 486; BJS, Correctional Population in the United States, 2010, December 2011, NCJ 236319, Appendix Table 2.

210. Pew Center on the States, *One in 100: Behind Bars in America 2008*, February 2008, emphasis added. *http://www.pewcenteronthestates.org/report_detail.aspx?id=35904.*

211. BJS, *Survey of State Prison Inmates*, 1991, p. 3.

212. BJS, *Criminal Offender Statistics, www.ojp.usdoj.gov/bjs/crimoff.htm*; and BJS, *Profile of Jail Inmates 2002*, July 2004, NCJ201932, *http://bjs.ojp.usdoj.gov/index.cfm?ty=pbdetail&iid=1118.*

213. *StatAbst—2003*, Table 589, p. 386; and BJS, *Profile of Jail Inmates 2002*, p. 9.

214. U.S. Census Bureau, *Current Population Survey*, 2003 Annual Social and Economic Supplement, Table PINC-01, *http://pubdb3.census.gov/macro/032003/perinc/new01_010.htm.*

215. BJS, *Profile of Jail Inmates 2002*, p. 9.

216. Ibid, p. 9.

217. Ibid, p. 2; and *StatAbst—2003*, Table 229, p. 154.

■ ■ ■ ■ ■

To the Vanquished Belong the Spoils
Who Is Winning the Losing War against Crime?

*In every case the laws are made by the ruling party in its own
interest; a democracy makes democratic laws, a despot autocratic
ones, and so on. By making these laws they define as "just"
for their subjects whatever is for their own interest, and they
call anyone who breaks them a "wrongdoer" and punish
him accordingly.*

—THRASYMACHUS, *in* PLATO'S *Republic*

Chapter 4 of *The Rich Gets Richer* examines how a failing criminal justice system
that neither protects society nor achieves justice is allowed to continue. The
criminal justice system actually fails in three ways: It fails (1) to implement
policies that stand a good chance of reducing crime, (2) to treat as crimes the
harmful acts of the rich and powerful, and (3) to eliminate economic bias in
the criminal justice system itself. The chapter argues that this happens because
the current system's failure produces benefits for the wealthy in America.
This is due, not to a conspiracy, but to historical inertia—the persistence of a
criminal justice system dating from pre-industrial times, which does not
recognize many of the harmful acts of the well-off. They can go on performing
harmful acts without punishment, while the country remains focused on
street crime and poor minority criminals.

A key idea here is that the criminal justice system contributes to an *ideology*,
a widely held set of beliefs that justify the status quo and its inequalities. The
criminal justice system does this by conveying the message that the poor are
the worst threat to society, and that their criminality is the result of individual
failings rather than social inequities.

WHY IS THE CRIMINAL JUSTICE SYSTEM FAILING?

The streams of our argument flow together at this point in a question: *Why is it happening?* We have shown how it is no accident that "the offender at the end of the road in prison is likely to be a member of the lowest social and economic groups in the country."[1] We have shown that this is not an accurate group portrait of who threatens society—it is a picture of whom the criminal justice system *selects* for arrest and imprisonment from among those who threaten society. It is an image distorted by the shape of the criminal justice carnival mirror. This much we have seen, and now we want to know: *Why is the criminal justice system allowed to function in a fashion that neither protects society nor achieves justice? Why is the criminal justice system failing?*

Answering these questions will require looking at who benefits from this failure and who suffers from it. We will argue that the rich and powerful in the United States—those who derive the greatest advantage from the persistence of the social and economic system as it is currently organized—reap benefits from the failure of criminal justice that has been documented in this book. However, as noted in the Introduction, this should not lead the reader to think that our explanation for the current shape of the criminal justice system is a "conspiracy theory."

A conspiracy theory would argue that the rich and the powerful, seeing the benefits to be derived from the failure of criminal justice, consciously set out to use their wealth and power to make it fail. There are many problems with such a theory. First, it is virtually impossible to prove. If the conspiracy succeeds, then this is possible only to the extent that it is kept secret. Thus, evidence for a conspiracy would be as difficult to obtain as the conspiracy was successful. Second, conspiracy theories strain credibility precisely because the degree of secrecy they would require seems virtually impossible in a society as open and fractious as our own. If there is a "ruling elite" in the United States that comprises a group as small as the richest *one-thousandth of 1 percent* of the population, it would still be made up of around 3,000 people. To think that a conspiracy to make the criminal justice system fail in the way it does could be kept secret among this number of people in a country like ours is just unbelievable. Third, conspiracy theories are not plausible because they do not correspond to the way most people act most of the time. Although there is no paucity of conscious mendacity and manipulation in our politics, most people most of the time seem sincerely to believe that what they are doing is right. Whether this is a tribute to human beings' creative capacities to rationalize what they do or merely a matter of their shortsightedness, it seems a fact. For all these reasons, it is not plausible that so fateful and harmful a policy as the failure of criminal justice could be purposely maintained by the rich and powerful. Rather, we need an explanation that is compatible with believing that policy makers, on the whole, are simply doing what they sincerely believe is right.

To understand how the Pyrrhic defeat theory explains the current shape of our failing criminal justice policy, note that this failure is really *three* failures that work together. First, there is the failure to implement policies that stand a good chance of reducing crime and the harm it causes. (This was argued in Chapter 1.) Second, there is the failure to treat as crimes the harmful acts of the rich and powerful. (This is the first of the hypotheses listed on page 75 in Chapter 2, and it is confirmed by the evidence presented in Chapter 2.) Third, there is the failure to eliminate economic bias in the criminal justice system, so that the poor continue to have a substantially greater chance than better-off people of being arrested, charged, convicted, and penalized for committing the acts that are treated as crimes. (This corresponds to the second through fourth hypotheses listed in Chapter 2, and is confirmed by the evidence presented in Chapter 3.) The effect of the first failure is that there remains a large amount of crime—even if crime rates dip largely as a result of factors outside the control of the criminal justice system, such as the declining use of certain drugs and the reduction of lead in the environment. The effect of the second failure is that the acts treated as crimes are those done predominantly by the poor. The effect of the third failure is that the individuals who are arrested and convicted for crimes are predominantly poor people. The effect of the three failures working together is that we are largely unprotected against the harmful acts of the well-off, while at the same time we are confronted on the streets and in our homes with a real and large threat of crime, and in the courts and prisons with a large and visible population of poor criminals. And lest it be thought that the public does not feel threatened by crime, consider that polls shows that, though crime was down from the early 1990s through 2011, 68 percent of Americans that year believed that there was more crime than there was the year before. During roughly 20 years of declining crime rates, never has a majority of the public expressed a belief that there was less crime than the previous year.[2] In short, the effect of current criminal justice policy is at once to narrow the public's conception of what is dangerous to acts of the poor and to present a convincing embodiment of this danger.

The Pyrrhic defeat theory aims to explain the *persistence* of this failing criminal justice policy, rather than its origins. It is not the origin of criminal justice policy and practices that is puzzling. The focus on one-on-one harm reflects the main ways in which people harmed each other in the days before large-scale industrialization; the refusal to implement policies that might reduce crime (such as gun control or legalization of heroin or amelioration of poverty) reflects a defensive and punitive response to crime that is natural and understandable, if not noble and farsighted; and the existence of economic bias in the criminal justice system reflects the real economic and political inequalities that characterize the society in which that system is embedded. What is puzzling, then, is not how these policies came to be what they are, but why they persist in the face of their failure to achieve either security or justice. The explanation we offer for this persistence is called "historical inertia."

The historical inertia explanation argues that current criminal justice policy persists because it fails in a way that does not give rise to an effective demand for change, for two reasons. First, this failing system provides benefits for those with the power to make changes, while it imposes costs on those without such power. Second, because the criminal justice system shapes the public's conception of what is dangerous, it creates the impression that the harms it is fighting are *the real threats* to society—thus, even when people see that the system is less than a roaring success, they only demand more of the same: more police, more prisons, longer prison sentences, and so on.

Consider first the benefits that the system provides for those with wealth and power. We have argued that the triple failure of criminal justice policy diverts attention from the harmful noncriminal acts of the well-off and confronts us in our homes and on our streets with a real, substantial threat of crime, and in the courts and prisons with a large and visible population of poor criminals. This conveys a vivid image to the American people, namely, that *there is a real threat to our lives and limbs, and it is a threat from the poor.* This image provides benefits to the rich and powerful in America. It carries an *ideological message* that serves to protect their wealth and privilege. Speaking generally, the message is this:

- The threat to law-abiding Middle America comes from below them on the economic ladder, not above them.
- The poor are morally defective, and thus their poverty is their own fault, not a symptom of social or economic injustice.

The effect of this message is to create (or reinforce) in Americans fear of, and hostility toward, the poor. It leads Americans to ignore the ways in which they are injured and robbed by the acts of the affluent (as catalogued in Chapter 2), and leads them to demand harsher doses of "law and order" aimed mainly at the lower classes. Most importantly, it nudges Americans toward a *conservative* defense of American society with its large disparities of wealth, power, and opportunity—and nudges them away from a *progressive* demand for equality and a more equitable distribution of wealth and power.

On the other hand, but equally important, is that those who are mainly victimized by the failure to reduce our high rates of street crime are by and large the poor themselves. The people who are hurt the most by the failure of the criminal justice system are those with the least power to change it. Households with an annual income of less than $7,500 were victims of violent crimes at a rate nearly four times that of households earning $75,000 and above. Indeed, as Table 4.1 shows, rates of victimization by crimes in all categories are substantially higher for the poorest segment of the population, and drop dramatically as we ascend the economic ladder.

The difference in the rates of property-crime victimization between rich and poor understates the difference in the harms that result. The poor are far less likely than the affluent to have insurance against theft, and because they have little to start with, what they lose to theft takes a much deeper bite out of their ability to meet their basic needs. Needless to add, the various noncriminal harms documented in Chapter 2, (for example, occupational hazards, pollution, poverty, and so on) also fall more harshly on workers and those at the bottom of society than on those at the top.

TABLE 4.1 Criminal Victimization by Family Income (2008 Estimated Rate of Personal Victimization per 1,000 Persons Age 12 and Older; and 2010 Estimated Rate of Property Crime per 1,000 Households)

Type of Victimization	Less than $7,500	$7,500 to 14,999	$25,000 to $34,999	$75,000 or More
Crimes of violence	43.5	40.4	25.4	12.6
Robbery with injury	1.8*	1.7*	0.6*	0.3*
Rape/sexual assault	4.4*	2.1*	0.6*	0.5*
Aggravated assault	9.3	8.6	3.4	1.9
Household burglary	44.4	47.2	27.1	16.7
Theft	120.4	117.3	99.4	97.5

*Based on 10 or fewer cases.

Source: BJS, *Criminal Victimization in the United States, 2010*, September 2011, NCJ 235508, Table 10 (Burglary and Theft); BJS, *Criminal Victimization in the United States, 2008—Statistical Tables*, March 2010, NCJ 227669, Table 14.

To summarize: Those who suffer most from the failure to reduce street crime (and the failure to treat noncriminal harms as crimes) are not in a position to change criminal justice policy. Those who are in a position to change the policy are not seriously harmed by its failure—indeed, there are actual benefits to them from that failure. Note that we have not said that criminal justice policy is created to achieve this distribution of benefits and burdens. Instead, the claim is that the criminal justice policy that has emerged piecemeal over time and usually with the best of intentions happens to produce this distribution of benefits and burdens. And because criminal justice policy happens to produce this distribution, there is no inclination to change the criminal justice system among people with the power to do so. Moreover, because the criminal justice system shapes the public's conception of what is dangerous, it effectively limits the public's conception of how to protect itself to incremental changes in existing policy. Thus, though it fails, it persists.

Before proceeding, it is worth noting that private prisons and elements of the larger "criminal justice industrial complex" make money from the system as it is. They have a vested interest in more of the same and actively lobby to defeat reforms that would reduce their revenue. Private prisons are multibillion dollar for-profit businesses in which private firms are contracted to build and/or manage government prisons. "Get tough" policy initiatives such as mandatory minimum sentences and the "three-strikes-and-you're-out" statutes led to the rapid and enormous increase in the U.S. prison population over the past 40 years. That growth placed strains on government budgets—strains that continue because of the financial crisis, even as lawmakers work to reduce the number of inmates in order to control expenditures on corrections. This has given states an incentive to hire out their prison facilities to private contractors, who claim to be able to run prisons at 10 to 20 percent less cost than state governments, though the National Institute of Justice found it was about one percent![3] The result has been a dramatic increase in the number of prisoners under private control. In the 10 years from 1985 to 1995, the number of prison beds under private management grew from 935 to 63,595, an increase of nearly 7,000 percent! Since then, the rate of growth has slowed. Nonetheless, there were 128,195 inmates in private prisons in 2010, and private prison contractors are expanding their operations into various aspects of community corrections.[4]

Wall Street noticed and supported this trend, and many stock analysts urged their clients to invest in the major corporations in the field, such as Corrections Corporation of America (CCA) and Wackenhut Corrections (now the Geo Group). An article in the *Wall Street Journal* carried the headline: "Shares of Wackenhut Break Out as Prisons Become a Hot Industry." An article on private prisons in *Forbes* was titled "A Surefire Growth Industry."[5] Writes Paulette Thomas, in a *Wall Street Journal* article titled "Making Crime Pay,"

> The gritty work of criminal justice has become the kind of big-ticket commerce to attract the loftiest names in finance. Goldman Sachs & Co., Prudential Insurance Co. of America, Smith Barney Shearson Inc., and Merrill Lynch & Co. Inc. are among those competing to underwrite prison construction with private tax-exempt bonds—no voter approval required.[6]

Ms. Thomas likens the new development to that of the old "military-industrial complex," of which President Eisenhower warned in his farewell address. Eisenhower's concern was that the presence of a large and permanent defense industry would drive policy.[7] The expansion of the criminal justice system, combined with the involvement of Wall Street investment banks, created a similar critical mass that can distort policy in its own interests. The American Legislative Exchange Council, an organization that lobbies state legislators and that receives contributions from CCA, says proudly that lawmakers on its crime task force have been actively leading in the drive for more incarceration in the states.[8] The National Institute on Money in State Politics reports, "Private prison companies gave more than $1.1 million in campaign contributions to state-level candidates in 14 Southern states during the 2000 elections."[9]

In *Punishment for Sale*, Donna Selman and Paul Leighton critique the growth of incarceration and note that private prisons were born from an incarceration binge "that has fostered injustice—and that these entities, pursuing their own economic interests rather than the public good, perpetuate policies causing injustice because they profit from them."[10] Consider that the two largest private prison firms are traded on the stock exchange and required to discuss "risk factors" to their business in their Securities and Exchange Commission filings. GEO Group's recent annual report noted: "the demand for our correctional and detention facilities and services could be adversely affected by changes in existing criminal or immigration laws, crime rates in jurisdictions in which we operate, the relaxation of criminal or immigration enforcement efforts, leniency in conviction, sentencing ..., and the decriminalization of ... drugs."[11]

CCA's annual report includes similar language and adds as factors that may limit growth: "Legislation ... that could lower minimum sentences for some non-violent crimes and make more inmates eligible for early release based on good behavior."[12] In short, a multibillion dollar industry has a powerful economic interest in maintaining existing harsh policies. Beyond private prisons, the prison-industrial complex includes companies that regard the $80 billion in corrections expenditures each year, "not as a burden on American taxpayers but as a lucrative market."[13] There's also a larger criminal justice-industrial complex, which includes the prison-industrial complex plus all those who supply goods or services to police and private security.

Thus far in this book we have been pointing out how *the rich get richer* WHILE *the poor get prison*, but the privatization movement and analysis of the criminal justice-industrial complex point to how *the rich get richer* BECAUSE *the poor get prison!* Our argument in the remainder of this chapter turns from considering the direct influence of big business to examining ideological messages. Ideology involves ideas that distort reality in ways that hide society's injustices, and thus secure uncritical allegiance to the existing social order. The people who have little far outnumber those who have plenty, so the wealthy need the poor to believe that they are not being exploited or treated unfairly and that the existing distribution of wealth is about the best that human beings can create. The criminal justice system plays a role in promoting this belief.

The section titled "The Poverty of Criminals and the Crime of Poverty" spells out in detail the content of the ideological message broadcast by the failure of the criminal justice system. The section titled "Ideology, or How to Fool Enough of the People Enough of the Time" discusses the *nature* of ideology in general and the *need* for it in America. For those who doubt that our legal system could function in such questionable ways, we also present evidence on how the criminal justice system has been used in the past to protect the rich and powerful against those who would challenge their privileges or their policies. These sections, then, flesh out the historical inertia explanation of the failure of criminal justice by showing the ideological benefits that the failure yields and to whom.

Ultimately, the test of the argument in this chapter is whether it provides a plausible explanation of the failure of criminal justice and draws the arguments of the previous chapters together into a coherent theory of contemporary criminal justice policy and practice.

THE POVERTY OF CRIMINALS AND THE CRIME OF POVERTY

Criminal justice is a very visible part of the American scene. As fact and fiction, countless images of crime and the struggle against it assail our senses daily, even hourly. In every newspaper, in every TV or radio newscast, there is at least one criminal justice story and often more. It is as if we live in an embattled city, besieged by the forces of crime and bravely defended by the forces of the law, and as we go about our daily tasks, we are always conscious of the war raging not very far away. Newspapers bring us daily, and newscasts bring us hourly, reports from the "front." Between reports, we are vividly reminded of the stakes and the desperateness of the battle by fictionalized portrayals of the struggle between the forces of the law and the breakers of the law. There is scarcely an hour on television without some dramatization of the struggle against violent crime. ("Before the average American child leaves elementary school, researchers estimate that he or she will have witnessed more than 8,000 murders on television." By 18, the average child will have seen some 200,000 acts of violence on television, according to the American Academy of Pediatrics. Although a few of these are performed by science-fiction monsters, the figure still suggests that the extent of the impact of the televised portrayal of crime and the struggle against it on the imaginations of Americans is nothing short of astounding—particularly on children, who are said to "spend as much as 28 hours a week watching television.")[14] In the mid-1980s, it was estimated that "detective, police, and other criminal justice–related programs accounted for some eighty percent of prime-time TV viewing."[15] A quick look at the television section of the newspaper suggests that, if anything, this has only increased in recent years, with certain cable channels largely devoted to crime and justice programming. If we add to this the news accounts, the panel discussions, the movies, the novels, the video games, the comic books, and the TV cartoon shows that imitate the comics, as well as the political speeches about crime, there can be no doubt that as fact or fantasy or both, criminal justice is vividly present in the imaginations of most Americans.

This is no accident. Everyone can relate to criminal justice in personal and emotional terms. Everyone has some fear of crime, and as we saw in Chapter 3, just about everyone has committed some crime. Everyone knows the primitive satisfaction of seeing justice done and the evildoers served up their just deserts. Furthermore, in reality or in fiction, criminal justice is naturally dramatic. To identify with the struggle against crime is to expand one's experience vicariously to include the danger, the suspense, the triumphs, and the meaningfulness—in a word, the drama—often missing in ordinary life. How else can we explain the seemingly bottomless appetite Americans have for the endless repetition, in only slightly altered form, of the same theme: the struggle of the forces of law against the forces of crime? Criminal justice has a firm grip on the imaginations of Americans and is thus in a unique position to convey a message to Americans and to convey it with drama and with conviction.

Let us now look at this message in detail. Our task falls naturally into two parts. There is an ideological message supportive of the status quo built into *any* criminal justice system by its very nature. Even if the criminal justice system were not failing, even if it were not biased against the poor, it would still—by its very nature—broadcast a message supportive of established institutions. This is the *implicit ideology of criminal justice*. Beyond this, there is an additional ideological message conveyed by the *failure* of the system and by its *biased* concentration on the poor. This is the *bonus of bias*.

The Implicit Ideology of Criminal Justice

Any criminal justice system like ours conveys a subtle yet powerful message in support of established institutions. It does this for two interconnected reasons. First, it concentrates on *individual* wrongdoers. This means that *it diverts our attention away from our institutions, away from consideration of whether our institutions themselves are wrong or unjust or indeed "criminal."*

Second, the criminal law is put forth as the *minimum neutral ground rules* for any social living. We are taught that no society can exist without rules against theft and violence, and thus the criminal law seems to be politically neutral: the minimum requirements for *any* society, the minimum obligations that any individual owes his or her fellows to make social life of any decent sort possible. Because the criminal law protects the established institutions (the prevailing economic arrangements are protected by laws against theft, and so on), attacks on those established institutions become equivalent to violations of the minimum requirements for any social life at all. In effect, the criminal law enshrines the established institutions as equivalent to the minimum requirements for *any* decent social existence—and it brands the individual who attacks those institutions as one who has declared war on *all* organized society and who must, therefore, be met with the weapons of war. Let us look more closely at this process.

What is the effect of focusing on individual guilt? Not only does this divert our attention from the possible evils in our institutions, but it also puts forth half the problem of justice as if it were the *whole* problem. To focus on individual guilt is to ask whether the individual citizen has fulfilled his or her obligations to his or her fellow citizens. *It is to look away from the issue of whether the fellow citizens have fulfilled their obligations to him or her.* To look only at individual responsibility is to look away from social responsibility. Writing about her stint as a "story analyst" for a prime-time TV "real crime" show based on videotapes of actual police busts, Debra Seagal describes the way focus on individual criminals deflects attention away from the social context of crime and how television reproduces this effect in millions of homes daily:

> By the time our 9 million viewers flip on their tubes, we've reduced fifty or sixty hours of mundane and compromising video into short, action-packed segments of tantalizing, crack-filled, dope-dealing, junkie-busting cop culture. How easily we downplay the pathos of the suspect; how cleverly we breeze past the complexities that cast doubt on the very system that has produced the criminal activity in the first place.[16]

Seagal's description illustrates as well how a television program that shows nothing but videos of actual events can distort reality by selecting and recombining pieces of real events.

A study of 69 TV law and crime dramas finds that fictional presentations of homicide focus on individual motivations and ignore social conditions: "Television crime dramas portray these events as specific psychological episodes in the characters' lives and little, if any, effort is made to connect them to basic social institutions or the nature of society within which they occur."[17]

To look only at individual criminality is to close one's eyes to social injustice and to close one's ears to the question of whether our social institutions have exploited or violated the individual. Criminologists James Unnever and Shaun Gabbidon, in their important book *A Theory of African American Offending*, link black criminality with a "long history of public dishonor and ritualized humiliation"—including by the criminal justice system—because of racism.[18] As a result, African-Americans are more likely to have less respect for the law and weaker bonds with conventional institutions. Focusing only on individual responsibility obscures the contribution of racism to African-American criminality.

Justice is a two-way street—but criminal justice is a one-way street. Individuals owe obligations to their fellow citizens because their fellow citizens owe obligations to them. Criminal justice focuses on the first and looks away from the second. *Thus, by focusing on individual responsibility for crime, the criminal justice system effectively acquits the existing social order of any charge of injustice!*

This is an extremely important bit of ideological alchemy. It stems from the fact that the same act can be criminal or not, unjust or just, depending on the circumstances in which it takes place. Killing someone is ordinarily a crime, but if it is in self-defense or to stop a deadly crime, it is not. Taking property by force is usually a crime, but if the taking is retrieving what has been stolen, then no crime has been committed. Acts of violence are ordinarily crimes, but if the violence is provoked by the threat of violence or by oppressive conditions, then, like the Boston Tea Party,[19] what might ordinarily be called criminal (even terrorist) is celebrated as just. This means that when we call an act a crime, *we are also making an implicit judgment about the conditions in response to which it takes place.* When we call an act a crime, we are saying that the conditions in which it occurs are not themselves criminal or deadly or oppressive or so unjust as to make an extreme response reasonable or justified or noncriminal. This means that when the system holds an individual responsible for a crime, *it implicitly conveys the message that the social conditions in which the crime occurred are not responsible for the crime,* that they are not so unjust as to make a violent response to them excusable.

Judges are prone to hold that an individual's responsibility for a violent crime is diminished if it was provoked by something that might lead a "reasonable person" to respond violently and that criminal responsibility is eliminated if the act was in response to conditions so intolerable that any "reasonable person" would have been likely to respond in the same way. In this vein, the law acquits those who kill or injure in self-defense and treats leniently those who commit a crime when confronted with extreme provocation. The law even occasionally treats understandingly the man who kills his wife's lover, and the woman who kills her brutal husband even when she has not acted directly in self-defense. By this same logic, when we hold an individual completely responsible for a crime, we are saying that the conditions in which it occurred are such that a "reasonable person" should find them tolerable. In other words, by focusing on individual responsibility for crimes, *the criminal justice system broadcasts the message that the social order itself is reasonable and not intolerably unjust* (due to inequality of opportunity, racism or other forms of discrimination, or the widespread poverty that our rich nation tolerates). Thus, the criminal justice system focuses moral condemnation on individuals and deflects it away from the social order that may have either violated the individual's rights or dignity or pushed him or her to the brink of the crime. This sends the message that the justice of our institutions is obvious, not to be doubted.

The second way in which a criminal justice system always conveys an implicit ideology arises from the presumption that the criminal law is nothing but the politically neutral minimum requirements of any decent social life. As already suggested, this presumption transforms the prevailing social order into justice incarnate and all violations of the prevailing order into injustice incarnate. This process is so obvious that it may be easily missed. Consider, for example, the law against theft. It does seem to be one of the minimum requirements of social living. As long as there is scarcity, any society—capitalist or socialist—will need rules to deter individuals from taking what does not belong to them. The law against theft, however, has more to it: It is a law against stealing what individuals *presently own*. Such a law has the effect of making the present distribution of property a part of the criminal law.

Because stealing is a violation of the law, this means that the present distribution of property becomes the implicit standard of justice against which criminal deviations are measured. Because criminal law is thought of as the minimum requirements of any social life, the result is that the present distribution of property is treated as the equivalent of the minimum requirements of *any* social life. The criminal who would alter the present distribution of property becomes someone who is declaring war on all organized society. The question of whether this "war" is provoked by the injustice or brutality of the society is swept aside. Indeed, this suggests yet another way in which the criminal justice system conveys an ideological message in support of the established society.

We have observed that by blaming the individual for a crime, the society is acquitted of the charge of injustice. But there is more: By blaming the individual for a crime, the society is acquitted of the charge of *complicity* in that crime. This is a point worth developing, because many observers have maintained that modern competitive societies such as our own have structural features that tend to generate crime. Thus, holding the individual responsible for his or her crime serves the function of taking the rest of society off the hook for their role in sustaining and benefiting from social arrangements that produce crime. Let us take a brief detour to look more closely at this process.

Cloward and Ohlin argued in their book, *Delinquency and Opportunity*,[20] that many crimes are the result of the discrepancy between social goals and the legitimate opportunities available for achieving them. The same point is basic to "strain theory," including variations like Messner and Rosenfeld's *Crime and the American Dream*.[21] Simply put, in our society everyone is encouraged to be a success—usually defined in terms of possessing wealth—but the legitimate avenues to success are open only to some. The conventional wisdom of our free-enterprise democracy is that anyone can be a success if he or she has the talent and the ambition. Thus, if one is not a success, it is because of one's own shortcomings: laziness, lack of ability, or both. On the other hand, opportunities to achieve success are not equally open to all. Access to the best schools and the best jobs is effectively closed to all but a few of the poor and becomes more available only as one goes up the economic ladder. The result is that many are called, but few are chosen. Many who have accepted the belief in the importance of success and the belief that achieving success is a result of individual ability must cope with feelings of frustration and failure that result when they find the avenues to success closed. Cloward and Ohlin argue that one method of coping with these stresses is to develop alternative avenues to success. Crime is such an alternative avenue.

Crime is a means by which people who believe in the American dream pursue it when they find the traditional routes barred. Indeed, it is plain to see that the goals pursued by most criminals are as American as apple pie. One of the reasons that American moviegoers enjoy gangster films—movies in which gangsters such as Al Capone, Bonnie and Clyde, or Butch Cassidy and the Sundance Kid[22] are the heroes, as distinct from police and detective films, whose heroes are defenders of the law—is that even when we deplore the hero's methods, we identify with his or her notion of success, because it is ours as well, and we admire the courage and cunning displayed in achieving that success. It is important to note that the discrepancy between success goals and legitimate opportunities in America is not an aberration. It is a structural feature of modern competitive industrialized society, a feature from which many benefits flow. Cloward and Ohlin write that

> a crucial problem in the industrial world is to locate and train the most talented persons in every generation, irrespective of the vicissitudes of birth, to occupy technical work roles. Since we cannot know in advance who can best fulfill the requirements of the various occupational roles, the matter is presumably settled through the process of competition. But how can men throughout the social order be motivated to participate in this competition?
>
> One of the ways in which the industrial society attempts to solve this problem is by defining success-goals as potentially accessible to all, regardless of race, creed, or socioeconomic position.[23]

Because these universal goals are urged to encourage a competition to select the best, there are necessarily fewer openings than seekers. Also, because those who achieve success are in a particularly good position to exploit their success to make access for their own children easier, the competition is rigged to work in favor of the middle and upper classes. As a result, "many lower-class persons are the victims of a contradiction between the goals toward which they have been led to orient themselves and socially structured means of striving for these goals."[24] "[The poor] experience … a desperation made all the more poignant by their exposure to a cultural ideology in which ... failure to become mobile" is proof of moral deficiency."[25] The outcome is predictable. "Under these conditions, there is an acute pressure to depart from institutional norms and to adopt illegitimate alternatives."[26]

This means that the very way in which our society is structured to draw out the talents and energies that go into producing our high standard of living has a costly side effect: *It produces crime.* By holding individuals responsible for this crime, those who enjoy that high standard of living can have their cake and eat it too. They can reap the benefits of the competition for success and escape the responsibility of paying for the costs of the competition. By holding the poor crook legally and morally guilty, the rest of society denies that it is the beneficiary of an economic system that exacts such a high toll in frustration and suffering.

William Bonger, the Dutch Marxist criminologist, maintained that competitive capitalism produces egotistic motives and undermines compassion for the misfortunes of others, and thus makes human beings literally *more capable of crime*—more capable of preying on their fellows without moral inhibition or remorse—than earlier cultures that emphasized cooperation rather than competition.[27] Here again, the criminal justice system relieves those who benefit from the American economic system of the costs of that system. By holding criminals morally and individually responsible for their crimes, we can forget that the motives that lead to crime—the drive for success, linked with the beliefs that success means outdoing others and that violence is an acceptable way of achieving one's goals—are the *same motives* that powered the drive across the American continent and that continue to fuel the engine of America's prosperity. (Appendix I presents the Marxian critique of criminal justice, and spells out the Marxian understanding of the motives and moral status of criminals.)

Political economist David Gordon maintains "that nearly all crimes in capitalist societies represent perfectly *rational* responses to the structure of institutions upon which capitalist societies are based."[28] Like Bonger, Gordon believes that capitalism tends to provoke crime in all economic strata. This is so because most crime is motivated by a desire for property or money and is an understandable way of coping with the pressures of inequality, competition, and insecurity, all of which are essential ingredients of capitalism. In capitalism, Gordon writes, "Individuals must fend for themselves, finding the best available opportunities to provide for themselves and their families. Driven by the fear of economic insecurity and by a competitive desire to gain some of the goods unequally distributed throughout the society, many individuals will eventually become 'criminals'."[29]

To the extent that a society makes crime a reasonable alternative for a large number of its members from all classes, that society is itself not very reasonably or humanely organized and bears some degree of responsibility for the crime it encourages. Because the criminal law is put forth as the minimum requirements that can be expected of any "reasonable person," its enforcement amounts to a denial of the real nature of the social order to which Gordon and the others point. Here again, by blaming the individual criminal, the criminal justice system serves implicitly but dramatically to acquit the society of its criminality.

The Bonus of Bias

We now consider the additional ideological bonus derived from the criminal justice system's bias against the poor. This bonus is a product of the association of crime and poverty in the popular mind. This association, the merging of the "criminal classes" and the "lower classes" into the "dangerous classes," was not invented in America. The word *villain* is derived from the Latin *villanus*, which means a farm servant.[30] In this respect, our present criminal justice system is heir to a long tradition of associating crime with the lower classes.

The value of this association was already seen when we explored the average citizen's concept of the Typical Criminal and the Typical Crime. It is quite obvious that throughout the great mass of Middle America, far more fear and hostility are directed toward the predatory acts of the poor than toward the predatory acts of the rich. Compare the fate of politicians in recent history who call for tax reform, income redistribution, prosecution of corporate crime, and any sort of regulation of business that would make it better serve American social goals with that of politicians who erect their platform on a call for "law and order," more police, fewer limits on police power, and stiffer prison sentences for criminals—and consider this in light of what we have already seen about the real dangers posed by corporate crime and "business as usual."

It seems clear that Americans have been effectively deceived as to what are the greatest dangers to their lives, limbs, and possessions. The very persistence with which the system functions to apprehend and punish poor crooks and ignore or slap on the wrist equally or more dangerous individuals is testimony to the sticking power of this deception. That Americans continue to tolerate the comparatively gentle treatment meted out to white-collar criminals, corporate price fixers, industrial polluters, and political-influence peddlers[31] while voting in droves to lock up more poor people faster and for longer sentences indicates the degree to which they harbor illusions as to who most threatens them. The vivid portrayal of the poor—and, of course, blacks—as hovering birds of prey waiting for the opportunity to snatch away the workers' meager gains serves also to deflect opposition away from the upper classes. A politician who promises to keep working-class communities free of blacks and the prisons full of them can get votes even if the major portion of his or her policies amount to continuation of the favored treatment of the rich at their expense. The sensationalistic use, in the 1988 presidential election, of photos of Willie Horton (a convicted black criminal who committed a brutal rape while out of prison on a furlough) suggests that such tactics are effective politics.[32]

The most important "bonus" derived from the identification of crime and poverty is that it paints the picture that the threat to decent Middle Americans comes from those below them on the economic ladder, not from those above. For this to happen, the system must not only identify crime and poverty, *but also fail enough in the fight to reduce crime so that crime remains a real threat*. By doing this, it deflects the fear and discontent of Middle Americans away from the wealthy.

There are other bonuses as well. For instance, if the criminal justice system sends out a message that bestows legitimacy on the present distribution of property, its dramatic impact is greatly enhanced if the violator of the present arrangements is without property. The crimes of the well-to-do "redistribute" property among the haves. They do not pose a symbolic challenge to the larger system in which some have much and many have little or nothing. If the criminal threat can be portrayed as coming from the poor, then the punishment of the poor criminal becomes a morality play in which the sanctity and legitimacy of the system in which some have plenty and others have little or nothing are dramatically affirmed. There is yet another bonus for the powerful in America, produced by the identification of crime and poverty. It might be thought that the identification of crime and poverty would produce sympathy for the criminals. But, in fact, it produces or at least reinforces the reverse: *hostility toward the poor.*

There is little evidence that Americans are very sympathetic to poor criminals. Very few Americans believe poverty to be a cause of crime (6 percent of those questioned in a 1981 survey, although 21 percent thought unemployment was a cause—in keeping with our general blindness to class, these questions are not even to be found in recent surveys). Other surveys find that most Americans believe that courts do not deal harshly enough with criminals (62 percent of those questioned in 2010), and that the death penalty should be used for convicted murderers, most of whom are poor (64 percent of those questioned in 2010).[33] Our view is that, because the criminal justice system, in fact and fiction, deals with *individual legal and moral guilt,* the association of crime with poverty does not mitigate the image of individual moral responsibility for crime, the image that crime is the result of an individual's poor character. It does the reverse: It generates the association of poverty and individual moral failing and thus *the belief that poverty itself is a sign of poor or weak character.* The clearest evidence that Americans hold this belief is to be found in the fact that attempts to aid the poor are regarded as acts of charity rather than as acts of justice. Our welfare system has all the demeaning attributes of an institution designed to give handouts to the undeserving and none of the dignity of an institution designed to make good on our responsibilities to our fellow human beings. If we acknowledged the degree to which our economic and social institutions themselves breed poverty and maintain economic inequality, we would have to recognize our own responsibilities toward the poor. If we can convince ourselves that the poor are poor because of their own shortcomings, particularly moral shortcomings, such as incontinence and indolence, then we need acknowledge no such responsibility to the poor. Indeed, we can go further and pat ourselves on the back for our generosity in handing out the little that we do, and, of course, we can make our recipients go through all the indignities that mark them as the undeserving objects of our benevolence. By and large, this has been the way in which Americans have dealt with their poor.[34] It is a way that enables us to avoid asking the question of why the richest nation in the world continues to produce massive poverty. This conception of the poor is subtly reinforced by our criminal justice system.

Obviously, no ideological message could be more supportive of the present social and economic order than this. It suggests that poverty is a sign of individual failing, not a symptom of social or economic injustice. It tells us loud and clear that massive poverty in the midst of abundance is not a sign pointing toward the need for fundamental changes in our social and economic institutions. It suggests that the poor are poor because they deserve to be poor, or at least because they lack the strength of character to overcome poverty. When the poor are seen to be poor in character, then economic poverty coincides with moral poverty and the economic order coincides with the moral order. As if a divine hand guided its workings, capitalism leads to everyone getting what he or she morally deserves!

If this association takes root, then when the poor individual is found guilty of a crime, the criminal justice system acquits the society of its responsibility not only for the crime *but for poverty as well.*

With this, the ideological message of criminal justice is complete. The poor rather than the rich are seen as the enemies of the majority of decent Americans. Our social and economic institutions are held to be responsible for neither crime nor poverty, and thus in need of no fundamental questioning or reform. The poor are poor because they are poor of character. The economic order and the moral order are one. To the extent that this message sinks in, the wealthy can rest easily—even if they cannot sleep the sleep of the just.

We can now understand why the criminal justice system is allowed to create the image of crime as the work of the poor, and to fail to reduce it so that the threat of crime remains real and credible. The result is ideological alchemy of the highest order. The poor are seen as the real threat to decent society. The ultimate sanctions of criminal justice dramatically sanctify the present social and economic order, and *the poverty of criminals makes poverty itself an individual moral crime!*

Such are the ideological fruits of a losing war against crime whose distorted image is reflected in the criminal justice carnival mirror and widely broadcast to reach the minds and imaginations of America.

IDEOLOGY, OR HOW TO FOOL ENOUGH OF THE PEOPLE ENOUGH OF THE TIME

What Is Ideology?

The view that the laws of a state or nation are made to serve the interests of those with power, rather than to promote the well-being of the whole society, is not a new discovery. It is a doctrine with a pedigree even older than Christianity. Writing during the fourth century B.C., virtually at the dawn of Western thought, Plato expressed this view through the lips of Thrasymachus.[35] A more contemporary and more systematic formulation of the idea is found in the works of Karl Marx, written during the nineteenth century, not long after the dawn of Western industrialism. Marx (and Engels) wrote in *The Communist Manifesto* that the bourgeoisie—the class of owners of businesses and factories, the class of capitalists—has "conquered for itself, in the modern representative State, exclusive political sway. The executive of the modern State is but a committee for managing the common affairs of the whole bourgeoisie."[36]

Anyone who thinks this is a ridiculous idea ought to look at the backgrounds of our political leaders. The vast majority of the president's cabinet, the administrators of the federal regulatory agencies, and the members of the two houses of Congress come from the ranks of business or are lawyers who serve business. Many still maintain their business ties or law practices, with no sense of a conflict of interest with their political role.[37] Even those who start from humble beginnings are usually quite rich by the time they finally make it into office. If either Thrasymachus or Marx is right, there *is* no conflict with their political role because that role is to protect and promote the interests of business.

It is clear that the most powerful criminal justice policy makers come from the have-plenties, not from the have-littles. It is no surprise that legislators and judges—those who make the laws that define criminality and those who interpret those laws—are predominantly members of the upper classes, if not at birth then surely by the time they take office. Richard Quinney compiled background data on key members of criminal justice policy-making and policy-advising committees and agencies, such as the President's Commission on Law Enforcement and Administration of Justice, the Federal Bureau of Investigation, and, last but not least, the U.S. Department of Justice. With few exceptions, Quinney's report reads like a *Who's Who* of the business, legal, and political elite.[38]

Further, there is considerable evidence that the American criminal justice system has been used throughout its history in rather unsubtle ways to protect the interests of the powerful against the lower classes and political dissenters. The use of the FBI and local police forces to repress dissent by discrediting, harassing, and undermining dissident individuals and groups has been abundantly revealed. The FBI, often with active cooperation or tacit consent of local police, has engaged in literally hundreds of illegal burglaries of the offices of law-abiding left-wing political parties,[39] and in political sabotage against the Black Panthers (e.g., "a Catholic priest, the Rev. Frank Curran, became the target of FBI operations because he permitted the Black Panthers to use his church for serving breakfasts to ghetto children").[40] It conducted a campaign to discredit the late Martin Luther King Jr. ("the FBI secretly categorized King as a 'Communist' months before it ever started investigating him").[41] Directors of the FBI have said that the bureau is "truly sorry" for these past abuses and that they are over. Later reports indicate that abuses have continued.[42] The latest chapter is police arresting and discharging pepper spray in the faces of nonviolent Occupy Wall Street protesters.[43]

These acts of repression are part of a long tradition. The first organized uniformed police force in the English-speaking world was established in London in 1829. They came to be called "bobbies" because of the role played by Sir Robert Peel in securing passage of the London Metropolitan Police Act, which established the force. The first full-time uniformed police force in the United States was set up in New York City in 1845.[44] It was also in the period from the 1820s to the 1840s that the movement to build penitentiaries to house and reform criminals began in New York and Pennsylvania and spread rapidly through the states of the young nation.[45] That these are also the years that saw the beginnings of a large industrial working class in the cities of England and America is a coincidence too striking to ignore.

The police were repeatedly used to break strikes and harass strikers.[46] The penitentiaries were used mainly to house the laborers and foreigners (often one and the same) whom the middle and upper classes perceived as a threat.[47] Throughout the formative years of the American labor movement, public police forces, private police such as the Pinkertons, regular army troops, and the National Guard, were used repeatedly to protect the interests of capital against the attempts of labor to organize in defense of its interests. The result was that "the United States has had the bloodiest and most violent labor history of any industrialized nation in the world"—with most of the casualties on the side of labor.[48]

Marx, of course, went further. Not only are the laws of a society made to protect the interests of the most powerful economic class, but also, Marx argued, the prevailing ways of thinking about the world—from economic theory to religion to conventional moral ideas about good and evil, guilt and responsibility—are shaped in ways that promote the belief that the existing society is the best of all possible worlds. Marx wrote that "the ideas of the ruling class are in every epoch the ruling ideas. ... The class which has the means of material production at its disposal, has control at the same time over the means of mental production."[49]

Because those who have economic power own the newspapers, endow the universities, finance the publication of books and journals, and (in our own time) control television, radio and other electronic media, they have a prevailing say in what is heard, thought, and believed by the millions who get their ideas—their picture of reality—from these sources. This does not mean that the controllers of the "means of mental production" consciously deceive or manipulate those who receive their message. What it means is that the picture of reality held by these controllers—believed by them, no doubt sincerely, to be an accurate representation of reality—will be largely the picture of reality that fills the heads of the readers and viewers of the mass media. The average man or woman is almost wholly occupied with the personal tasks of earning a living, piloting a family, and the like. He or she lacks the time (and usually the training) necessary to seek out and evaluate alternative sources of information. Most people are lucky when they have the time to catch a bit of news on television, in the papers, or on the Internet. Moreover, except when there is division of opinion among those who control the media, the average person is so surrounded by unbroken "consensus" that he or she takes it simply as the way things are.

Consequently, the vast majority of people will accept, as a true picture of reality, the picture held by those who control the media. This is likely to be a distorted picture, even if those who create it act with the best of intentions and sincerity. The point is that, for a wide variety of reasons, people will tend to view the world in ways that make their own role in it (particularly the advantages and privileges they have in it) seem morally just, indeed, part of the best of all possible worlds. Thus, without any intention to deceive at all, without any "conspiracy," those who control the content of the mass media are virtually certain to convey a picture of reality that supports the existing social order.

As a result, even in a society such as ours, where freedom of expression has reached a level unparalleled in history, there is almost never any fundamental questioning of our political-economic institutions in the mass media, that is, television and radio, the major newspapers, or the news weeklies such as *Time* or *Newsweek*. There is much criticism of individuals and of individual policies. How often, though, does one find the mass media questioning whether the free-enterprise system is really the best choice for America, or whether our political and legal arrangements systematically promote the domination of society by the owners of big business? These issues are rarely, if ever, raised. Instead, it is taken for granted that, although they need some reform from time to time, our economic institutions are the most productive, our political institutions the freest, and our legal institutions the most just that there can be.

Thus, we are told that the interests of the powerful coincide with the common interests of us all,[50] that "what's good for General Motors is good for the country." (This old slogan echoes eerily now as GM has teetered on the brink of bankruptcy and the government copes with firms that are "too big to be allowed to fail.") Where this picture of reality shows up some blemishes, they will always be portrayed as localized problems that can be remedied without fundamental overhaul of the entire social order, aberrations in an otherwise well-functioning social system. Indeed, the very willingness to publicize these blemishes "proves" that there is nothing fundamentally wrong with the social system, because if the media are free, willing, and able to portray the blemishes, they would surely portray fundamental problems with the social system if there were any—and because they do not, there must not be any! When ideas, however unintentionally, distort reality in a way that justifies the prevailing distribution of power and wealth, hides society's injustices, and thus secures uncritical allegiance to the existing social order, we have what Marx called *ideology*.[51] (Appendix I discusses in greater detail the Marxian theory of ideology, and of the role of criminal justice in capitalist society.)

Ideology is not conscious deception. People may spout ideology because it is all they know or all they have been taught or because they do not see beyond the "conventional wisdom" that surrounds them. This can be just as true of scholars who fail to see beyond the conventional assumptions of their disciplines as it is of laypersons who fail to see beyond the oversimplifications of what is commonly called "common sense." Such individuals do not mouth an ideology out of a willful desire to deceive and manipulate their fellows, but rather because their own view of reality is distorted by untruths and half-truths—and criminal justice is one source of such distortion. One way in which this works without conscious lying is that we have become so used to the criminal justice carnival mirror (described in Chapter 2) that we don't notice its curves. It looks flat, and thus we take it as an accurate picture of who threatens us in society.

Not everyone uses the term "ideology" as Marx did and as we have, namely, to point to what is necessarily deceptive. Some writers speak of ideology as if it meant any individual or group's "belief system" or "value system" or *Weltanschauung,* that is, "worldview."[52] This moral neutralization of the concept of "ideology" dulls an instrument that thinkers such as Marx and others have sharpened into an effective tool for cutting through the illusions that dog our political life. Such tools are few and hard to come by. Once we have them, they should be carefully preserved, especially when concepts such as "belief system" and "worldview" are available to perform the more neutral function.

The Need for Ideology

A simple and persuasive argument can be made for the claim that the rich and powerful in America have an interest in conveying an ideological message to the rest of the nation. The have-nots and have-littles far outnumber the have-plenties. This means, to put it rather crudely, that the have-nots and the have-littles could have more if they decided to take it from the have-plenties. This, in turn, means that the have-plenties need the cooperation of the have-nots and the have-littles. Because the have-plenties are such a small minority that they could never *force* this cooperation on the have-nots and have-littles, this cooperation must be voluntary. For the cooperation to be voluntary, the have-nots and the have-littles must believe it would not be right or reasonable to take away what the have-plenties have. In other words, they must believe that for all its problems, the present social, political, and economic order, with its disparities of wealth and power and privilege, is about the best that human beings can create. More specifically, the have-nots and have-littles must believe that they are not being exploited or being treated unfairly by the have-plenties; and these beliefs must be in some considerable degree false, because the distribution of wealth and power in the United States is so evidently arbitrary and unjust. Ergo, the need for ideology.

A disquisition on the inequitable distribution of wealth and income in the United States is beyond the scope and purpose of this book. This subject, as well as the existence of a "dominant" or "ruling" class in America, has been documented extensively by others.[53] We will make only two points here. First, there are indeed wide disparities in the distribution of wealth and income in the United States. Second, these disparities are so obviously unjust that it is reasonable to assume that the vast majority of people who must struggle to make ends meet put up with them only because they have been sold a bill of goods, that is, an ideology.

In 2010, the richest 20 percent of American households were expected to receive 50.2 percent of the income received by all families, whereas the poorest 60 percent of American households will receive 26.4 percent of the total income. In crude terms, this means that while the wealthiest 24 million American households will have more than half the money pie to themselves, the least wealthy 72 million American households will share about a quarter of that pie among them. At the outer edges the figures are more extreme: For 2010, the richest 5 percent of households are expected to receive 21.3 percent of total income, substantially more than the poorest 40 percent of households, who will receive 11.8 percent. This means that the richest 6 million households have nearly twice as much money to divide among themselves than the 48 million households who make up the bottom 40 percent.[54]

The distribution of *wealth* (property such as homes and stocks, as well as ownership of businesses and land that generate income and tend to give one a say in major economic decisions) is even more unequal than the distribution of income.[55] According to an analysis by a senior economist at the Federal Reserve, in 2007 the top 10 percent of households owned 71.5 percent of the nation's wealth, and the remaining 90 percent shared 28.5 percent. In 2007, the top one percent owned 33.8 percent of the country's wealth, and that did not include the wealth of the *Forbes* 400—the 400 wealthiest families in the United States. Those 400 families own about 2.3 percent of the total wealth, almost the same as what the poorest 50 percent of the country collectively owns. The bottom half of the population collectively owned 2.5 percent of the nation's wealth and 0.6 percent of stocks.[56] A study of long-term trends in wealth inequality shows that the top one-fifth of households has owned at least three-quarters of the nation's wealth over the period from 1962 to 1989. The author writes, "If anything, wealth concentration increased during the 1980s. It is estimated that the top 1 percent of households in 1989 owned 33 percent of household wealth, compared to 30 percent in 1986 and 28 percent in 1983." Looking back over the whole period from colonial times to the present, the author concludes that "at no time has the majority of the U.S. adult population or households managed to gain title to any more than about 10 percent of the nation's wealth." And, she adds, "the governmental policies of the past two decades have been hostile to progressive tax rates and economic measures benefiting workers. Real per capita income began declining in the early 1970s, benefits eroded in the 1980s. ... This situation suggests that the lower four quintiles' share of total wealth may well shrink in future years."[57] According to the *Washington Post* for January 23, 2003, "The rising economic tide of the late 1990s lifted the boats of almost all American families but also sharply increased the wealth gap between the rich and the rest of society, according to a survey released yesterday by the Federal Reserve."[58]

Americans generally underestimate the amount of inequality in the country, and when asked to construct their ideal distribution of wealth, it is more equal still. Some of the results of Michael Norton and Dan Ariely's survey of 5,522 Americans are shown in Table 4.2. They note that analysis of responses by sex, political party, and current income showed "much more consensus than disagreement among these different demographic groups."[59] Ideology is at work in making people perceive a lower level of inequality than

TABLE 4.2   Actual, Perceived, and Ideal Distributions of Wealth in the United States

Wealth of poorest 60%		Wealth of richest 20%
5%	Actual amount of wealth	84%
20%	Perceived amount of wealth	59%
45%	Ideal amount of wealth	32%

Source: Michael Norton and Dan Ariely, "Building a Better America—One Wealth Quintile at a Time" *Perspectives on Psychological Science 6(1),* p. 10, (2011).

actually exists and in accepting the vast difference between what exists and what they believe is fair.

We offer no complicated philosophical argument to prove that these disparities are unjust, although such arguments abound for those who are interested.[60] It is a scandal that, in a nation as rich as ours, some 46 million people (somewhat less when reckoned with the most generous valuation of in-kind benefits, such as food stamps) live below what the government conservatively defines as the poverty level, and that many millions more must scramble to make ends meet.[61] It is shameful that more than a third of the individuals below the poverty line are children! It is tragic that in our wealthy nation, so many millions cannot afford a proper diet, a college education, a decent place to live, and good health care. Because we are nowhere near offering all Americans a good education and an equal opportunity to get ahead, we have no right to think that the distribution of income reflects what people have truly earned. The distribution of income in America is so fundamentally shaped by factors such as race, educational opportunity, and the economic class of one's parents[62] that few people who are well-off can honestly claim they deserve *all* that they have. Those who think they do should ask themselves where they would be today if they had been born to migrant laborers in California or to a poor black family in the Harlem ghetto.

Enough said. We take it, then, as established that the disparities of wealth and income in America are wide and unjustified. For the vast majority, the many millions struggling hard to satisfy basic needs, to acquiesce to the vast wealth of a small minority, it is necessary that the majority come to believe that these disparities are justified, that the present order is the best that human beings can accomplish, and that they are not being exploited by the have-plenties. In other words, the system requires an effective ideology to fool enough of the people enough of the time.

This account of the nature and need for ideology, coupled with the historical inertia explanation of the persistence of criminal justice in its current form and the analysis of the ideological benefits produced by the criminal justice system, adds up to an explanation of the continued failure of criminal justice in the United States and its persistent bias against the poor. Thus, we believe that we have proven the Pyrrhic defeat theory of American criminal justice.

Summary

This chapter has presented the Pyrrhic defeat theory's explanation of the triple failure of criminal justice in the United States (1) to institute policies likely to reduce substantially the high incidence of crime, (2) to treat as crimes the dangerous acts of the well-off, and (3) to eliminate the bias against the poor in the treatment of those acts labeled "crimes." The persistence of this triple failure was explained by appeal to the notion of "historical inertia": the current shape of criminal justice policy emerged at an earlier time when it corresponded to the real threats to people's bodies and possessions; and it has persisted, in spite of its failures, because its failures mainly harm the poor, while they benefit the well-off; thus criminal justice policy does not generate incentives to change the system for those with the power to do so. The failing criminal justice system benefits those with the power to change things by broadcasting the message that the threat to Americans' well-being comes from below them on the economic ladder, not from above them, and that poverty results not from social causes but from the moral depravity of the poor. It was also argued that, aside from these "bonuses of bias," there is an implicit ideological message of any criminal justice system, insofar as such systems, by focusing on individual guilt, implicitly broadcast the message that the social system itself is a just one.

Study Questions

1. What is a conspiracy theory? What are the shortcomings of such a theory? Is the Pyrrhic defeat theory a conspiracy theory?
2. What is meant by "ideology"? What is the difference between ideology and propaganda? Is ideology needed in the United States?
3. How does any criminal justice system broadcast an ideological message supportive of the prevailing social and economic arrangements?
4. What additional ideological benefits result from the bias against the poor in the definition and treatment of crime?
5. Why are poor people in the United States poor?
6. Now that you have reviewed the historical inertia explanation of criminal justice in the United States, has the Pyrrhic defeat theory been proven?
7. What problems are posed by the privatization of prisons and the criminal justice-industrial complex?

Additional Resources

Jeffrey Reiman and Paul Leighton, *The Rich Get Richer and Poor Get Prison: A Reader* (Boston: Pearson, 2010). This volume is a collection of accessible articles that were either used as reference material for *The Rich Get Richer* or provide lively complementary examples or analysis. The reader is divided into sections that parallel the chapters of *The Rich Get Richer*, and each section of the reader opens with a substantial introduction, written by the editors, that provides article summaries, context, and linkages to *The Rich Get Richer*.

The authors also maintain a companion website to the text at *http://www.paulsjusticepage.com/reiman.htm*

Notes

1. *Challenge*, p. 44.
2. Lydia Saad, "Most Americans Believe Crime in U.S. Is Worsening," *Gallup*, October 31, 2011, *http://www.gallup.com/poll/150464/americans-believe-crime-worsening.aspx*.
3. "For example, it was discovered that, rather than the projected 20 percent savings, the average saving from privatization was only about 1 percent, and most of that was achieved through lower labor costs. Nevertheless, there were indications that the mere prospect of privatization had a positive effect on prison administration, making it more responsive to reform." James Austin and Garry Coventry, *Emerging Issues on Privatized Prisons by James Austin and Garry Coventry*, U.S. Department of Justice, Office of Justice Programs, Bureau of Justice Assistance, February 2001, NCJ 181249, p. iii.
4. BJS, *Prisoners in 2010*, December 2011, NCJ 236096, Appendix Table 19.
5. Karen L. Tippett, "Shares of Wackenhut Break Out as Prisons Become a Hot Industry," *The Wall Street Journal*, April 10, 1996, p. F2; and Michael Schuman, "A Sure-Fire Growth Industry," *Forbes*, January 16, 1995, p. 81.
6. Paulette Thomas, "Making Crime Pay," *The Wall Street Journal*, May 12, 1994, p. A1.
7. Quoted in Paul Leighton and Donna Selman, "Private Prisons, the Criminal Justice-Industrial Complex and Bodies Destined for Profitable Punishment," in Walter DeKeserdy and Molly Dragiewicz (ed.) *Routledge Handbook of Critical Criminology* (New York: Routledge, 2012), p. 270.
8. John Biewen, "Corrections, Inc: Corporate-Sponsored Crime Laws," American Public Media (no date), *http://americanradioworks.publicradio.org/features/corrections/laws1.html*.
9. National Institute on Money in State Politics, "Prison Companies Give $1.1 Million to Campaigns in Southern States," 2002, *http://www.followthemoney.org/press/ReportView.phtml?r=90*.
10. Donna Selman and Paul Leighton, *Punishment for Sale* (Lanham: Rowman and Littlefield, 2010), p. 21.
11. Quoted in Leighton and Selman, "Private Prisons, the Criminal Justice-Industrial Complex and Bodies Destined for Profitable Punishment," p. 270.
12. Ibid.
13. BJS, *Justice Expenditure and Employment extracts, 2009—Preliminary*, May 2012, NCJ 237913, Table 1; Eric Schlosser, "The Prison-Industrial Complex," *Atlantic Monthly*, December 1998, p. 54.
14. Joint report of the American Academy of Pediatrics, American Medical Association, American Academy of Child and Adolescent Psychiatry, and American Psychological Association available at *www.aap.org/advocacy/releases/jstmtevc.htm*. The joint report also says that "well over 1000 studies—including reports from the Surgeon General's office, the National Institute of Mental Health, and numerous studies conducted by leading figures within our medical and public health

organizations—our own members—point overwhelmingly to a causal connection between media violence and aggressive behavior in some children." See also "FRONTLINE Examines Impact of Television on Society in 'Does TV Kill?'" National Center for Children Exposed to Violence: Media Violence, *http://www.nccev.org/violence/media.html#statistics*; *Media Literacy Review,* Media Literacy Online Project of University of Oregon–Eugene, *http://www.nordicom.gu.se/clearinghouse.php?portal=special&main=themes.php&cat=12&me=14.* The Frontline program was aired in 1995. Brandon Centerwall, "Television Violence: The Scale of the Problem and Where to Go from Here," *Journal of the American Medical Association* 267, no. 22 (June 10, 1992): 3059, 3062; Jean Tepperman, "TV: The Violence Teacher," *www.4children.org*; report of the American Psychological Association cited in Sisela Bok, *Mayhem: Violence as Pubic Entertainment* (Reading, MA: Perseus, 1998), p. 57.

15. Graeme R. Newman, "Popular Culture and Criminal Justice: A Preliminary Analysis," *Journal of Criminal Justice* 18 (1990): 261.

16. Debra Seagal, "Tales from the Cutting-Room Floor: The Reality of 'Reality-Based' Television," *Harper's Magazine,* November 1993, p. 52. "Junkie-Busting Cop Culture" refers to the raids, arrests and round-ups of drug addicts. "Junkie" is a pejorative for a drug abuser, usually of heroin. It is less formal English to emphasize deep addiction and all the bad that happens to people in that condition.

17. David Fabianic, "Television Dramas and Homicide Causation," *Journal of Criminal Justice* 25, no. 3 (1997): 201.

18. James Unnever and Shaun Gabbidon, *A Theory of African American Offending* (New York: Routledge, 2011), p. 168.

19. On December 16, 1773, the group of colonists who raged against British colonial policies boarded the British ships and destroyed the tea of the East India Company, valued then about $1 million, by throwing it into Boston Harbor, Massachusetts. The incident, an early skirmish of American Independence, protested a tea tax imposed by the British and grew out of colonists' beliefs that they could only be taxed by their own elected representatives.

20. Richard A. Cloward and Lloyd E. Ohlin, *Delinquency and Opportunity: A Theory of Delinquent Gangs* (New York: Free Press, 1960), esp. pp. 77–107.

21. Steven Messner and Richard Rosenfeld, *Crime and the American Dream,* 3rd ed. (Belmont, CA: Wadsworth, 2000).

22. All of the above are mafia gangsters or cowboy outlaws who committed felonies from the end of the 19th to 20th century in the U.S. See Paul Kooistra, *Criminals As Heroes* (Bowling Green: Bowling Green State University Popular Press, 1989).

23. Cloward and Ohlin, *Delinquency and Opportunity,* p. 81.

24. Cloward and Ohlin, *Delinquency and Opportunity,* p. 10.

25. Ibid., p. 107.

26. Ibid., p. 10.

27. Willem Bonger, *Criminality and Economic Conditions,* abridged and with an introduction, by Austin T. Turk (Bloomington: Indiana University Press, 1969), pp. 7–12, 40–47. Willem Adriaan Bonger was born in Holland in 1876 and died by his own hand in 1940 rather than submit to the Nazis.

28. David M. Gordon, "Capitalism, Class and Crime in America," *Crime and Delinquency* (April 1973): 174.

29. Ibid.

30. William and Mary Morris, *Dictionary of Word and Phrase Origins,* vol. 2 (New York: Harper & Row, 1967), p. 282.

31. The full phrase "political-influence peddler" is meant to refer to political corruption and those in government who use their public authority to illegally benefit those who pay the politicians. Bribery is the most obvious form and political lobbying/campaign donations are the legal aspect of this.

32. See, for example, Jon Hurwitz and Mark Peffley, "Playing the Race Card in the Post–Willie Horton Era: The Impact of Racialized Code Words on Support for Punitive Crime Policy," *Public Opinion Quarterly* 69, no. 1 (2005): 99–113.

33. Roper Center, "Topics at a Glance: Crime," 2010, *http://www.ropercenter.uconn.edu/data_access/tag/crime.html#.TxmcpNVkjPo*. Frank Newport, "In U.S., 64% Support Death Penalty in Cases of Murder," 2010, *http://www.gallup.com/poll/144284/Support-Death-Penalty-Cases-Murder.aspx*.

34. Historical documentation of this can be found in David J. Rothman, *The Discovery of the Asylum: Social Order and Disorder in the New Republic* (Boston: Little, Brown, 1971); and in Frances Fox Piven and Richard A. Cloward, *Regulating the Poor: The Functions of Public Welfare* (New York: Pantheon, 1971).

35. *The Republic of Plato*, trans. F. M. Cornford (New York: Oxford University Press, 1945), p. 18 [I. 338]. Plato was born in Athens in the year 428 B.C. (or 427, depending on the reckoning) and died there in 348 B.C. (or 347). See S. J. Frederick Copleston, *A History of Philosophy, Volume 1: Greece and Rome* (Westminster, MD: Newman Press, 1946), pp. 127–141.

36. Karl Marx and Friedrich Engels, *Manifesto of the Communist Party*, in *The Marx–Engels Reader*, ed. Robert C. Tucker (New York: Norton, 1972), p. 337. Marx was born in Trier, Prussia (now in Germany), on May 5, 1818, and died on March 14, 1883. *The Manifesto* was first published in London in February 1848—when Marx was nearly 30 years old. Ibid., pp. xi–xiv.

37. An article on congressional ethics in *Newsweek* (June 14, 1976) makes the point so graphically that it is worth quoting at length:

    Some of the Hill's most powerful veterans have long earned part of their income from outside business interests—and may be tempted to vote with their own bank accounts in mind when legislation affecting those interests has come before Congress. House whip Thomas P. (Tip) O'Neill is active in real estate and insurance in Massachusetts, Minority Leader John Rhodes of Arizona is a director and vice-president of a life insurance company and scores of other senior members are involved with the banking industry, oil and gas companies and farming operations. Do these connections destroy their judgment? Not necessarily, argues Russell Long of Louisiana, chairman of the powerful Senate Finance Committee and a reliable defender of oil interests—who nevertheless refuses to disclose the size of his personal oil and gas holdings, most of them inherited from his father, former Gov. Huey Long. "A long time ago I became convinced that if you have financial interests completely parallel to your state, then you have no problem," says Long. "If I didn't represent the oil and gas industry, I wouldn't represent the state of Louisiana." Even more difficult to trace is the influence of representatives who keep their law practices—and their clients, many of whom do business with the Federal government—when they become members of Congress. (p. 25)

    For other analyses of the marriage of economic and political power, see William Greider, *Who Will Tell the People? The Betrayal of American Democracy* (New York: Touchstone/Simon & Schuster, 1993); Phillip Stern, *Still the Best Congress Money Can Buy*, rev. and expanded ed. (Washington, D.C.: Regnery Gateway, 1992); John Jackley, *Hill Rat: Blowing the Lid off Congress* (Washington, D.C.: Regnery Gateway, 1992); Donald Axelrod, *Shadow Government: The Hidden*

World of Public Authorities—and How They Control over $1 Trillion of Your Money (New York: Wiley, 1992); Michael Useem, *The Inner Circle: Large Corporations and the Rise of Business Political Activity in the US and UK* (New York: Oxford University Press, 1984); and Kim McQuaid, *Big Business and Presidential Power: From FDR to Reagan* (New York: Morrow, 1982).

38. J. A. Schmidhauser, "The Justices of the Supreme Court: A Collective Portrait," *Midwest Journal of Political Science* 3 (1959): 2–37, 40–49, cited in William J. Chambliss and Robert B. Seidman, *Law, Order and Power* (Reading, MA: Addison-Wesley, 1971), p. 96; and Richard Quinney, *Critique of Legal Order: Crime Control in Capitalist Society* (Boston: Little, Brown, 1973), pp. 60–82, 86–92.

39. See Ross Gelbspan, *Break-ins, Death Threats and the FBI: The Covert War against the Central American Movement* (Boston: South End Press, 1991); Margaret Jayko, *FBI on Trial: The Victory in the Socialist Workers Party Suit against Government Spying* (New York: Pathfinder Press, 1988); "F.B.I. Burglarized Leftist Offices Here 92 Times in 1960–66, Official Files Show," *The New York Times*, March 29, 1976, p. A1; and "Burglaries by FBI Listed in Hundreds," *The Washington Post*, July 16, 1975, p. A1. See also Cathy Perkus, ed., *Cointelpro: The FBI's Secret War on Political Freedom*, intro. Noam Chomsky (New York: Monad Press, 1975).

40. "Hill Panel Raps FBI's Anti-Panthers Tactics," *The Washington Post*, May 7, 1976, pp. A1, A22.

41. "FBI Labeled King 'Communist' in '62," *The Washington Post*, May 6, 1976, pp. A1, A26; and Michael Friedly and David Gallen, *Martin Luther King, Jr: The FBI File* (New York: Carroll & Graf, 1993). See also Carson Clayborne and David Gallen, *Malcolm X: The FBI File* (New York: Carroll & Graf, 1991); and Kenneth O'Reilly, *"Racial Matters": The FBI's Secret File on Black America, 1960–1972* (New York: Free Press, 1989).

42. "Kelley Says FBI Is 'Truly Sorry' for Past Abuses," *The Washington Post*, May 9, 1976, pp. A1, A14; and "FBI Break-Ins Still Go on, Panel Reports," *The Washington Post*, May 11, 1976. For more recent accounts, see "FBI Tactics Questioned in Probe of Activists," *The Chicago Tribune*, March 2, 1990, p. 1:5; "Here Come the '60s, with FBI in Tow," *Los Angeles Times*, June 26, 1990, p. A3; Peter Matthiessen, *In the Spirit of Crazy Horse* (New York: Viking, 1983), which discusses the FBI and the American Indian Movement (AIM), regarding which the FBI sued the author and delayed publication for several years; and Rex Weyler, *Blood of the Land: The Government and Corporate War against First Nations* (Philadelphia: New Society Publishers, 1992), which covers FBI and AIM. For other agencies of the government see, for example, "Military Spied on King, Other Blacks, Paper Says: Army Reportedly Targeted Southern Churches," *The Washington Post*, March 21, 1993, p. A16.

43. Note that J.P. Morgan Chase gave the New York police a $4.6 million gift: Yves Smith, "Is JP Morgan Getting a Good Return on $4.6 Million "Gift" to NYC Police? (Like Special Protection from OccupyWallStreet?)" (2012). *http://www.nakedcapitalism. com/2011/10/is-jp-morgan-getting-a-good-return-on-4-6-million-gift-to-nyc-police-like-special-protection-from-occupywallstreet.html*.

44. James F. Richardson, *Urban Police in the United States* (Port Washington, N.Y.: Kennikat Press, 1974), pp. 8–13, 22. See also Richardson's *The New York Police: Colonial Times to 1901* (New York: Oxford University Press, 1970).

45. Rothman, *The Discovery of the Asylum*, pp. 57–108, especially pp. 79–81. Cf. Michel Foucault, *Discipline and Punish: The Birth of the Prison* (London: Allen Lane, 1977).

46. Richardson, *Urban Police*, pp. 158–61. See also R. Boyer and H. Morais, *Labor's Untold Story* (New York: United Electrical, Radio & Machine Workers of America, 1976).

47. Rothman, *The Discovery of the Asylum*, pp. 253–54.

48. Philip Taft and Philip Ross, "American Labor Violence: Its Causes, Character, and Outcome," in H. D. Graham and T. R. Gurr (ed.) *The History of Violence in America* (New York: Bantam, 1969), pp. 281–395, especially pp. 281, 380; and Richard E. Rubenstein, *Rebels in Eden: Mass Political Violence in the United States* (Boston: Little, Brown, 1970), p. 81 inter alia. See also Center for Research in Criminal Justice, *The Iron Fist and the Velvet Glove* (Berkeley: University of California Press, 1975), pp. 16–19.

49. Karl Marx, *The German Ideology*, in Tucker (ed.) *The Marx-Engels Reader* p. 136.

50. Each new ruling class "is compelled, merely in order to carry through its aim, to represent its interest as the common interest of all the members of society." Marx, *The German Ideology*, p. 138.

51. Marx was not the first to use the term "ideology." The term was coined by a Frenchman, Antoine Destutt de Tracy, who was among the intellectuals named in 1795 to direct the researches of the newly founded Institut de France. The *idéologues* of the Institut generally believed that existing ideas were prejudices rooted in individual psychology or in political conditions and that the path to liberation from these prejudices and thus toward a rational society lay in a science of ideas (literally, an "idea-ology"), which made human beings aware of the sources of their ideas. Thomas Jefferson tried (albeit unsuccessfully) to have Destutt de Tracy's theory made part of the original curriculum of the University of Virginia. See George Lichtheim, "The Concept of Ideology," *History and Theory* 4, no. 2 (1965): 164–95; and Richard H. Cox, ed., *Ideology, Politics, and Political Theory* (Belmont, CA: Wadsworth, 1969), pp. 7–8. Needless to say, Marx used the term "ideology" in ways that neither Destutt de Tracy nor Jefferson anticipated.

52. Lichtheim's essay provides a good discussion of the philosophical antecedents of the gradual separation of the notion of ideology from that of false consciousness. Undoubtedly, this separation is of a piece with the current wisdom that insists that all views of the world are conditioned and rendered partial by the limits of the viewer's historical and social vantage point, and thus shrinks from trying to say anything true about the human condition. An illuminating example of this "current wisdom" applied to the criminal justice system is Walter B. Miller, "Ideology and Criminal Justice Policy: Some Current Issues," *Journal of Criminal Law and Criminology* 64, no. 2 (1973): 141–62. I shall use the concept of ideology in the Marxian sense, that is, to include that of false consciousness.

53. What follows is just a smattering of the literature documenting the wide and abiding disparities of wealth in America or the existence of a very small, not necessarily organized, group of individuals who, in addition to being extremely wealthy, make most of the economic and political decisions that shape America's destiny: Douglas Massey and Nancy Denton, *American Apartheid* (Cambridge, MA: Harvard University Press, 1993); Thomas Dye, *Who's Running America: The Bush Era*, 5th ed. (Englewood Cliffs, N.J.: Prentice Hall, 1990); G. William Domhoff, *The Power Elite and the State: How Policy Is Made in America* (New York: de Gruyter, 1990); Michael Parenti, *Democracy for the Few*, 5th ed. (New York: St. Martin's, 1988); William Julius Wilson, *The Truly Disadvantaged: The Inner City, the Underclass, and Public Policy* (Chicago: University of Chicago Press, 1987); J. Quirk, *Industry and Influence in Federal Regulatory Agencies* (Princeton, N.J.: Princeton University Press, 1981); Bertram Gross, *Friendly Fascism: The New Face of Power in America* (Boston: South End Press, 1980); G. William Domhoff, *The Powers That Be: Processes of Ruling Class Domination in America* (New York: Vintage,

1979); Edward S. Greenberg, *Serving the Few: Corporate Capitalism and the Bias of Government Policy* (New York: Wiley, 1974); Philip M. Stern, *The Rape of the Taxpayer* (New York: Vintage, 1974); Richard C. Edwards, Michael Reich, and Thomas E. Weisskopf, *The Capitalist System: A Radical Analysis of American Society* (Englewood Cliffs, N.J.: Prentice Hall, 1972); John Kenneth Galbraith, *The New Industrial State* (New York: Signet, 1968); G. William Domhoff, *Who Rules America?* 5th ed (New York: McGraw-Hill, 2005); and C. Wright Mills, *The Power Elite* (New York: Oxford University Press, 1956).

54. U.S. Bureau of the Census, *Income, Poverty and Health Insurance Coverage in the U.S.: 2010*, Table 3.

55. Alan S. Blinder, "The Level and Distribution of Economic Well-Being," in Martin Feldstein (ed.) *The American Economy in Transition* (Chicago: University of Chicago Press, 1980), p. 466.

56. Arthur Kennickell, "Ponds and Streams: Wealth and Income in the U.S., 1989 to 2007," Federal Reserve Board, January 7, 2009, *http://www.federalreserve.gov/pubs/feds/2009/200913/200913pap.pdf*.

57. Carole Shammas, "A New Look at Long-Term Trends in Wealth Inequality in the United States," *American Historical Review* 98, no. 2 (April 1993): 420, 421, 429. See Denis Kessler and Edward N. Wolff, "A Comparative Analysis of Household Wealth Patterns in France and the United States," *Review of Income and Wealth* 37 (1991): 249–66, which concludes, "The major finding of this study is that wealth is distributed more unequally in the U.S. than in France. The differences are considerable" (p. 262).

58. Albert Crenshaw, "Gap between Rich and Poor Grows: Fed Report Details Families' Income Situations," *The Washington Post*, January 23, 2003, p. E1.

59. Michael Norton and Dan Ariely, "Building a Better America—One Wealth Quintile at a Time," *Perspectives on Psychological Science* 6, no. 1 (2011): 10.

60. Undoubtedly, the most interesting recent work on this topic is John Rawls's *A Theory of Justice* (Cambridge, MA: Harvard University Press, 1971; revised ed., 1999). The noted British philosopher Stuart Hampshire has called it the most important work in moral philosophy since World War II. It has largely dominated theoretical discussions of political, legal, and economic justice for the last three decades. Rawls's approach is essentially "naturalistic"; that is, he takes the "good" to be that which people rationally desire, and the "moral good" to be that which would best serve all people's rational desires. From this, he takes justice to be those social (legal, political, and economic) arrangements that best serve the interests of all. To reach specific principles of justice, he asks for those principles that it would be rational for all people to agree to if each could not use force or influence to tailor the principles to his or her own interest. On the question of the distribution of income or wealth, this way of questioning leads to the principle that economic inequalities are just only if they work to everyone's advantage, for instance, as incentives that work to raise the level of productivity and thus the level of well-being for all. It would be the task of government to rectify inequalities that exceed this point, by means of taxes and transfers. We cannot, of course, do justice here to what Rawls takes 600 pages to explain and defend. However, we offer this short summary to suggest that the disparities of income in the United States are far from just in the light of contemporary moral philosophy. Clearly, those disparities are far greater than anything that could be claimed to be necessary to increase the well-being of all. Indeed, one would have to be blind not to see that they are not increasing the well-being of all.

Robert Nozick has replied to Rawls in a book titled *Anarchy, State and Utopia* (New York: Basic Books, 1974), which no doubt represents the free-enterprise system's theory of justice. Nozick holds that no theory (such as Rawls's) that calls for government intervention to rectify income distribution can be just. His argument is that if people acquire their property (including money) legitimately, then they have the right to sell or spend it as they wish. If this leads to disparities in wealth, one cannot alter this outcome without denying that those sellers or spenders had the right to dispose of their property or money as they saw fit. I shall not try to answer Nozick here. It should be noted, however, that his view starts from the assumption that the property or money that is sold or spent was acquired legitimately. In light of the fact that so much U.S. property was stolen at gunpoint from Indians or Mexicans and so much wealth was taken from the hides of black slaves, applying Nozick's theory in the U.S. context would require a massive redistribution of wealth to reach the starting point at which we could say that individuals own what they own legitimately. For an extended discussion of these theories of justice, see Jeffrey Reiman, *Justice and Modern Moral Philosophy* (New Haven, CT: Yale University Press, 1990).

61. U.S. Bureau of the Census, *Income, Poverty and Health Insurance Coverage in the U.S.: 2010*, Figure 4: "Number in Poverty and Poverty Rates: 1959-2010," available at: *http://www.census.gov/hhes/www/poverty/data/incpovhlth/2010/tables.html*.

62. One study reports that "among high school graduates with equal academic ability, the proportion going on to college averages nearly 25 percentage points lower for males (and nearly 35 for females) in the bottom socioeconomic quarter of the population than in the top quarter." Another indicates that "the sons of families in the top fifth of the socioeconomic pyramid have average incomes 75 percent higher than those coming from the bottom fifth." Arthur M. Okun, *Equality and Efficiency* (Washington, D.C.: Brookings Institution, 1975), pp. 81, 75.

Conclusion
Criminal *Justice* or *Criminal* Justice

Justice being taken away, then, what are kingdoms
but great robberies?

—St. Augustine, *The City of God*

... unjust social arrangements are themselves a kind of
extortion, even violence.

—John Rawls, *A Theory of Justice*

... the policeman moves through Harlem, therefore,
like an occupying soldier in a bitterly hostile country;
which is precisely what, and where he is, and the
reason he walks in twos and threes.

—James Baldwin, *Nobody Knows my Name*

A criminal justice system is a system of *justice* only if it protects equally the rights and interests of all members of society. For that it must punish evenhandedly the rich as well as the poor who violate these rights or endanger these interests. When it does not do this, the system is *criminal*. The biased use of the system's coercive power—police, courts, prisons—is force used against some members of society to promote the interests of others. Which is to say, it does precisely what crime does, and thus its force is morally equivalent to criminal violence. The conclusion of *The Rich Gets Richer* points out several policies that must be put in place if our system is to be a system of *justice*.

THE CRIME OF JUSTICE

Robbers, extortionists, and *occupying soldiers* are terms used to characterize those who enforce an unjust law and an unjust order. This is not merely rhetoric. There is a very real and very important sense in which those who use force unjustly or who use force to protect an unjust social order are no different from a band of criminals or an occupying army. If this isn't understood, you are likely to think that what has been described in the first three chapters, and accounted for in the fourth, amounts to only another call for reform of the criminal justice system to make it more effective and fairer, when in fact it is much more. A criminal justice system that functions like ours—that imposes its penalties on the poor and not equally on all who threaten society, that does not protect us against threats to our lives and possessions equal to or graver than those presently defined as "crimes," and that fails even to do those things that could better protect us against the crimes of the poor—*is morally no better than the criminality it claims to fight.*

Later in this chapter, we propose some reforms of the system. These should not be taken as proposals aimed merely at improving the effectiveness or fairness of American criminal justice. If the argument of this chapter is correct, then these proposals represent the necessary conditions for establishing the moral superiority of criminal justice to criminality. They are the conditions that must be fulfilled if the criminal justice system is to be acquitted of the indictment implicit in the statements above from St. Augustine, Rawls, and Baldwin. Bear in mind that the "criminal justice system" does not mean only police, courts, and prisons; it includes the entire legal system, from lawmakers to law enforcers to judges and prison guards and parole boards.

What is common to the charge implicit in the statements of St. Augustine, Rawls, and Baldwin is the idea that *injustice transforms a legal system into its opposite.* What is common to the robber, the extortionist, and the occupying soldier is that each uses force (or the threat of force) to coerce people to serve the interests of others at the expense of their own. The robber and the extortionist use force to make other people hand over things of value. The occupying soldier uses force to subject one people to domination by another. The injustice that characterizes criminal acts is the forcing of people to serve the interests of others.

A legal system, of course, also uses force. Its defenders, however, maintain that it uses force to protect people's control over the things they value and over their own destinies. They claim that the legal system protects people's possessions against robbers and extortionists and protects their autonomy against those who would try to impose their will on them by force. In short, although both a legal system and its opposite, either criminality or military domination, use force, the moral superiority claimed for the legal system lies in the fact that it uses force to protect the interests of all people subject to its force equally, whereas criminals and occupying troops use force to subject some people to the interests of others. The moral legitimacy of a legal system and the lack of legitimacy of crime and military domination hinge, then, on the question of whether coercion is being used in the interests of all equally, or to promote some people's interests at the expense of others.

This adds up to something that should be obvious but is not: *A criminal justice system is criminal to the extent that it is not truly a system of justice.* A criminal justice system is a system of justice to the extent that it protects equally the interests and rights of all and to the extent that it punishes equally all who endanger these interests or who violate these rights. To the extent that it veers from these goals, the criminal justice system is guilty of the same sacrificing of the interests of some for the benefit of others that it exists to combat. It is, therefore, morally speaking, guilty of crime. Which is it?

The experience of the twentieth century has taught us that we should not take for granted that every legal system is a system of justice. Hitler's Germany and Stalin's Soviet Union, as well as South Africa when it practiced apartheid, are testimony to the fact that what is put forth as law may well be outrageously unjust. An example closer to home would be the U.S. legal system, which, under the Supreme Court's *Dred Scott* decision of 1857, defined black slaves as property. In such instances, we easily recognize the truth implicit in the statements of St. Augustine, Rawls, and Baldwin that open this chapter: What is put forth under color of law[1] may be morally no better than crime or tyranny. Therefore, we can no longer uncritically take for granted that our own legal order is just merely because it is legal. We must subject it to the moral test of whether it serves and protects the interests of all to make sure it is not injustice disguised as justice, criminality wearing the mask of law. (Appendix II, "Between Philosophy and Criminology," argues that criminology requires a moral evaluation of crime as part of its identification of its object of study.) It is, of course, not our aim to place the U.S. legal system on par with that of Hitler's Germany or Stalin's Soviet Union. There is much in the system that is legitimate, and many are caught by the system who should be. Stated precisely, our claim is this:

> *To the extent that* the American criminal justice system fails to implement policies that could significantly reduce crime and the suffering it produces (as argued in Chapter 1),
>
> *To the extent that* the American criminal justice system fails avoidably to protect Americans against the gravest dangers to their lives and property (as argued in Chapter 2),
>
> *To the extent that* the American criminal justice system apprehends and punishes individuals not because they are dangerous but because they are *dangerous and poor* (as argued in Chapter 3),
>
> *Then, to that same extent,* the American criminal justice system fails to give all Americans either protection or justice, aids and abets those who pose the greatest dangers to Americans, and uses force in ways that do not serve equally the interests of all who are subject to that force, and *thus its use of force is morally no better than crime itself.*

REHABILITATING CRIMINAL JUSTICE IN AMERICA

The criminal justice system in America is morally indistinguishable from criminality insofar as it exercises force and imposes suffering on human beings *while violating its own morally justifying ideals: protection and justice.* Once this is understood, the requirements for rehabilitating the system follow rather directly. The system must institute policies that make good on its claim to protect society and to do justice. The remainder of this chapter briefly sketches the outlines of a "treatment strategy" for *helping the system go straight.* It cannot be reiterated too frequently that these proposals are not offered as means of *improving* the system. Nor are we under any illusion that these proposals will be easily adopted or implemented. They are presented as the necessary requirements for establishing the criminal justice system's moral difference from, and moral superiority to, *crime;* and even if not implemented or not likely to be implemented, they stand as a measure against which this moral difference and superiority can be judged. The proposals fall under the headings of the two ideals that justify the existence of a criminal justice system: protecting society and promoting justice.

Protecting Society

Every day that we refuse to implement those strategies that have a good chance of cutting down on the predatory and violent street crimes people fear, the system is an accomplice to those crimes and bears responsibility for the suffering they impose. Thus,

We must put an end to the crime-producing poverty in our midst.

Throughout this book we have documented the striking persistence of large-scale poverty in the United States as well as the link between that poverty and much of the crime people fear the most. The elimination of poverty is the most promising crime-fighting strategy there is and, in the long run, the most cost-effective. It is sometimes observed that poverty itself doesn't cause crime, because, for example, there was more poverty in earlier times than now and yet less crime. There is an important truth here, but it is easy to miss it. The truth is that it is not poverty as such that breeds crime, but the things that poverty brings with it in a modern, free, and free-enterprise society like ours: lack of good education (because public schools are financed primarily out of local property taxes; and the best schools are expensive private ones), lack of parental authority (because unemployed parents easily lose their children's respect), lack of cohesive local community (because those who can will escape the poor inner cities as quickly as possible), lack of allegiance to social institutions (due to feeling left out—recall the discussion of John Rawls's views in Chapter 1), and so on. It is these things, rather than lack of money itself, that lead to crime. Investing in our inner cities and providing high-quality public education, job training, and jobs for the unemployed will give us more productive citizens with a stake in playing by the rules. And it will be cheaper than paying for police and prisons to house those who break the rules.

Eliminating the debilitating and crime-producing poverty around us is essential to any serious, long-term effort to protect society from crime. But along with it, we must

---

Let the crime fit the harm and the punishment fit the crime.

For the criminal justice system to justify its methods, it must make good on its claim to protect society. This requires that the criminal law be redrawn so that the list of crimes reflects the real dangers that individuals pose to society. We must make new and clear laws against imposing certain dangers on workers and citizens generally, and then hold people to those laws no matter what their economic class is. Crime in the suites should be prosecuted and punished as vigorously as crime in the streets.

The law must be drawn carefully so that individuals are not punished for harm they could not foresee or could not have avoided, or that others have freely consented to risk. Moreover, this is not a matter of punishing people for anything and everything they do that might lead to harm. The pursuit of security must not swamp the legitimate claims of liberty and progress. Some risks are the inevitable companions of freedom, and some are part of modern life. For every mile of highway we build, we can predict the number of people who will be killed in accidents on it. This does not justify treating the highway engineer as a murderer. Rather, we must have an open and ongoing discussion about risk and decide together which risks are worth taking and what level of risk is reasonable to impose on workers or citizens generally. Within this framework, we must stop treating *indirect* harm as merely a regulatory matter and start *treating all intentional harm-producing acts in proportion to the actual harm they produce. We must enact and implement punishments that fit the harmfulness of the crime without respect to the class of the criminal.* Because responsibility for corporate actions tends to be spread or even blurred in large organizations, we need legal requirements that make corporations identify in advance the individuals who are legally responsible for specific acts. Kip Schlegel recommends that a standard of "reckless supervision" be built into sentencing guidelines for corporate offenses, so that individuals with supervisory authority could be held responsible for failure to exercise that authority when there is substantial risk of harm.[2] The Sarbanes-Oxley financial reform legislation takes a step in this direction by requiring executives to certify the accuracy of financial statements, so that they cannot get paid big money to run a company and then claim they had no idea about massive, systemic, billion-dollar frauds. The principle is sound and should be applied more widely in the business world.

But this is only the beginning. There is much more that can and should be done. In his book, *Corporate Crime and Violence*, Russell Mokhiber sets out a "50-Point Law-and-Order Program to Curb Corporate Crime."[3] Mokhiber's suggestions are quite realistic, and many fit well within the framework just outlined. A current list of recommendations for new laws would require corporate executives to report activities that might cause death or injury, make it a criminal offense to willfully or recklessly fail to oversee an assigned activity that results in criminal conduct, enable federal prosecutors to bring federal homicide charges against companies that have caused death on a national scale (such as Manville or the tobacco companies), hold corporations responsible for how they respond to wrongful acts (do they cover up or take measures to prevent recurrence, etc.?), facilitate class action suits against corporations, require convicted companies to make their misdeeds public by advertising them, better protect whistleblowers from reprisal, increase the penalties for convicted corporate executives, make it a crime for a corporation to have a faulty system for ensuring compliance with the law, use fines to support independent watchdog organizations, track the extent and cost of white collar crime, establish a specialized corporate crime task force within the Department of Justice and—for serious or repeated offenses—"execute" corporations (by stripping them of their corporate charters). Such laws, duly applied, would begin to make the criminal justice system's response proportionate to the real dangers in our society.[4]

The other side of the coin is the decriminalization of "victimless crimes," acts such as prostitution, gambling, vagrancy, drunkenness, and recreational drug use. As long as these acts involve only adults who have freely chosen to participate, they are no threat to the liberty of any citizen. This also means that there is generally no person who is harmed by these acts and who is ready and able to press charges and testify against the wrongdoers. Therefore, police have to use a variety of shady tactics involving deception and actions bordering on entrapment, which undermine the public's respect for the police and the police officers' respect for themselves. The use of such low-visibility tactics increases the likelihood of corruption and arbitrariness in the enforcement of the law. Beyond this, because these acts produce no tangible harm to others, laws against them make criminals out of people who have no intention to injure or take advantage of others. In short, such laws fill our prisons with people who aren't dangerous, while we leave truly dangerous people on the streets. To make good on its claim to protect society, the criminal justice system must not only treat the dangerous acts of business executives as crimes, but also decriminalize those acts that are not clearly dangerous.[5]

More than 150 years ago, John Stuart Mill formulated a guiding principle, still relevant to our time, for the design of legislation in a society committed to personal liberty:

> That principle is, that the sole end for which mankind are warranted, individually or collectively, in interfering with the liberty of action of any of their number, is self-protection. That the only purpose for which power can be rightfully exercised over any [sane adult] member of a civilized community, against his will, is to prevent harm to others.[6]

Although this principle needs to be modified in recognition of some of the ways in which individuals can cause future harm to themselves in a complex modern society where people must deal with machines and chemicals beyond their understanding,[7] the core of the principle is still widely accepted. This is the notion that a necessary condition of any justifiable legal prohibition is that it prohibits an act that does foreseeable harm to someone other than the actor himself. Because priority should be given to freedom of action, this harm should be *demonstrable* (i.e., verifiable by some widely agreed-upon means, say, those used by science), and it should be of sufficient gravity to outweigh the value of the freedom that is to be legally prohibited.[8]

This principle not only should guide legislators and those engaged in revising and codifying criminal law, but also should be raised to the level of an implicit constitutional principle. The U.S. Supreme Court recognizes certain traditional principles of legality as constitutional requirements even though they are not explicitly written into the Constitution. For instance, some laws have been held unconstitutional because of their vagueness[9] and others because they penalized a condition (such as being a drunk or an addict) rather than an action (such as drinking or using drugs).[10] The tenor of the Bill of Rights is to enshrine and protect individual liberty from the encroachment of the state, and thus Mill's principle is arguably already implicitly there.

Whether as a legislative or a judicial criterion, however, applying Mill's principle would undoubtedly rid our law of the residues of our puritanical moralism. And it would eliminate the forced induction into criminality of the individuals, mainly those of the lower class, who are arrested for "victimless crimes." It would eliminate the pressure toward secondary crime (the need of the prostitute for a pimp to provide protection, theft by drug addicts to support their habits, violent turf wars between drug gangs, and so on). And it would free up resources for the fight against the really dangerous crimes. Thus

We must legalize the production and sale of "illicit drugs" and treat addiction as a medical problem.

When drug addicts cannot obtain their fix legally, they will obtain it illegally. Because those who sell it illegally have a captive market, they will charge high prices to make their own risks worthwhile. To pay the high prices, addicts must, will, and do resort to crime. Thus, every day in which we keep the acquisition of drugs a crime, we are using the law to protect the high profits of drug black marketeers, *and* we are creating a situation in which large numbers of individuals are virtually physically compelled to commit theft. There can be little doubt that our present "cure" (arrests and incarceration) for narcotics use is more criminal (and crime-producing) than the narcotics themselves. Ethan Nadelmann, of the Woodrow Wilson School of Public and International Affairs, points out that "there is no single legalization option.

Legalization can mean a free market, or one closely regulated by the government, or even a government monopoly. ... Legalization under almost any regime, however, does promise many advantages over the current approach. Government expenditures on drug-law enforcement would drop dramatically. So would organized crime revenues."[11] Many observers seem to agree that the British system in which doctors may prescribe heroin for addicts is superior to our own punitive system. For example, an editorial in the *Montreal Gazette* states, "A Dutch study ... found prescribing heroin to abusers is not only cost-effective, but provided better quality of life to addicts. Savings to society were estimated at more than $20,000 a year per addict in reduced policing costs and property crime. Without this program, addicts on average were spending $1,500 a month on heroin, and were involved in a crime every three days to get extra money for drugs."[12]

A number of experts have gone even further. Norval Morris and Gordon Hawkins urge that narcotics use be decriminalized and the drugs be sold in pharmacies by prescription. Arnold Trebach urges that doctors be permitted to prescribe heroin for the treatment of addicts and as a powerful painkiller. Kurt Schmoke (who, prior to being mayor of Baltimore, was Maryland's State Attorney) has called for permitting health professionals to give drugs to addicts as part of a treatment and detoxification plan. Jerry Wilson, former Washington, D.C. police chief, has suggested the possibility of selling and taxing marijuana in the way that tobacco is currently sold and taxed, and treating opiates and cocaine derivatives the way alcohol currently is treated, while keeping some psychoactive drugs available only at pharmacies with a doctor's prescription.[13]

Any reasonable plan of legalization will start by decriminalizing marijuana, which is virtually harmless. On the other hand, there may be some drugs that are so addictive or so likely to stimulate people to violence that we must keep them illegal. This may be the case with "crack" and with PCP, also known as "angel dust." If this turns out to be true (and the government has so exaggerated the dangers of illicit drugs over the years that healthy skepticism is warranted about these recent claims), it may be necessary to exclude these from the general program of decriminalization. With less dangerous drugs decriminalized, however, many users of crack or PCP might switch to the less dangerous ones, and, in any event, already overstretched law enforcement resources would be freed up to concentrate on the really dangerous drugs and on the crucial problem of keeping drugs away from youngsters.

Ending poverty, criminalizing the really dangerous acts of the well-off, and decriminalizing victimless crimes will reduce crime, protect society, and free up our police and prisons for the fight against the criminals who really threaten our lives and limbs. For these, however,

We must develop correctional programs that promote rather than undermine personal responsibility, and we must offer ex-offenders real preparation and a real opportunity to succeed as law-abiding citizens.

The scandal of our prisons has been amply documented. Like our drug policy, our prisons seem more calculated to produce than reduce crime. The enforced childhood of imprisonment may be the painful penalty that offenders deserve, but if it undermines their capacity to go straight after release, we are cutting off our noses to spite our faces. Philosopher Richard Lippke contends that, if we punish people because they have failed to act morally, we must respect and preserve their capacity to act morally.[14] But, people cannot learn to control themselves responsibly if they have spent years having every aspect of their lives—the hour they wake, the number of minutes they spend washing up, the time and content of eating and working and exercising, and the hour at which lights go out—regulated by someone else. Add to this the fact that convicts usually emerge with no marketable skill and little chance of getting a decent job with the stigma of a prison sentence hanging over them. The result is a system in which we never let criminals finish paying their debt to society and instead give them every incentive to return to crime. What's needed is the encouragement of restorative justice, the adoption of proven rehabilitative programs, and a transformation of prisons to infuse hope, personal responsibility, and respect for human dignity into our correctional practices.[15]

Numerous experts on corrections believe that our prison sentences are far too long, in light of the extreme deprivations of prison life and the lack of evidence that lengthy sentences significantly reduce crime. Andrew von Hirsch and Andrew Ashworth argue that recent increases in sentence length in the United States and in England achieve neither proportionality between punishment and crime, nor significant crime reduction. In their view, these increases are due to cynical attempts by politicians to "mobilize and exploit resentment at crime or criminals." These experts urge substantial reductions in sentences.[16]

Lippke also argues for sentences considerably less draconian than those commonly meted out in the United States. He contends that the harsh conditions that generally characterize American prisons should be replaced with what he calls the minimum conditions of confinement. These minimum conditions are already enough to deprive offenders of freedom of movement and association, attenuate their ties with loved ones and friends, curtail their privacy, subject them to low levels of amenities, limit their work options and access to forms of entertainment, make them subservient to extensive bureaucratic control, and impose upon them a lasting stigma. Greater deprivations than these cause "near-extinction of the agency [meaning the capacity to form responsible judgments and act on them] of inmates," and thus run afoul of the requirement that offenders be respected and preserved as autonomous moral agents. Thus, Lippke holds that prisoners should retain all their civil rights that are compatible with the minimal conditions of confinement, under which he includes their rights to work for prevailing wages; to have extensive contact with friends and loved ones both inside and outside of prison; to vote, exercise free speech, and even run for public office; and to have moderate access to recreation and entertainment.[17]

Former National Institute of Justice Director, Jeremy Travis, points out that 630,000 people leave prison each year and reenter society. He writes that "reentry is not an option. Reentry reflects the iron law of imprisonment: they all come back."[18] Thus, if we are going to continue to punish people by depriving them of their liberty, we must do it in a way that prepares them for the life they will lead when their liberty is returned. Anything less than this is a violation of the Constitution's Eighth Amendment guarantee against "cruel and unusual punishment." Depriving a person of his or her liberty may be an acceptable punishment, but *depriving people of their dignity and a chance to live a law-abiding life when their punishment is supposed to be over is cruel and* (should be but sadly is not) *unusual!*

If depriving people of a chance to live a law-abiding life after prison is a cruel and unusual punishment, then pursuant to the guarantee of the Eighth Amendment, every imprisoned person should have a right to training at a marketable skill as well as a right to compete equally with non-ex-convicts for a job once the punishment is over. This might require making it illegal to discriminate against ex-convicts in hiring and illegal to require job applicants to state whether they had ever been arrested, convicted, and/or imprisoned for a crime. This requirement might have to be modified for particularly sensitive occupations, although on the whole it would be fairer and more effective in rehabilitating ex-cons to enact it across the board and to have the government finance or subsidize a fund to insure losses incurred as a result of hiring ex-convicts. This would surely be much less costly than paying to support ex-cons in prison and their families on welfare when they return to crime for lack of a job. And, if prison industries paid inmates at something closer to prevailing wages, that money could be used for restitution to victims and to purchase privileges and possibly increased privacy or freedom for the prisoners—all of which would give them greater practice at controlling their own lives so that they will be prepared to do so after release.

To release them back into a safer and more peaceful society, however,

We must enact and vigorously enforce stringent gun controls.

Americans are armed to the teeth. The handgun is the most easily concealed, the most effective, and the deadliest weapon there is. Its ubiquity is a constant temptation to would-be crooks who lack the courage or skill to commit crime without weapons or to chance hand-to-hand combat. Its ubiquity also means that any dispute may be transformed into a fatal conflict beyond the desires or expectations of the disputants. A large number of accidental injuries and deaths are also linked to the prevalence of guns. And the problem is not limited to handguns. In recent years, it has become relatively easy to obtain rapid-firing assault rifles. Trying to fight crime while allowing such easy access to guns is like trying to teach a child to walk and tripping him each time he stands up. In its most charitable light, it is hypocrisy. Less charitably, it is complicity in murder.[19]

If, because of the Second Amendment, we continue to allow private individuals to own guns, we can at least require that gun owners be registered and perhaps certified after completing a course on safe use of guns (safety classes are already commonly required as part of qualifying for gun permits). We can surely ban assault rifles and require all guns to have trigger locks that children and gun thieves cannot open.[20] These changes, taken together, would be likely to reduce dangerous crime and to bring us a legal order that actually punished (and, it is hoped, deterred) all and only those acts that really threaten our lives, limbs, and possessions; and punished them in proportion to the harm they really produce. Such a legal system could be truly said to protect society.

Promoting Justice

The changes recommended above would, in part, make the criminal justice system more just, because people would be punished in proportion to the seriousness of their harmful acts, and the number of innocent persons victimized by those acts would be reduced. At the same time, however, we have seen that the criminal justice system is biased against the poor, and until poverty is eliminated, much must be done to assure justice for the poor people who get caught up in the criminal justice system.

A criminal justice system should arrest, charge, convict, and sentence individuals with an eye only to their crime, not to their economic class. More frequent arrests or harsher penalties for poor persons than for others accused of the same crime constitute a grave injustice that undermines the legitimacy of the criminal justice system. Because many of the decisions that work to the disadvantage of the poor—police decisions to arrest, prosecutors' decisions to charge, and judges' decisions on how long to sentence—are exercises of discretion often out of public view, they are particularly resistant to control. Because, unlike prosecutors' or judges' decisions, the police officer's decision *not* to arrest is *not* a matter of record, it is the least visible exercise of discretion and the most difficult to control. Our best hope to make arrests by police more just lies in increased citizen awareness and education of police officers so that they become aware of the operation and impact of their own biases and are held more directly accountable to, and by, the public they serve and sometimes arrest.

As for prosecutorial and judicial discretion, two approaches seem potentially fruitful. First, lawmakers ought to spell out the acceptable criteria that prosecutors may use in deciding whether or what to charge. The practice of multiple charging (charging an accused burglar with "the lesser included crimes" of breaking and entering, possession of burglar's tools, and so on) should be eliminated. It is used by prosecutors to "coax" accused persons into pleading guilty to one charge by threatening to press *all* charges.

Of all the dubious features of our system of bargain justice, this seems most clearly without justification because it works to coerce a plea of guilty that should be uncoerced if it is to be legally valid.[21] Federal sentencing guidelines (followed by the adoption of sentencing guidelines by many states) are an important step toward reducing discretion, and thus discrimination, in the criminal justice system. But they are only a step. They have not eliminated discrimination. D'Alessio and Stolzenberg found that lower-socioeconomic-status (SES) offenders were likely to receive harsher sentences for nonproperty and morals offenses than higher-SES offenders, and that sentencing guidelines did not reduce these disparities.[22] And, as pointed out in Chapter 3, for similar charges white defendants are more likely to get sentences below the guideline minimums than blacks. It appears that such guidelines have not so much eliminated discretion as shifted it from judges to prosecutors (who decide what to charge), and because prosecutors are less insulated from political pressures than judges, that is counterproductive. Thus, sentencing guidelines must be matched with charging guidelines.[23] Neither sort of guidelines should be so rigid as to leave no room for the expert judgment of judges or prosecutors. (In 2005, the Supreme Court decided that sentencing guidelines are only advisory and not legally binding on judges; but research by the U.S. Sentencing Commission indicates that sentencing practices in the year following the Court's decision are consistent with earlier sentencing under the guidelines, so all the problems with them remain.)[24] Rather than rigid rules, we need public accountability, timely release of data about the status of cases, and explanations for decisions about cases that are dropped.

Moreover, the sentencing guidelines that we have arose during the Reagan era, with its emphasis on extreme punitiveness. They often either include or are accompanied by draconian mandatory minimum sentences for small crimes, particularly drug crimes, or life sentences for a third offense no matter how minor. In response to this, an advocacy group called "Families Against Mandatory Minimums" was formed, whose "files bulge with cases of citizens serving drug sentences of 5, 10 and 20 years without parole chances for first and often minor offenses."[25] California recently sentenced a man to 50 years in prison for two shoplifting incidents involving stealing 11 blank videocassettes from K-Mart, and the Supreme Court upheld the sentence in 2003 as not unreasonable or disproportionate.[26] Because this very punitive approach has dramatically expanded our prison populations with only small gains in reducing crime, it is time to separate the task of assuring even-handed sentencing from that of hard-fisted sentencing. Whichever way we achieve it, it is clear that to make the criminal justice system function justly,

We must narrow the range in which police officers, prosecutors, and judges exercise discretion, and we must develop procedures to hold them accountable to the public for the fairness and reasonableness of their decisions.

All these changes still leave standing what is probably the largest source of injustice to the poor in the system: *unequal access to quality legal counsel*. We know that privately retained counsel will have more incentive to put in the time and effort to get their clients off the hook. The result is that, *for equal crimes,* those who can retain their own counsel are more likely to be acquitted than those who cannot. The present system of allocating assigned counsel or public defenders to the poor, and privately retained lawyers to the affluent, is little more than a parody of the constitutional guarantee of *equal protection under the law.*

In our system, even though lawyers are assigned to the poor, justice has a price. Little over a century ago, before there were public police forces in every town and city, people got "police protection" by hiring private police officers or bodyguards if they could afford it. Protection was available for a price, and so those who had more money were better protected under the law. Today, we regard it as every citizen's right to have police protection, and we would find it outrageous if police protection were allocated to citizens on a fee-for-service basis. *But this is precisely what we do with respect to the legal protection provided by lawyers!*

Both police officers and lawyers are essential to the individual's legal protection. It is sheer hypocrisy to acknowledge everyone's right to equal protection under the law by the police and then to allocate protection under the law by lawyers on the basis of what individuals can pay. As long as this continues, we cannot claim that there is anything like equal treatment before the law in the criminal justice system. Therefore,

> We must transform the equal right to counsel into the right to equal counsel as far as it is possible.

Although this would appear to be a clear requirement of the equal protection and due process clauses of the Constitution, the Supreme Court has avoided it, perhaps because it poses great practical problems—and surely it does. The creation of public police forces to protect everyone posed great practical problems in its time as well.

It would not be appropriate to use the police as a model for resolving the problem of equal counsel. To establish a government legal service for all—in effect, to nationalize the legal profession—might make equal legal representation available to all. It would, however, undermine the adversary system by undercutting the independence of defense attorneys from the state. Some form of national legal insurance to enable all individuals to hire private attorneys of their own choice, however, could bring us closer to equal legal protection without compromising the adversarial relationship.

Such insurance would undoubtedly have to be subsidized by the government, as are the police, courts, and prisons; but it would not necessarily have to be totally paid for out of taxes. People can rightly be expected to pay their legal bills up to some fraction of their income, if they have one. The rest would be paid for by a government subsidy that would pay the difference between what the accused could afford and the going rate for high-quality legal counsel. Nothing in the system need interfere with the freedom of the accused to select the lawyer of his or her choice (an option closer to the hearts of free enterprisers than the present public defender system allows) or interfere with the independence of the lawyer.

Undoubtedly, such a system would be costly. Our commitment to equal justice, however, remains a sham until we are willing to pay this price. Americans have paid dearly to protect the value of liberty enshrined in the Constitution. Is it too much to ask that they pay to realize the ideal of justice enshrined there too?

One final recommendation remains to be made. We have already argued that the criminal justice system, by its very nature, protects the prevailing economic distribution with its laws. Therefore, it is an error to think of the criminal justice system as an entity that can be reformed in isolation from the larger social order. A criminal justice system protects that social order, and it can be no more just than the order it protects. A law against theft may be enforced with an even and just hand. But if it protects an unjust distribution of wealth and property, the result is *injustice evenly enforced*. A criminal justice system loses its right to hold individuals guilty of the injustice of breaking the law if the law itself supports and defends an unjust social order.

Without economic and social justice, the police officer in the ghetto is indeed an occupying soldier with no more legitimacy than his or her gun provides. When the criminal justice system protects an unjust distribution of property, it uses coercion to force some to serve the interests of others at the expense of their own and is thus morally indistinguishable from the criminal. *A criminal justice system can be no more just than the society its laws protect.* Along with the other recommendations made in this chapter, the achievement of economic and social justice is a necessary condition for establishing the criminal justice system's moral superiority to crime.

We must establish a more just distribution of wealth and income and make equal opportunity a reality for all Americans.

This is not merely a matter of throwing money in the direction of poor people. It is a call for investment in our most important resource—human beings—and for targeting that investment where it is most urgently needed and morally required: to rebuild our squalid inner cities, to educate our young, and to offer real opportunity to poor people to lift themselves out of poverty without lowering themselves into dependency. This would amount to a redistribution of wealth and income in the direction of greater social and economic justice. Because it would also reduce the temptations to crime produced by poverty, as well as the alienation

from social institutions that it produces, it brings us
recommendation that we made for protecting soci
ments of safety and justice converge.

Summary

Every step toward reducing poverty and its debilitating effects, toward criminalization of the dangerous acts of the affluent and vigorous prosecution of
white-collar crime, toward decriminalization of recreational drug use and
other "victimless crimes," and toward domestic disarmament; every step
toward creating a correctional system that promotes human dignity, toward
giving ex-offenders a real opportunity to go straight, toward making the exercise of power by police officers, prosecutors, and judges more accountable
and more just, toward giving all individuals accused of crime equal access to
high-quality legal expertise in their defense; and every step toward establishing economic and social justice are steps that move us from a system of *criminal* justice to a system of criminal *justice*. The refusal to take those steps is a
move in the opposite direction.

Study Questions

1. What do the three quotations at the beginning of this chapter mean? How do they
   apply to the American criminal justice system?
2. What are the necessary conditions for establishing the moral superiority of criminal justice to criminality?
3. What is meant by "victimless crimes"? Why do the authors believe they should not
   be kept criminal?
4. Would you be willing to have your taxes pay for equal-quality legal counsel for
   the poor?
5. Is the distribution of wealth and income in America just? How is this related to the
   justice of the criminal justice system?
6. Are the recommendations made in this chapter likely to be instituted? What does
   your answer imply about your view of the American legal system?

Additional Resources

Jeffrey Reiman and Paul Leighton, *The Rich Get Richer and Poor Get Prison: A Reader*
   (Boston: Pearson, 2010). This volume is a collection of accessible articles that
   were either used as reference material for *The Rich Get Richer* or provide lively
   complementary examples or analysis. The reader is divided into sections that
   parallel the chapters of *The Rich Get Richer*, and each section of the reader opens
   with a substantial introduction, written by the editors, that provides article summaries, context, and linkages to *The Rich Get Richer*.
The authors also maintain a companion website to the text at *http://www.paulsjustice-
   page.com/reiman.htm*

1. "Acting under color of law" is a phrase that basically means "acting under the authority of law." A police officer may arrest under color of law (using legitimate power duly delegated to him), but the arrest can still be illegal or unjust. "Color of law" does not imply race or racism, although many circumstances where this question is raised involve race.
2. Kip Schlegel, *Just Deserts for Corporate Criminals* (Boston: Northeastern University Press, 1990), p. 137.
3. Russell Mokhiber, *Corporate Crime and Violence: Big Business Power and the Abuse of Public Trust* (San Francisco: Sierra Club, 1988), pp. 38–65.
4. Ibid; David Friedrichs, *Trusted Criminals* (Belmont: Wadsworth/Cengage, 2010), pp. 364–366; Mary Ramirez Kreiner, "Prioritizing Justice: Combating Corporate Crime from Task Force to Top Priority." *Marquette Law Review* 93 (2010): 971–1018.
5. See Norval Morris and Gordon Hawkins, *The Honest Politician's Guide to Crime Control* (Chicago: University of Chicago Press, 1970), Ch. 1, "The Overreach of the Criminal Law," pp. 1–28; Herbert Packer, *The Limits of the Criminal Sanction* (Stanford, CA: Stanford University Press, 1968); and Jeffrey H. Reiman, "Can We Avoid the Legislation of Morality?" in Nicholas N. Kittrie and Jackwell Susman (ed.) *Legality, Morality and Ethics in Criminal Justice* (New York: Praeger, 1979), pp. 130–41.
6. John Stuart Mill, *On Liberty* (1859; reprint, New York: Appleton-Century-Crofts, 1973), p. 9.
7. See, for example, Gerald Dworkin, "Paternalism," in Richard Wasserstrom (ed.) *Morality and the Law* (Belmont, CA: Wadsworth, 1971), pp. 107–26; and Joel Feinberg, "Legal Paternalism," in Richard Wasserstrom (ed.) *Today's Moral Problems* (New York: Macmillan, 1975), pp. 33–50.
8. See, for instance, the excellent discussion of the principle in Peter T. Manicas, *The Death of the State* (New York: Putnam, 1974), Ch. 5, "The Liberal Moral Ideal," pp. 194–241; and H. L. A. Hart, *Law, Liberty and Morality* (New York: Vintage, 1963).
9. Jerome Hall, *General Principles of Criminal Law*, 2nd ed. (New York: Bobbs-Merrill, 1960), pp. 36–48. For a constitutional and philosophical argument for treating Mill's harm principle as an implied constitutional principle, see David A. J. Richards, *Sex, Drugs, Death, and the Law: An Essay on Human Rights and Overcriminalization* (Totowa, N.J.: Rowman and Littlefield, 1982), pp. 1–34, inter alia.
10. See *Robinson v. California*, 370 U.S. 66 (1962), in which the court held that a state law penalizing a person for a "status" such as addiction constitutes "cruel and unusual punishment" in violation of the Eighth Amendment [Prohibition of excessive bail and cruel and unusual punishment]. Cited and discussed in Nicholas N. Kittrie, *The Right to Be Different: Deviance and Enforced Therapy* (Baltimore: Johns Hopkins University Press, 1971), pp. 35–36, inter alia.
11. Ethan Nadelmann, "U.S. Drug Policy: A Bad Export," in Robert Lang (ed.) *Drugs in America* (New York: Wilson, 1993), p. 232.
12. "Prescription Heroin? It Just Might Work," *Montreal Gazette*, June 8, 2005, p. A24.
13. Jerry V. Wilson, "Our Wasteful War on Drugs," *The Washington Post*, January 18, 1994, p. A20.

14. Richard L. Lippke, *Rethinking Imprisonment* (New York: Oxford University Press, 2007), pp. 111–12.

15. Francis Cullen and Karen Gilbert, *Reaffirming Rehabilitation* (Cincinnati: Anderson, 1982). Francis Cullen, "Make Rehabilitation Corrections' Guiding Paradigm," in Jeffery Reiman and Paul Leighton (eds) *The Rich Get Richer: A Reader* (Boston, MA: Allyn & Bacon, 2010) pp. 180–189. John Braithwaite, "Encourage Restorative Justice," in Jeffery Reiman and Paul Leighton (eds) *The Rich Get Richer: A Reader* (Boston, MA: Allyn & Bacon, 2010), pp. 174–180. Lynn Branham "The Mess We're In: Five Steps Towards The Transformation of Prison Cultures," *Indiana Law Review* 44 (2011): 703.

16. Andrew von Hirsch and Andrew Ashworth, *Proportionate Sentencing: Exploring the Principles* (Oxford, UK: Oxford University Press, 2005), pp. 86–87, 132 note a, 140–43, 163 note 19. See also, von Hirsch, *Doing Justice: The Choice of Punishments* (Boston: Northeastern University Press, 1986), esp. Ch. 16.

17. Lippke, *Rethinking Imprisonment*, pp. 105–08, 111–13, 150, 241.

18. Jeremy Travis, *And They All Come Back* (Washington, D.C.: Urban Institute Press, 2005), p. xxi.

19. See the thoughtful recommendations for gun control and their rationale in Morris and Hawkins, *The Honest Politician's Guide to Crime Control*, pp. 63–71.

20. Joseph Blocher, "The Right Not to Keep or Bear Arms," *Stanford Law Review* 64 (2012): 104. The author argues that people who believe they are safer without guns are attempting to protect themselves from a risk of future violence, just like those who choose to keep a gun. The author then asks, "If self-defense is the 'core' of the Amendment, why should only one of these decisions be constitutionally protected?"

21. We have already pointed out (Chapter 3) that the vast majority of persons convicted of crimes in the United States are not convicted by juries. They plead guilty as the result of a "bargain" with the prosecutor (underwritten by the judge), in which the prosecutor agrees to drop other charges in return for the guilty plea. Kenneth Kipnis argues that the entire system of bargain justice is a violation of the ideal of justice because it amounts to coercing a guilty plea and often to punishing an offender for a crime other than the one he or she has committed. See Kenneth Kipnis, "Criminal Justice and the Negotiated Plea," *Ethics* 86, no. 2 (January 1976): 93–106.

22. Stewart D'Alessio and Lisa Stolzenberg, "Socioeconomic Status and the Sentencing of the Traditional Offender," *Journal of Criminal Justice* 21 (1993): 71, 73, 74.

23. This proposal is also made in Note, "Developments in the Law: Race and the Criminal Process," *Harvard Law Review* 101 (1988): 1550–1. The authors recommend that charging guidelines be supplemented with an "impact-inference standard." Under this standard, a defendant who believes that he or she has been discriminatorily charged would have to show that (1) he or she is the member of an identifiable class, (2) there is statistical evidence of discriminatory impact of prosecutorial decisions in the jurisdiction, and (3) the prosecutor's office lacked internal guidelines and procedures adequate to prevent abuse. If a defendant succeeded in showing these three elements, the burden of proof would shift to the government to explain its actions. Ibid., pp. 1552–3.

24. See John Council, "Survey Reveals Little Change in Sentencing Habits after 'Booker,'" *www.law.com/jsp/article.jsp?id=1123684510748*. The U.S. Sentencing Commission regularly monitors sentencing practices, and the latest reports are available at U.S. Sentencing Commission, *www.ussc.gov/bf.HTM*.
25. Colman McCarthy, "Justice Mocked: The Farce of Mandatory Minimum Sentences," *The Washington Post*, February 27, 1993, p. A23.
26. *Lockyer v. Andrade*, 538 U.S. 63 (2003). This case is discussed in Jeffrey Reiman and Paul Leighton, *A Tale of Two Criminals: We're Tougher on Corporate Criminals, But They Still Don't Get What They Deserve* (Boston, MA: Allyn & Bacon, 2004), *http://www.paulsjusticepage.com/RichGetRicher/fraud2004.htm*. See also, von Hirsch and Ashworth, *Proportionate Sentencing*, pp. 78–79.

APPENDIX I

The Marxian Critique of Criminal Justice*
by Jeffrey Reiman

In the first appendix,[1] I shall try to present the reader with an overview of Marxian theory that goes from Marxism's theory of capitalism to its theory of law and from there to criminal justice. This addresses some of the same aspects of criminal justice discussed in the main text of this book, but it sets them in a theoretical framework different from (although not incompatible with) the Pyrrhic defeat theory, with its historical inertia explanation of the peculiar failure of criminal justice. I shall close with comments on the ethical implications of the Marxian analysis.

Criminal justice has a concrete reality comprising police, prisons, courts, guns, and the rest. What is most important for our purposes, however, is the particular shape that this concrete reality takes in capitalism. This shape is governed according to certain principles that spell out what shall count as violations, what shall be done to violators, and so on. (For simplicity's sake, I shall use the term *criminal justice* as shorthand for the principles that normally govern criminal justice practices and practitioners in capitalism, and use the term *criminal justice system* as shorthand for the concrete reality of the practices and practitioners so governed.) Marxian analysis is in the first instance directed toward these governing principles. It aims to show that these principles are "economic reflexes," that is, they reflect and thus support the existing economic arrangements—in our case, the capitalist mode of production.

Criminal justice plays an ideological role in support of capitalism because people do not recognize that the principles governing criminal justice practices are reflections of capitalism. The principles of criminal justice appear instead to be the result of pure reason, and thus a system that supports capitalism is (mistakenly) seen as an expression of rationality itself! Engels—Marx's longtime collaborator—writes that "the jurist imagines he is operating with *a priori* [i.e., purely rational] principles, whereas they are really only economic reflexes; so everything is upside-down. And it seems to me obvious that this inversion ... so long as it remains unrecognized, forms what we call *ideological conception*."[2] As a consequence of this "inversion," criminal justice embodies and conveys a misleading and partisan view of the reality of the whole capitalist system. Because capitalism requires laws that give individual capitalists the right to own factories and resources, a view of these laws that makes them appear to be purely rational makes capitalism appear purely rational as well.

Before proceeding, a few words about the nature of Marxian theory are in order. First of all, Marx's theory of capitalism is separate from his advocacy of socialism and communism. Marx might be right about how capitalism works or about capitalism's unjust nature, even if socialism or communism would in fact be worse or even if they are merely utopian dreams that cannot be made real. This is important because of the tendency to think that the collapse of communism in Eastern Europe and the former Soviet Union (as well as the unpalatable features of that communism before it collapsed) refutes Marxian theory generally. This is quite untrue. What the collapse of Eastern European and Soviet communism refutes is, if anything, the theories of Lenin and Stalin about how to establish communism. Marx himself said very little about such things, and what he does say generally favors a much more democratic kind of socialism and communism than what Lenin and Stalin managed to bring about. Accordingly, it is still useful to look at what Marx thought about capitalism, even if one is convinced by recent events of the undesirability of actual communism or the impossibility of ideal communism.

Second, when we turn to Marx's theory of capitalism, we see that Marx portrays capitalism in pure form. He does so not to claim that that is how it actually exists anywhere, but rather to show the shape to which it tends everywhere. Actual systems will be a product of the force of that tendency versus the force of local factors, traditions, talent, innovation, luck, resources, the success or failure of particular human actions, and so on. Likewise, a Marxian analysis of criminal justice will indicate the pure form toward which criminal justice systems tend insofar as they support the functioning of capitalism. Actual criminal justice systems will be approximations of this tendency. Actual criminal justice systems will also clearly be shaped by human actions—often substantially so. No Marxist need to deny that the criminal justice system in the capitalist United States is much different from the criminal justice system in, say, capitalist Chile. What she must claim, rather, is that as capitalism develops in both countries, their criminal justice systems will increasingly tend to take on the shape that the theory implies.

I shall try to show how Marxism leads to a theory of the structure that criminal justice systems tend to have under capitalism, while at the same time recognizing that any existing criminal justice system is only an approximation of this structure. To give the reader as complete a picture as possible (in this short space) of the whole of Marxian theory—from general theory of capitalism to particular theory of criminal justice, and from there to ethical evaluation—I will have to sacrifice a lot of detail. I shall largely ignore the differences that individual actions may make in determining the shape of actual systems. I hope I have said enough to suggest that this in no way implies that human actions are irrelevant to actual historical outcomes.

I proceed in the following way. In the first section, "Marxism and Capitalism," I sketch out enough of Marx's theory of the capitalist mode of production as is necessary to lay the foundation for a Marxian theory of law. Because law is, for Marxism, a form of ideology, we shall have to see how ideology works in capitalism. I take this up in the next section, "Capitalism and Ideology." In "Ideology and Law," I develop the Marxian theory of law and from it the Marxian theory of criminal justice. Then, in the final section, "Law and Ethics," I consider the characteristic Marxian moral judgments about criminal justice—particularly about guilt and punishment—that are appropriate in light of the Marxian account.

MARXISM AND CAPITALISM

Marx says that capitalism is a system of "forced labour—no matter how much it may seem to result from free contractual agreement."[3] Here is both the truth that Marx asserts about capitalism and the legal ideology that shrouds that truth. To understand precisely how this works, we must consider the nature of the coercion that Marx discovered in capitalism.

For Marx, the value of any commodity is equivalent to the average amount of labor-time necessary to produce it.[4] Under capitalism, the worker's ability to labor—Marx calls this *labor-power*—is sold to the capitalist in return for a wage. Because labor-power is also a commodity, its value is equivalent to the average amount of labor-time necessary to produce it. *Producing labor-power* means producing the goods needed to maintain a functioning worker. The value of labor-power then is equivalent to the labor-time that on the average goes into producing the goods (food, clothing, shelter, and so on) necessary to maintain a functioning worker at the prevailing standard of living, which Marx understood to differ among countries depending on their respective histories (*Capital*, vol. 1, p. 171). The worker receives this in the form of a wage, that is, in the form of the money necessary to purchase these goods.

The capitalist obtains the money she pays as a wage by selling what the worker produces during the time for which he is employed. If the worker produced an amount of value equivalent only to his wage, there would be nothing left over for the capitalist and no reason for her to hire the worker in the first place. Labor-power, however, has the unique capacity to produce more value than its own value (*Capital*, vol. 1, pp. 193–94). The worker can work longer than the labor-time equivalent of the value of the wage he receives. Marx calls the amount of labor-time that the worker works to produce value equivalent to his wage *necessary labor*. The additional labor-time that the worker works beyond this is called *surplus labor*, and the value it produces, *surplus value*. The surplus value, of course, belongs to the capitalist and is the source of her profit (*Capital*, vol. 1, pp. 184–86); that is, when the capitalist sells the product made by the worker, the capitalist gives some of the money she gets back to the worker as wage (this corresponds to the value that the worker put into the product during his necessary labor-time), and the capitalist keeps the rest as profit (this corresponds to the surplus labor-time that the worker puts in after his necessary labor-time).

Profit, then, rests on the extraction of unpaid surplus labor from the worker. To see this, one need to only recall that although all products in the economy are produced by labor, only a portion of those products are wage-goods that the workers get paid with (wages only have value because they can be traded for wage-goods). The remainder belongs to their bosses and is effectively uncompensated. The wage-goods only compensate necessary labor-time to which they are equivalent in value. What workers produce beyond this goes to the capitalist gratis. Thus, writes Marx, "The secret of the self-expansion of capital [that is, the secret of profit] resolves itself into having the disposal of a definite quantity of other people's unpaid labour" (*Capital*, vol. 1, p. 534).

For Marx, however, capitalism is not only a system in which unpaid labor is extracted from workers, it is also a system in which workers are *forced* to provide this unpaid labor. Workers are not merely shortchanged; they are enslaved. Capitalism is "a coercive relation" (*Capital,* vol. 1, p. 309). The coercion, however, is not of the direct sort that characterized slavery or feudal serfdom. It is, rather, an indirect force built into the very fact that capitalists own the means of production and laborers do not. Means of production are things, such as factories, machines, land, and resources that are necessary for productive labor. Lacking ownership of means of production, workers lack their own access to the means of producing a livelihood. *By this very fact,* workers are compelled to sell their labor to capitalists for a wage because the alternative is (depending on conditions) either painful or fatal: relative pauperization or absolute starvation.

This compulsion is not in conflict with the fact that the terms upon which the worker works for the capitalist are the result of free contractual agreements. Indeed, the compulsion works *through* free agreements. Because the agreements are free, each side must offer the other a reason for agreeing. If workers offered capitalists only as much labor as went into the wage-goods they will get back in return from the capitalists, the capitalists would have no reason to purchase their labor. It follows that, no matter how free the wage contract is, as long as it occurs in a context in which a few own all the means of production, those who do not own means of production will be compelled to give up some of their labor without compensation to those who do. Thus, Marx describes the wage-worker as a "man who is compelled to sell himself of his own free will" (*Capital,* vol. 1, p. 766). The compulsion of the worker operates through the structure of property relations: "The dull compulsion of economic relations completes the subjection of the labourer to the capitalist. Direct force, outside economic conditions, is of course still used, but only exceptionally" (*Capital,* vol. 1, p. 737).

The very existence of the social roles of capitalist and worker—defined by ownership and nonownership of means of production, respectively—is what coerces the worker to work without compensation. It coerces in the same way that a social structure that allotted to one group ownership and thus control of all the available oxygen, would coerce. Beyond what was necessary to defend this group against challenges to its ownership of the oxygen, no additional force would be necessary for the coercion to operate. Indeed, it would operate quite effectively by means of bargains freely struck in which the nonoxygen-owners had to offer something to the owners to get the chance to breathe. They, too, would be compelled to sell themselves of their own free will. The same can be said of capitalism. Once its structure of social roles is in place, all that is necessary is that individuals choose, from among the alternatives available to them in their roles, the course of action that best serves their self-interest, and the extraction of unpaid surplus labor is enforced without further need for overt force.

As with the oxygen-owning society, so too with capitalism: Overt force is used or threatened to defend owners against challenges to their ownership.

That is just another way of saying that, in capitalism, the state uses overt force to protect private property. And this force is used to protect both the property of the capitalist (her factories and resources) and the property of the worker (his labor-power). This differs crucially from the way in which overt force is exercised in social relations like slavery. In slavery, the use of overt force is part of the normal exercise of the master's power. In capitalism, overt force is used to defend all against forceful interference with their right to dispose of whatever property they happen to own, be it means of production or labor-power. Accordingly, such force is not part of the capitalist's power, but is left to a third party that, in this respect, functions neutrally toward all owners—the state.

With both capitalists and workers protected in their capacity to dispose of what they own, the process by which workers are forced to work gratis can proceed apace. This effect can be achieved with the state functioning neutrally. Although the state normally favors the interests of capitalists over workers,[5] it can serve the process of forced extraction of unpaid labor by protecting both capitalists and workers alike in their freedom to dispose of what they happen to own. Thus, the state can treat capitalists and workers as having the same or "equal" property rights over what they own. It just turns out that what capitalists happen to own is means of production, and what workers happen to own is the muscles in their arms. Capitalism, then, naturally appears as a system of free exchanges between people with equal rights (over unequal amounts of property). This brings us to the phenomenon of ideology.

CAPITALISM AND IDEOLOGY

Of the study of social revolutions, Marx writes,

> In considering such transformations a distinction should always be made between the material transformation of the economic conditions of production, which can be determined with the precision of natural science, and the legal, political, religious, aesthetic or philosophic—in short, ideological forms in which men become conscious of this conflict and fight it out.[6]

The legal, then, is an ideological form. This is not to say that it is merely mental. It has a material reality in the form of police and prisons and guns and courts and legislators and law books, and the rest. What is crucial is how this material reality is shaped, and for that we must understand how ideology is shaped.

As its etymology suggests, *ideology* means the science of ideas, where science can be taken in the ordinary sense as the study of causal connections. (Recall the discussion of ideology in Chapter 4.) In the context of Marxian theory, ideology comes to mean the ideas caused by the mode of production (in our case, the capitalist mode of production), and, equally important for Marxism, the caused ideas are in some important way false. Thus understood, for Marxism, the study of ideology denotes the study of how the mode of production gives rise to people's false beliefs about society. In *The German Ideology*, Marx writes,

> If in all ideology men and their circumstances appear upside down as in a camera obscura, this phenomenon arises just as much from their historical life-process as the inversion of objects on the retina does from their physical life-process. ...
>
> The phantoms formed in the human brain are also, necessarily, sublimates of their material life-process, which is empirically verifiable and bound to material premises.[7]

As this statement makes clear, the study of ideology requires that both the existence and the falsity of ideological beliefs be given a *materialist* explanation.

To understand this requirement, consider that Marxian materialism is the conjunction of two distinct claims, an ontological claim and a social scientific one. The *ontological* claim is that what exists is material, that is, physical objects in space. Mind and spirit, in any immaterial sense, are chimera. ("From the start the 'spirit' is afflicted with the curse of being 'burdened' with matter, which here makes its appearance in the form of agitated layers of air, sounds, in short, of language" [*German Ideology*, p. 19].) The *social scientific* claim is that the way in which a society is organized for the production of the material conditions of its existence and reproduction ("the mode of production") plays the chief (though by no means the only) causal role in determining the nature and occurrence of social events. ("The mode of production of material life conditions the social, political and intellectual life process in general.")[8] According to this social scientific claim, the belief that societies are shaped primarily by their members' attitudes, or that history is shaped by the progressive development of knowledge or ideals, is false. Rather, it is primarily the organization of production that shapes people's attitudes, and the progressive development of modes of production that shapes history. ("That is to say, we do not set out from what men say, imagine, conceive, nor from men as narrated, thought of, conceived, in order to arrive at men in the flesh. We set out from real, active men, and on the basis of their real life-process we demonstrate the development of the ideological reflexes and echoes of this life-process" [*German Ideology*, p. 14]; "it is not the consciousness of men that determines their being, but, on the contrary, their social being that determines their consciousness.")[9]

Of these two claims, the social scientific is more restrictive than the ontological. The ontological claim requires only that we attribute ideology to material realities, be they brains or agitated layers of air or modes of production. The social scientific claim requires that among these material realities, priority be given to the mode of production as the primary cause of ideological beliefs. This means that the *main* source of false ideology is to be found not in the perceiving subject but in the perceived objects. It is not a "subjective illusion," the result of faulty perception by individuals of their material conditions, but an "objective illusion," the result of more or less accurate perception of those conditions.[10] Viewing ideology this way has the added benefit of leaving the door open just wide enough so that the theory of ideology does not exclude the possibility of all true beliefs—and thus of the very science upon which it is based. A materialist theory of ideology, then, must show that false ideology is an *objective illusion* arising primarily from more or less accurate perception of the organization of material production, rather than from some subjective error.[11] Bear in mind that this is a matter of placing primary emphasis on objective factors, not of absolutely excluding subjective ones.

We can fix the idea of an "objective illusion" by considering a very common example of one, namely, the illusion that the sun goes around the earth. Any illusion, any erroneous belief that an individual holds, can be *stated* as a subjective error—but not every erroneous belief arises primarily *because* of a subjective error. A person who believes that the sun rises above a stationary horizon in the morning makes a mistake. However, this sort of mistake differs crucially from, say, the mistake that a color-blind person might make of believing that the light is green when it is red, or the mistake a person balancing her checkbook might make of believing that a number is 4 when it is 2. In these latter cases, the mistaken beliefs are not merely held by the individuals; they arise in the individuals primarily as the result of a defective perceptual faculty or misuse of a sound one. These are subjective illusions. In these cases, correcting the defect in the perceptual faculty (or in its use) should undo the mistake. The mistaken belief that the sun goes around the earth, by contrast, arises as a result of a sound perceptual faculty properly exercised. This is an objective illusion. Neither healthier vision nor looking more carefully will enable an individual to correct this mistake and see that what occurs at dawn is not the sun rising above the horizon, but the horizon tipping down below the sun.

The ideology of capitalism is the illusion that capitalism is noncoercive. This illusion is a mistake of the same type as the illusion that the sun goes around the earth. What corresponds in capitalism to the movement of the sun seen from the earth is the free exchange of wages and labor-power between capitalists and workers. That the sphere of exchange is the objective basis of ideology is recognized in effect by Marx, when he writes that this sphere,

> within whose boundaries the sale and purchase of labour-power goes on, is in fact a very Eden of the innate rights of man. There alone rule Freedom, Equality, Property. Freedom, because both buyer and seller of a commodity, say of labour-power, are constrained only by their free will. (*Capital*, vol. 1, p. 176)

The normal perception of what goes on in exchange gives rise to the ideological illusion that capitalism is uncoercive. This is not because the freedom in exchange is an illusion. The fact is that, for Marx, capitalism works only because the moment of exchange, through which the circuit of capital continually passes, is truly free.

> For the conversion of his money into capital, therefore, the owner of money must meet in the market with the free labourer, free in the double sense, that as a free man he can dispose of his labour-power as his own commodity, and that on the other hand, he has no other commodity for sale, is short of everything necessary for the realization of his labour-power. (*Capital*, vol. 1, p. 169)

That the second of these senses of freedom is the worker's "freedom from" ownership of means of production does not deny the reality of the first sense, without which we would have slavery or serfdom rather than capitalism.

In exchange, the power that capitalists have over workers recedes from view. If we distinguish two sorts of power—the power to withhold one's commodity until offered something preferable, and the power to command obedience and back this up with violent force—then it is clear that, in the sphere of exchange, the latter power is suspended and all that remains is the former power. This former power is a power that all parties to the exchange have equally. Thus, the unequal power of capitalist and worker appears as their equal power to withhold from exchange what they happen to own, and their social inequality appears as the difference between the things that they happen to own. To use the famous words of Marx's analysis of the fetishism of commodities, a "social relation between men assumes, in their eyes, the fantastic form of a relation between things" (*Capital*, vol. 1, p. 72).

If this accurate perception of what goes on in exchange is to explain how capitalism appears uncoercive, we need to understand how the sphere of exchange—which is only part of capitalism—should be the source of beliefs about the whole of capitalism. Why should the experience of freedom in exchange, rather than, say, the experience of taking orders on the production line, determine the beliefs that members of capitalist societies come naturally to have? How is the representation of exchange *generalized* into a view of capitalism as a whole?

Marx offers a clue to the answer to this question when he says that the fetishism of commodities results because "the producers do not come into contact with each other until they exchange" (*Capital*, vol. 1, p. 73). Exchange transactions are the salient points of social contact for economic actors in capitalism. They punctuate capitalist social relations. Every social interaction between individuals playing roles in the capitalist mode of production begins with such a transaction (say, the signing of a wage contract exchanging labor-power for money) and can be ended with such a transaction (say, the dissolution of the wage contract). Each of these beginnings and endings is characterized by the absence of either party having the power to command the other's obedience and use violence to get it. Each party knows that he can enter or withdraw from any capitalist social interaction without being subject to the command or the overt force of the other. What constraint either feels seems to be only a matter of what they happen to own, which naturally appears as a feature of their own good or bad fortune rather than a condition coercively imposed by the other. Thus, *all* capitalist social interactions, *not just the exchanges themselves*, appear as voluntary undertakings between equal people who happen to own different things.

Exchange accurately perceived and then generalized is what leads workers in capitalist societies to believe that they are free, although they take orders most of their waking lives. Thus, ideologically false beliefs about capitalism result from accurate perception of exchange, when the rest of capitalism is, by default, assumed to be more of the same. The law follows suit.

IDEOLOGY AND LAW

"Law," wrote Marx in *The Poverty of Philosophy*, "is only the official recognition of fact."[12] For capitalist law, the fact is exchange. Law in capitalism is the official recognition of the fact of the economic relations in which the exchangers stand to one another. This insight—which will guide the materialist explanation of criminal law that I shall develop in this section—must be credited to the work of the Soviet legal theorist Evgeny Pashukanis, whose *General Theory of Law and Marxism* was published in Russian in 1924.[13] Among the things for which Pashukanis argued was that law was a product of capitalism and consequently had no legitimate place in socialism. As Stalin took firm control of the Soviet Union and saw fit to use the law to shore up that control, Pashukanis came eventually into disfavor. He recanted his views to some extent, but it was too late. By 1937 he had been declared an enemy of the people, and he "disappeared" shortly thereafter. Recently rediscovered by Western Marxists, Pashukanis's work was first the object of lavish praise and subsequently the target of harsh criticism. I do not intend to endorse or defend the whole of Pashukanis's theory. He aimed at a general theory of law and made only a few observations about criminal law, which is my main concern here. I shall try to show that his basic insight about the relation between law and exchange can be developed into an explanation of the content of the criminal law and of the constitutional protections relevant to criminal justice.

Marx writes that parties to an exchange

> must behave in such a way that each does not appropriate the commodity of the other, and part with his own, except by means of an act done by mutual consent. They must, therefore, mutually recognize in each other the rights of private proprietors. This juridical relation, which thus expresses itself in a contract, whether such contract be part of a developed legal system or not, is a relation between two wills, and is but the reflex of the real economic relation between the two. (*Capital*, vol. 1, pp. 88–89)

Exchangers must in fact refrain from forcing those with whom they would trade to part with their goods or services or money. Official recognition of this fact takes the form of granting to exchangers "the rights of private proprietors." Because this recognition is related to the ideological failure to perceive the coerciveness reproduced in exchanges between proprietors of capital and proprietors of labor, exchanges are understood legally as acts of the free will of the parties as long as no overt violence is used or threatened. Consequently, exchangers treat one another as *free subjects* whose freedom is expressed in their right to dispose of their property without interference from others.

It is the difference between what capitalists own and what workers own that, for Marx, makes it possible to reproduce a coercive relation through free exchange. If the law follows ideology in representing the relation between exchangers as noncoercive, then the law must abstract from this difference in what is owned and treat each party as having the same right to dispose of his property regardless of what that property is. The law reflects this in its formality. The legal right of property is an empty form to be filled in with different content, depending on what an individual owns. Capitalists and workers have the same right of property; they just happen to own different things. It just happens that what some people own are factories and what others own are their bodies, but their property rights in these things are the same. Their freedom to dispose of their property also is the same.[14] Thus, exchangers treat each other as *equal* free subjects with equal property rights—that is to say, as legal *persons*.[15]

We saw in the previous section that ideology is not to be understood as merely a subjective illusion. Ideology reflects the real way in which capitalism appears to its participants. By the same token, the ideological nature of law reflects the real relations in which exchangers stand to one another. The written law, even the institutions of law (from lawmakers to law enforcers), are not the source of law. They reflect real, objective relations between members of a capitalist society, relations that exist, so to speak, on the ground first and only later on the page or in the courts for that matter. It is here that the "inversion" of which Engels wrote does its ideological work. Although the law is a reflection of the relations of exchangers on the ground, it appears that the law is an expression of rationality itself, with the consequence that the relations among exchangers seem so as well.

Here, however, a problem arises for the Marxian materialist: If law is the reflection of the actual practice of economic exchange, how does law come to function as a norm? A simple reflection would represent whatever occurs and thus could not identify some actions as infractions. How can the materialist account for the normative dimension of law that arises as a reflection of economic relations?

The answer to this is that law is not a simple reflection of economic relations, but an *idealized* reflection. Actual exchanges will be characterized by the full range of violations and deviations, from failure to meet agreed-upon deadlines to gross expropriation with the threat or use of violence. Such violations tend to undermine the likelihood of the same parties exchanging again. Because it is generally in people's long-term interest that stable trading relationships be maintained, it will generally be in people's interest to eliminate such violations. Accordingly, over time the vast majority of exchanges, particularly those between people in continuing exchange relationships, will tend to be free of violations. Thus, an average core of exchange, characterized by absence of violence and fraud as well as by dependable fulfillment of agreements, will emerge as the norm. The law in general will represent this norm.

This tendency to go from what happens "on average" to what is normative is a common feature of human social existence. People tend to take what usually happens as what should happen. This tendency of the statistical norm (what people can generally be expected to do) to become the moral norm (what is expected of people) is visible in early civilization (where, for example, natural and moral law are not distinguished from each other) and in advanced civilization (where, for example, existing business practice is often taken by courts as creating legally enforceable obligations).

This brings us to a second question. It would seem that law that reflects (even the idealized "average" core of) exchanges would include not only the criminal law but also what we currently understand as contract or civil law. How can the theory that traces law to exchange account for the nature of the criminal law per se, with its special content and its unique remedies?

To answer this, note first that there is considerable overlap in the content of criminal and civil law; criminal acts, such as theft or battery, also can be causes of civil action. This overlap, however, is largely asymmetrical: Virtually any criminal act can be a cause of civil action, but only some civil causes are subject to criminal prosecution. This suggests that the criminal law is more distinctive in its remedies than in its content. In general, criminal prosecution seeks punishment of the guilty, and civil action seeks recovery of damages from the one responsible for a loss. Now, on the materialist theory, both sorts of law—criminal and civil—represent the "essential core" of normal exchange and aim to rectify violations of or deviations from that core. Thus, to explain the nature of the criminal law per se, we must show why some class of deviations from normal exchange is singled out for the distinctive "criminal" remedy, namely, punishment. Because punishment is generally a graver matter than recovery of damages, we should expect the criminal law to be addressed to the most serious violations of normal exchange, whereas the civil law can be addressed to all violations.

Violations of normal exchange can be distinguished in the following way: Some threaten the very possibility of free exchange by depriving people of the ability to dispose of their property. Other violations threaten not the possibility of free exchange but its success in meeting the wishes of the exchangers. What threatens the very possibility of exchange are acts of violence that overtly block the capacity of individuals to exercise their wills, acts of theft that overtly bypass the capacity of individuals to choose how their property is disposed of, and acts of deception that have the same effect, so to speak, behind the backs of their victims. These are so serious that they must be prevented in advance— and that requires a standing threat of punishment. Accordingly, the criminal law is primarily aimed at acts of violence, theft, and fraud.[16]

Less serious violations are compatible with the existence of exchange, but cause exchanges in some way to fall short of the legitimate expectations of the exchangers. These violations are mainly failures to live up to the terms of explicit or implied contracts. They can be remedied by requiring performance or payment from the one responsible. These are suitable targets for the civil law, although nothing is lost by allowing the civil law to apply to recovery of losses due to the more serious violations as well.

On the whole, then, although the entire law in capitalism reflects the conditions of normal exchange, the content of the criminal law is composed of those acts that threaten the very possibility of normal exchange. These are the acts that are identified as "crimes." Moreover, because the normal relations of exchange are not only idealized but also (as we saw in the previous section) generalized to the whole of capitalism, they will shape people's normative expectations beyond exchange. Thus, they determine the limits that will be imposed on officials taxed with the job of finding and prosecuting criminals, the shape of court proceedings, the relation of punishment to offense, and the emphasis on the free will of the offender. Accordingly, by tracing law to its source in exchange, we can account for at least the general content of criminal law and the general shape of the criminal justice system and of the constitutional limits within which that system operates. Here, briefly sketched and numbered for ease of identification, are the main ways in which this works.

1. Normal exchange presupposes that people are treated as having property rights in whatever they are to trade, and that must mean not only goods but their bodies as well, because bodily actions are what workers trade with capitalists for their wage. Crime, then, is any violation by one individual of the property rights of another in whatever he owns, including his body. This explains why the criminal law is directed primarily against acts of violence, theft, and fraud. Moreover, because criminal law protects an individual's body because he owns it (and not, say, because it is the earthly vessel of his immortal soul), the law will be concerned primarily with injuries done to people's bodies against their will—otherwise, such injuries do not violate the individual's ownership of his body. This accounts for the liberal principle *volenti non fit injuria* (no injustice is done to one who consents) and thus, via generalization, for the tendency in capitalism to decriminalize (or reduce in importance) "victimless crimes" or "morals offenses."

2. This account also tells us what we are not likely to see as crime in capitalist society, namely, exercises of the power inherent in the ownership of property itself. Thus, we will not generally find that death due to preventable dangers in the workplace will be taken as murder because that would assume that the worker was somehow forced into the workplace by the power inherent in his boss's private ownership of the means of production. Because that is just the power that is invisible in capitalism, the worker is taken as freely consenting to his job and thus freely accepting its risks. Accordingly, when the criminal law is used against employers to get them to eliminate occupational hazards, it is never with the understanding that employers who do not eliminate such hazards are violent criminals. If the criminal law is used in these cases at all, it is as a regulatory mechanism applied to employers because this is the most efficient way to reduce the social costs of occupational injury and disease. The treatment of guilty employers is generally light-handed, even though far more people lose their lives due to preventable occupational hazards than as a result of what the law currently treats as murder. In capitalism, subjection to one person is seen as arbitrary and thus unlawful coercion, but subjection to the capitalist class is not seen at all. (Here is how the Marxian theory understands the phenomena discussed in the main text of this book and accounted for with the historical inertia explanation.)

3. The other side of criminal law—the limits placed on legal officials in their pursuit of suspected criminals (for example, in the Bill of Rights)—likewise reflects the generalized conception of people as owners of their bodies and other property. Accordingly, we find protections against official invasions of suspects' property (for example, the Fourth Amendment protections against unreasonable search and seizure) and against penetration of suspects' bodies or minds (for example, the Fifth Amendment protection against self-incrimination). Moreover, this explains why corporal punishment, which was the norm in feudalism and slavery, tends to be eliminated in capitalism. The bodies of slaves are literally owned by their masters, and lords have natural (that is, parent-like) authority over their serfs. In those cases, corporal punishment fits the existing social relations. In capitalism, employer and employee meet as owners of their respective bodies, and thus corporal punishment looks increasingly out of place.

The existence of these various limitations on what can be done to enforce the law is evidence that the Marxian view of law includes recognition of the way law functions not only to control the working class but also as a limit on the behavior of the ruling class. Indeed, the Marxian view can be taken as claiming that it is precisely as a system that protects everyone alike in their property (including their body), by limiting both what citizens and law enforcers can do to the bodies (and other property) of other citizens, that the law most effectively serves the purpose of keeping the working class selling its labor-power to the owners of means of production—both classes safe in the knowledge that no one can interfere with their right to dispose of what they happen to own.

4. As crime is a violation of normal exchange, punishment is thought of on the same model of equivalence as exists in exchange. "Punishment emerges as an equivalent which compensates the damage sustained by the injured party."[17] The commercial model doesn't end here. The adversary system reproduces it in court. "The public prosecutor demands a 'high' price, that is to say a severe sentence. The offender pleads for leniency, a 'discount,' and the court passes sentence in equity."[18] Crime deforms exchange by taking with force rather than payment. Punishment restores exchange by using force to pay back the criminal for his force. This is the *tribute* in retribution. The court is the extraordinary market where this extraordinary exchange is negotiated. The scales in Justice's hands are the same as those used by the merchant.

5. Because exchange normally brings payment to an individual only when she freely chooses to offer up her goods or services for it, the payment of punishment comes due only when the offender has freely chosen to commit the offense for which the punishment is payment. Accordingly, liability for punishment is subject to conditions of the same sort as apply to liability to contractual obligations. One is not bound by a contract that she has not signed freely, or that she signed while insane or in ignorance of its contents, and so on. Likewise, the offender is liable to punishment, and thus is truly a criminal, only if he has committed his violation freely, sanely, and with knowledge of what he was doing. By the same logic, the law generally prohibits ex post facto attribution of criminal liability because a person cannot choose freely to violate a law before it has been passed.

Here, then, we read off the face of exchange, albeit idealized and generalized, the main contours of criminal justice as it develops in capitalism. As I suggested at the outset, this is no more than a skeleton. It does not aim to account for the full, rich detail of any particular criminal justice system. Actual criminal justice systems exist in societies with other modes of production present alongside capitalism are affected by the complex interplay of human actions, and so on, so that each actual system—like each actual face—will have a distinct physiognomy while sharing in the basic structure. Some criminal justice systems will be slower in eliminating "morals offenses," some will be stricter on occupational hazards, some will abolish the death penalty while others will retain it, and so on.[19] These specific outcomes will be a function of the strength that various social groupings (such as religious organizations, labor unions, academia, the press, and the like) come to have in the specific history of specific countries, and of all the largely unpredictable features that determine the outcome of particular battles over the content of the law and the funding of the legal apparatus. This notwithstanding, the Marxian claim is that criminal justice (principles and systems) in capitalist countries will tend toward the shape sketched out above.

LAW AND ETHICS

We now reach the question of the moral stance toward capitalist criminal justice that is appropriate if the Marxian account is correct. Marxism describes capitalism as an exploitative system, meaning one in which workers are forced to work for capitalists without compensation. Marxists characteristically regard exploitation, and consequently capitalism, as unjust or immoral. Broadly speaking, they reach this condemnation by one of three routes. One is to view capitalist exploitation as wrong because it promotes antagonistic or alienated relations between human beings.[20] The second way is to view capitalist exploitation as wrong because it is a form of forced servitude or slavery.[21] The third way is to view capitalist exploitation as wrong because it is based on an unjust distribution of wealth, namely, the unjustifiable exclusive ownership by a few of the means of production.[22] I shall call these three views, respectively, the *alienation charge*, the *slavery charge*, and the *maldistribution charge*. Each of these has moral implications for capitalist criminal justice. The task of identifying these implications is simplified by the fact that the second and third charges incorporate each other. The slavery charge accepts that private ownership of means of production is a case of unjust maldistribution (because it is a means of forcing servitude), and the maldistribution charge accepts that private ownership of means of production is a means of enslavement (because it is a power wrongly monopolized by a few). For our purposes, then, the charges against capitalism can be reduced to two: the alienation charge and the slavery–maldistribution charge.

Those who raise the alienation charge point out that capitalism is a system in which each person's well-being is in conflict with that of others. Capitalism pits class against class (competing over the division of the economic product into wages versus profit), worker against worker (competing for jobs), and capitalist against capitalist (competing for market shares). Moreover, proponents of this charge hold that antagonism of interests is neither a necessary feature of human life nor a desirable condition. It is caused by capitalism. It was less marked in feudalism and might be eliminated in the future if a more cooperative arrangement, such as socialism, could be established. Criminal justice as it emerges in capitalism is understood as a means to regulate this antagonism of interests. Because it assumes that this antagonism is inevitable, criminal justice serves to confer permanent validity on capitalism. Moreover, criminal justice promotes this antagonism by teaching people that the rights of each are in conflict with the rights of others rather than mutually supportive, that freedom is *freedom from* invasion by others rather than freedom to develop with others, that what people owe each other is noninterference rather than a helping hand.

Also important is the fact that a society based on antagonism of interests is one in which people earn their daily bread only as long as someone else can profit as a result. When that changes, workers may find themselves in need and with little in the way of help from the rest of society. On this view, then, the high crime rates characteristic of capitalism are due to the fact that people in capitalism are taught to see their interests as in conflict with others' and thus they are trained to have limited altruism and fellow feeling, and to the fact that a society based on antagonism of interests is one in which economic need and insecurity are endemic. When limited fellow feeling meets economic need and insecurity, the result is crime. (Recall the views of Bonger and Gordon, discussed in Chapter 4.) The same system that calls criminals individually guilty, then, is responsible for the antagonism of interests that breeds crime in the first place. The upshot of this charge is that criminals are not—or at least not wholly—guilty of the crimes they commit. On this charge, criminals are in large measure unjustly punished for actions caused by the very system that punishes them.

On the slavery–maldistribution charge, the emphasis is on the wrongness and coerciveness of private ownership of means of production. Capitalism promotes a system of criminal justice based on protecting the freedom of individuals to dispose of what they rightly own; but the system itself is based on the wrongful appropriation of means of production, and with it the power to coerce others to labor without compensation. On this view, socialism would cure capitalism not so much by replacing antagonism of interests with harmony, but by replacing private ownership of means of production by a few with social ownership by everyone.

To understand the moral implications for criminal justice of this charge, imagine for a moment that we see someone take a sheep from a field owned by another. In response, suppose that we make the normal judgment that a theft, an unjust expropriation, has occurred. Now suppose further that we learn that the field owner had himself stolen the sheep from the sheep taker some time before. According to these new facts, we shall change our views about the moral status of the sheep taking. Now we are likely to say that the one we saw take the sheep was not, morally speaking, a criminal but the opposite, a victim responding justifiably to an earlier crime. Likewise, if we come to see ownership of means of production as itself a violation of justice (because it is unjustly maldistributive or unjustifiably coercive), we will see the "crimes" that people do in response to it as more just than they appeared when we didn't question the justice of ownership of means of production. Recall the discussion in Chapter 4 of how a judgment that an individual is guilty of a crime presupposes that the social context in which his act occurred was just. By the same logic, judgment that the social context is unjust, weakens the judgment that the individual is guilty of a crime.

On the slavery–maldistribution view, then, the individuals normally labeled "criminal" are seen as the victims of a prior "crime" to which they are responding. That criminals may not (and usually do not) see themselves as doing this only reflects the fact that they are taken in by capitalist ideology no less than law-abiding folks are. The "criminal," then, is not a doer of injustice, but the reverse. He is a victim of injustice trying to improve his situation by means that have been made necessary by the fact that capitalism leaves him few alternatives. The upshot of this charge is that criminals are not really morally guilty. They are in large measure unjustly punished for reacting against crimes perpetrated by the very system that punishes them.

In sum, the Marxist critique of criminal justice does lead to a moral condemnation of criminal justice under capitalism. This moral condemnation comes in two forms, both of which share the claim that capitalist criminal justice wrongly punishes people who do not deserve to be punished. In the first form, the alienation charge, criminals are thought not to deserve punishment because their acts are caused by socially conditioned antagonism to their fellows in conjunction with limited and unstable opportunities to satisfy their needs and desires. In the second form, the slavery–maldistribution charge, criminals are thought not to deserve punishment because their apparent crimes are legitimate reactions against conditions that are themselves, morally speaking, criminal. Needless to say, it is possible for the same person to endorse both forms of condemnation.

Several things that apply to both charges are worth noting. First of all, in both cases, the features of capitalist criminal justice that come in for ethical condemnation reflect the failure to see the way criminal justice reflects the mode of production—mentioned at the outset. In the case of the alienation charge, the failure is that of not seeing that capitalist criminal justice emerges to regulate the antagonistic relations between human beings that capitalism produces. Seeing capitalist criminal justice as the product of independent reason, it sees those antagonistic relations as a natural feature of human life that always must be so regulated. Then, capitalist criminal justice rather than protecting the interests of capitalists appears merely to be the necessary condition of any peaceful social coexistence.

In the case of the slavery–maldistribution charge, the failure is of not seeing how property in capitalism is an expression of a particular and morally questionable constellation of social forces. Seeing capitalist criminal justice as the product of independent reason, it sees the property that criminal justice protects as a natural feature of human life that is always in need of such protection. Then, capitalist criminal justice, rather than protecting the interests of capitalists, appears merely to be protecting everyone's interest.

What's more, it follows that the continued and heavily publicized activities of criminal justice serve to reinforce ideological blindness: on the first view, blindness to capitalism's role in causing the alienated and antisocial attitudes and conditions that lead to crime; and, on the second view, blindness to the moral dubiousness of capitalist property relations.

It also must be borne in mind that the ethical implications of both charges are general propositions that will fit actual criminals in varying degrees. For example, while the alienation charge suggests that criminals are not culpable because they are shaped by an antagonistic society, in actual cases the degree to which individual lawbreakers have been so shaped will vary. There may be some who have largely escaped the deleterious influences and yet, out of selfishness or greed, commit crimes. Marxism naturally claims that the number of criminals of this sort is small compared with the number of criminals all told. Marxism, however, need not deny that there are some criminals like this and that they deserve punishment. Likewise, on the slavery–maldistribution charge, whereas criminals are generally taken to be victims of the prior injustice of private ownership of means of production, actual criminals differ in the degree to which they are so victimized and in the degree to which their actual crimes can be thought of as reactions thereto. Relatively privileged persons, or others whose crimes bear little relation to their class position (some rapists, for example), may well be more culpable than the general run of criminals. It seems to me appropriate for Marxists to view responsibility—and thus guilt—as existing in varying degrees, relative to the actual impact of the social structure on a given individual's criminal act.

Finally, note that on neither of the two views we have discussed does the criminal emerge as any kind of "proto-revolutionary," as is sometimes asserted of Marxism. On the alienation charge, the criminal is at best relieved of responsibility because he has been shaped by the social system to have antisocial attitudes and fated by that system to experience need and insecurity that, together with those attitudes, lead to crime. On the slavery–maldistribution charge, the criminal is at best a victim because he is the object of the unjust coercion or expropriation characteristic of private ownership of means of production. His crime, rather than being a kind of rebellion against what victimizes him, is most often a narrowly self-interested striking out against whatever he can get his hands on. On both charges, Marxism does imply reduced or no blame for (most) criminals; but it does not imply any celebration of their acts. This is particularly so in light of the fact that most victims of crime are other exploited people, members or would-be members of the working class. Crime and criminality must on the whole be placed by Marxism among the costs of capitalism, lined up alongside poverty, unemployment, pollution, and the rest.

Notes

1. This essay is a revised and shortened version of an article that appeared in *Criminal Justice Ethics* 6, no. 1 (Winter–Spring 1987): 30–50. Peter Darvas assisted me with the research for that article.
2. Frederick Engels, "Letter to Conrad Schmidt (October 27, 1890)," in Karl Marx, *Selected Works*, ed. V. Adoratsky (Moscow: Cooperative Publishing Society of Foreign Workers in the USSR, 1935), vol. 1, p. 386.
3. Karl Marx, *Capital* (New York: International Publishers, 1967), vol. 3, p. 819.
4. Note that Marx does not hold that the value of a commodity is equivalent to the actual amount of labor-time that goes into producing it. On that view, commodities would increase in value the more inefficiently they were produced. Instead, recognizing that a commodity will command a price no higher than that for which commodities like it are selling, Marx takes the commodity's value to be determined by the average or socially necessary labor-time it takes to produce commodities of its kind. See *Capital*, vol. 1, p. 189. Furthermore, although Marx claims that value is equivalent to average labor-time, he assumes that values and market prices coincide only for the purposes of the argument of volume 1 of *Capital* about the fundamental nature of capitalism. In the subsequent volumes, Marx shows at length the mechanisms in capitalism that lead prices to diverge from values. Even after these common misinterpretations of the theory are eliminated, it must be admitted that Marx's labor theory of value has come in for so much criticism in recent years that many, even many Marxists, have given it up for dead.
5. See, for example, G. William Domhoff, *Who Rules America?* 4th ed. (New York: McGraw-Hill, 2001); M. Green, J. Fallows, and D. Zwick, The Ralph Nader Congress Project, *Who Runs Congress?* (New York: Grossman, 1972); Edward S. Greenberg, *Serving the Few: Corporate Capitalism and the Bias of Government Policy* (New York: Wiley, 1974); and Ralph Miliband, *The State in Capitalist Society* (New York: Basic Books, 1969).
6. Karl Marx, "Preface to *A Contribution to a Critique of Political Economy*," in Robert Tucker (ed.) *The Marx-Engels Reader*, 2nd ed. (New York: Norton, 1978), p. 5.
7. Karl Marx and Friedrich Engels, *The German Ideology*, pts. 1 and 3 (New York: International Publishers, 1947), p. 14.
8. Marx, "Preface to *A Contribution to a Critique of Political Economy*," p. 4.
9. Ibid.
10. "It is not the subject who deceives himself, but reality which deceives him"; Maurice Godelier, "Structure and Contradiction in Capital," in Robin Blackburn (ed.) *Ideology in Social Science* (Glasgow: Fontana/Collins, 1977), p. 337.
11. Examples of theories of ideology that trace its distortions to subjective illusions are the attempt by some members of the Frankfurt School to explain the affection of German laborers for fascism by means of a Freudian account of the persistence of irrational authoritarian attitudes and the attempt of some sociologists to trace ideology to an existential need to reify a mythic worldview as protection against the terrors of meaninglessness. For the former, see Martin Jay, *The Dialectical Imagination: A History of the Frankfurt School and the Institute for Social Research, 1923–1950* (Boston: Little, Brown, 1973). For the latter, see Peter Berger and Thomas Luckmann, *The Social Construction of Reality* (New York: Doubleday, 1966).

12. Karl Marx, *The Poverty of Philosophy* (Moscow: Progress Publishers, 1955), p. 75.

13. Evgeny B. Pashukanis, *Law and Marxism: A General Theory,* trans. B. Einhom, ed. C. Arthur (London: Ink Links, 1978).

14. As Frederick Engels wrote,

The labor contract is to be freely entered into by both parties. But it is considered to have been freely entered into as soon as the law makes both parties equal on paper. The power conferred on the one party by the difference of class position, the pressure thereby brought to bear on the other party—the real economic position of both—that is not the law's business. (Frederick Engels, *The Origin of the Family, Private Property, and the State* [New York: International Publishers, 1942], p. 64)

15. Pashukanis, Law and Marxism, pp. 112–13, inter alia.

16. Pashukanis approvingly attributes to Aristotle "the definition of crime as an involuntarily concluded contract" (ibid., p. 169).

17. Ibid., p. 169; see also Alan Norrie, "Pashukanis and 'the Commodity Form Theory': A Reply to Warrington," *International Journal of the Sociology of Law* 10 (1982): 431–434.

18. Pashukanis, *Law and Marxism,* p. 177.

19. See Georg Rusch and Otto Kirchheimer, *Punishment and Social Structure* (New York: Russell & Russell, 1968), for a classic Marxian-inspired historical study of the relationship between penal policy and the supply and demand for labor.

20. This is the view of, for example, Allen Buchanan in *Marx and Justice* (Totowa, NJ: Rowman & Littlefield, 1982).

21. This is essentially the view argued for by, for example, Allen Wood in "The Marxian Critique of Justice," *Philosophy & Public Affairs* 1, no. 3 (Spring 1972): 244–82.

22. This is the view of, for example, G. A. Cohen in "Freedom, Justice and Capitalism," *New Left Review* 126 (March–April 1981): 3–16. There is, by the way, a substantial literature on the question of whether Marxism holds that capitalism is wrong because it is unjust or that justice is part of what's wrong with capitalism. See articles in M. Cohen, T. Nagel, and T. Scanlon, eds., *Marx, Justice, and History* (Princeton, NJ: Princeton University Press, 1980); K. Nielsen and S. Patten, eds., *Marx and Morality, Canadian Journal of Philosophy* 7 (suppl., 1981); and J. Pennock and J. Chapman, eds., *Nomos XXVI: Marxism* (New York: New York University Press, 1983); as well as Norman Geras's review of the whole discussion, "The Controversy about Marx and Justice," *New Left Review* 150 (March–April 1985): 47–85. My own views are presented in "The Possibility of a Marxian Theory of Justice," in Nielsen and Patten, *Marx and Morality,* pp. 307–22.

APPENDIX II

Between Philosophy and Criminology
by Jeffrey Reiman

Though *The Rich Get Richer and the Poor Get Prison* is more frequently assigned in criminology courses than in philosophy courses,[1] it raises a philosophical question, perhaps *the* central philosophical question of criminology, namely, "What should be a crime?"; and it aims to use that question to shed a special kind of light on the criminal justice establishment in the United States, but I suspect as well on just about any criminal justice system anywhere.[2]

I say this by way of introduction because my aim here is to explore the relationship between philosophy and criminology. In light of criminology's multidisciplinary nature, however, criminology might be thought already to include philosophy. Thus, to be precise, I should say that I want to explore the relationship between philosophy and the nonphilosophical aspects of criminology, that is, between philosophy and criminology considered as a social science. In general, this is what I shall mean when I speak of *criminology*.

To give you a hint about where I am headed, I shall argue that criminology needs philosophy, and not only in the way that, as I also believe, everything and everyone need philosophy, but also in very special ways. For example, I shall argue that criminology has a special need for philosophy because criminology is in the unusual position of being a mode of social inquiry whose central concept—*crime*—is defined officially, by governments. We hear a lot these days about the politics of knowledge and of research, but this is politics with a vengeance. Politics openly, necessarily, insinuates itself into the heart of criminology. Political systems hand criminology a ready-made research agenda. And so I shall argue that criminology needs philosophical reflection on the concept of crime in order to establish its intellectual independence of the state, which to my mind is equivalent to declaring its status as a social science rather than an agency of social control, as critical rather than servile, as illumination rather than propaganda.

This is not, however, where I shall start. Rather, I will start, so to speak, at the outer ring of a series of concentric circles, by indicating the philosophical assumptions that I think are necessary to all forms of social science. I shall proceed from there to talk about the philosophical assumptions that I think are special to criminology, the ones it especially needs. And then, arriving at the smallest inner circle, I shall say something about my own particular philosophical commitments, the ones that underlie *The Rich Get Richer and the Poor Get Prison*. I hope that somewhere along the line, readers will recognize some of their own philosophical assumptions, and thus be in a better position to reflect on them, to consider what else they entail, and to decide whether in the end they are ready to endorse them explicitly, or want to consider others.

Before starting this, I want to make one thing clear. I shall be talking about "what criminology needs," but this is shorthand for what I think people who practice criminology need in order to do criminology in a coherent and plausible way. Moreover, when I say, for example, that criminology needs a theory of crime, I do not mean that it needs one particular theory. This too is shorthand, in this case for the idea that everyone who practices criminology needs *some* theory of crime, not that all need the same one. I put these all as claims about "what criminology needs" rather than as about what criminologists need, to emphasize that the needs are disciplinary and conceptual, not personal or psychological.

PHILOSOPHICAL ASSUMPTIONS OF SOCIAL SCIENCE GENERALLY

First of all, to engage in social science, you must believe that there is such a thing as society, and that it can become an object of knowledge. That there is such a thing as society means that there are real human beings, in real social relations, in a real world, manipulating real objects, and so on. That there can be knowledge of society means that knowledge is possible, and that we can know when we have got some. In short, a social scientist cannot be a thoroughgoing *ontological* skeptic or agnostic.[3] He or she cannot suppose that society is only an idea or a construct, and all the more so, he or she cannot suppose society to be an illusion. Nor can a social scientist be a thoroughgoing *epistemological* skeptic or agnostic.[4] To seek knowledge of society is to assume that such knowledge is possible for us.

Along the same lines, I believe that social scientists must believe it is important to aim at *scientific objectivity*, and that this aim can be adequately achieved. Some authors writing about the development of modern science in the time of Bacon and Galileo speak of the attempt at scientific objectivity as nothing but following certain conventions aimed at giving science a higher status than, say, religious inspiration.[5] My claim is that, even if the attempt at scientific objectivity is this, it cannot be *only* this.

No one could use conventions of objectivity without believing that they were effective ways of getting at the way things are, anymore than one can use language without believing that one is speaking about things beyond the words one uses. Even those who think of objectivity as just so many conventions, think that *that* is the objective truth! They think that they are telling us the way things are, not the way they would like them to be. Notice here that I am not claiming that we always succeed in freeing ourselves of our biases. What a social scientist must believe is that the attempt to represent the world as it is, as opposed to how we wish it were, can succeed generally and does succeed in many particular cases.

In affirming that, as social science, criminology must presuppose that there are real people performing real actions in a real world and that we can have knowledge of them, I do not mean to resurrect some hoary positivistic model of science. I grant that the facts we study may be the product of the interaction of beliefs and language and objects. However, for the study of those facts to be fruitful, the process by which beliefs and language and objects interact must itself be knowable as an objective reality. It is a general philosophical requirement of social theorizing that one's theory leave open the possibility of its own status as knowledge—this is a test that many statements of postmodernist theory, and of relativism generally, seem to me to fail, even as their practitioners produce valuable *objective* knowledge in spite of what they say they are doing.

Before leaving the discussion of the general philosophical requirements of social science, I want to say a word about *value-neutrality*. Value-neutrality is related to objectivity, but it's not the same thing. Later I shall suggest that criminology needs some value commitments, at least to some conception of justice. Thus, I do not think that criminology should be value-neutral all the way down, even though I think it should aim at objective knowledge. There is no contradiction here.

The point is this. I believe that the proper study of crime requires taking some position on the justice of the social system in which certain acts are treated as criminal. Suppose that I make explicit the ideal of justice that I endorse. This doesn't mean I am no longer objective. First of all, I believe, and I may try to show, that my ideal of justice is appropriate, not merely what I want or what serves my interests. Second and equally important is that, once I have stated my ideal of justice, I want to know objectively whether or to what extent that ideal is realized. If I misperceive or bend the facts because I want to show that the criminal justice system is unjust, I fool myself as much as anyone else. I am not honestly committed to my ideal of justice unless I am willing to apply it as objectively as I can.

I turn now to consider the special philosophical needs of criminology.

SPECIAL PHILOSOPHICAL NEEDS OF CRIMINOLOGY

I shall make three arguments aimed at showing that criminology has a special need for philosophical reflection. First, I will contend that criminology has such a need because it is a multidisciplinary study and thus requires an explanation for why crime is worthy of its own organized inquiry. Second, I will make the political argument for criminology's need for philosophy, at which I hinted in my opening remarks. And, third, I will argue that the need for philosophy arises from the topic itself, that crime cannot be studied without coming to some judgment about its moral status, which requires philosophical reflection.

Consider first the fact that criminology is a multidisciplinary mode of inquiry. The traditional disciplines, history or sociology or philosophy, are not defined by their topics. Rather than study *something* in the world, some problem or problem area, they study *everything*, but from a particular angle. Criminology is the reverse. It studies the problem area of crime and criminal justice, from a wide variety of angles. But, then, why *this* problem area?

What makes crime an interesting focus of study? That it is crime, or a violation of a rule, is not enough of an answer. Why not study people who cheat at solitaire, or those who arrive late for dates with friends, or drivers who fail to put on their turn signal before turning left, or folks who have bad manners, or speakers who say *ain't?* They are all rule violators. And these rule violations are all subject to penalties of some sort, but hardly worth devoting a special discipline to their study. What makes crime worthy of its own study?

Since the mere fact that crime is a rule violation does not earn it special treatment, the mere fact that it is a law violation will not do so either. Responding to this need for explanation requires you to say what you think crime is, such that it is an important occurrence in a society. Is crime a breakdown in social order, an alternative career route, a way of coping with acute need or insecurity, a rebellion against injustice, a cry for help, a form of play, a form of self-defense, an exciting walk on the wild side, a symptom of individual or social pathology, a label—and accompanying treatment—applied for political purposes? Choosing among alternatives like these requires you to say what you think a society is, such that crime is important to it. Is society a rational association among individuals, a site of conflict or consensus or of continual negotiation between the two; is it a mechanism of control of labor and resources, a struggle among classes, a pluralistic ragbag of interest groups?

I do not mean to suggest that these ways of thinking about crime and about society exhaust the possibilities. My point is that unless you have some thought like this about crime and society, you don't really have an answer to why crime is worth studying. And, then, you do not have an answer to why there should be a field of social inquiry devoted specially to the study of crime. A thought like this about crime is a theory of crime, and a theory of crime is a part of a theory of society. And a theory of society is a work of philosophizing.

To move now to the political dimension of the issue, consider this question: What's the difference between what criminologists do and what the FBI does in compiling the annual *Uniform Crime Report (UCR)?* Both seek to amass and disseminate knowledge about crime; both chart trends and correlations. There are numerous differences, but one is, to my mind, of chief importance. The *UCR* simply accepts the legal system's definitions of crimes as well as the legal system's grading of their gravity. It needs no more; in fact, it would exceed its mandate if it varied from this. But criminology cannot simply accept the legal definition of crimes and the legal system's determination of their gravity, because criminology is not a branch of law or of the legal system.

Unless criminologists have their own view of what crime is and what makes it especially important, if they simply study what the legal system calls crimes in the order of gravity the legal system assigns them, then criminology accepts the research agenda handed to it by the government. Criminology is then an arm of the state. Even if it comes up with some news that the state would rather not hear, it is doing the state's work, which is to amass and disseminate knowledge about law violations.

To affirm its intellectual independence from the state as a social science, criminology must look at crime while staying open to the idea that the legal definitions and, just as crucially, all the righteous beliefs that normally surround the legal enterprise are less than the whole truth, and perhaps even misleading or ideological. This means that criminology must keep its distance from the legal system as such, and this in turn requires that criminology seek its own understanding of what crime is. And I contend again that this requires a theory of crime, and a theory of crime is part of a theory of society, and a theory of society is a work of philosophizing.

You may think that this argument only amounts to showing that criminologists need a bit of social theory, which may be an interesting fact, but not very startling. You may think that social theory is a thing different from social philosophy, something that sociologists do rather than philosophers. I disagree. I think that social theorizing is philosophizing, but that doesn't mean that it can or should only be done by philosophers.

Every discipline has a place where it overlaps with philosophy, where its questions become philosophical questions. When art historians ask what art or beauty is, when psychologists ask what a mind is, when political scientists ask what a state is, and when sociologists or criminologists or anyone else asks what crime or society is, the questions they ask are philosophical ones. One clear reason that they are philosophical questions is that they are distinctively about the *validity* of norms or criteria—what makes the *Mona Lisa* beautiful, what makes a property mental rather than physical, when is a group a state, what should be prohibited by criminal law? To be sure, sociologists and others also study norms and criteria. Their focus is on the existence and consequences of norms and criteria. The questions that are distinctive to philosophy are those about the *justification* of norms and criteria. Philosophy aims to evaluate their credentials and, where those credentials pass muster, to defend the norms and criteria as valid ones.

That said, be clear that I do not think that philosophical questions can *only* be asked or competently answered by people with PhDs in philosophy. I think rather that whoever answers them should recognize that he or she is no longer in the realm of empirical scientific endeavor, but is engaged in the conceptual and normative reflection that is properly philosophy's domain.

I do not want to leave the issue here. There is a dimension to the theorizing needed about crime that I think is uncontroversially philosophical. We reach this dimension by recognizing that crime is a *violation*, and not just any old violation. It is not just the sort of rule violation that is involved in saying *ain't*. It's not the sort of violation that occurs when someone cheats at solitaire.

Because crime affects other people and often in very serious ways, it is a morally consequential act. And, as a result, you cannot say *what crime is* without taking a position on its moral status. That in turn will require a position on the moral obligation to obey the law. I am not saying that you must believe that the criminal does a moral wrong or violates a moral obligation. My point rather is that you must have *some* position on this. You cannot be neutral. If you are neutral, you treat crime as no different from any old rule violation, which is less than what crime is, and thus a distortion of your object of study.

This, then, is my third argument. Crime itself requires moral assessment. To be studied, it must be identified for what it is, and that includes its moral nature. Even if you do not think that criminals violate a moral obligation in committing crimes, you probably do think that many, if not most, crimes would, under normal circumstances, constitute immoral actions. After all, all crimes with victims violate the Golden Rule. The criminal does things to people that he wouldn't want done to him. And this is important. It constitutes, so to speak, the default position on the moral status of crimes. Suppose you think that violating laws against illicit drug use or prostitution involves no violation of a moral obligation. Then, you probably think that those acts should not be crimes. This implies that you assume that the sorts of things that should be crimes are the sorts of things the doing of which do violate moral obligations.

Or, suppose you think something rather radical, say, that inner-city violence against the police is not immoral because it is a kind of legitimate self-defense or even retribution. Even here, you are taking a position on the moral status of criminal acts. Most importantly, calling an act *self-defense* or *retribution* is a way of saying that an act that is normally immoral is morally permissible in light of what it is a response to. You are assuming that the same acts, if not done in self-defense or as retribution, would be immoral.

That is what I mean by saying that the view that crime is a moral violation is the default position. Crime is prima facie a moral violation; that is, it is a moral violation, unless reasons to the contrary can be given. To hold that crime is a moral violation is to affirm part, not just of a social theory of crime, but of a moral theory about what human beings owe to their fellows in the way of conduct. And, insofar as you affirm such a moral theory, not blindly, but after reflecting on its validity, you are squarely in philosophy's jurisdiction.

There's another way to make this argument. Many criminologists believe—as I do—that the legal catalogue of crimes is biased in certain ways; for example, it focuses on the acts of poor people and ignores much of the antisocial behavior of the well-off. Those criminologists may also believe—as I do—that this bias weakens in some measure the obligations of the poor to obey the law. Other criminologists disagree on both the claim of bias and on the weakening of obligation, or they might accept one of these and not the other. What is this disagreement about?

Well, certainly, it is a disagreement about what should be crime. This is clearly a normative disagreement. In disagreeing about what should be crime, we are disagreeing more generally about what kind of conduct individual human beings owe to each other. This is a disagreement about the requirements of *interpersonal justice*. In disagreeing about how bias in the legal determination of crime affects the moral obligations of the victims of that bias, we are disagreeing about what society as a whole owes its members. This is a disagreement about the requirements of *social justice*. Both are philosophical disagreements that arise from trying to say what crime really is in the society that we are studying. And since all criminologists must believe either that the definitions of crime are biased or that they aren't or that some are and some aren't, and they must believe as well that this does or does not weaken obligation, it follows that all criminologists must hold philosophical views that fill out their notions of what crime is. And the reflection that leads them to believe that these philosophical views are valid is philosophical reflection.

I now turn to the specific philosophic commitments that underlie *The Rich Get Richer and the Poor Get Prison.*

THE RICH GET RICHER AND THE POOR GET PHILOSOPHY

I got the idea for *The Rich Get Richer* while reading Richard Quinney's seminal work, *The Social Reality of Crime.*[6] That provocative book contended that crime was not some real, objective event in the world, but the creation of a labeling process, the crucial step in which was the definition of crimes by lawmakers. In short, crime has a social rather than a physical reality. What's more, Quinney held that this social reality was created in a politically biased way. Quinney contended that the labeling of some acts as crimes by lawmakers reflected the interests of the wealthy and powerful in the society at the expense of the rest. I found this conclusion very believable, but I was dissatisfied with the argument by which Quinney arrived at it. In effect, he contended that lawmakers were from the wealthy and powerful groups in society; that they tended to act in their own self-interest; and consequently, that the criminal laws they wrote must reflect their interests, which is to say, the interests of the wealthy and powerful and not the interests of the rest of society.[7]

This argument has the advantage of being neat and economical, but the disadvantage of being inconclusive. It assumes that, because people *tend* to act in their self-interest, then we can conclude of anything they do that it is in their self-interest. But, sometimes people act contrary to their self-interest. They may occasionally act to do their duty, or to do what they think is right. Think, for example, of people who risked their own lives and the lives of their families to hide Jews from the Nazis during the Second World War—it can happen that people are motivated to do the morally right thing! And it's just possible that lawmakers were doing this at the moment that they were writing criminal laws, even if in general they tend to act in their own interest.

Moreover, that something is in the interest of the wealthy and powerful doesn't entail that it is *not* in the interests of others. It might be that what is in one person's interest is also in that of others, such that when the person acts in his own self-interest, he serves the interests of the others in spite of himself. And this is arguably the case regarding the criminal law, since both wealthy people and poor ones have an interest in, say, not being robbed or murdered.

Then, even if the wealthy and powerful draw up laws against robbery and murder to serve their own interests, they would be serving the interests of the rest of society at the same time.

To get to the politically critical conclusion that Quinney wanted to reach, a different sort of argument was needed. What sort? First of all, as I have been suggesting all along in this essay, it was necessary to take some distance from the legal system's list of crimes. That required establishing some normative standard of what *should* be crime, against which the actual legal definitions could be assessed as fair or biased. The normative standard with which I stated in *The Rich Get Richer* was simple and uncontroversial. I contended that a criminal justice system ought to be protecting the lives and limbs and possessions of the citizenry, and thus the legal list of crimes ought to follow this imperative. The most serious crimes should be the gravest threats to life, limb, or property; and the gravest threats to life, limb, or property should be the most serious crimes.

With this notion in mind, I looked at the most serious threats to life, limb, and property in society and compared them to the law's list of crimes. What I found was that, while the criminal law did treat some acts that posed great threats as crimes, many equally or even more dangerous acts were not treated as crimes: Either they were not labeled crimes, or they were not labeled serious crimes in proportion to the danger they threatened, or, if they were labeled serious crimes, they were rarely treated as such in practice. I noted as well that some acts labeled crimes did not seem to be threatening or dangerous to society at all—here I have in mind the so-called "victimless crimes" of voluntary recreational drug use by adults, consensual commercial sex, and so on.

This, in turn, led me to ask what the acts labeled crimes had in common and what the dangerous acts not labeled crimes had in common. And my conclusion was that the acts labeled crimes, instead of being all dangerous acts, were predominantly acts of the poor in society. And the dangerous acts not labeled crime were predominantly acts of the well-off. With these conclusions, I could show that Quinney's conclusion was indeed largely correct: The law's definitions of crimes serve the interests of the wealthy and powerful at the expense of the rest of society. I say *largely correct* because there are crimes in the law's list that are acts that threaten the poor (many of the crimes tracked in the FBI's *UCRs* certainly do), and there are dangerous acts of the well-off that are occasionally treated as serious crimes (as Enron's Andrew Fastow and WorldCom's Bernard Ebbers have recently learned). But *largely correct* is correct enough to support the critical conclusion.

My point here is that reaching this conclusion required a reflection on what crime is that could not rest satisfied with legal or conventional understandings. It had to be a normative, and thus philosophical, reflection on what crime should be in order to compare reality to this and find it lacking. The route from which acts are and are not crimes to the conclusion that the legal definitions of crime serve the interests of the wealthy and powerful had to pass through a theory of what *should* be crime. In sum, the social inquiry that leads to the view defended in *The Rich Get Richer*, namely, that the criminal justice system is biased against the poor, relies on an irreducibly normative and thus philosophical conception of crime.

Moreover, this conception of crime was not simply pulled out of a hat. It was the product of philosophical reflection. This philosophical conception of crime is based on an equally philosophical conception of social and political justice. I contend that the ways in which the coercive apparatus of the law is used must be justified in principle to all citizens. This is so for three reasons.

First, both our tradition and our social order take freedom—the right of sane adults to do what they want—as a paramount value. Freedom is important because people tend to enjoy acting as they wish, and because it is the necessary condition of having a life that can be seen as one's own accomplishment, a life of which one can be proud. Without freedom, we are playing out a script of which we are not the author. Freedom is also important as a source of new ideas and creativity and thus of social progress. For these reasons and others, I start with the idea that freedom is a great value and thus that those who would limit it owe a satisfactory justification to those whose freedom is to be limited.

Second, on the social contract tradition in political and moral philosophy (which is enshrined in the *Declaration of Independence*) and, indeed, on any democratic view, the coercive power of the state—police, prisons, and so on—represents the people's own power, and thus can only legitimately be used for the people's own purposes. Consequently, the exercise of that power must be justifiable to the people in terms of their own purposes.

Third, the legal system appeals to the citizens morally, that is, it implicitly and explicitly asserts that the citizens are morally obligated to comply with it. But, on the contract model, obligation is a matter of owing fair compensation for benefits one receives. And, thus, only laws that benefit people can obligate people. Ultimately, this has to be cashed out individually, because it is as individuals that we are obligated or not. The law must benefit me, protect me against something that really threatens me, for me to be morally obligated to obey it. The law must serve people's interests to be morally binding on them. And thus the claim of the law to morally obligate citizens requires that it be justifiable to them in light of their interests.

This is not the whole story. I am, for example, also benefited by the fact that the law is the product of a democratic process, whose benefits are only available on the assumption that laws will be binding even on those who do not approve of them or find them in their interest. And, I am benefited by order itself, by the predictability and regularity of my fellow citizens' conduct that come of their obeying the law even if they are unhappy with it. Consequently, the argument as to whether I am or am not obligated to a particular law starts with consideration of whether it serves an interest I have, but it doesn't end there. Even if a particular law doesn't benefit me, some weight must be given to the fact that democratic lawmaking systems are beneficial generally, and order is as well, and that both democracy and order require people to accept laws which they don't think serve their interests. Nonetheless, if a law or a whole legal system significantly veers from serving all citizens' interests and toward serving the interests of some segment of society at the expense of the rest, the weight of democracy and order will not be enough to preserve the obligatory nature of the law. Such veering away from serving all citizens' interests will weaken, if not eliminate, the obligations of those whose interests are served less or not at all.

This is the philosophical reflection that underlies the simpler claim that the criminal law should be protecting citizens' life and limb and possessions generally. Because it must serve all citizens' interests, a just legal order must criminalize behavior that threatens the interests of all citizens, and it must do so in proportion to the gravity of the threat posed. It must not be protecting citizens only or even mainly against threats posed by the poor, while leaving the threats posed by the wealthy either untouched or only lightly grazed. This philosophical argument also creates a presumption against the legitimacy of laws against victimless crimes because laws that criminalize actions that do not clearly have victims—actions that some people detest but others accept— will surely appear to many in society as nothing more than the majority building its moral preferences into the law with no more justification than that they are the majority. Large numbers of citizens will tend not to view themselves as obligated by such laws and, in my view, they will often be correct. Thus, not only does my argument pass through a normative theory of crime but also that theory is itself based on a theory of social justice.

Moreover, since a theory of crime is part of a theory of society, this conception of crime reflects a conception of how society works that is, to my mind, equally a matter of philosophical reflection. Basically, my view of U.S. society is that it works roughly the way Marx supposed it would. It is dominated by the capitalist mode of production, which brings with it a crucial class divide between those who own means of production and those who don't. This has the consequence that, in a certain significant sense, the nonowners are forced to work for the owners. The divide between owners and nonowners amounts to an inequality in power between the two classes, which goes far toward explaining what is and what is not treated as crime in capitalist societies.

However, the Marxian view has even richer resources for explaining this bias. It holds that the capitalist mode of production is accompanied by an ideology, the core of which is blindness to the coerciveness of ownership of means of production vis-à-vis nonowners.[8] I believe, by the way, that, within these coercive relations, a capitalist economy works pretty much the way neoclassical economists—such as Milton Friedman—think it does (and Marx generally believed this as well). This accounts for the general success of neoclassical economics, while its blindness to the coerciveness explains how neoclassical economics can be ideological even as it accurately describes market tendencies.

Blindness to the coerciveness of private ownership of means of production is not primarily due to active deception by those in power. It is rather the way in which capitalism normally looks to its participants who view it, so to speak, up close. The illusion that capitalist transactions are fully free is similar to the illusion that the sun goes around the earth—it's just what you would expect people to see from where they are standing. Up close, the fact that capitalists, unlike feudal lords or slave owners, cannot use violence to get people to work for them makes the transactions between owners and nonowners of means of production appear free. They are, of course, free in important ways, but not as free as they seem. Workers are free to choose among capitalists, but not free to avoid working for one of them after all (leaving aside the marginal alternatives, working for the church or the government, stealing, or begging—and, for the few who have the initiative and willingness to sacrifice as well as plenty of luck, the possibility of going into business on one's own).

Since most of the ways that the wealthy pose dangers to the rest of society are as threats either to employees (subjecting them to preventable occupational hazards) or to consumers (subjecting them to shoddy products or to higher prices due to corporate skullduggery), blindness to the coerciveness of capitalism makes it appear as if employees and consumers—who are, of course, the same people—have signed on freely to the risks involved. Consequently, those responsible for these threats don't seem like criminals, because criminals characteristically force dangers on their victims. In light of the coerciveness of capitalism, however, this difference is largely illusory. For all intents and purposes, occupational harms are forced on workers (they must choose among the jobs that are available), and product risks as well as corporate financial shenanigans are forced on consumers (they must choose among the products that are available, and they must pay for the losses due to corporate misdeeds when they are passed on in the form of higher prices). Nonetheless, the law in capitalism continues the illusion that these dangers are voluntarily accepted, by focusing mainly on one-on-one theft and violence, while treating deadlier preventable occupational hazards as well as consumer risks and costlier financial misdeeds as merely regulatory matters. Consequently, the Marxian view will lead us to expect just the bias in the legal definition of crimes that *The Rich Get Richer* documents.

I should add that my Marxism is tempered by recognition of two interconnected failings in Marxian analysis. One is the failure to see how dangerous to human freedom socialism could be, even though there is a good Marxian reason for expecting socialism to be dangerous. If ownership of the means of production is the main instrument of coercion in a society, one must have a very idealistic view of human beings to be willing to place that instrument of coercion, whole and entire, into the hands of a single institution, the government. Socialism only has a chance of being a truly liberating social form for a society in which democracy is already very well developed, and in which citizens are already extremely sophisticated about the exercise of their democratic power. This leads me to believe that the likelihood of a truly liberating socialism is way off in the future. For the foreseeable future, the future in which we are all likely to live and die, I can see no truly liberating alternative to capitalism. And, sad to say, the current and recent examples of socialism—China, North Korea, and the former Soviet Union—confirm this bleak conclusion.

On the other hand, there is a good Marxian reason to expect capitalism to maintain individual freedom. As a system of multiple competing owners of means of production, capitalism distributes the main instrument of social coercion among a multiplicity of separate agents. Thus, capitalism maintains a space for individual freedom that results, not from an enlightened citizenry or officialdom, but rather from the material conditions of capitalist production itself. In a kind of Madisonian fashion, the multiple competing owners each have an interest in resisting the control of the economy by other firms and thus in keeping the market generally open and the government in a wide variety of hands. Moreover, capitalism does, as Marx very explicitly noted, create enormous technological progress that reduces unwanted toil and increases the material income of the workers. The impoverishment to which Marx thought capitalism led is a matter of workers' decreasing relative share of the product of their labor—but, since this is caused by the fact that labor under capitalism becomes increasingly productive, this share buys more and more goods.

To be sure, capitalism is also a system that generates large (and, recently, growing) inequalities, which in turn give some people great power to determine the way others live. That is, capitalism not only makes some people richer than others, but also makes some people freer than others. Moreover, capitalism subjects all of us, but the poor most of all, to forces and developments beyond our control, making life uncertain for most and painful for many. These facts, taken together with the dangerousness of socialism and the freedom-maintaining tendency of capitalism, mean that Marxism implies of capitalism roughly what Winston Churchill said of democracy, namely, that it is the worst form of economic system, except for all the others.

The second failing in Marxian analysis offers some compensation for this conclusion, which some readers may find too dismal. The second failing is that of not seeing how progressive capitalism is culturally, that is, in the dimension that Marx called the *relations of production*. Marx and Marxists saw clearly that capitalism is progressive with respect to the *means of production*, that is, the development and implementation of labor-saving technology. But, Marx and Marxists did not (though Marx did more so than Marxists) see that capitalism is also progressive with respect to the relations of production, that is, *the growth and spread of liberal values and institutions.*

Under these, I include the preference for greater personal freedom (tending toward the requirement of harm as a justification for restricting freedom, and against victimless crimes or other restraints based on faith or tradition or custom), the inclination toward using rational criteria for evaluating people (tending toward use of merit and conduct to judge people rather than race or gender or creed or age), and the insistence on more effective and responsive government (demanding freedom to vote and the progressive extension of eligibility to vote, freedom to assemble, and the rest). These progressive tendencies are, of course, very imperfectly realized. Nonetheless, that does not mean that they are unimportant or without effect. I think that Jürgen Habermas has gone some distance toward integrating this progressive dimension of capitalism's liberal culture into Marxian theory.[9]

The second failing is connected to the first in several ways. One way of explaining why existing or recent socialist societies have been as unattractive as they have is that they embraced capitalist technology without embracing capitalist liberalism. Socialists failed to realize that socialism itself is sure to be oppressive unless it is staffed by officials who are deeply imbued with liberal values, and held democratically accountable by a populace that is equally so imbued.

But the second failing has a bright side as well. In recognizing the progressiveness of capitalism with regard to the relations of production, we can see a way in which the fact that we are probably stuck with capitalism for our lives and beyond presents a special opportunity. Capitalism produces the cultural tools needed to push it to become fairer. The struggle to make people freer and more equal is a struggle to make capitalism live up to its own liberal ideals. And, there is reason to hope that this struggle can succeed, since the values that guide it are the very ones affirmed by cultural institutions within capitalism.

This, to my mind, locates *The Rich Get Richer and the Poor Get Prison* in philosophical space. *It is a radical critique of criminal justice in capitalism that works by confronting capitalist criminal justice with capitalism's own liberal moral philosophy.*

Notes

1. This paper is a revised version of my article of the same title appearing in the *Journal of Law* 1 (2004): 42–58, which in turn was a revised version of my keynote address to the second annual conference of the Canadian Society of Criminology, Toronto, April 1, 2004.

2. For its relevance to Canadian criminal justice, see, for example, Stuart Henry, "Law Commission of Canada's Discussion Paper 'What Is a Crime?' A Commentary on the Issue of Power," paper presented at the annual meeting of the American Society of Criminology, Denver, November, 19–22, 2003.

3. *Ontology* is the philosophical study of what is real. An ontological skeptic about society doubts that society exists, and an ontological agnostic about society believes we cannot know if society exists.

4. *Epistemology* is the philosophical study of what knowledge is and how or if it is possible. An epistemological skeptic about social science doubts that social science provides knowledge; an epistemological agnostic about social science believes that we cannot know whether social science provides knowledge.

5. See, for example, Julie R. Solomon, *Objectivity in the Making: Francis Bacon and the Politics of Inquiry* (Baltimore: Johns Hopkins University Press, 1998).
6. Richard Quinney, *The Social Reality of Crime* (Boston: Little, Brown, 1970).
7. Quinney, *Social Reality*, p. 15 inter alia; and see the section titled "Criminal Justice as Creative Art" in Chapter 2 of the present book.
8. This analysis of Marxian theory and its relationship to the issue of what is and what is not treated as crime in capitalist societies is developed in Appendix I of this book, "The Marxian Critique of Criminal Justice." That appendix is a shorter version of an article that was originally published in *Criminal Justice Ethics* 6, no. 1 (Winter–Spring 1987): 30–50.
9. See, for example, Jürgen Habermas, *Communication and the Evolution of Society* (Boston: Beacon Press, 1979), esp. Chapters 4 and 5.

INDEX